MW01201644

Return Migration and Identity

Return Migration and Identity

A Global Phenomenon, A Hong Kong Case

Nan M. Sussman

香港大學出版社

HONG KONG UNIVERSITY PRESS

Hong Kong University Press
14/F Hing Wai Centre
7 Tin Wan Praya Road
Aberdeen
Hong Kong
www.hkupress.org

© Hong Kong University Press 2011

Hardback: ISBN 978-988-8028-83-2
Paperback: ISBN 978-988-8028-84-9

The author would like to thank Xu Bing for writing the book title on the cover in his Square Word Calligraphy.

"Square Word Calligraphy" is a system of writing developed between 1994–96 by artist Xu Bing (1955–). It presents English words in a Chinese format, challenging the preconceptions of readers of both languages.

The *Bauhinia blakeana* flower on the front cover, first discovered in Hong Kong, symbolizes the territory. It is also featured in the Regional Flag of the Hong Kong Special Administrative Region of the People's Republic of China.

British Library Cataloguing-in-Publication Data
A catalogue record for this book is available from the British Library.

This digitally printed version 2011

Contents

Illustrations

Figures

Tables

Preface and acknowledgments

The global trend for immigrants to return home has a special relevance to the people of Hong Kong. While the research that forms the core of this book was undertaken within the academic and theoretical framework of cross-cultural psychology, the book has been written to be accessible both to scholars of cultural transitions and to the immigrants and their families who uprooted their lives by leaving their home countries and, subsequently, by returning to them. I hope that my findings help explain the psychological and social experiences of these remigrants.

While I alone am responsible for the final product, such a research study required the assistance of many. First, my profound gratitude to the people I interviewed for this study. No scientific psychological investigation can be carried out without the participation of volunteers. In this case, we were strangers until we met to discuss their experiences of migration and remigration. The interviewees openly shared with me their anxieties, anticipations, joys, learning, and flexible world perspectives. They gave me insights into the cultural transition process as they discussed their relationships with their spouses, parents, children, friends, and coworkers. Although many volunteers were initially reluctant to give even one hour of their precious time to an unknown researcher, albeit one with an intriguing topic, once the interviews began, the respondents often spoke for two or three hours. For many participants, our discussions seemed cathartic, and I hope that they did find our conversations helpful in understanding the process they had undergone.

The remigrants introduced me to the cultural aspects of the Hong Kong world of work. I anticipated conducting interviews over lunch but quickly discovered that most local restaurants were too noisy with the buzz of diners and the frantic movements of waiters. When I suggested to one interviewee that we instead meet during the workday, he replied, "No, I am too busy during the day." "Perhaps we can meet after work?" I suggested. There was silence on the telephone. "You want to meet at 10 p.m.?" he responded, incredulous. I was the one who was amazed. "Saturday?" "No, I work on Saturday, too." "Sunday?" "That's for the family." Yet despite their dedication to their work and their families, most of the remigrants I contacted were eventually able to clear some time in their busy schedules for our meetings.

Second, many thanks to the colleagues who assisted me in the initial stages of this research project: Kay Deaux, Philip Kasinitz, Jennifer Holdaway, Bill Dickery, Gerard Postiglione, K. B. Chan, Ronald Skeldon, Lesley Lewis, Henry Steiner, Jan Selmer, Jane DeBevoise, and Michael DeGolyer. I am also appreciative of those individuals who helped pilot the interview schedule and psychological scales.

I am grateful to Kwok Leung, chair of the Department of Management, City University of Hong Kong, and to Wong Sui-lun, director of the Centre of Asian Studies, the University of Hong Kong. They graciously provided me with office space and equipment, included me in faculty events and colloquia, and shared with me their ideas. My adjustment was also aided by my new friends at City University, especially my office mate Anna Tsui and the other faculty and staff in the Department of Management. Thanks as well to David Zweig of the Hong Kong University of Science and Technology for his wise counsel and our good discussions. Big hugs and thanks to my two research assistants from the Chinese University of Hong Kong (CUHK), Lorraine Pun and Yat Yee Lee. They were cheerful, conscientious, and exceedingly well trained by their professor, and my friend, Michael H. Bond of the Department of Psychology, CUHK. Additional thanks to my CUNY student assistants Dianne Tyson, Nhan Truong, Deanna Quinlan, and Rachel Pascall-Gonzalez for their help in various phases of this study.

This research project was funded by the W. J. Fulbright Scholars Program, US Department of State. The funding and support provided by this program enabled me to move forward with my research project in multiple ways. Had it not included funding for my family (including tuition for my children's schooling), I could not have accepted the grant. I strongly urge the US Congress to continue "family funding" so that researchers who are parents can include their children in their research travel. As an aside, my children have continued their study of Mandarin, and both are now fluent and are pursuing university degrees in Asian studies. My thanks also to the staff of the Council for International Exchange of Scholars (CIES), to the Hong Kong Fulbright office, and to Glenn Shive of the Hong Kong-American Center for providing necessary support for my research. Their superb organizations made my predeparture, settling in, and investigative work go as smoothly as possible.

Thanks also to the various groups that aided me in the recruitment of interviewees: the American-Hong Kong Chamber of Commerce, the University of British Columbia Alumni Association, the Australian and Canadian Chambers of Commerce, the Island School, and members of the United Jewish Congregation and of the Union Church. Also, my thanks to Marti and Alan Law and Sue and Alistaire Heyman for their research and personal support.

The College of Staten Island, CUNY, also supported my research by granting me a Fellowship Leave and, subsequently, a Presidential Research Award.

A special note of appreciation to Colin Day, the former publisher of Hong Kong University Press. When I presented some preliminary research findings at the Centre of Asian Studies, he was in the audience. His enthusiasm for the topic and recognition of interest among both scholars and the Hong Kong public spurred me to develop my research project into its present book form. He has been a patient source of encouragement and constructive critical suggestions. I wish him well in his retirement and his repatriation.

Profound thanks to Richard Krupinski, longtime friend and writer extraordinaire. His comments and suggestions improved the manuscript and clarified my ideas. Thanks also to Janice Ewenstein and Susan Greenberg for copyediting assistance. Two anonymous reviewers provided invaluable suggestions that improved the flow and clarity of the manuscript. I am also grateful to my kindred spirit, the late Ira Caplan. For more than 20 years, our discussions of repatriation challenged and enriched my thinking. He regaled me with hilarious, irreverent, and insightful stories of his cultural transitions and kept my focus on the human consequences of moving across borders.

Finally, much gratitude and love to my husband, Jerald Rosenbloom, who is delighted at the prospect of reclaiming our dining room table from under the mound of migration books and remigration articles. When I first broached the subject of my applying for a Fulbright grant so that I could embark on this research in Hong Kong, he was immediately supportive.

He endured monthly flights from New York to Hong Kong to visit me and our children and cold meals at home while we were away. Luke and Peter also enthusiastically greeted the prospect of living and studying in Hong Kong. Once we arrived, they adjusted quickly and made this cross-cultural psychologist proud.

NMS
January 2010

About the author

Dr. Nan M. Sussman was born and raised in the United States but became enamored with international travel as a teenager. For Nan, culture and its psychological impact became a lifetime personal and professional interest. She holds a bachelor's degree in anthropology, sociology, and communications from the University of Pittsburgh (1973), and a master's and a doctoral degree in social and cross-cultural psychology from the University of Kansas (1975 and 1977, respectively). She was awarded a postdoctoral fellowship as a Professional Associate with the Culture Learning Institute of the East-West Center, Honolulu, Hawai'i. She received further education in intercultural training at the Intercultural Communication Institute at Stanford University. She has been honored by the International Society for Intercultural Education, Training and Research (SIETAR) for her accomplishments.

Early in her career, Nan focused on applied cross-cultural psychology. She became a Senior Program Coordinator at the Washington International Center, where she developed and conducted weekly intercultural workshops for mid-level managers from developing countries. She wrote and produced a training videotape and accompanying manual. Subsequently, she was a Cultural Specialist at the Orientation Resource Center at Georgetown University and Director of International Training for the International Council of Education for Teaching, Washington, DC.

In 1982, she became Director of the Center for International Service at the College of Staten Island, City University of New York, where she developed programs for overseas study, international students, and intensive English language study, and initiated the internationalization of the undergraduate curriculum. She also created a major in international studies and a concentration in international business within the Department of Business.

In 1985, she was awarded the first of two Fulbright research grants. Working from Japan's Keio University, she studied the returnee experience of Japanese and American executives. During the next 20 years, she continued to investigate the psychological issue of returning home for teachers, business personnel, and students. In recognition of the beginnings of a global trend in return migration, she was awarded a second Fulbright, in 2004, to Hong Kong. Using facilities at both the University of Hong Kong and the City University of Hong Kong, Nan examined the phenomenon of Hong Kongers' returning home following "hand-over" motivated migration. This book is a result of that research project.

Dr. Sussman is currently an associate professor of psychology at the College of Staten Island and a member of the doctoral faculty in industrial and organization psychology, the Graduate Center, City University of New York. She has lectured throughout Asia and presented papers at conferences all over the world. She has published in scholarly journals, books, and popular magazines. Her research is widely cited and serves as the inspiration for many doctoral dissertations. Nan has conducted cultural training for international organizations, governmental agencies, nonprofit organizations, universities, and multinational enterprises.

Dr. Sussman lives in New York with her husband, Jerald Rosenbloom. Their two sons are fluent in Mandarin and both are pursuing university studies in Asian studies and international relations. She can be contacted at nan.sussman@csi.cuny.edu.

Introduction:
"Anna" migrates and returns home

Anna (a pseudonym) was 35 years old when she and her husband decided to move to Australia in 1991. They returned to Hong Kong two and a half years later. Anna described herself as Hong Kongese before she emigrated, distinguishing this cultural identity from that of Chinese. *"There is a kind of cultural difference … Like my grandparents, they are really typical Chinese. I didn't really share the real feeling of behavior like this. They are traditional. But the Hong Kongese … they are energetic, enthusiastic, and they are eager on the job and career development."*

Like many residents of the territory, Anna emigrated because of the impending handover of sovereignty to the People's Republic of China. *"We moved because of '97. We really were not sure what would happen, and Australia is a really good place in terms of weather and the resources. And we think it is a good place to set up the rest of life there."* Her husband was a professional, and she worked as a secretary. They felt confident that they would find jobs in Australia, which, in fact, her husband easily did. He also enrolled in a university to pursue a second degree. Anna had more difficulty finding employment, despite having left a responsible position in Hong Kong. Her four-month job search left her demoralized. *"They said, 'You have no local experience, so I cannot hire you.' But if you don't even give me a chance, how can I demonstrate [my ability]? I sent out fifty applications, and I didn't get a job at all. But luckily I have friends [in Australia], and they encouraged me to try some other ways … Then I got a job."*

The Hong Kong community in Sydney was supportive of Anna in many ways and helped ease the couple's transition to living in Australia. In fact, Anna found living away from her family to be freeing. She had not lived away from home during her college years and was now enjoying the experience. *"It seemed like I was going to boarding school ... I could do whatever I like. And I got some close friends. So got me easily mixed together [adjusted to Australia]. Otherwise, I would feel sorry, miserable, and I would miss my family ... But I didn't."*

During her immigration period, Anna described herself as Hong Kongese, but she gradually adopted Australian values and behaviors. For example, she began to be less concerned about saving money for the future, reflecting Australian ways. *"They couldn't bother about saving much. They just earn and spend every week. They get the pay and they spend it all out. If I don't save up, I feel insecure because this is my traditional way, the Chinese way. But eventually I feel like ... I have confidence in the government; they will take care of me. So I spend whatever, and I just enjoy life."* Anna literally slowed down both her strides and her life in adjusting to the more leisurely pace of the locals. *"When I got to Australia, the first week I went to the park and someone spot me and said, 'Are you coming from Hong Kong?' I said, 'How do you know that?' They said, 'You walk so fast, and your foot pace is just like the Hong Kongese is. They walk very fast.'"* But over time, Anna changed, *"There's no need for me to hurry or rush."*

Anna began to appreciate the balance that Australians maintained in their lives, where the outdoors and their hobbies and leisure activities were as important to them as work was, or perhaps more important. *"I picked up some good points from the Australians, like they enjoy the life; they think that everything is beautiful even if taking care of the garden. You can enjoy in every aspect. While life in Hong Kong they just push all your achievements on work. So that's why I think when I have been staying abroad for two years, I feel like, 'well, working is not my sole achievement.' I need to develop some kinds of things that I can expand beyond, like reading more books, grow some plants if I am allowed to do on a piece of land."*

Once Anna found a job, she, her husband, and their young daughter came to enjoy life in Australia. She found the Australians welcoming and egalitarian. *"They treat you on an equal base."* And Anna liked meeting people from many different cultural backgrounds who were willing to help and assist her.

But after two years, the local economy gradually slowed down. Simultaneously, *"The Hong Kong economic situation is picking up, and they have the MTR [Mass Transit Railway] and those kind of construction thing; the opportunities are higher and someone ask for their ex [employees] to come back. So my husband said, 'Will I have the opportunity come back, maybe after that I can get back to Australia as well.' Since we feel good in Australia, like our hometown, we can go back anytime ... I will bring my children back to Australia someday."*

Anna's husband returned to Hong Kong first, and several months later Anna and their daughter followed. The climate and weather shocked her initially. *"The air pollution got me so stuff[ed]. And I get sick for the first month. And I am scared to go out. There are so many people!"* Additionally, Anna missed her Australian friends and colleagues, and her little flat, and the diverse and welcoming environment in Sydney. She also missed the Australian emphasis on family life. *"Straight after work, they [Australians] go back to take care of their family; or even you get pregnant or after you have a childbirth, even the father can take some time to take care of the wife. So the quality of life is much better than in Hong Kong."*

For some newly acquired behaviors, such as walking speed, Anna quickly resumed her Hong Kong style, readapting to her former customs and habits. Her Australian stroll speeded up. *"But just at the very first time I get there, I get used to the Hong Kong pace. No matter what happen [the immigration experience], I walk very fast."* She also again demonstrated a pragmatic approach to work, putting in long hours at her job. Once more, Anna was surrounded by her traditional extended family and by the obligations and behaviors that were entailed in family relationships. *"Since coming back here, my family, my in-laws, they are all around. So I can say I behave like a Hong Kongese. [But not] a typical Chinese because the way they think is too old."*

However, the profound cultural adaptations that Anna gradually made to living in Australia, perhaps out of her awareness, had become an important part of her value system and sense of self. She grafted Australian ideas and ways of thinking onto her "Hong Kongese self." *"I can't say I am an Australian because I've just stayed there for two years. But I really adapted to their way of life, and I like their style."* For example, Anna and her husband embraced the Australian style of family togetherness and they both wanted to spend more time with their daughter. *"I do want to have some kind of vacation with the family at least once a year. Not quite common [in Hong Kong] because they would devote into job or in some other issues [parents] and taking care of their children's studies."*

Their parenting decisions regarding their daughter's education also reflected a combination of Australian and Chinese values. Instead of sending their daughter to their local school in Hong Kong, Anna and her husband decided to enroll her in an English Schools Foundation (ESF) primary school, which followed British curriculum and teaching styles. *"I don't like the Chinese kids being pushed too hard. And they just don't have physically free or mentally free, just studying for the exam. It's not preparing for their growing up ... I am not pushing my daughter very much because I want her to adapt to her way of studying instead of me, at the back to push her. That's what I think maybe that's what I am different with the traditional Chinese."*

Anna had a clear sense of the difference between Chinese and Western teaching and learning styles, and she preferred the latter, in which active learning and individual effort are rewarded. *"They [ESF teachers] have a very good way of teaching. They [students] come to explore by themselves, and she read many different kinds of books to get the knowledge there by herself ... 'This is a science subject and you need to study. I will give you a quiz. You couldn't answer because you are not concentrating' ... That's the Chinese way of teaching. But in the Western way, they would say: 'How did you explore? What is the water cycle? The rainwater goes back to the sewage.' She tells me that this what she discovered. She told me how it goes for the water cycle. So I mean, this is the way they learn. A natural way. But if it is in the traditional Chinese way, they push it in but after the quiz and exam they forget because it's not in your brain, it does not go through your memory. You can't retrieve it."*

Anna and her husband were also planning for a future time when they would return to Australia and their daughter would complete her education there. Placing her in a Hong Kong school system in which English was the medium of instruction and Western methods predominated would enable her to readapt to Australian education more easily.

Through her brief immigrant experience in Australia, Anna had incorporated a more individualistic approach not only to making her own life decisions but also to allowing her daughter freedom to make decisions for herself separate from what her parents or extended family might wish for her. Integrating Chinese and Western modes of thinking was a struggle for Anna, but the newly added Western ideas frequently influenced her actions. *"In the Chinese traditional way, you want your daughter to be more ladylike, be more obedient. But in the foreign way, Western way, they give them more opportunities to show their view and feeling. So sometimes I feel like I was struggling. The traditional way would say, because I am a mother, I say that you must eat up and clear the plate, and not [be] messing around. Like my daughter would think, 'I am not going to eat it. I want ice cream instead, for the meal.' Something like that, she would have a say. But in the Chinese way we would say, 'You must finish your proper meal before you can have the ice cream for your meal.'"*

Traditional parents in Hong Kong were very involved in career decisions for their children, as Anna's were with her. However, acculturation to Australian values and ideas changed Anna's relationship to her daughter. She declined to select her daughter's career path *"because I feel that if she's really not that kind of person in that area, why should I force her? She won't be happy. Or maybe she like to be a farmer, or she would like to be a scientist, or she would like to be a musician. That's her way to go. She would feel more happy. If she does not enjoy the job, she would look for other things. I can give her some idea, but I cannot influence her because of my own feeling. I think this is the Australian way or Western style."*

The introduction of Australian customs into the lives of Anna and her family played out in domains other than education and child rearing. The family's choice of neighborhood after they returned to Hong Kong reflected their immigrant experience. *"We wanted to find a place not too crowded. Because we are used to the Australian way, not too crowded. So we want to get somewhere not too crowded. So we picked Ma On Shan [New Territories] because that place is a newly developed suburb, not so crowded, not too many buildings, something like that. And there is a nice beach over there and a park, and it seems like I am in Australia."* The suburban-like environment also attracted other returnees and expatriates from many countries, adding to a multicultural environment that appealed to Anna and her husband.

Relationships with friends were also influenced by immigration and return. Anna divided her friends into three categories: Hong Kong immigrants who remained in Australia, Hong Kong immigrants who returned to Hong Kong (but may have again boomeranged to Sydney), and Hong Kongers who never left Hong Kong. *"I can say, it's [my relationship with the last group] a bit different. Like in terms of raising the kids, they would put them in the traditional Chinese school; they push the kids. And then need them to study very hard. They join in the study so that they coach them. But for those who came back from overseas, they tend, like my idea, to put them in an ESF school or something like that. So they [the children] can learn more freely."*

Despite some significant changes in thought and behavior, Anna did not suffer from depression or anxiety after her return to Hong Kong. She never expressed feelings of isolation or of not fitting in again with Hong Kong society. Her explanation: *"I didn't leave for quite long. I leave Hong Kong for two years."* She successfully incorporated those aspects of Western thinking that felt comfortable to her into her combined Chinese/Hong Kong ideas and family concepts. And Anna and her husband continued to actively plan for the future, with both short-term and long-term goals.

In the short run, Anna planned to complete a college degree while her daughter completed primary school and her husband expanded the business he started when they returned to Hong Kong. Their long-term plan is for the family to return to Australia; Anna's husband would move his business there, and their daughter would attend secondary school. Always flexible and pragmatic, however, Anna adds, *"or even go to China, I don't know. Or maybe just stay here because there are so many situations which make you change your mind. And I feel that Australia is a good place."*

Hong Kong return migration

Between 1984 and 1997, nearly 800,000 Hong Kongers emigrated from the territory, a sixth of the total population. This historic exodus has been matched by an equally unrivaled occurrence: since 1997, an estimated 500,000 immigrants have returned to Hong Kong, now as citizens of Canada, Australia, the United States, the United Kingdom, and more than a dozen other Western and Asian nations. This book tells the psychological story of individuals who have been a part of this movement. It highlights their altered identities, acculturation, and readaptation, and their flexibility and pragmatism, as well as the transnational movements, global politics, and local cultures that also played roles in the migration and return of these Hong Kongers. "Anna's" account of immigrant life and return to Hong Kong reflects this process and the attitudes, values, and behaviors exhibited by many of the returnees. The experiences of Anna and 49 others have been captured and are discussed in the succeeding chapters.

Hong Kong's narrative may or may not be the most dramatic, but it is definitely at the leading edge of a worldwide return migration chronicle. The United Nations has estimated that annually as many as 100 million people return to their homelands because of seasonal migration,[1] and untold hundreds of thousands more experience repatriation for a wide range of reasons following either short- or long-term stays in host countries. Seasonal workers, temporary emigrants, sojourner repatriates, and return migrants are all part of a diverse but growing global phenomenon in which individuals returning to their families, workplaces, and home societies must make psychological and social adjustments.

The number of people returning to their homelands is growing. It is estimated, for example, that 40,000 Chinese returned to Mainland China in 2006 compared to 7,000 in 1999 and the brain drain of the past has been replaced by a brain gain — in 2006, approximately 42,000 students returned from their studies abroad compared to 25,000 in 2004.[2] It is projected that 20,000 Indian first- and second-generation immigrants returned home between 2004 and 2006.[3] Hi-tech executives from California's Silicon Valley, many of whom completed their graduate education in the United States, were at the forefront of the wave of Indian returnees, but it now includes doctors, engineers, and artists. The Indian government is actively luring second-generation Indians back to India by creating the Overseas Citizens of India (OIC) program. Between 2006 and 2008, the government issued more than 200,000 OIC cards providing holders with visa-free entry to India for life.[4] In Europe, immigrants are returning to Ireland, Turkey, and the Czech Republic. It was estimated that 400,000 Poles would return home from Britain in 2008.[5] In Asia, returnees are streaming back to Bangladesh, Taiwan, and Korea. South Americans are returning to Colombia, and Africans are remigrating to Nigeria and South Africa. Some plan to permanently resettle in their countries of origin; others are preparing for a life of transience. For all, it is still too soon to know the full personal and societal consequences of their global wanderings.

We do have an idea, however, regarding aspects of the psychological consequences of returning home. Curiously, the experiences of return sojourners worldwide are diametrically opposed to those of most Hong Kongers. For those returning to North America or Europe, to Africa or South America, the process of coming home is fraught with negative emotions, resulting in depression, anxiety, isolation, strained family relationships, and loss of employment. These returnees are alienated from their compatriots and no longer feel at home in their home countries. But this is not the situation with most Hong Kong returnees. Why are their psychological experiences so different from those of the rest of the world? What unique factors in their history and culture explain their psychological responses to cultural transitions?

The Hong Kong Remigration Project

The Hong Kong Remigration Project (HKRP) was created by the author in 2003 and was conceived to fulfill twin objectives: first, to capture the ongoing psychosocial experience of a major remigrant population, and second, as an extension of research conducted to test and validate the Cultural Identity Model (CIM) of Cultural Transitions. Pre- and post-data collection research was supported by the College of Staten Island, City University of New York. The data collection phase in Hong Kong, January to

July 2004, was supported by a Research Fellowship awarded to the author of this study by the Fulbright Commission of the US Department of State. Her work in Hong Kong was additionally supported by the Department of Management of City University of Hong Kong and the Centre of Asian Studies of the University of Hong Kong. Colleagues at both institutions were generous with their time and ideas.

The research findings from the Hong Kong Remigration Project presented in this book assess how the Hong Kong experience fits within a larger theory of cultural transitions, explaining both the reactions of Hong Kongers that are distinctive and those that overlap with the reactions of other nationalities. Chapter 1 examines the origins of the Hong Kong identity, starting with the indigenous inhabitants from southern China, and continuing through the nineteenth-century imposition of British sovereignty, modern identity, and, finally, the late twentieth-century handover to China. Chapter 2 steps back from the pin-light focus on Hong Kong movement and identity, scrutinizing the sojourner transition cycle through the lenses of social science theory, novelistic narratives, and artistic endeavors, each of which adds clarity to our understanding of the psychological responses to population shifts. Chapter 3 refocuses our attention on the issue of remigration, first historically and then psychologically. The author's model of repatriation and cultural identity (CIM) is explicated and provides the theoretical backdrop for the Hong Kong Remigration Project. The methodology used in this investigation is described at the end of the chapter. Those readers whose primary interest is in the results of the Hong Kong Remigration Project may want to skip Chapter 2 and the first half of Chapter 3, and proceed directly to Chapter 4. The remainder of this book describes the project's research outcomes. Chapter 4 summarizes participant responses to questions regarding predeparture identity, reasons for emigration, and the adaptation/acculturation process to either Australia or Canada. These are the antecedents to the remigration experience and may serve as causal elements in understanding the transitions that follow. In-depth excerpts from immigrant narratives show remarkable similarities in expectations and experiences, while giving insight into some demographically related variability. This chapter ends with a discussion of the decision-making process that led the migrants home to Hong Kong. Chapters 5 through 7 describe the remigrant experience through a comprehensive examination of the four CIM identity profiles, additive, subtractive, global, and affirmative. Again, the rich interview narratives give voice to the remigration story, as do the outcomes of the quantitative analyses of the psychological scales used in the study. Statistical outcomes are described in greater specificity in Appendix C.

Chapters 8 and 9 focus on two essential aspects of remigrant life: the family and the workplace. The actions and behaviors of remigration chosen by the returnees in these two personal spheres form a crucial intersection. How will they chose to live their lives, educate their children, resume their relationships, interact with their supervisors and subordinates, and conduct the minutiae of everyday life? In their own words, the remigrants explain their sometimes deliberative and sometimes off-handed decisions.

Chapter 10 looks to the past to Chinese philosophy, religion, and history to help us in understanding the unique Hong Kong response to remigration and identity. The teachings of Confucius and Laozi, among others, form a four-thousand-year-old foundation for looking at the migrant psychology of contemporary Hong Kongers. These formative schools of thought are contrasted with those of the ancient Greek philosophers whose work similarly shaped Western culture, including psychological responses to cultural transitions. The concluding Chapter 11 looks to the future. What will be the long-term effect of remigration on the identity and sense of self and of belonging of Hong Kong residents? How will the massive return migration influence the civic life, societal attitudes, and popular culture of Hong Kong? And what is the next layer of identity for Hong Kongers, as an increasingly larger portion of the population regularly interacts with the Chinese people and government for work and pleasure? Will there be a recapturing of or a return to the core Chinese identity, a double additive identity, or an affirmation of Hong Kong's unique identity roots?

1 A short history of two hundred years of Hong Kong migration and identity

Origins of Hong Kong identity

In order to understand the experiences of return Hong Kong immigrants in 1999, one needs to examine the complexity of their Chinese identity, which began to form in 1841. The British had claimed the island of Hong Kong at the terminus of their first Opium War with the Chinese. Yet while the battles ceased more than 150 years ago, the identity turmoil continues today. To comprehend the early development of the identity of the Hong Kong Chinese, though, one must first look at Hong Kong's location, bounded by the sea and adjacent to a vast continent. In his groundbreaking book *Guns, Germs and Steel*,[1] Jared Diamond, a professor of physiology, develops the notion that culture (and identity) was first and foremost

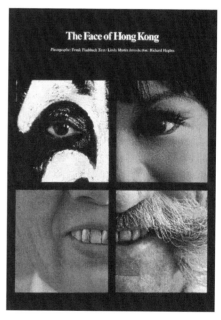

Figure 1.1 Henry Steiner, book cover of *The Face of Hong Kong* (1970). Courtesy of the designer.

a consequence of geographic location, climate, and natural resources. He suggests that topography, the ratio of sun and rain, accessibility to rivers and the sea, and the ways in which a population sustains itself all shape ideas of culture and self. Hong Kong political scientist Michael DeGolyer agrees, asserting that "Hong Kong exists solely because of a gift of geography: its deep water harbor. There would be no city without that central geographic feature."[2] That feature, the sea and its harbor, has shaped the way Hong Kongers traditionally and currently craft a living as fishermen, boat workers, international global port employees; the way Hong Kong interacts with a continuous flow of seaborne invaders, travelers, traders, and immigrants; the way Hong Kong protects itself from typhoons and creates its neighborhoods; and the way in which Hong Kongers create an identity.

More essential than Hong Kong's reliance on and struggle with the sea and what it brought, was its status as an island of rocky, barren mountains with limited land on which to grow food and to house inhabitants. Hong Kongers have one of the highest population densities on earth, and they typically live in tiny, cramped dwellings. The survival of Hong Kong's residents is due to their persistence, hard work, shrewdness, and cooperation.

The land and its location shaped Hong Kong culture and identity in another way: the island's proximity to the great landmass of China has created a complicated and evolving relationship between the two regions. Initially severed by war, and officially kept separate by first the British and then the Chinese governments, China and Hong Kong have maintained a continuous, albeit unofficial, flow between their territories. The movements of goods and information were at times reciprocal; the movement of people has historically been one-way but is increasingly bidirectional. This ever-changing relationship has also forged the culture and identity of Hong Kongers.

Once located within the sea and by land, Hong Kong identity is influenced by another set of variables, connected to time and events, with four distinct historical periods shaping each of the identity layers that envelop the Hong Kong residents. These historical/identity events can be divided into the era prior to the Opium Wars; the postwar British sovereignty period; the prehandover period (1984–97), which included large-scale emigration; and the posthandover, remigration period.

Before 1841, four separate Chinese indigenous communities of farmers and fishermen existed in Hong Kong, governed loosely by a fifth, landowning group, the Cantonese,[3] who were former residents of the southern Chinese province of Guangdong. The indigenous and immigrating settlers brought with them to Hong Kong more than the Cantonese dialect. They brought the core Chinese values, rooted in Confucian teachings and transmitted by parents and teachers, that have recently been highlighted by social science research.

One category of these values focused on relationships within the family. Individuals defined themselves according to their obligations to their families[4] and limited their associations with groups outside of the family.[5] Social structures and hierarchies were fixed according to factors such as age, gender, and ranking within the family, but individual behavior could be flexible,[6] depending on the environment in which the interaction takes place (researchers refer to Chinese culture as "high context," meaning that behavior varies based on the situational context).[7]

A second grouping of values, focused on nonfamilial interpersonal relationships, demonstrated a preference for harmonious social relations and the avoidance of conflict.[8] This was accomplished by valuing tradition and by restraining emotional responses,[9] as well as through conformity to group practices and obedience to authority figures. A third category of values focused on a pragmatic approach to learning coupled with social discipline. These traits were inspired and reinforced by the moral teachings of social, educational, and political leaders.[10] Many of these Chinese values can be summarized as a collectivist approach to life, defined as emphasizing loyalty to and the well-being of family and friends.[11] Thus the needs of the social group take precedence over individual needs and desires.

Immigrants from Guangdong also carried with them to Hong Kong traditional Chinese ways of thinking, or what is known as cognitive style. This style features a particular pattern for the interpretation of other people's behavior. The inclination is to attribute the motivation behind people's actions to group norms and beliefs rather than to individual preferences or personality types.[12] Chinese cognitive style also tends to perceive objects and events as continuous and whole rather than as discrete and separate. Finally, in contrast to Western thinking, which stresses an "either-or" preference to decision making and conflict, Chinese thinking is characterized as dialectical or accepting of contradictions as a step toward harmonious goals.[13]

By the mid-nineteenth century, Hong Kong was serving as an entrepôt or transit point of emigration from Mainland China through the Pearl River Delta and onward to the global market, bringing to the territory thousands of individuals seeking economic gain. The worldwide demand for laborers drew men from the far reaches of China. The majority were Cantonese speakers, but the influx included Fujianese-, Chaozhou-, Shanghainese-, and Hakka-speaking groups.[14] Their intended destination may have been Singapore, Canada, or the United States, but many found the opportunities in Hong Kong alluring and their immigration journey ended there. Although the core identity of these migrants was Chinese, their primary identification remained with their regional and dialect-based groups, especially among the non-Cantonese-speaking population. A speaker of the Chaozhou dialect, for example, would refer to himself as a Chaozhou person.

British sovereignty over Hong Kong Island in 1841, at the end of the first Opium War, began the next historical identity era. As Kowloon, by treaty (1860), and later the New Territories (1898), by long-term lease, also came under British rule, Hong Kong's foreign population grew. However, then as now, the population of Hong Kong remained 98% Chinese in origin and language. Its role as an entrepôt intensified as the island's infrastructure in support of immigrant needs developed: steamship companies were created and expanded; employment brokers matched emigrants with labor needs throughout the world; government bureaucrats ensured that territorial immigration policies were upheld; hospitals and aid societies tended to the social service needs of the lost, sick, and lonely; and businessmen, the honest and the unscrupulous, moved payments and formed nascent banking systems. It has been calculated, using the detailed records maintained by British harbormasters, that between 1868 and 1939 more than 6 million Chinese emigrated through and from Hong Kong.[15] Local residents, primarily from the small villages in the New Territories, joined in the emigration as well. Records summarized by the historian Elizabeth Sinn indicate that villagers from Yuen Long, Tsuen Wan, Sha Tau Kok, and Sha Tin immigrated in the late nineteenth century to the United States and Australia but also to Panama, Peru, Borneo, Jamaica, and Singapore.[16]

Amid the mass departures from Hong Kong, both voluntary and forced repatriations to Hong Kong began. One of the first reports of a returnee was for a Chinese woman who had been taken by an American family to Hawaii in 1837 and who returned to Hong Kong in 1843. She also represents the beginnings of the cyclical migration and the globalization of Hong Kongers, as traveling with still another American family, she left the island again in 1848, settling in California.[17] Forced repatriation to Hong Kong ebbed and flowed in response to world conditions. Sinn reports that owing to the Great Depression more than 28,000 persons were repatriated to Hong Kong in 1931.[18] These early experiences of emigration and repatriation formed the next strata of the Hong Kong psyche. As Sinn states, "Emigration both as practice and idea had become commonplace to the people in Hong Kong … emigration was accepted as a way of life. In sum, not only did the practice of emigration become an essential part of Hong Kong's material life, but the idea of emigration, one might say, had also become a basic element of Hong Kong's common mentality."[19]

The permanent population of the island grew slowly during the first 100 years of British sovereignty (1841–1941), shrinking to a low of 650,000 during the Japanese occupation (1941–45) and rebounding to 1.8 million by 1949. The territory experienced dramatic growth beginning in 1949, on the heels of the Chinese Communist Revolution, and then again following several cataclysmic events in China, including the Great Famine (1959–61) and the Cultural Revolution (1965–76), reinforcing the fates of these two locales. Hundreds of thousands of Chinese, many from southern China, poured into Hong Kong and became the workforce that transformed Hong Kong from an entrepôt of Chinese and foreign goods to an independent manufacturing, production, and financial center.

In the 30 years following World War II, Hong Kong's Chinese population doubled. Small-scale emigration from Hong Kong, estimated to be 2,000 to 3,000 people annually, many of whom were again drawn from the villages of the New Territories, continued through the postwar period. Despite their intentions to return to their home villages, many of these emigrants did not do so, and in time, entire villages were emptied of their residents.

The movements of other Hong Kongers were circular throughout this period, although temporary. During such major holidays as the Lunar New Year, hundreds of thousands of Hong Kongers returned to their villages and towns in China. By the 1990s, more than one million were making the annual trek back to their ancestral villages.[20] This circular movement was primarily Hong Kong-based until the late 1980s when China-based tourism and short-term visits reached larger proportions.

Modern identity

From 1841 to 1984, the colonial administration of the territories brought to Hong Kong thousands of British citizens, who ran the territory's government, schools, businesses, entertainment, sports, and so on. Other European expatriates also lived and worked in the colony. Collectively, they brought with them values, social and behavioral structures, communication styles, and cognitive preferences common to British and northern European culture. These Western values can be categorized in several ways. Some values were related to conceptions of the self in which the person was viewed as independent from his or her family and friends in decision making and in the pursuit of individual life goals.[21] A person's actions were propelled by the need to increase self-esteem and toward individual success and achievement. Furthermore, rather than being shaped by situational contexts, each person's behavior depended on the distinctive attributes that the individual possessed.[22] Other values focused on social relationships and the Western preference for an egalitarian style. However, if the relationships were unequal, the person's inclination would be to assume the superior position.[23] Cognitive values tended toward logical, rational thinking and the classification of people, objects, and events.[24] These Western concepts became layered over the Hong Kongers' core Chinese identity. Chinese and British values were not always incompatible; both cultures had long histories of successful and creative entrepreneurship with elaborate trade relationships beyond their borders.

Although the British were a numerical minority in Hong Kong, as its colonial rulers they established institutions and public laws, and rites and rituals that reflected their Western cultural preferences. The Chinese population, during the nearly 150 years between 1841 and 1984, when the Sino-British treaty was signed stipulating that Hong Kong would revert to the political control of the People's Republic of China, was exposed to a dual system of Chinese and Western cultural elements.[25] Chinese values and behaviors were primarily operational in the home among family and friends while Western values and behaviors were displayed in the public realm. Many residents saw themselves as "sampling the best from both cultural traditions, the Chinese providing the spiritual grounding, the Western, the technical prowess."[26] Identity was often described in oppositional terms as "we" (Chinese) versus "they" (British), but behaviorally a hybridization was emerging. Partly in response to industrialization and to higher levels of education, Hong Kongers incorporated Western values of personal competence and autonomy, signaling a shift toward more individualism and less collectivism.[27] H. F. Siu has suggested that the Chinese of Hong

Kong avoided rigidly defined identities; they were comfortable with their multicultural qualities and had learned how to "be flexible in themselves."[28] Similarly, S. M. Cheng and S. H. Ng have observed that the movements of people in and out of Hong Kong created "a highly mobile and culturally cosmopolitan society."[29]

Western values and behaviors became more salient for and infused into the lives of the middle- and upper-class families who chose to have their children educated in the West. In the latter half of the twentieth century, thousands of Hong Kong Chinese children attended high schools and universities in the United Kingdom, in Australia, and, to a lesser extent, in Canada and the United States. In a 2003 survey of 863 Hong Kongers, 23% indicated that they had lived outside Hong Kong for one year or more,[30] and many others aspired to international experience. These sojourner transitions deepened and broadened the Western cultural layer surrounding the individual.

Exposure to Western culture was also pervasive for Hong Kong residents who did not leave Hong Kong but found themselves part of the local workforce employed by international companies on the island and thus spent their working days communicating in the Western corporate style with Western managers and, to a lesser extent, with Western coworkers. A comparative study of managers in Hong Kong, China, and the United States found that the penchant for blended identities extended to managerial styles and values.[31] The responses of Hong Kong managers reflected more Western values than did the responses of Chinese managers. However, those same managers also embraced more Asian values than did the American managers.

Hong Kong identity: 1984 and migration decisions

By 1984, the specter of Britain's 1997 handover of political control of Hong Kong to China was becoming a reality. While Hong Kong and the world discussed the political and economic consequences of this move, a more personal cultural identity crisis was brewing. Not prepared to abandon their sophisticated, urbane behaviors and cultural identities for the drab and autocratic Chineseness of the People's Republic of China (PRC), Hong Konger began to develop a new identity, or *Xianggang ren* identity,[32] this time in opposition to the Chinese rather than to the British.[33] Utilizing her optimal distinctiveness theory, the social psychologist Marilyn Brewer suggests that Hong Kong Chinese needed to fulfill the twin motivations of being connected to the Chinese (through ethnicity and origin) yet of remaining distinctive from them.[34] That is, Hong Kongers' Chinese cultural identity served to differentiate them from their Western identity without their having to embrace the political aspects of the Chinese identity. Other social scientists have found evidence of the narrowness of the core Chinese identity.[35] Hong Kong research participants showed favoritism to people who shared their Hong Kong identity but not to all Chinese (e.g., mainland Chinese). Thus the modern Hong Konger identity appeared to be made up of three nested identities: a core Chinese identity surrounded by Western economic and civic values encased in a regional geographic identity. Another research study found that Hong Kong Chinese identified more with, were more similar to, *both* the British and PRC Chinese than the British identified with either PRC or Hong Kong Chinese.[36] Others perceived this same duality. Siu reports that designers of the Hong Kong Room in the Great Hall of the People in Beijing debated whether English and Ming furniture should be juxtaposed.[37]

As the 1997 handover approached, the motivation for keeping Hong Kong Chinese identity and PRC Chinese identity distinct became more salient and polarized yet the identity itself was unstable and fluctuating. A 1985 survey indicated that more than 60% of respondents identified themselves as "Hong Kongers" compared to approximately 36% who described themselves as "Chinese."[38] In a later survey (1988), investigators found a widening of this gap, 64% compared to 29%.[39]

S. L. Wong suggests that Hong Kong identities are rooted in family experience within China and Hong Kong and that individual preferences for cultural identity reflect that family history.[40] In a 1991 survey, he found that 45.9% of the population defined themselves as Chinese, while 48.4% chose the Hong Kong label. Wong defined the emerging Hong Kongese identity as characterized by the person's being mobile, pluralistic, flexible, situational, and pragmatic.

The political handover provided a unique opportunity for social scientists to track changing ideas and attitudes held by Hong Kongers. In 1989, a multi-university consortium established the Hong Kong Transition Project (HKTP) to chart a wide range of social and political attitudes in the years prior to and following the handover.[41] Using sophisticated sampling and polling methodology, the project conducted surveys and collected interview data, in Cantonese, Mandarin, Hakka, and English, two to four times per year. The number of respondents in each survey ranged from 550 to 1,200. Of particular note in the massive amounts of data collated and analyzed by the project staff, are the substantial swings in cultural identity from 1995 to 1997. Respondents were asked "How might you describe yourself?" and were given a choice of six responses: Chinese, Hong Kong Chinese, Hong Kong people (*Xianggang ren*), Hong Kong British, Overseas Chinese, and Other. Less than 5% of the respondents chose any one of the latter three descriptions. The percentage choosing the option of "Chinese" was initially 20%, jumped to 30% in 1996 and 1997 (surrounding the handover date), and has since settled at approximately 23%.

Most interesting is the identity shift among those Hong Kongers who combined Chineseness into their identity. In 1993, an equal number of respondents (36%) identified themselves as either Hong Kong people or Hong Kong Chinese (similar to the Wong study mentioned earlier). By 1994, respondents diverged — with 40% identifying as Hong Kong Chinese and 28% as Hong Kong people. These percentages flipped dramatically in late 1996, with 45% identifying as Hong Kong people and 20% as Hong Kong Chinese. Just prior to the handover, there was a modest convergence, with 30% identifying as Hong Kong Chinese and 35% as Hong Kong people. On the evening of July 1, 1997, a resident of Yuen Long remarked, "Ten years ago I called myself British because no one supported us [Chinese]. If you said you were a Hong Kong person your image was downgraded. But China is great now and more open internationally. Last year, I started calling myself Chinese." Following the handover in July 1997, identity categorizations stabilized, with 45% of the respondents describing themselves as Hong Kong people and 25% as Hong Kong Chinese, the largest discrepancy yet recorded.

Ying-yi Hong and her colleagues, who measured social identity and attitudes toward Mainland China four times between 1996 and 1998, found that social identity on average did not change. This was in contradiction to the Wong and HKTP results. However, Hong did find that, as a whole, Hong Kong university students showed a more positive attitude toward Mainland China after the handover than before the handover. Moreover, the researchers found that social identity (measured in October 1996) was associated with a pro-China attitude (in March 1997) such that a Chinese identity predicted a positive attitude toward Hong Kong's merging with China. These results were limited to the prehandover time period. After the handover, negative attitudes toward Mainlanders were associated with stronger Hong Konger identity at a later time period.[42]

In an ambitious longitudinal study,[43] the sociologists Janet Salaff (University of Toronto) and Wong Siu-lun (the University of Hong Kong) interviewed 30 Hong Kong families repeatedly during the six-year transition period from 1991 to 1997. The families, initially drawn from a random sample, were then selected to represent both a social class and the decision to emigrate or not. The study's fundamental aim was to understand Hong Kongers' attitudes toward the handover. However, the investigators quickly discovered that political attitudes, that is, the extent to which individuals felt connected either to the Mainland or to Hong Kong, were closely linked to cultural identity. Through intensive interviews and ethnographies, four identity types were uncovered: China "loyalists," Hong Kong "locals," "waverers," and China's "class enemies."

While all interviewees were ethnically Chinese, each varied in his or her extended family's relationship to China (e.g., loyalists had more extended family currently living in China). Loyalists accepted the idea of Hong Kong's reverting to China, attributed much of Hong Kong's economic success to Chinese values, and had no plans to emigrate. Several, in fact, purchased homes in China. They did, however, hold negative stereotypes about Mainlanders and enjoyed their life and freedom in Hong Kong. Middle-aged men born in China were often "loyalists." Locals were primarily born and raised in Hong Kong and felt no connection to China. They did have a positive outlook on Hong Kong's economy, although a few families applied to emigrate as "insurance" against possible economic chaos. Importantly, this group had few family members who had emigrated; Hong Kong was the center of their lives and identity.

In opposition, those individuals in the latter two categories, waverers and China's class enemies, frequently had relatives who either lived abroad or planned to emigrate, and all made application to emigrate themselves. Among the waverers, though, while preferring the British to the Chinese, only one family actually migrated during the study's six years. The class enemies group feared the handover and the anticipated crackdown on civil liberties, corruption, and lawlessness. Families in this group were frequently victims of Mainland political upheavals (e.g., the Cultural Revolution) although few had kinship ties any longer to China. Being members of Hong Kong's upper-middle or upper class and having embraced British values to a greater extent than the other three identity groups, they believed that they had the most to lose both economically and culturally during the handover. Most of the class enemies group methodically planned for their emigration and carried it out sometime over the course of the study.

Hong Kongers on the move: Outbound migration

The handover of sovereignty for Hong Kong from Great Britain to the People's Republic of China was a unique historical phenomenon. The anticipated change from a frenetic capitalistic environment ruled by a democratic, Western country to a communist country with limitations on individual rights of speech and private property created fear and anxiety about what the future might bring under Chinese control. Gary Hamilton encapsulated these feelings when he stated that the entrepreneurs and professional classes needed to "assess whether the risks of being grounded in China ... outweigh[ed] the opportunities that might ensue from becoming China's broker to the world."[44]

As the Saloff and Wong study indicated, the decision-making process was family-focused and was influenced by identity labels. Cultural identity was more than a descriptive category; it had behavioral consequences. Among those interviewees identifying themselves as Chinese, 60% were committed to staying in Hong Kong, whereas among those claiming a Hong Kong identity, only 45% said that they would definitely stay after the handover.

Thousands of Hong Kong residents decided that the risks of staying put were too great; migration soared from 22,400 in 1980 to a high of 66,000 in 1992,[45] although demographer Ronald Skeldon suggests that this government figure underestimates the emigration by 10–15%. He estimates that total outflow of Hong Kongers from 1987–92 was more than 300,000.[46] More inclusive figures from 1984 to 1997 indicate that close to 600,000 emigrated from Hong Kong (Hong Kong government). The latest data collected from the Australian, Canadian and US governments plus estimates of emigration to other countries puts the grand total at approximately 800,000 (see Table 1.1).

Late twentieth-century emigration differed from earlier emigration in more than its quantitative dimension. Nineteenth- and early twentieth-century immigrants were primarily rural, lacked formal education, and represented the poor or working class. These were the Hong Kongers who built the railroads in the West and established the world's Chinatowns. In contrast, immigrants in the 1980s and 1990s were primarily urban, highly educated, middle or upper class. For example, in 1993, 5.2% of all Hong Kongers held university degrees, yet 15% of those Hong Kongers who emigrated were university graduates. Similarly, 12% of the total population was employed in high-level occupations, yet 35.5% of the immigrants were

Table 1.1   Immigrants to major destinations whose last previous residence was
Hong Kong, 1984–97

	Australia	Canada	United States
1984	3,691	7,696	12,290
1985	5,136	7,380	10,975
1986	4,912	5,893	9,930
1987	5,140	16,170	8,785
1988	7,942	23,281	11,817
1989	9,998	19,994	12,236
1990	11,538	28,825	12,853
1991	16,747	22,340	15,564
1992	15,656	38,841	16,741
1993	8,111	36,571	14,418
1994	4,075	44,146	11,953
1995	5,139	31,737	10,699
1996	6,187	30,007	11,319
1997	5,340	21,597	7,974
Total	109,612	334,478	167,554

Grand Total: 611, 644

Estimated Total Emigration to All Countries: 795,137[a]

Sources:

Australia: Department of Immigration and Ethnic Affairs, Australian Immigration, Canberra, Consolidated Statistics, No. 13, 1982 and No. 19, 1997; Department of Immigration, Local Government and Ethnic Affairs, Canberra, Statistical Note 36: Asian Immigration, 1988; Bureau of Immigration Research, Immigration Update, several issues.

Canada: Employment and Immigration Canada, Ottawa, *Annual Immigration Statistics;* Annual Demographic Statistics, No. 19, 1998.

United States: US Department of Justice, Washington DC, *Statistical Yearbooks of Immigration and Naturalization Service.*

Note:

[a]Skeldon (1994) estimated that emigration from Hong Kong to all countries (including the United Kingdom, Singapore, New Zealand, China, and Taiwan) may have been 35% higher than emigration to Australia, Canada, and the United States together. We have used a more conservative estimate of 30% to calculate total emigration during these years.

professionals. Handover emigrants also differed from the emigrants of earlier periods by frequently including three generations of a family rather than a husband migrating alone.[47]

Immigrant families obtained visas to traditional "settler" countries including the United Kingdom, United States, Canada, and Australia, along with neighboring countries such as Singapore and more exotic locales like Fiji, Panama, and Lesotho. Decisions to depart from Hong Kong coincided with changes in immigration policies in a number of countries that served to funnel the immigrants either toward or away from those destinations. One example of a country experiencing the effects of the liberalization of immigration policy was New Zealand, which enacted new laws in 1986. Soon thereafter, New Zealand became the fifth most popular country of destination, receiving 13,530 Hong Kong immigrants between 1987 and 1992.[48]

Combined, Canada, Australia, and the United States accounted for more than 80% of the total number of immigrants during the initial period of immigration (1987–93). Canada received more than 185,000 Hong Kongers during that time period, quadrupling the immigration from the prior seven years.[49] Australia received 75,000, increasing its number of Hong Kong immigrants threefold. The United States received 92,000, only a minor increase over the prior period, at a rate of 10,000 permanent visas granted per year under the Family Reunification Act.[50] Despite the commonalities among these settler countries, the Hong Kong emigrant experiences varied widely.

Hong Kongers on the move: Settling in

In general, emigrants found themselves in countries that differed dramatically from Hong Kong in many ways. One significant physical difference between Hong Kong and the Western countries of emigration is the density levels. Hong Kong is among the most densely populated territories on earth, averaging 6,380 people/square kilometer. The United States averages 31/square kilometer. And the countries that experienced the most immigration from Hong Kong are among the most sparsely populated: both Canada and Australia average 3/square kilometer.[51] Other features were distinctive by country as the Hong Kong newcomers began their adaptation.

Canadian settlement

As the recipient of the largest number of Hong Kong immigrants, Canada found itself in the midst of the largest single-country influx in its history. Hong Kong moved from a tenth place ranking in 1971 as an immigration source country to first place in 1987,[52] and immigration category shifted from family reunification to economic. The sheer number was multiplied in its effect in that the majority of Hong Kong immigrants moved either to the west coast province of British Columbia or to Ontario, in the middle of the country. While the Canadians needed to adjust to their new neighbors, Hong Kongers needed to adjust to a cold climate, mountainous regions, a new language, and a new culture. Chinese culturally derived social networks were the first line of assistance. Voluntary Chinese associations, initially formed to provide aid to the rural, unskilled mid-nineteenth-century gold rush immigrants, continued their efforts to assist the well-educated urban professionals during the difficult preliminary adjustment period in Vancouver, Toronto, and other cities that experienced large-scale immigration.[53] These associations were modeled on those found in villages throughout China.

The shift from the unaccompanied male immigrants in the nineteenth century to multi-generation families in the 1980s led to varied adjustment patterns during the acculturation process. Children straddled two cultural milieu: adapting to the cultural values of their school environments and newly made local friends while maintaining the ethnic values of their parents at home. Inevitable conflicts arose. Husbands and wives had to make differential adaptations as well. Men needed to adjust to a workplace that required more openness in expressing opinions, a flatter organization (fewer managers) with minimized status differences between managers and subordinates, and a slower and less driven work style. Women were thrust into domestic situations without the assistance of domestic help or extended family, resulting in their having increased responsibility for child rearing and for shopping and running a household, mostly in English.

A recent study compared similarities and differences in acculturation among parents and children of immigrant Chinese families in Canada.[54] Three domains of acculturation were investigated. Behavioral practices compared, among other overt actions, Chinese and Canadian language use and media preferences. Ethnic identity assessed the strength of the immigrants' feelings of belonging to their Chinese ethnicity. Cultural values measured the extent to which the families embraced Chinese or Canadian qualities (e.g., family cohesion vs. individualism). Overall, and not unexpectedly, children were more open to adopting the behaviors (speaking English and using English media) and values (more independent) of the Canadians than were their parents. Surprisingly, though, parents were only marginally more committed to Chinese culture than their children were. The families exhibited the most similarities to each other in the ethnic identity and Asian value dimensions, suggesting that, at home, parents were particularly concerned about transmitting aspects of Chinese culture. Yet while the children received and integrated Chinese values into their identities, their behavior frequently reflected Canadian ideals, an example of the duality and integrative flexibility of Chinese self-concept.

Demographic distinctiveness did not break down only along age lines, as the adults themselves did not hold uniform values or beliefs. One unexpected finding was the difference between immigrant mothers and fathers on most of the cultural dimensions. The mothers were more oriented toward Chinese culture and identity, while the fathers favored Canadian ones. These results had consequences for familial relationships, particularly in light of the differential residency in Canada of mothers versus fathers. As we will see, the mothers were more likely to be the sole caretaker of the family in Canada, whereas the fathers returned to Hong Kong.

Immigration has multiple constituents, both individual and institutional, social and cultural. Acculturation to Canada by Hong Kong immigrants must be seen against the backdrop of the prevalent Canadian philosophy of multiculturalism. The tenets of this concept permitted and subtly encouraged the private maintenance of ethnic values while simultaneously insisting on minimal public adherence to Canadian behaviors and values. An example of the outcome of this model is found in a study of immigrants from the Netherlands to Canada compared with those who immigrated to Australia and the United States.[55] Dutch immigrants to Canada were far more likely to identify themselves as Canadian and with an integrative acculturation strategy (i.e., maintaining both home and host culture values and attitudes) and be less marginalized than Dutch immigrants to the other two countries. In a similar study, Punjabi Sikhs were better acculturated to Canada than to Australia or the United Kingdom.[56]

K. B. Chan, a prominent Hong Kong sociologist, argues, however, that within the Hong Kong Canadian community, women and younger immigrants in particular preferred an alternative to multiculturalism. According to Chan, "The hyphen remains a hyphen forever. The multicultural policy has effectively prevented the hyphen (Chinese-Canadian) from being removed and replaced by an arrow (Chinese → Canadian)."[57] Chan advocates for a philosophy that would allow Hong Kong immigrants to better integrate and fuse Chinese and Canadian values, to experience "inclusion and exclusion, togetherness and separation, certainty and adventure, living out … life at the borders"[58] through a hybridization of behavior, identity, and values.

Canada and Canadians also have been transformed by the Hong Kong migration in both small, intimate, and large, structural, ways. New urban development projects such as Pacific Place connect Hong Kong and Vancouver and shift Canadian linkages from northern Europe to the Pacific Rim.[59] The Canadian preference for modest homes surrounded by lawns, trees, and shrubbery reflected the national value placed on open space and natural beauty. Hong Kong immigrants, longing for internal space denied them when they lived in the colony, purchased existing homes in Vancouver or Toronto, razed them, and replaced them with enormous houses fitting to the edges of the footprint of the building lots. Their Canadian neighbors chafed at the changes, whereas the Hong Kongers luxuriated in their new multi-bedroom, multi-bathroom mansions. Who needed a lawn?

Australian settlement

Australia received the largest per capita number of Hong Kongers, who gained entry under the nation's Independent Skills Program (based on educational and occupation skills); by 1990, Hong Kongers had become Australia's largest source of non-English-speaking immigrants, jumping from a 21st ranking in 1980.[60] In 1991–92, for immigrants categorized by place of last residence, Hong Kong was the number one source, with 15,656 new settlers. The total number of Hong Kong–born residents also dramatically increased, from 1,554 in 1954 to 80,000 in 1993.[61] In a comparative study of Asian immigrants to Brisbane, Australia, which included 23 Hong Kongers, parameters of this subgroup were described and they deviated noticeably from those of immigrants from the PRC, Taiwan, Japan, and Vietnam. Most Hong Kong respondents were married to other Hong Kongers, only half had children, and most owned their own homes or apartments in neighborhoods described as at the middle or upper socioeconomic level. Nearly half of the Hong Kong respondents had visited Australia prior to immigrating there and indicated that physical attributes of the environment (climate, cleanliness, open spaces) were important factors in their selecting Australia as their immigration destination. Mostly university-educated, they were employed as professionals.[62]

Although geographically proximal to Hong Kong, Australia offered differences in climate, topography, history, employment opportunities, and culture. A critical aspect of immigrant adjustment was economic, posing the question of whether these highly educated immigrants from Hong

Kong would find appropriate jobs within the Australian labor force. Anita Mak, a Hong Kong–born psychologist, educated partly in Hong Kong and partly in Australia, conducted an in-depth study of 111 Hong Kong Chinese who settled in Australia.[63] These mid-career professionals, both men and women, included newcomers (less than 3½ years in Australia) and settlers (3½–10 years).

Somewhat unexpectedly, two-thirds of the respondents were able to find positions in the same occupation as in Hong Kong although subsequently many found career advancement blocked. Two-thirds of the respondents also indicated that while generally satisfied with their jobs, they were uncertain or dissatisfied about career development. Nearly a quarter of the interviewees needed further study in a new academic area in order to secure a job, and obstacles to their finding relevant employment were particularly evident in the areas of engineering, teaching, and management.

Cross-cultural differences between the two countries were revealed most clearly in the employment arena. Study participants perceived that limitations both in finding pertinent employment and in career promotion were fueled by racial discrimination, the undervaluing of Hong Kong education and work experience, language barriers, and lack of local knowledge. Australian cultural values influenced workplace interactions and customs, leading to the need for adjustments on the part of the immigrants. In his groundbreaking work on cultural values and their influence in the workplace, Geert Hofstede, a Dutch organizational psychologist, found significant differences between Hong Kong and Australia.[64] On the continuum of collectivism (0) to individualism (100), Hong Kong scored a 25 (ranked 53) (more collectivist) while Australia scored a 90 (and was ranked 2) (more individualist). These differences were manifest in the relationship that the workers felt with the work institution and the amount of time and energy that would be spent on behalf of the institution. Hong Kongers were accustomed to working long hours, six to seven days a week, and to socializing with coworkers in the evening (eating, drinking, playing mah-jong). These behaviors were cultural signifiers and represented strong connections to the work group. Their hard work would support and maintain the organization, which in turn would reward the employee. For Hong Kongers, the balance of work life to family life inevitably fell on the side of work. For Australian workers, the balance fell on the side of family and personal leisure. In individualist Australia, the work day and the work week were short and individual effort was modest. Immigrants were often troubled by what they perceived as a weak work ethic and lack of concern about the organization. Conversely, Australians negatively attributed the workplace dedication and persistence of the Hong Kong immigrants to cloying deference to the boss or to an unfortunate lack of concern for family.

Respondents in the Mak study indicated that other problematic cultural differences included uncomfortably democratic work relationships between supervisor and subordinate, and preferences for the open expression of opinions. External factors, such as the struggling state of the Australian economy in the late 1980s and early 1990s, also resulted in dissatisfaction with financial compensation. One-third of the respondents were considering a return to Hong Kong. Not all cultural differences were met with distress, however. Increased workplace autonomy and responsibility resulted in increased satisfaction among the Hong Kong immigrants.

Overall, Hong Kong immigrants were happier with their personal and family life than they were with their jobs in Australia. The search for career satisfaction as well as the challenges of raising school-aged children appeared to be significant factors in immigrants' decision making regarding whether they remained in or departed from Australia.

United States settlement

Hong Kongers who emigrated to the United States did so under America's family reunification policy. Therefore, these immigrants had private mutual assistance groups ready to ease their acculturative stress. Despite the existence of supporting family and friends, the majority of social scientific research on the Hong Kong immigrant group has focused on the effects of acculturation on a wide variety of psychological outcomes. Few consistent findings enable us to generalize about the acculturation process for the Hong Kongers in the United States. Some studies demonstrated that acculturation levels (i.e., the extent to which an individual acculturated to US society) did not affect depression,[65] whereas others indicated that those immigrants with lower acculturation to the United States had higher expectations about the expertise of psychological counselors.[66] A more nuanced result indicated that the amount of stress related to acculturation was influenced by whether an immigrant held an internal versus external Chinese identity.[67]

An anthropological study, which used a case study method rather than an experimental one,[68] discussed Hong Kong immigrants' planned and intentional strategy not only to adjust to life in California but also to fit within the upper social classes and monied elites. Through interviews and observations, this author revealed that the immigrants used multiple tactics including selection of the "right" private schools, investment in self-improvement lessons (tennis, golf, music, chess), purchase or building of homes in geographically desirable locations (from both a local and a *feng shui* perspective), and philanthropic donations to and leadership volunteerism with favored charities and cultural institutions. This study was also critical of many current conceptualizations of globalization. The researcher's paradigm included immigrant choice or personal agency in emigration rationale and acculturation decision making.

New Zealand settlement

The New Zealand clinical psychologist Elsie Ho, herself an immigrant from Hong Kong, has examined New Zealand's Chinese community, particularly in Auckland, where the largest numbers of former Hong Kong residents reside.[69] Her profile of recent Hong Kong immigrants to New Zealand reflect those who have resettled elsewhere: well-educated, well-off, and moving as nuclear or extended families. New Zealand provided them with a stable, democratic, and English-speaking environment coupled with a comfortable climate, distinctively "clean and green" surroundings, and excellent educational opportunities.

Ho found that the new immigrants settled in easily economically, securing managerial, professional, and administrative positions. Eighty percent of their employment was in wholesale or retail trade, restaurants and hotels, business and financial services, and manufacturing. Socially, the atmosphere was more clouded. The large numbers of immigrants settling into a rather small geographic area over a short time period resulted in some public display of prejudice. Overt and subtle discrimination led to active attempts on the part of local and Chinese leaders to seek ways to increase tolerance and enhance understanding between the two communities. It also prompted the Hong Kongers to pursue dual goals of becoming more fully integrated into the host society while maintaining their Hong Kong identity through the establishment and growth of community self-help organizations.

Hong Kongers on the move: Coming home

On July 1, 1997, on a hot and rainy evening in Hong Kong, the British Union Jack was lowered and replaced by the five-starred flag of the People's Republic of China and by the smaller bauhinia flag of the new Special Administrative Region of Hong Kong. The HMY *Britannia*, carrying Prince Charles and Christopher Patten, the 28th and last Governor of Hong Kong, sailed away from Victoria Harbour as the People's Liberation Army, arriving from Shenzhen, assumed their positions guarding the former Prince of Wales Barracks in Admiralty. Revelers in Statue Square mixed with democracy protestors who shouted outside of the Legco (Legislative Council) Building. Amid the celebrations and the anxiety, the people of Hong Kong held their collective breath.

Despite the removal of symbols of the Crown, no calamitous changes occurred in Hong Kong in the next few months, and the island's population cautiously exhaled. So did the Hong Kong immigrants, who, while adapting to life in Vancouver, Los Angeles, Sydney, and London, kept their eyes trained on events in the former colony. For many, their immediate fears about the impact of Chinese sovereignty were not realized but neither were their optimistic expectations of life as immigrants. In their new countries, professionals found themselves either under- or unemployed, subtle discriminatory practices were uncovered, and English-language skills were found to be insufficient.

As a result, the immigration tide began to turn. What began as a trickle of husbands returning to Hong Kong to work turned into a steady flow of returnees. The structure of late twentieth-century Hong Kong immigration began with features both similar to and distinctive from immigrant patterns from other countries. As was noted earlier in the chapter, migrants most often departed as multi-generation families, and their middle-class status and advanced education distinguished them from past immigrant groups. Their return to Hong Kong was distinctive as well. Some men who had emigrated found themselves dissatisfied with their immigrant jobs, with the outlook for career advancement, and, most disturbing, with their low financial compensation. What then was the salient option? They decided to return to Hong Kong, where the economy was expanding, the labor pool depleted, and the salaries high. With an eye toward the future and Hong Kongers' characteristic flexibility, immigrant men had maintained their Hong Kong workplace networks throughout their overseas adjustment, communicating often with their former coworkers and supervisors and their university friends. Hong Kong businesses were in dire need of skilled and experienced workers because of the recent exodus and were luring immigrants back to Hong Kong with enticing compensation packages.

But who should return? Just the husband? The entire family? Only the parents, leaving the grandparents to care for the children in the settler country? Both the parents and children, leaving the grandparents as placeholders in the newly purchased home? All possibilities were tried. The patterns varied in format and over time.

Initially, the pattern was for the entire family to remain in the new homeland with the exception of the husbands, who accepted employment in Hong Kong. Often this option was undertaken as an expedient measure, with the expectation that the men would return frequently to their new homeland to visit the family and, conversely, that the family would travel to Hong Kong during school holidays and the summer. Thus was born the Hong Kong "astronaut" (*tai kong ren*). A play on words, this term also can be translated as "man without a wife." These men, flying back and forth between Kai Tak Airport and Vancouver or Sydney, led binational lives while their "satellite" families struggled to adjust to a new culture and a new identity. The long-term strategy was straightforward although rarely realized — after a year or so the solo husbands would earn enough in Hong Kong to return to their families and the country to which they had immigrated.

Although these astronaut tactics were born of economic underemployment,[70] they had psychological motivations as well. In the settler country, husbands did not only feel the pinch of declining income. They also experienced the ego-deflating effect of having less prestigious jobs than they had had in Hong Kong, which often necessitated that their wives now seek employment. The possibility of lowered self-esteem surely was behind the comments of one male returnee: *"When you are not able to find a job, or earn enough money or work at your former position, especially for a male, they'll feel that they are useless. Some people who are used to being a boss, [but] after they went to Canada they had to distribute newspapers or to work as a driver for a living. As their social class lowered dramatically, they also suffered serious psychological depression. I think, other than money, this is another important reason why many have returned to Hong Kong."*[71]

These personal inclinations and desires to return home were fanned by the Hong Kong government's active attempts to lure the migrants back home. Recruitment teams from the private sector and the government traveled throughout North America, Australia, and New Zealand seeking to entice the immigrants back with the promise of hefty salaries and bonuses, and appealing to their loyalty to the territory.[72]

A secondary remigration strategy began to develop. The pragmatic characteristics of the Hong Kong identity began to coalesce around the issue of child rearing. Parents wanted to raise bilingual and bicultural children. Perhaps a developmental interlude back in Hong Kong would ensure that their children would have their Cantonese skills reinforced and would begin to learn Mandarin, all the while maintaining their newly polished English-language fluency. Wives and children began to depart from their countries of immigration, often leaving behind a parent, or keeping ownership of a house, now rented to newer immigrants. Thus behavioral decisions to return to the territory were based on both macro and micro forces. On the macro side were fluctuating economies, political decisions by the Chinese government, and human rights concerns. On the micro side were depressed husbands, unhappy children, ill and aging parents, and lifestyle preferences.

The plan was now a reversed journey: move to Hong Kong but return to the new passport countries during school holidays to reunite with extended family and for linguistic maintenance, in anticipation several years hence of their children's matriculating at the University of British Columbia or the University of New South Wales. The solo astronaut was gradually replaced by the familial boomerang,[73] careening back and forth from Hong Kong.

Counting the remigrants

How many Hong Kongers have returned in their former homeland? Accurately tracking the movement of people is a notoriously difficult task. Government statisticians and academic demographers frequently disagree about population figures. Estimates of migrants returning to their home countries are just that, estimations based on shipboard manifests, census information, occasional surveys, and anecdotal evidence. The historian Mark Wyman investigated early twentieth-century return migration from the United States back to the immigrants' native European homelands.[74] He used many sources to estimate the numbers and suggests that more than 4 million immigrants returned home. Researchers attending a 1981 European conference on International Return Migration estimated that 20–30% of the Europeans returned home. But these numbers varied dramatically by ethnicity and by reason for migration, primarily economic compared with political. For example, 50–60% of southern Italians, whose immigration to the United States was motivated by financial reasons, returned to Italy, whereas only 5% of Eastern European Jews, migrating to avoid anti-Semitic programs and mass displacements, returned to Russia and neighboring countries. Cinel also investigated return migration from the United States focusing on Italians.[75] His estimates were based on extensive banking records and on archival documents from local municipalities. Despite the numerical statements, most historians admit to uncertainties in their estimates and to inconsistencies in early censuses and surveys.

Similarly, it is impossible to accurately assess how many Hong Kongers have returned to live and work in the territory. Surveys on intentions to remigrate are not necessarily an accurate reflection; there is no assurance that the migrating behavior will match the intention.[76] There were those returnees intending to return briefly to Hong Kong who stayed. Then there were those who intended to remain in Hong Kong but who returned to their country of migration. And many found themselves leading a peripatetic existence creating the Hong Kong migrant boomerang.

The outflow of emigrants from and inflow of returnees to Hong Kong are particularly difficult to track because individuals departing for Commonwealth countries prior to 1997 were not required to relinquish their Hong Kong residency cards when they left and therefore were not required to apply for a visa or for re-entry permission when they returned. Despite its speculative nature, I will not shirk from the task of suggesting some return migrant assessments. Early surveys by the Hong Kong government claimed that in 1992 alone, 8,000 people returned,[77] or an estimated 16% of the total emigrant group.[78] Academic study has suggested that 30% of those who settled in Australia in 1990/91 returned to Hong Kong by 1993.[79] Ronald Skeldon revised these estimates, suggesting that "it is not improbable that one-fifth of the more than 300,000 who are said to have left Hong Kong between 1987 and 1992 might have returned, or some 60,000 people."[80]

Later surveys by the Hong Kong government estimated that 120,000 emigrants had returned.[81] This figure, however, is generally acknowledged by social scientists to substantially undercount the actual number. The profile and a similar census in 2001 indicated that most returnees were young adults (aged 20 to 29, 37.5%) or middle-aged (aged 30 to 39, 21.5%); very few were children or retirees.

DeGolyer's annual Hong Kong Transition Survey inquired as to the respondent's identity. Approximately 7% describe themselves as either remigrants or Hong Kong expatriates. Extrapolating to the current population of nearly 7 million, this would translate to 490,000 returnees — nearly a half million remigrants.

Another enumerative methodology is to measure the number of foreign nationals living in Hong Kong. This method may give an indication of the numbers of return migrants as many entered Hong Kong under their new foreign passports. Ley and Kobayashi summarized media reports that estimated that between 500,000 and 700,000 Hong Kongers had returned by the mid-1990s.[82] The Hong Kong Immigration Department indicated that the number of Australians living in Hong Kong was approximately 8,500 for much of the 1980s. That number jumped to 18,700 by 1994, and to 50,000 by 2005. One can reasonably assume that the majority of these Australian passport holders are Hong Kongers returning home. Similarly, the number of Canadians living in Hong Kong hovered between 8,000 and 10,000 in the 1980s; in 1994, the number was 24,700. By 2005, the Canadian Consulate of Hong Kong indicated that 250,000 Canadian passport holders were residing in Hong Kong and the Canadian Chamber of Commerce in Hong Kong provided the high estimate that 500,000 Canadian citizens were living in Hong Kong.

Less dramatic are the increases in the numbers of US and UK passport holders residing in Hong Kong. The number of British citizens living in Hong Kong during the 1980s and early 1990s stayed flat, at 16,000, which was not a surprisingly large number given that Hong Kong remained a colonial territory. However, the number began to rise and reached 23,700 by 1994 and by 2005 was 250,000. There was a different trajectory for US citizens residing in Hong Kong, with a slow and steady increase in the number from 14,000 in 1986 to nearly 30,000 in 1994; in 2009 there were 54,000.

One might be tempted to assume that the increases in Western representation in Hong Kong were due to an influx of business expatriates. But there are indications that the number of corporate expatriate employees in Hong Kong has declined in the first decade of the twenty-first century. Several reasons account for this change, including the cost of living for expatriate workers, corporate relocation of Asian headquarters to Shanghai or Beijing, and changes in the US tax codes that are less beneficial for expatriates.

Therefore, increases in the numbers of Australian, Canadian, UK, and US passport holders in Hong Kong can reasonably be attributed to Hong Kong Chinese migrants returning under the passport of their newly acquired citizenship. In summary, conservative estimates would put the number of remigrants from all countries of settlement at 500,000, that is, 83% of those who migrated and nearly 7% of the total population of Hong Kong.

Returning home: Psychological consequences for identity

Psychologically, what is the nature of the cultural identity of the returnee to Hong Kong, whether the husband or the entire family? On to the multilayered Hong Kong identity, Chinese, British, Hong Kong identity vis-à-vis British, Hong Kong identity vis-à-vis China, and Canadian/Australian, is now added yet another — the identity of return migrant. Who are these individuals and what is the configuration of their identity? Do they feel at home again in Hong Kong, or has their identity transformation led to a new global transnational identity? This book, and the Hong Kong Remigration Project that it summarizes, was designed to answer such questions so that we might better understand the identity changes that return migrants face. Antecedents to remigration, such as characteristics of the adaptation process to the settlement country, and consequences of remigration, in terms of behavior, thought, and emotion, will be investigated. To assist in the analysis of these questions, a theoretical framework was utilized. The Cultural Identity Model (CIM) of Cultural Transitions was initially developed to conceptualize the repatriation of sojourners, those travelers who are temporarily living in a foreign country.[83] However, the CIM has proven to be a functional framework with which to understand the repatriated immigrant identity as well. A detailed discussion of the features and variables in the CIM will be explored in Chapter 3.

The case has been made in this chapter that residents of Hong Kong have developed complex identities. Triggered by situational cues, Hong Kongers have learned how to negotiate these identities within the Hong Kong regional and global context. Wong Siu-lun provides a rich example of the ability to switch cultural identities among Hong Kong textile manufacturers who were born in Shanghai:

> According to the situation, a Shanghainese can activate regional ties of various scope … In international forums such as textile negotiations, the cotton spinners usually present themselves as industrialists from Hong Kong … Vis-à-vis their foreign buyers or the senior British officials of the colony, they are Chinese. Meeting in regional associations, they are people from Ningpo or Shanghai city who enjoy their local cuisine and theatrical entertainment. When they participate in the activities of their trade associations, they are modern, westernized businessmen.[84]

The large-scale movement of people from and back to Hong Kong allows us not only to understand the psychological consequences of Hong Kong return migration but also to illuminate an emerging worldwide phenomenon. Migrants are returning in large numbers to Asian countries including China, Korea, Vietnam, and India. Particular European countries, such as Ireland, the Czech Republic, and Turkey, are also experiencing a rise in return migrants, as is Israel. Results of the limited number of social scientific investigations focusing on the experiences of these remigrants will be summarized throughout the book, starting in Chapter 3, and contrasted with the findings of the Hong Kong Remigration Project.

2

Sojourner adjustment and adaptation to new cultures:
Art, literature, and the social science perspective on identity

Humans are a peripatetic species, traveling widely for food and territory. Recent biological anthropology research indicates that 3,500 years ago, residents of coastal China migrated eastward across the Pacific Ocean, populating hundreds of islands that make up Micronesia and Polynesia.[1] No doubt, early clans and tribes experienced problems in maintaining rigid boundaries and separate identities from neighboring groups. Early documents reveal in some instances the struggle to assimilate into other societies, while in other situations the admonitions by community leaders were to avoid such integration. Individual internal struggles to blend cultural identities introduced through proximity and enculturation, political change and geographic transition have been revealed in art, both visual and textual, as well as through social scientific analysis.

Art and cultural adaptation

Artists have been among the most frequent culture travelers, their movements pulled by their muses or pushed by government censorship, or initiated through artistic training, increasingly global exhibitions, or the transnational business of art. Irrespective of the catalyst, the consequences have been artistic renderings that mirror either the personal anguish of or their effortless adaptation to their cultural displacement. These artists focus on combining home and host country images, symbols echoing the psychological experience of overlapping, hybrid, or replaced identities that result from the need to adapt to life away from their homeland. Several artists provide vivid examples of cultural transition and identity art.

Masami Teraoka, a painter born in Japan, moved to Los Angeles at the age of 25 and then settled in Hawaii, itself a location of mixed cultures and identities. After the artist's more than 40 years of artistic work in America, his paintings focus on many universal themes, including power, popular culture, the degradation of women, and worldwide health epidemics. But the themes of his early work echoed his personal cultural journey in both style and content. He was struck by the sharp differences in values between Japan and the United States, especially those of respect for tradition, familial responsibility, and discretion on the one hand and freedom, individual liberty, and materialism on the other.[2] He embarked on a series of watercolors that resembled the traditional Edo-period woodblock prints (*ukiyo-e*) filled with kabuki actors and ninja, with a humorous but clear reference to American symbols and values. The series, *McDonald's Hamburgers Invading Japan*, completed in the 1970s, portrays kimono-clad geishas stepping with their wooden geta on half-eaten hamburgers and their wrappers (Figure 2.1); a traditional Japanese broom sweeping away McDonald detritus (Figure 2.2); and a Western woman, wearing a slightly disheveled kimono, attempting to use chopsticks to dine on slippery noodle soup while a hamburger-eating geisha appears in the background (Figure 2.3). In his *Hawaiian Snorkel Series/View from Here to Eternity*, Teraoka utilizes the style of the famous ukiyo-e artists Hiroshige and Hokusai but inserts Western icons such as snorkeling equipment.[3]

Contemporary Chinese artists, who began to exhibit internationally in the late 1980s, also incorporated cultural transitions and blendings into their works, as travel and study outside China became more available to and the urge to depict cultural struggles and identity became compelling for these artists. Hung Wu suggests that "instead of taking the global and local as two external frames ... we should consider them as internal experiences and perspectives. The key to understanding these artists and their works is to discover how such experiences and perspectives were negotiated through specific art forms."[4] One example is the work by Zhu Jinshi entitled *Impermanence* (1996). Using 50,000 pieces of *xuan* paper, the material used for traditional calligraphy paintings, he built a fortress-like structure, first in Beijing and then in Berlin. Zhu had emigrated to Berlin several years prior to creating this piece and within it he combined elements of his dual cultural experience and identity. The works of the artists Zhou Chunya and Ai Weiwei also mixed traditional Chinese icons with modern or Western ones. The paintings of the German-trained Zhou present the Chinese concept of scholars' rocks in a German Expressionist

Figure 2.1 Masami Teraoka, *McDonald's Hamburgers Invading Japan/Chochin-me* (1982). Courtesy of the artist and Catharine Clark Gallery, San Francisco, CA.

Figure 2.2 Masami Teraoka, *McDonald's Hamburgers Invading Japan/Broom and Hamburger* (1974). Courtesy of the artist and Catharine Clark Gallery, San Francisco, CA.

Figure 2.3 Masami Teraoka, *McDonald's Hamburgers Invading Japan/Geisha and Tattooed Woman* (1975). Courtesy of the artist and Catharine Clark Gallery, San Francisco, CA.

style, while Ai deconstructs Ming-style furniture and reassembles the pieces as postmodern sculpture.[5]

Xu Bing emigrated to the United States in the early 1990s from Beijing. Following the dislocation and disassociation in the countryside during the Cultural Revolution, Xu had created his own 4,000-pictograph language that was strikingly reminiscent of Chinese characters yet different enough to confuse even Chinese gallery-goers. This Chinese scholar's tradition was reinforced when he displayed the language in long and flowing printed pages in an installation entitled *A Book from the Sky* (1987–91). Once Xu settled in America and began his work there, his pictographs morphed into English words but rendered in Chinese calligraphic style. He calls this technique Square Word Calligraphy, and entitled one of his first projects using it *Case Study for a New English Calligraphy* (1998). Simplification of Chinese characters by the Communist leaders of the PRC had severed the people from their ancient texts, which were written in more elaborate configurations. Xu's creative work, however, opens the elegance and wonder of Chinese calligraphy to millions of English speakers.[6] Simultaneously, the artist has recognized that language and thought are inseparable and that learning a new, although created, language involves viewers' readjusting "their ingrained thought."[7] Xu has noted, as he gives Chinese traditional modes his own unique interpretation, that combining his history and China's history has allowed him to forge a new path, separate from the East and the West, an artistic hybridization.[8]

Another Chinese artist transplanted to the United States is Cai Guoqiang. He was born in Fujian Province and worked in Japan for nearly ten years prior to relocating to New York. Cultural misunderstandings are often represented in his work, placing Chinese elements such as *feng shui*, herbal medicine, and funerary customs in a Western or global context. In 1997, at an exhibit at the Queen's Museum in New York, he created the installation *Cultural Melting Bath*, in which a hot tub infused with herbal medicine was surrounded by stones imported from China. In his 2002 solo exhibition at the Shanghai Art Museum, five new installations underscored his cross-cultural themes. As one art critic noted, "He [Cai] has joined the ranks of the art-world nomads for whom the idea of home is largely theoretical. For such an artist, the discomfort of exile is mitigated by the advantage of an external perspective. No longer a Chinese insider, yet not a Western native, Cai is able to reveal the unstable material out of which such identities are constructed."[9]

America and Europe have not been the sole destinations for Chinese painters and sculptors. Guan Wei is a Chinese-born artist now living and working in Australia. Deborah Hart describes Guan's art, which combines Chinese brushstrokes and acupuncture points with Western figures, as having "evolved a distinctive visual language that brings together ideas from East and West."[10] Although Guan's work covers a wide range of subjects, cross-cultural migrations have informed many of his installations and multi-paneled paintings. Representative of this grand style is *Echo* (2005), a series of 42 panels painted as mythological maps of Australia, using figures from European colonial exploration and Chinese landscape painting. Guan intersperses real animals and mythological creatures in *Towns Called Dread and Bathe* (2007), and the work includes Chinese characters but with additional strokes leading to an invented language. For Guan, the search for home appears to be both an artistic and a personal subject. In his major work, *Looking for Home* (2000), the panels show humans floating through a starry sky and looking perhaps for a spiritual home. Guan's own history is revealed in much of his art. Born to an aristocratic Manchu family and educated in Beijing, Guan enjoyed a short artistic residency in Tasmania in the late 1980s. Returning to Beijing in 1989, he lived through the demonstrations and turmoil of the Tiananmen Square student demonstrations and then left China again for Australia. On his return there, first to Tasmania and then to Sydney, he felt isolated and lonely and was hampered by his minimal English. Despite these psychological difficulties, or perhaps in a reaction to them, his art has flourished. One of his largest works, *Dow: Island* (2002), with its 48 panels, explores the plight of refugees, employing the visual language of traditional Chinese paintings and borrowing from the look of early Western maps from the Middle Ages.

One final example of a bicultural Mainland artist is Gu Xiong. Born and educated in Sichuan Province, Gu now lives and works in Canada. He is a multimedia artist for whom the merging and remerging of cultural identities is a persistent theme. Reflecting on his art, Gu states, "All cultures are complex but the one into which you are born is the one you come to understand most profoundly. Thus, this influence is what finds its way into the work of an artist, and I believe it is expressed almost instinctively. If a person should move to another culture, he or she must make both a conscious and instinctive adjustment in seeking to understand what at first is a strange new world … This inevitable conflict of two cultures within my 'artistic being' has entered my work since coming to Canada permanently."[11] Gu had already experienced the dizzying effects of displacement during the Cultural Revolution when he was banished to the countryside for his political artwork. That experience along with the cultural dislocation of being an immigrant influenced many of his works. For example, *To Belong* (1995) places his daughter, representing his Chinese past, in a Canadian Rockies landscape, and *Ding Ho/Group of Seven* (2000), a collaboration with a Canadian artist, represents stereotypes, national identities, and the perceptions and realities of second-culture living. Gu continued to explore these ideas in a piece he contributed to a 2004 exhibit, *Here Is What I Mean*, held at the Museum London (Ontario, Canada), which focused on artistic representations of the immigrant experience. Gu submitted a collection of 16 square charcoal drawings on canvas conveying the complicated relationship between his two cultures and two identities (*Here, There, Everywhere*, 1995).

Hong Kong artists were concerned about East-West issues two decades earlier than were their neighboring colleagues. Beginning with Lui Shoukwan and his students such as Wucius Wong in the 1970s, their art was an attempt to harmonize and hybridize Chinese and Western themes and styles, years before these attempts were seen elsewhere.[12] Perhaps the awareness of and struggle with opposing cultural identities within the same geographic space made the issues salient without the sojourner experience. By the time Mainlander artists began experimenting with conflicting East-West identities in the 1990s, the Hong Kong artists were addressing the anxiety of maintaining their "Hong Kongness" in advance of the handover to Chinese sovereignty by imbuing their work with local linguistic and material concepts. The sculpture of Antonio Mak (*Bible from Happy Valley*, 1992) and Kith Tsang (*Guong Guen*, 1998) and the art of Oscar Ho (*Stories around Town*, 1991) all incorporated Cantonese verbal puns — what could be a more direct way of drawing distinctions between themselves and the Putonghua speakers of the Mainland? Identity challenges had shifted from the far to the near.

Are both the East and the West interrelated within the sphere of art and identity when it is the Westerner who has relocated to Asia? The answer is emphatically *yes* in the case of Henry Steiner, one of the premier graphic designers working in Hong Kong. Born in Europe and raised in New York, Steiner arrived in Hong Kong as a young man in the early 1960s. He quickly made his mark in the design of corporate brands and imaging for the most powerful companies in the territory, many of which had been established in the nineteenth century by British entrepreneurs. His complex personal mixture of cultural venues and values has informed his art, which he calls cross-cultural design. Reflecting on his style, Steiner states that "designers are representative of their own culture yet adaptive to new surroundings. The goal is to achieve a harmonious juxtaposition; more of an interaction than a synthesis."[13] His words echo his work. One culturally satisfying example is an image in the 1980 Annual Report of the Hong Kong and Shanghai Bank (HSBC) in which two split photographs form one image: one combines halves from two lions' heads, one from the lion sculpture guarding the entrance to the HSBC headquarters in Hong Kong and the other from one of the literary lions majestically welcoming patrons to the New York City Public Library's main branch (Figure 2.4). The second split image portrays the masked face of a Cantonese opera performer on the left side while the right side is a close-up of the face of the Statue of Liberty. In addition to reporting the HSBC's financial status, the Annual Report was celebrating the corporation's acquisition of a New York-based bank.

Steiner was as adept at juxtaposing culturally distinct languages as he was images. On the cover of the Hong Kong Mass Transit Railway's Tenth Annual Report, he spelled out the word "ten" replacing the Roman-style letter "t" with the calligraphically brushed Chinese character for the number ten (*shi*), which resembles the letter "t."

Figure 2.4   Henry Steiner, cover I and II of the *HSBC Annual Report* (1980). Courtesy of the designer.

Steiner is clear that whereas Western icons and identities can be juxtaposed or added to Eastern ones, they should not be merged or hybridized with them (he would support the concept of the additive/bicultural identity described in Chapter 5). These concepts appear to have been shaped by Steiner's own sense of self and identity. On the cover of *Idea* magazine,[14] he appears wearing a Western business suit, seated in a black leather office chair (Figure 2.5). His face, however, is painted to resemble the Cantonese opera mask that he favors in his designs. He explains his design, and perhaps his personal philosophy, further: "The individual character of the

Figure 2.5 Henry Steiner, cover of *Idea Magazine 162* (1980). Courtesy of the designer.

elements should be retained, each maintaining its own identity while also commenting on and enriching the other, like the balance of *yin* and *yang*. Combination, mixture, blending — these are useless concepts as they will result in a kind of mud. Street stalls in Hong Kong serve an understandably unique beverage called 'Yin-yang,' a combination of tea and coffee. It tastes as you would imagine: the worse characteristics of both are enhanced."[15]

Critiques of Steiner's cross-cultural design ideas claim that he fails to acknowledge the cultural iconic and identity syntheses already present in Hong Kong, the colonial roots of many of the "local" corporate institutions, the modernity of the city, and the fact that Hong Kongers love the taste of "Yin-yang."[16] These essayists would no doubt support the additive/hybrid concept of cultural identity, also described in detail in Chapter 5.

Surprisingly, while artistic visions of migration and cultural identity proliferate, the art of the remigrant has been absent to date. Perhaps those artists who have returned to live in Hong Kong or China have not yet had the time or psychological distance they need to integrate the remigration experience into their art.

Literature and cultural adaptation

The immigrant experience and identity

For hundreds of years, fiction has captured the tumultuous experiences of leaving one's home, either by choice or exile, either for temporary sojourns or permanent immigration, and has narrated the paths to and the consequences of two cultures' clashing, merging, and submerging within a single individual or multigenerational family. Among the most experienced writers of this genre are Indian authors, perhaps because of the hundreds of thousands of Indians living in the diaspora who have generated stories of loss and adjustment. Common themes involving intergenerational conflict, friendship patterns, and marriage have emerged. One of the newest young writers is Jhumpa Lahiri, author of *The Namesake* (2003), a tale of loneliness, ethnic bonding, self-discovery, and generational conflict among Indian immigrants to the United States. Lahiri provides a unique window on the assimilation narrative through the cultural and personal prerogatives of the public and private naming conventions used in India. What Indians are called by their family, friends, schoolmates, and work colleagues, and, most essentially, how they refer to themselves, shapes and reflects their sense of the cultural self.

Chinese writers, many possessing immigrant or bicultural identities themselves, have also felt compelled to explore adaptation and its identity consequences in their writings. Two of the earliest contemporary writers on this theme are Maxine Hong Kingston and Amy Tan. Both Kingston's *The Woman Warrior* (1976) and Tan's *The Joy Luck Club* (1989) examine the immigrant narrative through the lens of Chinese experience, describing the struggles of both FOBs (fresh-off-the-boat immigrants) and ABCs (American-born Chinese). The next generation of immigrant writers may well be represented by Gish (Lillian) Jen, an American-born writer of Shanghai parents. Her identity was shaped both by her ethnic and cultural identity and by growing up in a predominantly Jewish neighborhood in suburban New York. Despite her parents' desire for her to become a doctor or lawyer, she pursued writing and published her first book, *Typical Americans*, in 1991. In this novel, she departs from the formulaic story of "immigrant struggles, immigrant succeeds," to depict a multidimensional and somewhat dark characterization of assimilation of Ralph Chang and his family. Author and essayist Begoña Simal suggests that the characters who inhabit Jen's novel resort to a more hybrid sense of identity, one that is rooted in "multiple anchorages."[17] This theme of creating a cultural identity and self-identity is furthered in Jen's second novel *Mona in the Promised Land* (1996) which continues the story of the Chang family and of Ralph's American-born daughters. Additional layers of identity are selected and merged when Ralph's younger daughter, Mona, rebels against her Chinese roots and decides to convert to Judaism, causing her parents to question their own assimilative philosophy. "No more typical American parents ... No go out ... From now on we are Chinese parents."

The Hong Kong-born novelist Timothy Mo was raised in England by his British mother, and his bicultural identity informs his books in both style and storyline. He has been described as writing with the eye of a Westerner but also with a keen and intimate understanding of Chinese history, literary modes, and voice.[18] Two of his early works, *The Monkey King* (1978) and *Sour Sweet* (1982), explore cultural identities, first that of a Portuguese-Chinese hero living in Macau and then those of Chinese immigrants to London. Mo understands the identity-straddling dilemma of the newcomer, as evidenced in the opening lines of *Sour Sweet*: "The Chens have been living in the UK for four years, which was long enough to have lost their place in the society from which they had emigrated but not long enough to feel comfortable in the new."

Migrant literature, either as thinly veiled autobiographical fiction or overt memoir, allows readers to hear the authentic voice of the immigrant portraying both the rosy remembrances of the homeland and the adaptive struggle in the adopted country. This literature allows for the interpretations and perceptions of the immigrants rather than those of the local and powerful dominant population. As T. A. Koh reflects, "The migrant literature is a means of indigenizing or naturalizing the self, of creating and expressing a new identity, of taking psychic possession of the new land. This last phase is truest of the experience of the descendants of immigrants who are born in the country of their parents' or grandparents' adoption."[19]

Adaptation and the return home

The full cultural transition cycle has been described for more than four millennia. These early travelers were more often than not living in another culture involuntarily and owing to their own wits and courage or to a benevolent ruler were able to return to their homelands. The Old Testament traces the Jewish exile to Babylonia and back to Jerusalem, commenting throughout on the changes in and adjustments made by the ancient Hebrews. In Homer's eighth century BCE epic poem *The Odyssey*, Odysseus' homecoming to Ithaca is as crucial a segment of his journey as were his adventures along the way. But for Odysseus readjusting to home proved to be surprisingly difficult: "Odysseus rose to his feet and stood staring at what was his own land, crying mournfully: 'Alas! And now where on earth am I? What do I here myself?'"

The historian Mark Wyman has noted that the theme of the difficulty of return migration has appeared in nineteenth- and early twentieth-century novels by Irish, German, Finnish, Italian, and Jewish authors.[20] Stories abound in which the emigrant returns to Europe from America a changed person, confronting with difficulty the behaviors and beliefs of his or her former homeland.

Nathaniel Hawthorne's *Marble Faun* recounts the story of Americans in Italy and addresses their concerns about returning home:

> And, now that life had so much human promise in it, they resolved to go back to their own land; because the years after all, have a kind of emptiness, when we spend too many of them on a foreign shore. We defer the reality of life, in such cases, until a future moment, when we shall again breathe our native air; but by-and-by, there are no future moments; or, if we do return, we find that the native air has lost its invigorating quality, and that life has shifted its reality to the spot where we have deemed ourselves only temporary residents. Thus, between two countries, we have none at all, or only that little space of either, in which we finally lay down our discontented bones. It is wise, therefore, to come back betimes — or never. [21]

Through anecdote and personal experiences, contemporary novelists make us aware of the psychological tribulations not only of the sojourner returnee but also of the growing number of immigrants returning home, presaging the scientific analyses of these demographic trends and psychological challenges. Loida Maritza Perez's *Geographies of Home* (1999) describes identity struggles among Dominican immigrants and returnees; similarly, Samia Serageldin's *The Cairo House* (2003) tells of a young woman who returns to Egypt after living ten years in New Hampshire. Many of the tales of return immigration from East Asia focus on Indians returning home and include themes of postcolonial identity search. In Bharti Kirchner's *Darjeeling: A Novel* (2002) the author traces the story of two sisters who return to Northern India following a decade of living in North America, and in Vikram Chandra's *Red Earth and Pouring Rain* (1995), an Indian student returns home from his studies in America.

Inheritance of Loss (2005) by Kiran Desai examines three generations of Indians who return to India after sojourns in Britain and the United States. Their adaptation to foreign lands had been traumatic, and their return home was equally so. After several months in England, "Jemubhai's mind had begun to warp; he grew stranger to himself than he was to those around him, found his own skin odd-colored, his own accent peculiar. He forgot how to laugh, could barely manage to lift his lips in a smile ... he could barely let any of himself peep out of his clothes for fear of giving offence. He began to wash obsessively, concerned he would be accused of smelling ... To the end of his life, he would never be seen without socks and shoes and would prefer shadow to light, faded days to sunny, for he was suspicious that sunlight might reveal him, in his hideousness, all too clearly" (p. 45).[22]

The themes of the anguish of return migration, class distinctions, nationalism, globalization, colonial legacies, and terrorism mingle in this novel. Forty years after his return from student life at Cambridge, the retired judge Jemubhai Patel remains estranged from his Indian homeland, his elevated status as an educated man and returnee further distancing him from common people. As an Indian Anglophile, he is insensitive toward his traditional Indian wife and lacks understanding of the social and political calamities brewing in modern India. "He sat up, fidgeted, looked at the winged dinosaur, purple-beaked banana tree with the eye of one seeing if for the first time. He was a foreigner — a *foreigner* — every bit of him screamed." His father agreed with this assessment. "It was a mistake to send you away. You have become like a stranger to us." Patel's granddaughter, Sai, the product of a colonial-style education within India, also suffered from identity confusion and discomfort with core Indian values and daily behaviors.

Paralleling the Patel family's narrative is the story of their devoted cook's son, Biju, and his illegal migration to the United States, squalid work experiences in New York, and traumatic return home. Yet at least Biju found, on returning to India, that he could shed the label of "immigrant" and not suffer the negative perceptions that accompanied that identity. Upon landing at the Calcutta airport, "Biju stood there in that dusty tepid soft sari night. Sweet drabness of home — he felt everything shifting and clicking into place around him, felt himself slowly shrink back to size, the enormous anxiety of being a foreigner ebbing — the unbearable arrogance and shame of the immigrant. Nobody paid attention to him here, and if they said anything at all, their words were easy, unconcerned." Desai, however, takes a dim view of multiculturalism and of what her fellow author, Salman Rushdie, has called "hybridity, impurity, intermingling, the transformation that comes of new and unexpected combinations of human beings, cultures, ideas, politics, movies, songs."[23]

The Japanese-British writer Kazuo Ishiguro, in his novel *When We Were Orphans* (2000), also explores the identity issues of people returning to a simultaneously familiar and unfamiliar place. Although British, Christopher Banks grows up in 1920s Shanghai and frets about not behaving sufficiently "British." "Uncle Philip, I was just wondering. How do you suppose one might become more English?" "Now why would you want to be more English than you are? ... Well, it's true, out here, you're growing up with a lot of different sorts around you. Chinese, French, Germans, Americans, what have you. It'd be no wonder if you grew up a bit of a mongrel. But that's no bad thing ... Perhaps one day, all these conflicts will end, and it won't be because of great statesmen ... It'll be because people have changed. They'll be like you. More of a mixture. So why not become a mongrel? It's healthy." "But if I did, everything might ..." "Everything might scatter ... I suppose it's something we can't easily get away from. People need to feel they belong. To a nation to a race. Otherwise who knows what might happen" (p. 80).[24]

But at the age of nine, following the mysterious disappearance of his parents, Christopher finds himself on a steamship to London, accompanied by a British army officer. "Look here, old fellow, you really ought to cheer up. After all, you're going to England. You're going home." "It was this last remark, this notion that I was 'going home' which caused my emotions to get the better of me for — I am certain of this — the first and last time on that voyage. Even then, my tears were more of anger than sorrow. For I had deeply resented the colonel's words. As I saw it, I was bound for a strange land where I did not know a soul, while the city [Shanghai] steadily receding before me contained all I knew" (p. 30).

As yet, Chinese writers have not joined this small but growing band of novelists specializing in the remigrant narrative. No doubt as the numbers returning to Hong Kong, China, and Taiwan continue to increase, the literary exploration of the returnees' experience will also develop.

Social science: General immigrant adaptation

Painters and sculptors, novelists and essayists were describing creatively and with insight the conflicts, anguish, and identity disturbances of human global movement long before the scholarly community systematically addressed the topic. Issues surrounding the movement of peoples are only now, somewhat belatedly, being examined by historians, demographers, anthropologists, sociologists, communication theorists, and, most recently, psychologists, each discipline having its own perspective on the process. In the 1980s, a second major wave of twentieth-century immigration began and was matched by a substantial increase in sojourner travel. These demographic events inspired an increase in scholarly theory and research, resulting in a fresh understanding of the complexity of the cultural adaptation experience. In the section that follows, I have summarized several of the theories that demonstrate the range of ideas regarding the factors influencing the psychological outcomes of migration.

Theory

In 1989, Grinberg, Grinberg, and Festinger provided one of the first psychoanalytic treatments of the topic of transition.[25] Having examined both individual and group responses, they proposed a two-element reaction to immigration — that of the immigrant and that of those left behind. The authors outlined a broad framework in which immigration and the process of losing family relationships are viewed as a type of mourning. The guilt felt by the immigrant at leaving others behind and the envy and resentment felt by the abandoned family and friends are proposed to explain the psychological consequences of immigration, which include anxiety, depression, and other dysfunctional responses.

Moving beyond the medical model of transition psychopathology, psychologists theorized that cultural transition and the subsequent "shock" resembled, in its precedents and antecedents, the explanatory model of life stress and the ways in which people cope with stress.[26] The affective variables of the psychological well-being and satisfaction of people in transition are examined in the Stress and Coping Model, a well-articulated framework that looks at individual differences and situational variables as determinants of transition adjustment. Cultural transitions are viewed as stress-provoking life-changing events, and the extent of psychological distress they engender is seen to be moderated by such internal factors as personality, demographic considerations (gender, age, etc.), cognitive interpretation of the transition experience, coping styles, and experience with transitions. External or situational variables, such as coping resources from social support, also affect transition distress. Cultural distance between the home country and the host country and changes in satisfaction over time are two additional unique factors that influence transition-related stress and adaptation.

A wide-ranging and multidisciplinary theory on the process of cultural adaptation of immigrants, refugees, and sojourners was proposed by Kim, building on the stress paradigm.[27] Effective intrapersonal and social communication is seen as the heart of successful adaptation. Positive outcomes such as personal growth are envisaged as a consequence of a stress-adaptation-growth model. Kim emphasizes the host country's role (its attitudes toward immigrants, political and social environment, etc.) in influencing the adaptation trajectory rather than the role of individual-level variables.

A related model focuses on the behavioral aspects of cultural learning, with an emphasis on social interaction. This theory uses a social-psychological lens through which to analyze intercultural encounters.[28] In this model, successful adaptation to a new culture is bolstered through the acquisition of both micro level social skills and knowledge of gestures and postures, and macro interactions such as greeting and leave-taking, making friends, or having a conversation.[29] Conversely, prejudice, conflict, and interpersonal misunderstandings can ensue when cultural skills are absent from the behavioral repertoire of the sojourner or immigrant. The Culture Learning Approach, developed by Furnham and Bochner[30] and expanded by Ward and Kennedy,[31] suggests that social skills acquisition forms the foundation for cultural adjustment and adaptation.

At its core, psychology has always explored issues of the self and identity. While other social sciences have shared this interest, resulting in conceptualizations of political, linguistic, class, and geographic identity theories, the essential element of psychological thought has been the individual, and so it is with identity. Personal identity, that is, those characteristics that are unique to an individual and sets him or her apart from others, and relational identity, or those features in which the self and familiar others interact, have been the major focus of attention in psychology. Social psychological writings, however, have broadened the concept of identity by examining group membership in which members do not necessarily interact with or even know each other. This approach has been developed by both social identity theory[32] and self-categorization theory.[33] In these theories, individual identity is transformed into social identity as a result of the individual's being part of a group (perhaps family, ethnic, or religious) and through comparisons between that person's group ("in-group") and all other groups ("out-groups"). Several scholars have recently suggested replacing the term "social identity" with "collective identity," which they consider to be less ambiguous and more meaningful. Ashmore, Deaux, and McLaughlin-Volpe[34] define "collective identity" as a multidimensional concept that serves as an acknowledgment by an individual of the different groups in which the individual belongs ("subjective claim").[35]

Individuals possess a multiplicity of collective identities, including their gender and family position (ascribed characteristics) and their occupation or hobby (achieved characteristics). Cultural identity, which can be construed as one element or subset of collective identity, has not been well explored in the psychological literature. Cultural identity can be defined as that identity that, through geography, ancestry, or perceived similarity, links an individual to a membership group that encompasses emotional ties, frameworks of thinking, and ways of behaving. Cultural identity may overlap with national (or passport) identity, but it is not a requirement for that identity. In nations with multiple cultural groups, it often will be distinct.

Extrapolating from the collective identity framework developed by Ashmore, Deaux, and McLaughlin-Volpe,[36] cultural identity has several fundamental elements. These include an evaluation of the cultural identity ("I feel positive about being a member of my group"), a sense of belonging ("I feel a part of my group"), behavioral involvement ("I do the activities, cook the food, speak the language of my group"), and an ideology (i.e., a narrative about the cultural group and the individual's link to it). However, it is suggested here that, distinct from other collective identities, cultural identity may occasionally be reflected more in the ways that people think and act than in self-categorization; that is, individuals may not have to make the self-categorization statement ("I am a Hong Konger") that is considered necessary for collective identities in general. As Baumeister points out, not all beliefs about oneself are simultaneously part of one's self-awareness.[37]

Finally, note that the individual experience of cultural identity, as with other individual-level elements of collective identity, develops over time and may have considerable variability. This is particularly true for the individual experience of Hong Kong identity in which developmental changes (e.g., progress from adolescence to adulthood) intersect with historical events (e.g. the 1949 Communist Revolution, the 1989 Tiananmen Square student demonstrations, the 1997 handover, the 2003 SARS epidemic).

Owing to both geographic mobility and increasing cultural heterogeneity within national borders, individuals may possess several cultural identities, often referred to in the psychological literature as "frames" (e.g., an Italian American, a Japanese living in Peru, a Dutch citizen as a permanent resident in Thailand). These multiple cultural identities or frames interact in a variety of ways, and several competing theories have been developed to account for individual responses to multiple cultural identities: identity maintenance, identity conflict, integration, biculturalism, hybridization, and situationalism.

John Berry's elaborated acculturation theory is simultaneously among the widest disseminated and tested and the most controversial. It proposes four identity responses to multiple cultural identities, namely, assimilation, integration, marginalization, and separation, with different acculturative stress levels associated with each response.[38] Berry's model was devised to explain identity issues facing indigenous individuals who are confronted with an imposed dominant or ruling culture, although later it was applied to sojourner adaptation as well. Other writers have focused attention on the movement of individuals (sojourners or immigrants) from one culture to another and the competence associated with biculturalism. LaFromboise, Coleman, and Gerton reviewed this literature,[39] which tends to stress the positive outcomes of an integrated or bicultural identity; Rudmin disputes this claim and demonstrates that biculturalism does not necessarily result in more satisfied or less disturbed immigrants.[40]

Hermans and Kempen have suggested that the increasing cultural connections experienced by the world population will result in the phenomenon of cultural hybridization, and they speculate that this will lead to new forms of cultural identities.[41] Other researchers have more deeply explored the layering of two cultures and the situational occurrences that activate one cultural mindset rather than the other one,[42] and the cultural frame switching of biculturals.[43] Rather than focusing on smooth transitions between multiple cultural identities, Baumeister and his colleagues have proposed a theory of identity conflict in which individuals have irreconcilable components of their identities.[44] Additionally, individuals may have positive emotional responses to both identities yet incompatible ways of behaving. In a test of this model, Leong and Ward found that among Chinese sojourners in Singapore, increased contact with the host nationals positively predicted cultural identity conflict.[45]

It has been noted that Chinese people can be found everywhere in the world, making them purportedly the most ubiquitous nonnative group.[46]

With Hong Kong in the early twenty-first century as a case study, what is the genesis of multiple cultural identities among a population of nearly 7 million inhabitants, and how are these identities negotiated in the public and private arenas?

Social sciences: Chinese immigrant adaptation

Chinese living, studying, and working throughout the world may be sojourners living temporarily in another country with the intention of returning to their homeland, or they may be immigrants intending permanent transition. In either case, the structure, antecedents, and consequences of cultural transition for persons of Chinese background and their hosts are important to investigate and understand. Although Chinese migrant workers have traditionally constituted the major portion of the sojourner population, psychological research has overly sampled the student population, and some researchers speak critically of the conceptualization of a unitary and timeless Chineseness among the diaspora.[47]

K. B. Chan is one of the most prolific theorists and investigators on the topic of Chinese immigrants to the West and their adaptation and identity transformations, which he refers to as cosmopolitanism. Chan argues that the geographically dispersed Chinese family is a strategic and positive development, although certainly not a new development if one reviews both Chinese and non-Chinese immigration over the past 200 years.[48] However, contemporary ease of travel and communication leads these dispersed families to what Chan suggests a new type of Chinese identity, that of the Chinese cosmopolitan, or *chonggen*, meaning multiple rootedness. "The Chinese character *chong* has three meanings: first, multiple, not singular; second, regenerative, as in 'born again'; third, to reassure, to value. It conjures up an image of a succession of sinking roots as process, and multi-stranded roots as outcome."[49] The cosmopolitan is neither *wugen* (rootless) nor *zancao chugen* (total assimilating to the host culture, or "to eliminate grass, one must pull out its roots"). In fact, the cosmopolitan resembles the psychological profile of additive identities (described in Chapters 3 and 5) as those rooted in two different places simultaneously.[50] Although this appears to be contradictory, the Chinese cosmopolitan may find this identity best suits the familial goals of economic and educational success.

Wang put forth an earlier model of Chinese immigration in which, using variants of the word *gen* (roots), he distinguishes five types of Chinese immigrant identities and the diasporic immigrant relationship to host and homeland.[51] Similar to the acculturation model developed by Berry, Wang suggests the following distinctions: *yelou guigen* (fallen leaves return to the roots, or immigrants' desire to return to China but may only be buried there), *zancao chugen* or *luodi shenggen* (accommodate, or sink roots in the host country), *xungen wenzu* (ethnic pride, or search for one's roots), and *shigen lizu* (uprooted, or losing contact with one's roots).

Both Hong Kong sojourner and immigrant adaptation to Canada and Australia have been examined in a variety of empirical studies although none was specifically designed to test the theories mentioned earlier. Some findings indicate profound acculturative stress and discrimination. Other studies report host nationals' holding positive attitudes toward Hong Kong and Chinese sojourner students and immigrants, specifically that of their being the "model minority." However, these stereotypes can come at a cost to the students and may explain why Chinese students in Canada had higher levels of anxiety associated with taking tests than did Anglo- or European-Canadian students.[52] Chinese women, in particular, whether in Hong Kong or Canada, had high levels of psychological distress, but for Chinese women students in Canada, the greater the impact of stressful events, the fewer the reported distress symptoms.[53] These results suggest that women are masking the emotional response to stress or failing to report symptoms. Poorer mental health was also reported among Hong Kong university students in Canada; these students exhibited higher levels of dysfunctional behavior than did French- or English-Canadian students,[54] but their anxiety was modified if the Hong Kong students believed that they had friends and family who would support them. Further, Hong Kong students who engaged in positive thinking as a coping strategy were found to be more satisfied with their ability to cope with stress. In assessing transition-related stressors, Chinese student-sojourners in Canada reported difficulties similar to those of Chinese-Canadians and non-Chinese Canadians — love, marriage, and academic concerns — and only a few stressors that, not surprisingly, were distinctive from those of the residents: language and communication problems, homesickness, and loneliness.[55]

Rosenthal and Feldman studied Hong Kong–born adolescent immigrants in Australia and the United States, examining the acculturation process and comparing the immigrants with locally born Hong Kongers, Australians, and Canadians.[56] There were expected differences in acculturation outcomes in part due to the differential size and power of these Hong Kong communities in Melbourne and San Francisco, the sites of the studies. At the time of the survey, in the late 1980s, the Australian Hong Kong community was small and fragmented, while the United States had a denser and more cohesive Chinese community.

Focusing on values, immigrant youth differed from their Hong Kong–based peers in placing less value on tradition, on helping others, and on the family as a residential unit and placing more value on success. As predicted, second-generation Hong Kong adolescents in Australia acculturated most completely (being nearly indistinguishable from the locally born) compared to those in the United States, demonstrating the influence of the wider community on the adaptation of the individual migrant. These studies also looked at the emotional outcomes of the acculturation process, namely, at behavioral autonomy (independence), misconduct, and distress levels. In general, Hong Kong children exhibited more dependence on their families. They also displayed less behavioral misconduct but more emotional distress, perhaps because they turned their anxieties "inward." Immigrant youth showed slower emotional acculturation, although with similar patterns to the values shifts; Hong Kong adolescents in Australia showed higher levels of misconduct (more acculturation) than adolescents in Hong Kong. Hong Kong immigrant youth in the United States, however, resembled youth living in Hong Kong in autonomy, misconduct, and distress levels, thus showing no evidence of behavioral acculturation.

Rosenthal and Feldman extended their studies of Hong Kong immigrant youth by exploring the issue of Chinese identity, which they defined in multiple ways: self-description ("How Chinese do you feel?"), social relations (e.g., percentage of Chinese friends), Chinese knowledge and behavior (e.g., language, food preferences), and pride in being Chinese.[57] In general, in both Australia and the United States, second-generation Hong Kong adolescents reported feeling less Chinese and being less knowledgeable about Chinese culture than did first-generation immigrants. However, they felt similarly high levels of pride in their Chinese identity. Similar to the pattern of results regarding values and emotional outcomes, the Hong Kong youth in Australia were more acculturated in terms of social relations: they were less likely to spend time with Chinese friends or to desire a Chinese marriage partner than were the youth in the United States.

Chinese student sojourners in the United States trace their origins to 1854, when Yung Wing graduated from Yale and became the first Chinese student to receive a degree from an American university.[58] Hundreds of thousands have followed, either as lone students or as part of family immigration. It has been noted that in the US context, there were twin pressures on these students: those placed by their parents that they succeed academically and those placed by the wider American community that they assimilate to American culture; both pressures threatened the students' Chinese identity. One correlate of adaptation for Chinese students was their decision to anglicize their names;[59] although the relationship between cultural adjustment to the United States and name change could be bidirectional, selecting an English name might speed the adjustment process. But some studies have indicated, to the contrary, that English competency can be identified as a variable associated with acculturative stress and difficulty in adjusting.[60]

Other studies of adaptation to the West can be divided by domains of acculturation in continuity and change between East Asian countries and the United States, Britain, Canada, and Australia. Researchers have examined independence and autonomy, values and identity conflicts, child-rearing practices, family relationships, women's roles, and intermarriage. Psychological studies of the immigrant and adaptation, especially with samples of Chinese, have tended to focus on clinical outcomes such as depression[61] and eating disorders.[62] Building on another discipline tradition, the psychosocial issue of cultural identity and its antecedents and outcomes has been examined among Chinese and Hong Kong immigrant youth and adults. One study by Lieber and colleagues collected data from individuals in the second large wave of Chinese immigration to the United States (late 1960s–1970s) and investigated the balance between maintaining Chinese identity and acculturating to the United States and how this balance affects perceptions of quality of life.[63] Prior research suggested that individuals who successfully maintain homeland identity while simultaneously acculturating to US identity, that is, bicultural individuals, would feel more satisfied with their lives.[64] Results from the Lieber study, however, found that among adult Chinese immigrants (primarily from China, Taiwan, and Hong Kong) the most satisfied were those who had high Chinese identity but low acculturation to the United States; it appears that this was due to high support from spouses.

More in-depth investigations of the home/host identity balance found striking differences between individuals based on personality traits. One such study investigated how, among Chinese-Americans, switching between Chinese and American thinking styles can be influenced by two factors: by cultural priming (being shown symbols of one of their two cultural identities) and by a personality trait — whether individuals see their two identities (Chinese and American) as compatible or in opposition.[65] The researchers proposed that perceiving two identities as either compatible or in opposition will influence the effect of cultural cues on the interpretation of social events. They found that Chinese biculturals who saw their two identities as compatible shifted their cultural mindsets appropriately when primed by cultural cues. For example, if they were shown American symbols (e.g., Mickey Mouse or the Statue of Liberty), the Chinese participants adopted a thinking style common among Americans. When the biculturals were shown Chinese symbols (e.g., the Great Wall or a picture of a rice farmer) they used a Chinese thinking style. For those subjects who perceived their dual cultural identities as contradictory, there was a reverse effect on thinking style from the cultural cues' priming.

In one final glimpse at Chinese adjustment and adaptation, Ward and Kennedy summarized and compared sociocultural difficulties during cross-cultural transitions among 20 different sojourn samples. Chinese (Hong Kong and Mainland groups) sojourners in Singapore had the lowest rate of difficulty, perhaps due to adjustment flexibility on the part of the students or to cultural similarity (low cultural distance) between the visitors and the host country.[66]

In summary, we have seen the struggle for adaptation to a new country as manifested in painting and sculpture; novels and essays; social scientific theory; and empirical studies of academic success, adolescent behavior, ethnic pride, familial stress, life satisfaction, and psychological disorders. Sociological and psychological paradigms have given us models of biculturalism, cosmopolitanism, and multiple-rootedness, all in an effort to better explain the complicated identities and behaviors of those who live in a new land. For the majority of immigrants, their narratives flow from one generation to the next through transformations from ethnic members into citizens and native-born. But for an increasing number of global transitors, another move and relocation is in store. Thus we turn our attention to those who return home, either by design or default, either temporarily or for a final place to rest their "discontented bones."

3 Returning home: Cultural transitions and the identity model

Historical perspective on remigration

Until recently, a popular and stubbornly persistent myth existed throughout the world: once individuals emigrated from their home countries, they were unlikely to return to those countries of origin. This belief was held no more fervently and embedded itself no more passionately into the national psyche than in the United States. As a country of immigrants, the narrative of the myth wove a story of impoverished families in their native lands, victims of vicious prejudice and injustice, who overcame near overwhelming odds to make their way to New York, Atlanta, Chicago, or San Francisco. The closing lines of the story followed the immigrants' successful albeit harrowing adjustment process to life in the United States. But the narrative omits the postscript. Among even the earliest immigrants to the "New World" of colonial New England (1640–60), those returning to Europe outnumbered those traveling west to the colony.[1] Moreover, in the mass migration to the United States from 1880 to 1930, one-quarter to one-third of all European immigrants permanently returned home, totaling nearly 4 million people.[2] Similarly, there are estimates that 30% of immigrants from Europe to the United States between 1908 and 1957 returned home;[3] among Finnish emigrants to the United States prior to 1930, 20% returned home.[4] Yet, as the historian Mark Wyman notes, "Ignored by Fourth of July orators, overlooked by historians who concentrate on the newcomers' assimilation, return migration looms so large in world history, with critical implications for the homelands and the United States that it cries out for attention."[5]

Wyman viewed remigration through many lenses. Psychological observations focused on individual changes in attitudes, beliefs, and behaviors, while sociological themes examined the effects of returnees on the politics, business, housing, language, and even the jokes of the citizens of their homelands. Frequently, remigrants returned home wealthier than they left, which allowed them to build bigger houses, acquire land, and create new businesses offering new products and services. This produced, in turn, a greater demand for goods in the home countries. In Finland, remigrants were credited with introducing new farm crops, livestock, farming equipment, and farming methods. Return migrants to Greece built better roads in rural areas and lobbied for improved public sanitation. Having experienced the rise and potential power of labor unions in the United States, return migrants became leaders in the nascent labor movement throughout Europe, campaigning for safer working conditions and livable wages. Human rights advocates also were often returnees, as exemplified by the Norwegian remigrant Aasta Hansteen, who spearheaded Norway's first feminist movement. The effects of returnees were wide-ranging, and Wyman credits the remigrants with "awakening a general spirit of modernism and a curiosity about the world."[6]

Compatriots were not always pleased with the new philosophies, concepts, or products brought home by the returnees. Of course, some immigrants returned to their homelands immediately following migration, having been rejected by the destination country for health, political, or legal (criminal) reasons and were treated with embarrassment by relatives and scorn by local officials. Upon their return, longer-term immigrants were considered to be a threat to the established social and spiritual order, and clergymen in Europe used words like "degenerated," "dechristianized," and "rushing to their own spiritual destruction" to describe them. Local politicians needed to contend with constituents among the returnees who had been exposed to a different political and economic system and who harshly judged land policies or the local political structure. Friends and neighbors struggled to understand newly accented native tongues, and Americanized phrases appeared in returnees' speech and in store signs and newspaper articles. Popular culture was altered by the inclusion of destination country jokes, slang, and songs.

One significant archival research project focused on nineteenth-century and early twentieth-century return migration to Italy from the United States.[7] It estimated that between 1945 and 1983, 8 million Italians left Italy and 5 million returned, for reasons that included retirement, serious illness, dissatisfaction with life in the United States, and deportation as a result of illegal immigration. As these remigrants reintegrated into Italian life, they were influenced by and had an impact on societal institutions. Historical records, specifically bank archives, reveal the role that the Italian government and the private sector, working in concert, had in encouraging migrants to send remittances back to their home villages and families, and in promoting remigrant investment in Italy in the optimistic belief that these investments would single-handedly modernize the country. These formal policies and informal endorsements supporting migration did result in a slightly improved economy for Italy in general and for southern Italy in particular. However, for many remigrants, readjustment to Italian life was uncomfortable, the economic benefits did not meet their expectations, and their social reimmersion in village life proved unhappy. Their return to Italy was short-lived for these remigrants; America beckoned to them once again, permanently for some and intermittently, albeit regularly, for others.

The current, early twenty-first-century wave of remigrants encompasses dozens of nationalities and includes both the migrant generation and, in a new twist on remigration, the second generation raised in the diaspora. Commentaries and anecdotes about this latest remigration have been captured by journalists; social scientists are just beginning to systematically investigate the phenomenon. Notable among the theories are those put forth by sociologists to explain the scope and consequences of people's continuous movement between their country of origin and their country of immigration. In contrast to the twentieth-century focus on immigration and assimilation, the theory of transnationalism and the development of diasporic citizenship focus on "the process by which immigrants forge and sustain simultaneous multi-stranded relationships that link together their societies of origin and destination."[8] Critics claim that transnational movements are nothing new. During the nineteenth and early twentieth centuries, substantial numbers of immigrants remained in contact with their families through remittance payments or, for some, by eventually remigrating back home,[9] yet there are qualitative and quantitative differences between the interactions of migrant and home country today compared to those of earlier immigrants. Modern transportation and communication allow immigrants to maintain frequent, sometimes daily, contact with their families and to stay closely involved with the culture and politics of their society of origin. Social scientists find that there are consequent improvements in the mental health of immigrants and the economic health of their hometown families.[10]

As a social science concept, transnationalism already has taken on diverse and distinct meanings and thus may have limited usefulness as an explanatory idea. Some researchers may view the trend as a local one, others may see it as a threat to the cohesiveness of the country of settlement, and still others may focus on the role of multinational political or social organizations or may explore the consequences of immigrant financial and ideological involvement in the political life at home.[11]

Psychologists, of course, are less interested in nation-state or societal perspectives and more focused on the development and stability of the self, aspects of identity, and mental health. Some psychologists assert that these transnational citizens develop a bipolar identity that is fragmented yet permits transcendence of national boundaries,[12] whereas others see a more positive bicultural identity that forms in the country of destination and allows the development of transnationalism.[13] It should be noted that transnationalism does not necessitate physical movement and geographic transition. As sociologists more often use the term, it includes remaining in the country of settlement but visiting the homeland, and sending remittances to and doing business with the country of origin. And, most often, transnational practices are the domain of the immigrant generation and not of their children.

Utilizing this definition, Chinese immigrants in the United States are among the least transnational of ethnic groups found in the New York–based Second Generation Study.[14] The Chinese subjects of this study rarely visited the homelands of their parents, and few were interested in relocating to Mainland China, Taiwan, or Hong Kong. While perhaps not yet identifying themselves as Americans, they did think of themselves as New Yorkers.

For our purposes, the crucial question is how does the concept of the transnational — the immigrant who may participate in home life from afar — intersect with that of the remigrant — the immigrant who physically returns to the country of origin? At least one category of transnationalist challenges the conventional way in which social scientists have described immigrants and the assumptions made about their trajectories (linear rather circular), their social and psychological transitions, and the status of their physical and mental health. Can we speak of return migrants and bicultural identities when a growing number of immigrants retain dual citizenship and demonstrate a vibrant involvement with at least two communities? Yet there are those immigrants whose return home is more permanent and who cannot be categorized as vacation sojourners or on an economic tether. What nomenclature should we use for these culture transitors, and what is the consequence of their status for their sense of self and identity?

Terminology: What do we call the people who return to their country of origin?

There is widespread agreement among scholars that the term *immigration* describes entering a new country for the purpose of long-term residence, whereas *emigration* pertains to a departure, typically from one's country of origin. There is little consensus, however, on the description of individuals who return to their home countries. Confusion over terminology turns on several variables, the most prominent being the range of permanence in the change in country of residence.

Those travelers for whom change in residence is intentionally temporary are referred to, within the cross-cultural psychology literature, as *sojourners*, or expatriates. Business executives, guest workers, missionaries, diplomats, military troops, educators, and students constitute these global travelers. A fixed period for an international assignment implies the eventual return to one's homeland. Early research in the 1960s investigated these populations and described the action of returning home as *re-entry*, borrowing the term from space travel concepts and implying the potential for serious psychological outcomes. Embedded in the notion of re-entry was the high risk that returnees could "crash and burn" when returning home. Later research on corporate returnees utilized the less negatively charged term "repatriates," but this concept was borrowed from the sociological literature on refugees, which in that context was referring to refugees forcibly returned to their home countries.

Other social science writings discussing immigrants have used a variety of terms both more descriptive and less evaluative, including "return migrants" or "remigrants." Wyman collected examples of historical vocabulary such as "repeaters" or "birds of passage" (for those who traveled for seasonal work), in addition to more pejorative nicknames such as "Yanks," "American-os," and "okay-boys."[15] The demographer Ronald Skeldon suggested the term "return movement" to describe the action of coming home as the term "migrant" implies permanency.[16]

A well-developed literature has investigated Japanese returned sojourners,[17] with a particular emphasis on the difficulties faced by returnee teenagers.[18] More than 50,000 young Japanese were estimated to be living overseas in 2001.[19] Their plight was captured by the term *kikokushijo*, which can be translated as sons and daughters (*shijo*) who return to the home country (*kikoku*). These young repatriates who accompanied their parents on overseas work assignments during the 1980s were seen as tainted when they returned to Japan, culturally contaminated and linguistically deficient. They faced bullying by peers, isolation at school, and difficulty finding employment. As the internationalization of the Japanese economy and consequently of the Japanese worldview slowly shifted from being a stigma to an asset, *kikokushijo* became sought after by domestic companies desiring bilingual and bicultural employees and by foreign companies wishing to secure a toehold in the Japanese market.

Another type of historical sojourner was the so-called Chinese sojourner (*huaqiao*), who is described as immigrating to the West but never assimilating to his or her adopted country.[20] These sojourners lived in Chinatown ghettos, retaining their language and customs and yearning to return home. They remained proud of their Chinese heritage and patriotic about their homelands despite the obvious fact that they never did return to their countries of origin. Some scholars have argued that the term *huaqiao* is too political and that more neutral terms, such as *huaren* (meaning ethnic Chinese, such as Chinese-Americans) or *huayi* for second and subsequent generations (Chinese descendants), would be appropriate.[21]

Today, returnees to China are somewhat derisively referred to as *hai gui pai* (sea turtles) or worse, *hai dai* (seaweed); those who were locally educated in China are labeled "land tortoises." Each group is imbued with different attitudes on social and political issues.[22]

Hong Kong reporters, pundits, and academics have used two terms to describe those who return: *huiliu* (return flow) and *huigui* (return to belong).[23] The former term applies to returnees to Hong Kong who have been drawn back for economic reasons. The implication of *huiliu* is that the returnees will go back to their adopted countries again,[24] reflecting the essence of the transnational. The latter term, however, refers to those who return to Hong Kong because that is where they feel at home, where they feel they belong.

It was also the Hong Kong media that coined the term "astronaut," again borrowing vocabulary from the aeronautics industry. An "astronaut" refers to the husband of a middle-class family who emigrated together but dispersed soon thereafter. Most often, the wife and children remained in the destination country and the husband returned to Hong Kong to work but frequently shuttled back to see them in Canada or Australia or wherever they had immigrated. K. B. Chan provides a sociological analysis of the term and suggests three meanings for "astronaut family":[25] the sense of travel, movement, or crossing borders; the straddling of two places connoting duality or perhaps marginality; and the separation of wife from husband, the family divided in space. He parses the Chinese characters as well — the word "astronaut" comprises two Chinese ideographs, *tai*, referring to wife, and *kong*, meaning lonely or solitary; thus "astronaut family" specifically underscores the psychosocial nature of *taikong*. The term has also been written as 太空人 and described from the opposite perspective — a "man without a wife."

The sparse psychological literature on cultural transitions uses the terms "return migrant" or "remigrant" even though the long-term prospects of the migrant's remaining in the country of origin are unknown. It is this latter nomenclature that will be used interchangeably in the succeeding chapters of this book.

Why people return home

For sojourners, why they return to their home countries is clear: their work assignment has concluded, the academic year has ended, the humanitarian crisis has abated, the tour of duty has finished, or the proselytizing has been successful. For the immigrant, the rationale and decision-making process for returning home is complex and varied, and includes both economic[26] and such noneconomic factors as patriotic or social ties to home, care for an aging relative,[27] or lack of assimilation into the host country.[28] Four useful categories have been proposed to clarify the rationale behind return migration: (1) a return of failure (unable to find satisfactory employment); (2) a return of conservatism (host culture not sufficiently traditional, miss family and friends); (3) a return of retirement (desire to retire comfortably in country of origin); and (4) a return of innovation (envision economic opportunities in their homeland).[29]

Political, economic, and social changes in the homeland strengthen its lure for emigrants; among these changes are strong and globalized economies, improved human rights, reduced government corruption, and restored individual freedoms.[30] Nearly 30% of Chinese respondents in one study,[31] for example, returned home because of favorable government policies that presumably were welcoming and forgiving. These institutional changes may be thought of as the minimal home country conditions that must exist for the migrant to consider returning home. Migrants are often queried as to their transition intentions. However, migrant intentions to return home and actual return behavior are frequently at odds as immigrants unexpectedly assimilate, their linkages to their home countries weaken, and migrant communities grow and strengthen. Thus, care must be taken in interpreting the data collected while immigrants remained in their adopted countries.

One early sociological study on the motivations for migration and remigration was conducted among Austrian scientists who spent more than 8 years in either the United States or Germany.[32] They pursued remigration for a variety of personal reasons including attachment to family and friends or to native country and culture. In particular, many of these scientists had small children, and the scientists' concerns about their children's cultural identity and security informed their decision making.

From the vantage point of population economics, Christian Dustmann has developed a "child-centered" decision-making model.[33] His simple but creative explanatory model suggests that return migration is influenced by parents' concerns about their children's future welfare. In particular, he argues that if they perceive career opportunities to be greater in the host country parents might deem return migration as detrimental to the child. However, return migration may appear beneficial to the child if the parents perceive the homeland environment as being more nurturing or traditional. Dustmann proposes that the detriment/benefit ratio is determined by the gender of the offspring: parents are more concerned about the economic future of their sons and therefore are less likely to return to their home country if career opportunities are greater in the host country; parents are more likely to remigrate if their offspring are daughters as the homeland environment is perceived as less threatening. The latter hypothesis is more pronounced when the parents' culture is traditional. The author uses the results of government surveys taken in the 1980s that sampled, among other groups, southern European immigrants to Germany. He finds modest support for the hypothesis in that parents with daughters were slightly more likely to return to their home countries. When country of origin was examined in this context, Turkish parents (the only Muslim group in the study and perhaps the most traditional) of daughters were the most likely to intend to return home, viewing the homeland as a better environment for their daughters.

A study of southern and southeastern European guest worker–immigrants in Germany examined, through the lens of a geographer, external or time-dependent variables and internal variables (such as personal characteristics or residential or job satisfaction) and their effects on intentions to return to countries of origin.[34] Again using German government surveys, in this case administered between 1970 and 1989, the researcher found few differences among migrants by nationality (Greeks, Italians, Spaniards, Turks, and Yugoslavs). Satisfaction with both housing and jobs was associated with lower intentions to remigrate, as were the time-related variables for as the duration of the stay increased, the probability of return diminished. A curvilinear relationship was observed in the relationship between age and intention to return — the lowest probability was when the immigrants were at age 32, with higher probabilities when they were in either their early twenties or as they neared retirement age in their late sixties Unexpectedly, personal characteristics, such as gender or marital status, had little effect on intentions to return.

Contemporary remigrants are primarily motivated by economics — either the push of their settlement country, the pull of their country of origin, or both. In the first decade of the twenty-first century, 2 million Poles left their home country to work in Great Britain and throughout the European continent, sending more than $18 billion back home in 2007 alone. By 2009–10, Poles were departing Britain, motivated by both the recession in the British economy and the strength of the Polish zloty against the pound and the plentiful jobs in Poland.[35] Illegal immigrants, many of whom work as day laborers, have also been streaming back to their respective home countries as their jobs are filled by unemployed native workers. In California, in 2008, the number of construction jobs fell by 84,000 compared to 2007, and anecdotal evidence indicates that fewer than 15% of the day laborers were being hired.[36] Mexican and Brazilian consulates throughout the United States reported a surge in passport renewals, and Mexico City expected the imminent return of 30,000 more immigrants.[37]

For immigrants in the United States, the economic crises of 2008–09 have combined with other factors to encourage remigration. These factors include the continual obstacles to obtaining legal status (an immigration bill had still not passed Congress by 2010), barriers to obtaining driver's licenses, increasingly overt prejudice and discrimination toward immigrants, the wish to be reunified with family in their home country, and the desire to ensure that their children receive an education of excellence.[38]

Return migration has also been examined by economists, development specialists, and government policy makers. One former development assistance specialist with the United Nations reviewed programs and policies, referred to colloquially as "brain gain" programs, implemented by governments and international organizations and designed to lure emigrants back to their home countries.[39] International aid organizations have been successful in linking technical assistance funding to the hiring of migrants. For example, the Aga Khan Foundation sought out expatriated Afghans to fill positions on a recent project in Afghanistan. Receiving countries that have been the target of increasing immigration are also developing their policies, which, in most cases, seek to assist or force immigrants to return home. The International Organization for Migration (IOM) compiled an extensive list of policies and programs developed by individual European governments.[40] Overall, the authors conclude that voluntary programs are both preferable to and more cost-effective than forced remigration.

Individual governments have also developed and implemented programs to lure compatriots back to their home countries. Extensive laboratories, new scientific parks, and lucrative incentive packages are now offered by the governments of Ireland,[41] Taiwan,[42] and China.[43] More than 50% of Chinese returnees report that government programs designed to recruit them back to China provided housing allowances. Other valuable and persuasive perquisites from the Chinese government included assistance in finding employment for the professional and for his wife, arrangements to ease the settling-in process, and financial assistance with children's education.[44] The Chinese government has also sponsored recruitment fairs throughout Australia, Europe, and the United States and provided its worldwide network of embassies and consulates with brochures about these incentive programs.

In 2007, the Ecuadorean government launched Plan Retorno, a program designed to facilitate immigrants' return home. Incentives include loans to build houses and start businesses, elimination of high import duties on cars, and ending ceilings on the amount of cash and the value of goods remigrants can bring into Ecuador.[45] While not encouraging remigration, the Polish government is responding to the wave of remigrants by setting up job banks on the internet and preparing for what policy makers believe will be a steady increase in the number of Polish returnees.[46] Countries of settlement may also encourage return migration. In Britain, the government-funded International Organization for Migration provides a wide-range of services and incentives to encourage the country's estimated 1 million illegal immigrants to return home. Free flights, a departure stipend, and excess luggage waivers entice the immigrant to leave Britain, and aid in developing a business plan, grants to purchase equipment and cars, salaries for the first few months, and funds to obtain needed training are intended to keep the remigrant in their country of origin. It is reported that 3,290 people took advantage of the program within the first nine months of 2007.[47]

Skeldon speculated that economics might have been behind the return movement of Hong Kong emigrants. If the economies of the host countries had been robust and vibrant, Hong Kongers would have had little need to return. Rather, it was the confluence of a Hong Kong market upswing and a Canadian and Australian economic downswing that fueled the astronauts' rockets. Skeldon's remarks were prescient, as the reader will see.

Social science views of the consequences of remigration

Contemporary investigations have begun to bring social scientific perspectives to examining the impact of returning home, although there remains a dearth of such studies. For example, in studying identity consequences, researchers found that if their personal and professional attachments intersected, Austrian remigrants' identification with Austria was strengthened.[48] Their country identity was likewise strengthened if they had not been absent from Austria for too long.

Greek remigrant children were investigated as part of a study of families returning to Greece from the former Federal Republic of Germany.[49] Based on a variety of self and other assessments, it was found that these young remigrants had few interpersonal adjustment problems. However, their school performance was poor.

In one of the few studies of Central American or South American remigrants, surveys, interviews, and field observations of Dominicans who had lived in the United States were collected.[50] More men than women returned home, as well as more individuals who were motivated by family interests. Migration frequently improved the returnees' socioeconomic status, and the remigrants' return home was financially beneficial to their families and to the Dominican economy. However, these returnees are more accurately described as transmigrants as they continued to move back and forth between the Dominican Republic and the United States, maintaining familial, social, and business ties.

An extensive survey of nearly 400 returnees from Australia to Bangladesh, China, Taiwan, and Vietnam examined their repatriation decision-making processes, the social and economic impacts of their return on their home countries, and the role of transnational communities in social transformation.[51] The researchers provided policy suggestions for the countries of origin to optimize the benefits they could receive from the skills of the remigrants. Although a common 20-page questionnaire was developed for use by all the local study partners, considerable latitude was allowed in method (some investigators added extensive interviews; some used only close-ended response options), administration (in person, by mail, by phone), and content (questionnaire items were added or subtracted based on local conditions). The survey's extensive findings in the area of economic and social consequences provided much needed comparative data but barely scratched the surface of the psychological outcomes of return migration for either the migrants themselves or their communities.

Data that gave a glimpse of some attitudinal outcomes were items assessing satisfaction ratings of employment and working conditions. In general, Chinese returnees were least satisfied (only 29% satisfied with their jobs), but returnees to all four countries found the cultural readjustment to workplace behaviors and attitudes difficult. Bangladeshis complained that there were too many formalities, too much red tape, not enough innovation, and too much emphasis on personal loyalty in the office environment compared to the personal freedom they had experienced abroad. Similarly, Vietnamese returnees observed that personal relationships at work reduced effectiveness and that subjective hiring, evaluation, and termination of employees undermined professionalism. Vietnamese returnees also commented on more general repatriation issues, as summarized by a 39-year-old female manager: "facilities in home, social safety, relationships in family and office are obstacles in reintegration process of skilled returnees ... in addition, relationships in the family neighborhood, and office are complicated." A 30-year-old male also complained: "I am ill because of the humid and polluted climate ... I feel that water is not clean and foodstuffs is not hygiene [sic]." A 24-year-old woman business owner worried because "the first month I feel as a stranger to slow and fond [sic] life in Vietnam." Approximately 20% of all four groups reported experiencing general readjustment difficulties. One unobtrusive measure of readjustment is the percentage of remigrants indicating that they were willing or eager to leave their home countries again: nearly 60% of Taiwanese returnees considered moving overseas once more. Finally, although the majority of the study's respondents were men, a sufficient number of women participated to allow for some gender comparisons. Overall, for all four groups, the men readjusted better to their return than did the women.

A psychological model of repatriation and cultural identity

As we have seen, nearly all of the past investigations of return migration examined external, or institutional, variables in an attempt to understand immigration and return migration. Missing is an exploration of the internal, or individual-level, variables. Psychological perspectives provide such a view, but psychological theory has been nearly silent on the topic of cultural transitions such as migration and their effects on identity. Until the past decade, immigration had been little researched,[52] and the study of remigration continues nearly absent. The return home of expatriates, however, has for more than three decades been the subject of research by a range of social and behavioral scientists.[53] Nearly all of this research has focused on Western sojourners who on returning to their home countries experienced substantial identity conflict,[54] negative emotions,[55] and confused thinking.[56] Frequently, their distress on their return home was so severe that repatriates left their jobs, home cities, and marriages.

The psychological perspective on remigrants, in contrast to repatriated sojourners, has been limited. A few studies have tried to identify symptoms of dysfunction and instances of therapeutic intervention. One early writer on these topics proposed a crisis-trauma-stability model of immigrant assimilation.[57] As something of an afterthought, he described the process of remigration and identified variables affecting the severity of re-entry shock such as duration of absence, age, loneliness, and previous individual/family pathology. Psychological symptoms present during the process of reassimilation included disturbances of cognitive function, affect, and values.

I have identified elements of repatriation distress and suggested remedies in several early studies.[58] Subsequently, I developed the Cultural Identity Model (CIM) of Cultural Transitions to bring a psychological perspective to the understanding of the antecedents and consequences of returning home.[59]

Model of repatriation and cultural identity

The CIM suggests that changes in a person's sense of self (labeled "self-concept disturbances") and subsequent shifts in home culture identity characterize cultural transitions. The model suggests that there are three fundamental elements in the transition process: identity salience, sociocultural adaptation, and cultural identity change. These features interact within a larger cyclical framework of cultural transition to predict consequences for the returnees transition process made evident during repatriation. Figures 3.1, 3.2, and 3.3 depict the significant psychological factors in the model.

Identity Salience. Although self-concept, emotion, and motivation may be shaped by the cultural context, few individuals are cognizant of culture's influence. Culture may be a part of the self, but cultural identity is not explicitly recognized as such. Like a fish in water, an individual is surrounded by his or her home culture but its impact is seldom a salient feature of the individual's self-concept; people rarely recognize the imprint of their own culture and its ubiquitous nature. Thus in my social psychology classroom in New York, few students, in describing themselves, ever list "American" among their top 20 attributes.

However, exceptions to the general lack of cultural identity awareness may be found, for example, among individuals who hold more than one identity, as either distinctly separate or embedded. They are more aware of culture's influence. The multiplicity of identities of the Chinese residents of Hong Kong makes for a heightened awareness of cultural identity generally and of embedded or overlapping identities specifically.

Cultural differences in the awareness of cultural identity may be differentiated by values domains. Americans and members of other individualistic cultures are more cognizant of their personal traits and characteristics, whereas residents of collectivist cultures tend to be more aware of their social and group interconnections and hence their cultural identity.

The CIM predicts that one situation in which a person's cultural identity will emerge or become heightened is at the commencement of a cultural transition. Enveloped in a new social environment where behavior and thinking diverge from a familiar cultural context, the individual's awareness of the profound influence of culture on behavior begins to grow. In close juxtaposition to the emerging cultural identity salience, a new social identity status develops, that of outsider — an expatriate or immigrant in a new cultural environment. These thoughts of cultural identity awareness and outsider status appear to strengthen, at least initially, identification with home culture. For the Hong Kong transitor, Chinese identity may be activated as a result of both an enhanced identity salience and the motivation to be distinct from the settlement country.

Sociocultural Adaptation. Following the cultural reaffirmation phase, the CIM proposes that immigrants recognize the discrepancy between their cultural selves (and the goals that direct their behavior and thought) and their new cultural context. In addition, immigrants may seek more information about themselves for practical reasons: by understanding the cultural differences and adapting to the new culture, they can achieve a better "fit" with their new country.[60] Cultural readjustment prompted by the lack of fit between a person's cultural thinking patterns and behavior and a new cultural context may lead individuals to modify their behavior or thought or both and, consequently, their cultural identity. For the Hong Kong resident, this phase may activate a dormant Western identity and set of behaviors.

Immigrants are faced with a continuum of accommodation choices that range from maintenance of their homeland values, beliefs, and cultural identity at one endpoint to a new cultural self with values and beliefs aligned with the destination country at the other end. This transformation is sometimes described as "going native." Additionally, newcomers might find the new culture too difficult to understand; they may suffer from what has been referred to as "confusionism,"[61] an immigrant's honest assessment that because cultures are so diverse it is impossible to comprehend the framework of another culture.

Distinct from adjustment, which is a process of ongoing change, adaptation is conceptualized as the successful endpoint of accommodation. Newcomers have adapted to their new culture if they utilize to some extent the values, behaviors, beliefs, and thought patterns of the host society. These changes enable immigrants to engage in smooth social relations and to understand and use the new culture's rules governing social and professional life.

The classic immigration story ends with the immigrant's gradual accommodation and adaptation to the new culture. The nature of the sojourner's experience is to return home, but not that of the immigrant. Parallel to the gradual awareness of home culture identity at the commencement of the stay, the CIM suggests that cultural accommodation and adaptation disturb the individual's self-concept. The consequent changes in cultural identity become obvious to the returnee at the commencement of repatriation.

In a process parallel to culture identity awareness when emigrating, though now against the backdrop of the home culture, repatriates evaluate their personal values, ideas, and customs against the prevailing cultural norms at home. For many repatriates, there is no longer a fit between their newly formed host culture identity and the identity called for by the culture-of-origin environment. The emotional response of most repatriates is overwhelmingly negative; repatriates report feelings of "not fitting in" with friends, family, and former colleagues. Behavior that was appropriate in the host country is now unacceptable and interpersonally ineffective. Home culture identity no longer matches the returnee's own, and the sojourner is now a member of a new outsider group within the home country, that of repatriate.

Cultural Identity Change. As sojourners and immigrants successfully adapt to their destination country by modifying their behavior and social thought, their cultural identity changes as well. However, newly learned cultural patterns that enabled the newcomer to function in the host environment are not appropriate back in the individual's home culture. Those traits both trivial and profound that together create a home culture identity are no longer actively engaged at the point at which one has adapted to a new culture. Behaving like an Australian while in Melbourne is adaptive, but what about when in Kowloon? The cultural identity changes that took place overseas become apparent when the migrant returns home. Many sojourners experience more severe stress upon repatriation than at any other time during their cultural transition. And repatriation may be more jarring still for the immigrant who did not anticipate returning home. Wendy Chan, who returned to Hong Kong following nine years in Canada, commented: *"I was very excited when I finally secured a job offer that enabled me to return to Hong Kong. My enthusiasm did not last long, however. Without my full awareness, a decade of living in Canada had obviously changed how I think and feel. I have found that I can no longer engage in meaningful conversation with the few old friends that are still living in Hong Kong and my world view on many things is also often not shared by my new friends."*[62]

The CIM proposes that four distinct types of identity shift might occur, with the shift hidden until repatriation reveals the change to the returnee. These cultural identity shifts have been labeled relative to the home culture identity as subtractive, additive, affirmative, or global/intercultural.

Subtractive and additive identity shifts (see Figure 3.1) begin the transition cycle identically with an obscured cultural identity (indicated by shaded first box of the figure) that becomes visible as the transition to the new culture begins (now indicated by an unshaded box). Home culture and new culture discrepancies are recognized, and the adjustment process is triggered.

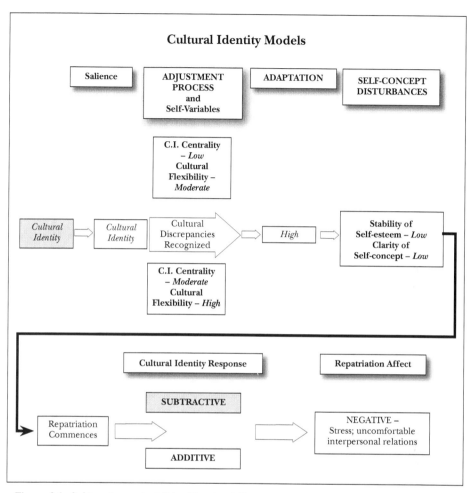

Figure 3.1 Subtractive and additive identity shifts

The two identity types diverge at this point, distinguished from each other owing to differences in personality factors: identity centrality and cultural flexibility. Centrality describes how important one's culture is to the individual. Flexibility describes the degree to which individuals are willing to bend or change cultural rules and patterns. People differ as to the importance of their home culture to their self-identity and the extent to which they are culturally flexible. For sojourners for whom home culture identity centrality is low and cultural flexibility is low to moderate (indicated by shading in the figure), a track begins that leads to a subtractive identity shift. For sojourners for whom home cultural identity centrality is moderate and cultural flexibility is high, additive cultural identity becomes the repatriate response.

Subtractive and additive identity shifts are both associated with high sociocultural adaptation to the immigrant country, and it is predicted that sojourners will experience a more difficult repatriation than those with low adaptation. A Japanese research study found that the more integrated the sojourner was into the host culture, the more distressing the re-entry and the more long-lasting the distress.[63]

The subtractive identity shift (in the shaded box) results in repatriates feeling less comfortable with their home culture's values and norms and less similar to their compatriots. An additive cultural identity shift would result in repatriates feeling more similar to their host culture, such that the repatriates' cultural identity more closely resembles the host culture's values, norms, and behaviors. One outcome of an extreme form of this shift category finds repatriates seeking opportunities to return to the host culture as soon and as often as possible.

Although both subtractive and additive identity shifters will experience similar negative emotion, the consequences for their behavior will vary. Subtractive repatriates might respond to home by seeking out other repatriates and by perceiving compatriots as less similar in culturally shaped values and behavior. At the extreme, the subtractive repatriates feel devoid of cultural identity and alienated. In contrast, additive repatriates might seek out opportunities to interact with members of the former host culture; participate in or attend entertainment, sports, or food representations of the host culture; or continue to study the host culture's language.

The model does allow for repatriates to adopt both types of identity shifts, subtractive and additive. This psychological state has been described as the "captive mind syndrome" whereby a sojourner rejects a home culture identity and uncritically adopts a host identity.[64] In both identity shift categories, interaction with the home culture collective is minimized, exacerbating the experience of isolation from the home culture and the perception of not fitting in with co-nationals.

The third proposed category of identity shift (see Figure 3.2), the affirmative identity shift, can be described as one in which the home culture identity is maintained and strengthened throughout the transition cycle. These newcomers also begin with an obscured cultural identity (indicated by the shaded box in the figure) that becomes obvious during the early stages of the cultural transition. In contrast to shifters having the subtractive or additive experience, affirmative shifters largely ignore

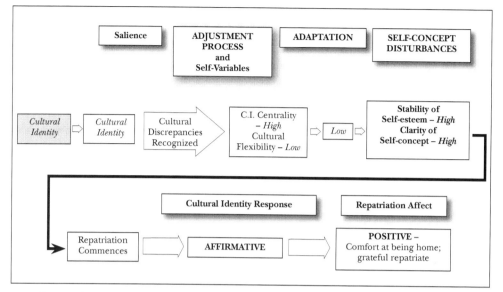

Figure 3.2 Affirmative identity shift

the cultural discrepancies between home and host cultures, resulting in low adaptation to the host culture environment. Cultural self-concept consequentially will be highly stable and unambiguous, which in turn will result in a repatriation experience that is low in repatriation distress. For affirmative sojourners who neither adapted successfully overseas nor experienced an identity change, it is predicted that repatriation comes as a welcomed relief.

The intercultural or global identity shift (see Figure 3.3), a less common identity modification, enables repatriates to hold multiple cultural scripts simultaneously and to draw on each as the working self-concept requires. The transition cycle commences for these transitors with an awareness of their own cultural identity (shaded box in the figure). Recognition of the cultural discrepancies between the sojourner's current cultural values and behaviors and that of the new sojourn site triggers the adjustment process. It is suggested that adjustment is facilitated by low cultural centrality and high cultural flexibility resulting in high adaptation.

The self-concept of the sojourner with an intercultural identity can be described as structurally complex. This identity shift paradigm is neither the integration of home and host culture values (hybridization) nor the bicultural strategy that results from the acculturation experience; rather,

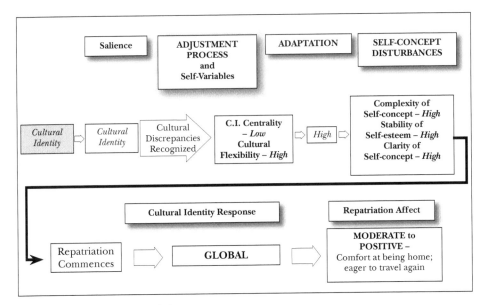

Figure 3.3 Global identity shift

it is an identity in which repatriates define themselves as world citizens and are able to interact appropriately and effectively in many countries or regions by switching cultural frames as needed.

Intercultural identity shifts will result in positive emotional responses and little repatriation distress. Behaviorally, intercultural repatriates may seek to develop friendships with individuals representing many different cultures, select a wide range of international entertainment (movies, sports, television programming) and reading material (books, newspapers), and participate in international electronic discussion groups and web sites.

It is important to note that multiple cultural transition experiences are not sufficient for a global identity to result. Self-concept complexity and subsequent positive response to the return home depend on two features: (1) that prior to the commencement of the transition, the sojourner is actively aware of his or her cultural identity and its consequences, that is, understands himself or herself as a cultural being, and (2) that during the adaptation and repatriation phases, the sojourner is actively cognitively processing cultural aspects of his or her self-concept and is aware of any changes in cultural identity. Physical movement home, then, is not coupled with an unexplained negative emotion, as is the case with additive and subtractive shifters. Rather, the intercultural identity shift evokes a positive response.

American, European, and Japanese identity response to repatriation

Neither the United States nor Japan has experienced significant remigration patterns, and thus, repatriation research on these geographic locations has been limited to the repatriated *sojourner* experience. While all four types of identity responses to repatriation have been found among Western and Japanese returnees, identities differ in the variability and typicality of response.

A negative response to returning home to the United States is most frequently associated with subtractive identity response, the most common reaction to re-entry. Repatriated Americans report feeling less American, less similar to other Americans, and less able to "fit in" compared to their predeparture identity.[65] As one American Peace Corps volunteer described his return to the United States after two years in Peru working with the indigenous peoples: "When I got back to my hometown in Ohio and went to work, I fell back into hanging out evenings in the neighborhood tavern with my old buddies. After about two weeks of that I gave up the tavern. They didn't care about the problems of the Indians in Peru and I didn't give a damn about what happened to the Indians [the local baseball team] in Cleveland."[66] The distress felt by returning sojourners is exacerbated by the unexpectedness of the identity response; the negative emotion is often misattributed to the re-entry job, to the city where the returnee is settling, or to spousal or familial relations.[67]

Affirmative identity responses are the second most frequent response of American returnees and are coupled with positive emotion and relief at returning home. These grateful repatriates rarely made cultural adaptations in their host countries and therefore did not experience self-concept or identity changes. A smaller percentage of American repatriates experience additive or global identity shifts. One "additive" expatriate commented: "I felt dejection at not being able to communicate to others the intensity of my China experience. I was expected to be much the same person I was before going to China. But I was no longer that person. I was so saturated with my Chinese experience that I felt I was half Chinese. I may have looked like the same blue-eyed, light-haired Westerner, but a significant part of me had changed radically. I wanted to discuss these changes and have them acknowledged."[68]

Recent research among Italian sojourner repatriates reports consistently negative effect and subtractive, additive, and global identity responses. Few returnees reacted positively to their return and to their

Italian identity. One young woman who repatriated to Italy following a sojourn in Sweden remarked, "I've experienced the feeling of no longer fitting into my home country, and talking with other students, they had the same feeling, the same distress."[69] A Swiss woman returned to her home city after living for nine years in the United States. Her coworkers chided her regularly, saying, "You're not in America anymore!" and her boss complained that she was not appropriately submissive. "They all teased me about having salads for lunch and having changed so much."

In a study of repatriates to Finland, subtractive identity appeared to be a common consequence of cultural transition. A woman returning from Australia noted, "Coming back home was more difficult than going abroad because I had expected changes when going overseas. During repatriation it was real culture shock! I felt like an alien in my own country. Surprisingly, I was totally unprepared for the long, harsh, cold, dark Arctic winter. My attitudes had changed so much that it was difficult to understand Finnish customs. Old friends had moved, had children, or just vanished. Others were interested in our experiences, but only sort of. Most simply could not understand our overseas experience or just envied our way of life." Additionally, emotional distress upon repatriation was correlated with a lack of communication with home family and friends while the sojourner was overseas.[70]

Adolescents returning to Turkey following many years of living in various European countries experienced more depression, anxiety, and academic achievement problems compared to adolescents who never left Turkey.[71] While this investigation found the repatriation affect to be negative, identity data was not collected.

After the collapse of the Soviet Union, Finns who lived in Russia or Estonia remigrated to Finland. Between 1994 and 1996, a small number of these remigrants were interviewed, comparing objective criterion of ethnic identity (language, religion, citizenship) with subjective identity (self-identity, commitment).[72] The age of the remigrants proved to be a crucial variable; those who were younger identified themselves as Russian, while the middle-aged Finns spoke of identity conflicts and difficulties reintegrating into Finnish society.

Japanese sojourners, due in part to the cultural homogeneity of Japan, report high cultural awareness prior to departure from Japan. Despite that awareness, Japanese repatriation is also often negative emotionally but is characterized as an additive response as a result of successful adaptation to the host culture. However, the negative affect is tempered by the awareness of self-concept and identity changes.[73] Japanese repatriates report knowing that despite additive identity changes, the norms of Japanese culture demand their adherence to Japanese behaviors and lifestyle once they return home — that is, low cultural flexibility is the norm. They negotiate an additive identity, bicultural type.

The prevalent identity response among adolescent Japanese returnees is subtractive, with participants reporting a sense of "feeling different" from mainstream society[74] in that they are usually more assertive and individualistic as compared to peers who have not left Japan,[75] resulting in prolonged emotional distress. Japanese women repatriates who accompanied their husbands on an overseas assignment also report "difficulty in fitting in to Japanese society" due to feeling "less Japanese."[76]

As the CIM predicts, an intercultural or global response is found among Japanese corporate executives who have had several overseas assignments. This is particularly evident when the overseas site was rural or suburban and the Japanese expatriate community was small; local adaptation therefore more compelling.

More than 50,000 Japanese moved to Brazil during the period 1953–62. In an unusual variation of remigration, more than 250,000 second- and third-generation Japanese-Brazilians have "returned" to Japan to work. Two anthropological studies of this population were recently conducted.[77] Many of these returnees assumed reverse affirmative identities: they embraced Brazilian culture and identity, established Portuguese newspapers, and supported the Brazilian soccer team and its victories. While the majority resisted Japanese assimilation, others adopted an additive identity, acting Japanese among the locals and Brazilian among their returnee peers. A portion of this returnee population settled in Japan, but many have become transmigrants, moving often between Brazil and Japan. In a bit of transcultural irony, those attempting to resettle in Brazil, double returnees if you will, expressed difficulty in readjusting to Brazilian society following their years of working in Japan.

Two magazine articles report increased return migration of Western-educated Chinese back to the People's Republic of China. Many of these returnees found work with multinational corporations or law firms or started their own venture capital or high-tech companies.[78] Anecdotes of successful returns are tinged, however, with cautionary tales of adaptation difficulties and value mismatches between old friends, new supervisors, and the culturally transformed returnees. But the rate of return migration remains low, and few studies have examined the psychological impact on those who have made the return journey. In a survey of Mainland Chinese in the United States, Zweig found only 9% indicating that they planned to return to China, citing economic, professional, personal, and political hindrances.[79] Another survey reported that return rates to China varied by host country, with the lowest number of Chinese (18.8%) planning to return from the United States and the highest (63.5%) from France.[80]

Hong Kong identity response to repatriation

Past research

Hong Kong-based researchers, many of whom personally experienced active cultural transitions, have begun examining the sociological and political consequences of remigration. Wendy Chan, herself a Canadian Hong Kong return migrant, used the concept of "home" as a central notion for the study of Hong Kong returnees. Chan's cultural identity was made salient (as theorized in the Cultural Identity Model) during her early years in Canada as she notes that "years of living as an immigrant ... made me acutely aware of my Chinese heritage. Although I desired deeply to call Toronto home and tried to learn everything 'Canadian,' I could not help but feel being an alien. I longed for going 'home-home' where I do not have to figure out the right words."[81]

Yet when she did return "home-home," she felt uncomfortable with her family and former friends and disoriented by Hong Kong culture. To uncover the reasons behind this discomfort, while still a student at the University of Science and Technology, she conducted detailed interviews with 18 returnees from Canada then living in Hong Kong to explore their sense of home and homelessness. Chan's methodology was somewhat unorthodox in that she conducted unstructured interviews, did not audiotape them, and took only minimal notes. At the conclusion of each interview, Chan created detailed field notes, and the narratives of her respondents yielded rich personal and psychological descriptions.

While most of the interviewees described their immigrant selves as "reluctant exiles" from Hong Kong, only 2 of the 18 had a plan to return as evidenced by retaining an apartment in Hong Kong. One could say that Chan's returnee respondents were again "reluctant exiles," though this time from Canada. The "brain drain" instigated by the mass emigration from Hong Kong resulted in creative and ultimately persuasive tactics to draw emigrants back. So too for Chan's remigrated respondents, as they were mostly drawn back to Hong Kong for economic reasons but their return home provided them with little comfort or sense of rootedness. Study participants can be characterized using the CIM profiles demonstrating both additive and subtractive identities. Details and narrative excerpts from Chan's study can be found in Chapters 5 and 6, respectively.

Gender differences emerged in a number of dimensions. Women in the study were more likely to have felt at home in Canada than in Hong Kong, especially among women who worked. They were willing to forsake career opportunities in Canada and stay at home to raise their families (because of the lack of domestic help) for the quality of life that Canada afforded them and their children. In contrast, men preferred to live in Hong Kong for the career satisfaction and job opportunities they found there.

Another comprehensive study of Hong Kong returnees was conducted by David Ley and Audrey Kobayashi,[82] two geographers at Canadian universities, who place the return of Hong Kong migrants into a transnationalism paradigm. They suggest that the return to Hong Kong was simply one transoceanic crossing among many, some planned and anticipated, others accidental. As one of the respondents aptly summarized his attitude, "The Hong Kong migrant would like to work in Hong Kong and sleep in Canada." In this creative study of returnees and migrants who had lived in Vancouver and returned to Hong Kong, as well as those who had remained in Canada, respondents were interviewed both individually and as part of focus groups.

The researchers summarized the reasons for the respondents' return to Hong Kong: weak job markets in Canada and Australia, limited opportunities to start and maintain a business, and the individual's lack of commitment to being an immigrant (emigrating primarily to obtain a Western passport either as political insurance or for travel flexibility). While interviewees generally held positive opinions about Canada, especially about its clean environment and slower pace of life, its perceived economic decline trumped quality-of-life issues for many of them.

For many of the respondents, movement back and forth between Canada and Hong Kong was timed in accordance with phases in the familial life cycle: to Canada after the children were sufficiently enculturated into Hong Kong culture and had learned Cantonese but in time for the Canadian provincial examinations or university; to Hong Kong as young adults for an exciting life or as middle-aged fathers for economic gain; to Canada for retirement. As one respondent remarked: "I will consider moving back after retirement, though I still have 30 years to go. My dream is to go back to Vancouver for retirement ... [My parents] plan to be there after retirement. My dad will retire in seven years. He will live there with my mum because there it's more comfortable."

In many ways, this methodology was unique because Ley and Kobayashi investigated Hong Kongers on both sides of the Pacific, underscoring the transnational cycle. However, they did not explore the psychological process of adjustment that accompanied each move or the issue of cultural identity.

The most recent lens through which returnees have been viewed is the human resources one. Salaff, Shik, and Greve examined the decision-making process of young Hong Kong–Canadian adults who spent their childhoods in Canada.[83] Approaching working age, these young people had to decide on which side of the Pacific to begin their careers. The investigators used a trilevel analysis, assessing macro- (how labor markets recognize training and credentials), meso- (family, social networks), and micro-level (personal ideas of home and identity) variables to explore the decision-making processes of these young immigrants and the factors that led them back to Hong Kong for employment.

The authors combined data from two small longitudinal studies in which young new migrants to Toronto were interviewed. In one case, the sample was reinterviewed a decade later; in the other case, the sample was intermittently interviewed over a 15-year period. In 2006, the sample ranged from unmarried college students to married adults in their 30s. All had received part of their education in Hong Kong and part in Canada. Most had "astronaut" parents during their youth, and 20 of the 24 study participants had at least one parent living in or owning a business in Hong Kong. In multiple ways, these young immigrants embraced aspects of both Hong Kong and Canadian culture and values. Their desire to return and work in Hong Kong appears to have been directly related to their familial networks there. Nine of the 24 respondents had already returned to work in Hong Kong, and 7 of them had parents living there. In contrast, 6 of the 24 had no plans to return to Hong Kong and of these, none had parents living there.

Those respondents who had already returned to Hong Kong found that their bilingual, bicultural experience and university training made them highly marketable in some industry sectors but disadvantaged in others in which local university graduates were given priority. These returnees maintained an open mind, though, about returning to Canada for advanced training and new career opportunities. The notion of a transnational career was beginning to take root among these individuals. Other interviewees were drawn back to Hong Kong to fulfill obligations to family-owned businesses, some willingly and some reluctantly. They were leaving behind in Canada close friendship networks born out of the anxiety of being young immigrants together. So, if one friend or dating partner decided to leave Canada and return to Hong Kong, others in the network found the courage to follow suit. Whether factual or not, returnees perceived that "ninety percent of my Toronto friends have returned" or "everyone I know in Hong Kong is a returnee."

A domain of concern within the personal, the academic, and the civic affairs sphere, but not within the scope of this book, is the legal and political role of the returnees. With nearly one-sixth of the population of Hong Kong holding foreign passports, often occupying senior positions within the banking and financial services sector or the public sector, concerns have been raised by Beijing, Canberra, and Ottawa. Where does the loyalty of the Hong Kong returnee lie? In a natural, political, or economic crisis, who supports the returnees? And what is the consequence of mass return for their passport countries?

Factors affecting repatriation

The case has been made that residents of Hong Kong have developed complex identities. Triggered by environmental cues, they have learned how to negotiate these identities within the Hong Kong, regional, and global contexts.

How will migration and remigration affect these cultural identity frames? As immigrants successfully adapt to their destination culture by modifying their behavior and social thought, their cultural identity changes as well. Among the professional/educated returnees, the CIM predicts that although identity profiles for Hong Kong repatriates will be found among all four types, the predominant one will be the global identity. This is partly due to their awareness of their cultural identity prior to emigration and to the multidimensional nature of the Hong Kong identity. The CIM also describes identity response as being affected by personality and by individual variables such as English proficiency, prior cultural experiences, and appropriateness of immigrant and repatriation employment.

In Hong Kong, because of the collectivist nature of the Chinese core culture, differences in familial variables are expected to influence individual identity responses to repatriation. Such familial factors include the number of family members accompanying the emigrant head of household, level of migrant adaptation by family members, number of years spent in the destination country, ages of the children, and nature of the immigrant/ home country experience (intact family vs. astronaut family).

Based on the global identity profile alone, one might expect an immigrant's emotional response to repatriation to be positive. However, there is reason to believe that Hong Kong remigration results in a more nuanced and complex identity response. Three factors, psychological, sociological, and economic, may contribute to the remigrants' repatriation distress. First, psychological expectations may not have been met for the transition experience. The basis for immigration — the imagined economic and political catastrophe resulting from the 1997 handover — did not materialize; that is, the "push" for immigration was unfounded. Further, the "pull" for immigration — financial success and smooth adjustment — may not have been completely realized. The attempt to minimize handover anxiety and provide for future family stability may not have worked out, and repatriation may have become a public statement of a failed strategy.

There does appear to be a category of immigrant for whom a multination residential life was purposely planned. These migrants may have already possessed a global identity; for them, obtaining a foreign passport was a hedge against political turmoil in Hong Kong and not a reflection of a desire for a either a new identity or a new permanent abode. However, there were unexpected consequences for some of these immigrants as well.

While husbands commuted between Hong Kong and their immigrant country, maintaining and strengthening bicultural identities, adolescent children in the family were developing new cultural identities that in many cases may have supplanted their Hong Kong or Chinese identity. Repatriation complicated the individualized identities within a family. Anecdotal evidence suggests that adolescents discovered that they now possessed a combination of "subtractive" and "additive" identities and, as a result, experienced discomfort on returning to Hong Kong. Frequently, these returnee children had to continue their education at international schools in Hong Kong because they lacked Cantonese proficiency, which further isolated them from the general population.

Second, sociologically, both migration and remigration may have resulted in unexpected family stresses. Changes in spousal roles resulted from absentee husbands who left their families behind in the country of emigration. For example, wives found themselves heading the household for long periods of time and being the sole decision maker for the family. Repatriation found families again united physically but now fractured culturally and structurally. One additional aspect of the acculturation process for many immigrated families involved their having joined Chinese Christian churches while they were abroad. In maintaining these affiliations on their return to Hong Kong, they exhibited yet another life choice that could possibly separate them from their nonimmigrating friends and family.

A final factor that may influence distress levels in the repatriation experience is economics. The cycle of the world financial markets was particularly unkind to 1980s/90s Hong Kong migrants. In the decade leading up to the colony's handover, property prices in Hong Kong fell as anxiety spread and departing immigrants sold their real estate and businesses at a loss. However, concurrent economic booms in Australia, Canada, and the United States led these same immigrants to invest in their settlement countries at high prices. By the late 1990s and early 2000s, when remigration begins, economies had slumped in the West and the Hong Kong remigrants again lost on their investments.

Past research supported the Cultural Identity Model of cultural transitions as an explanatory theory for understanding the *sojourners'* return home and its consequences. Does it also explain the psychological consequences for these *return migrants*? After all, migrants have strong motivation to make a significant adaptation to their new country as they generally anticipate that their immigration will be permanent. If the model is applicable to immigrants, it is unclear if the distribution of the four identity profiles will be similar to those of Western repatriates. Hong Kong in the early twenty-first century offers an excellent case study for examining large-scale remigration. In addition to the vast number of remigrants, this is a homogeneous population in several important ways. Hong Kongers emigrated during a narrow time period (1984–97) responding to political events in their environment, and they represent the well-educated and well-employed. They also emigrated in large numbers to just a very few Western countries. In short, this is an ideal population to investigate.

Hong Kong Remigration Project

The methodology for the Hong Kong Remigration Project combined qualitative interviews with quantitative psychological scales in measuring overseas adaptation, repatriation stress, life satisfaction, and self-concept. Interviews lasted two hours each and consisted of participant responses to a semi-structured interview followed by the completion of a questionnaire packet. The interview explored the nature of the immigration experience, reasons for returning home, and the remigration experience and included questions about changes in the remigrant's behavior and thinking; the perception of the remigrant by family, friends, and coworkers; and the remigrant's future plans. Most of the interviews took place in an office building conference room in Central, the business hub of Hong Kong. Two interviews took place in the living room of the interviewer, two were held in the interviewees' homes, seven were held in the interviewees' workplaces, and three were held in public cafes or restaurants.

The questionnaire included the Satisfaction with Life Scale,[84] the Repatriation Distress Scale,[85] a modified version of the Birman Cultural Acculturation Scale,[86] the Self-Construal Scale,[87] a modified Twenty Statement Test,[88] and demographic items. The research questionnaires were translated into Chinese (traditional characters) using the back-translation method. Participants were offered both versions; all selected the English version. Appendix A includes copies of the scales used in this study.

The methods chosen for this study were intentionally varied, employing a triangulation design to understand the remigration experiences of the returnees. By utilizing both qualitative inquiry and psychometrically sound quantitative scales, the goal was to increase confidence in the investigation's findings. The multiple methods were intended to provide support for and confirmation of the results.

The qualitative approach generally aims to understand, without the constraints of response categories or scales, human behavior as it exists in its lived form. Various qualitative techniques lead to direct observation of behaviors, individuals, and groups (e.g., ethnography) or to involvement in the group (e.g., participant observation). In another technique, narrative inquiry, individual participants construct and convey their experiences through the stories they tell. Their narratives reveal the connections individuals make between their identities and events in their lives. As Kanno suggests, "Narrative is indispensable not only for individual experiences but also for our understanding of our own identities and those of others."[89]

For all of the research participants, Cantonese was their first spoken language and English their second. However, English was the medium of instruction in the Hong Kong schools during the education of all participants and their immigration experiences were all in English-speaking countries (Australia and Canada). Thus the research interviews were conducted in English. The interviewer spoke no Cantonese, and there was concern that the psychological vocabulary embedded in the interviews and in the questionnaires might be confusing. Therefore, a bilingual research assistant accompanied the researcher to all the interviews to provide translation either for the researcher or for the interviewee. Minor explanations were provided for a few respondents.

Despite such attempts to provide translation/interpretation services to the interviewees, conducting the interviews in English may have impeded the participants' expressions, ideas, and identity constructs. There are empirical findings that indicate that, for bilinguals, the language of response (native vs. second language) may affect the content and intensity of response. For example, having taken a personality test once in their native language and once in English, Chinese and Korean bilinguals presented different personalities.[90] Although it was beyond the scope or intention of the Hong Kong Remigration Project, future or replication studies might gather data in both Cantonese and English to provide a direct comparison of the effect of language of interview on remigration narratives.

The "snowball sampling" method was used to recruit remigrants to participate in this study. Two returnees were introduced by their friends to the author. They agreed to take part, and, following their interviews, they were asked to recommend another returnee. Similar to the snowball that grows in size as it rolls, each interviewee provided an introduction to other potential participants, and the sample grew. Within six months, in 2004, 50 men and women volunteered to assist in the study. These remigrants departed from Hong Kong no earlier than the mid-1980s and returned to Hong Kong after living at least one year in either Canada or Australia. Returnees from these two countries were selected for the sample as these were the most common settler destinations. In a Hong Kong government survey of returnees,[91] 35% had lived in Canada and 24% had lived in Australia or New Zealand. Only 12% were returning from the United Kingdom and 11% from the United States. Appendix B provides additional detail regarding methodology and qualitative analysis. For those readers interested in the results of the statistical analyses used in this study, Appendix C will provide those specifications.

Some respondents returned to Hong Kong as early as 1986 (as soon as they qualified for citizenship in their new country of abode) and some not until 2003. The age range at the time of immigration was 13 to 47 years. All but one participant immigrated because of "handover" anxiety — concern about the aftermath of the PRC's assuming sovereignty. Reasons for remigration were slightly more diverse — the majority remigrated for economic reasons, a smaller minority was concerned with the education of their children (learning Cantonese and Mandarin), and the fewest remigrated owing to extended family obligations. These reasons closely match those that journalists and Hong Kong social scientists had speculated about and those that empirical research had uncovered during the past decade. Demographic variables, itemized for each interviewee, are found in Appendix D.

4 Results from the Hong Kong Remigration Project:
Departing, adjusting, returning

During the Hong Kong Remigration Project, 50 respondents were interviewed resulting in over 100 hours of tape-recorded discussion. Each respondent was asked the same questions, but the ensuing conversations varied as their different answers led to unique follow-up questions. The full interview schedule can be viewed in Appendix A. The recordings were transcribed and coded for specific information and cultural transition domains. See Appendix B for details on the coding process. The transcription is exact and does not correct for grammatical mistakes on the part of the interviewee. Although native English speakers may find clarity moderately impaired, it was important to report the thoughts and sentiments of the participants in their own words. Occasionally a question to an interviewee or a restatement of an answer will appear in the text. In that case, the question is preceded by an "I," indicating Interviewer; the interviewee's remarks are significd by the letter "P," indicating Participant response. Each participant was assigned a number that matches the demographic chart found in Appendix D. In this chapter, we will explore the findings related to why the interviewees left Hong Kong, issues of identity both predeparture and postadaptation, the adjustment period in either Canada or Australia, remigration decision making, and the initial emotional and behavioral responses to the interviewees' return to Hong Kong.

Why they left Hong Kong

A substantial portion of the emigrants (66%) identified the impending handover of sovereignty of Hong Kong to China as the impetus for their immigrating. The prospect of economic and political life under Communist Chinese rule frightened the residents of the territory in which an open and profoundly capitalist economy flourished. In particular, those Hong Kongers who witnessed firsthand the 1949 Communist Revolution or the Cultural Revolution of the late 1960s found the prospect of living under Chinese rule disturbing. Their concerns were exacerbated by the June 4, 1989, Tiananmen Square student democracy demonstrations in Beijing and the fatal consequences of the attempt by the People's Liberation Army to quell the unrest. The pace of emigration subsequently increased. In addition to political concerns, emigrants also identified personal and economic reasons that motivated their desire to leave Hong Kong.

A male respondent who left Hong Kong for Canada in 1988 at age 33 stated (P3):

> At that time, I think the British government is negotiating with the Chinese government of the handover. And when I was a kid, I was living in some of the islands in Hong Kong, and, you know, in the Cultural Revolution, at that time almost every day, I can see floating bodies coming from China. I was scared, about the Communism. And I don't trust them.

Similar sentiments were expressed by a female respondent who migrated to Canada in 1989 at age 28 (P28):

> Because our Chinese politic, they say that after takeover 1997 we don't know what happen. Then I am scared because in Chinese you don't have freedom of, no freedom, and then you don't have the right to talk, so I scare. Also when I doing business, not business, I working in a Germany company, [I: A German company?] Yes, I am working in Chinese department. Then I have some contact with the Chinese people, and then I am scare of them. Because their mentality is too, is no good. Then I am scared. That's why I think about it to move to other country. I want to have more freedom, I don't know what happen in 1997.

Note how this respondent refers to "Chinese people" as distinct from herself, a Hong Kong person. This distinction is one that has been identified by previous researchers and confirmed by many in our participant population as well. Identity issues will be discussed at length throughout this chapter.

Another male who left for Canada in 1989 at age 31 responded in the following way (P42):

> It's like I think a lot of Hong Kong people think political instability. Also influence from my father because he has experienced the old type Chinese government, the style. He said better go, never trust the Chinese government, at that time. That's why also, I listen to my parents and run away.

For a male who immigrated to Australia in 1990, the reasons for leaving were a bit more personal (P33):

> And also, I am quite interested to have some other countries living and working experience. At that time, maybe I was young, so I was prepared to have some new life and new working experience. As what I said, I never have the experience studying or living overseas. So that's the reason why made me and my wife because at that time I don't have any children. So I and my wife together want to have a different life at that time.

Another male's immigration to Australia in 1991 was in response to what he saw as a growing trend to seek overseas experience (P20):

> By that time a lot of people immigrate, and it becomes a kind of general practice, and you will feel a bit lost when you are not entitled to immigrate. [I: So everybody is doing it?] Everybody was doing that either to Canada and, in fact, there are other chances popping up, other countries then they also hand out immigrant proposal to people in Hong Kong. Less stringent than those offer by Canada and Australia. There is a trend by that time. Of course, I am very much influence by people of those colleague and as well as classmates in the university.

Thus the "push" of anticipated political crackdowns and economic downturns combined with the "pull" of gaining international work and living experience compelled nearly 800,000 Hong Kongers, including the 50 respondents in this study, to emigrate between 1984 and 1997. How did these émigrés construct their cultural identity at their point of departure? After more than 150 years of rule by the United Kingdom, did they describe themselves as thinking and acting British? Or did they imagine themselves as Chinese, reflecting their ethnic heritage and Confucian-laced upbringing? Or was their cultural self-concept derived from the layered history and multiple influences described as being a Hong Kong person?

Premigration identity

Chapter 1 revealed the variegated roots of the Hong Konger's complex identity, tracing it back to Hong Kong's historical origins. The confluence of British and Chinese traditions has led to a fluidity of self-definition that is unique to the Hong Kong people. This complexity is exemplified in an insightful reflection from a male participant who immigrated to Australia at age 32 (P33):

> For the Hong Kong person, it's a mixture of Western and Chinese culture. I am not born in Hong Kong. I was born in Macau. But I moved to Hong Kong at about 1966. I was only a boy. I worked in Hong Kong, I was educated in Hong Kong, and all my friends, my family, and my parents have a root in Hong Kong. So, at 1990, you ask what is my cultural background, I would say I am a Chinese, but Hong Kong is my original place. I would say I am proud to be a Chinese, but I also understand all the Western education, culture. So I would say a mixture.

When the 50 respondents were asked the question "*How would you have identified yourself prior to migration from Hong Kong?*" the most prevalent response (40%) was to identify themselves as Hong Kongers; 28% identified themselves as Chinese; 16% identified themselves as some mixture of Chinese and Western culture; 14% identified themselves as Hong Kong–Chinese; 10% identified themselves as British–Hong Kongers; 6% identified themselves as international; and 2% self-identified as British. Many of the respondents identified themselves as fitting into more than one category.

The variety of premigration identity responses found in this study confirms the Hong Kong Transition Project's findings.[1] However, that study also revealed the malleability and situationality of cultural identity and the effect of external events in shaping identity; that is, situational contexts, particularly political events, were the catalysts for individual cultural identity shifts. In Figure 4.1, note that as the handover deadline (July 1, 1997) approached, respondents were less likely to describe themselves as Hong Kongers but also less likely to ascribe the single Chinese identity to themselves. Once the handover was completed, the political context changed yet again, and it was reflected in the emergence of a new identity category, that of Hong Kong–Chinese.

Among the plurality in my study who identified themselves as Hong Kongers, the central influence hinged in part on their being born and educated locally while simultaneously experiencing a sense of detachment from China and the Chinese way of doing things. In fact, many were overtly critical of the Chinese Communist system. A male respondent who immigrated to Canada at age 17 stated (P17):

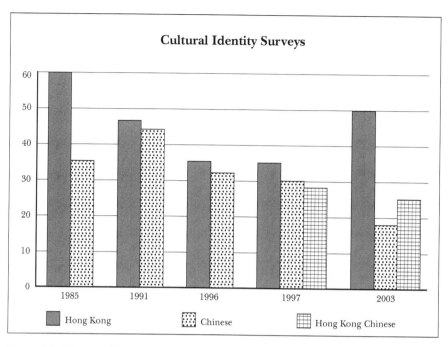

Figure 4.1 Identity of Hong Kong residents taken at five-time points (DeGolyer, 2007)

Even though I was educated in Catholic school, I was in Hong Kong. I didn't find much Western culture to attach myself. Perhaps it's family, I think. My mum is sort of "right wing" thinking, like she perceived communist as evil. So I was actually brought up … My mum actually influenced me a lot. The thinking, the value, so it's following her footsteps and say: Chinese, get rid of the communist … So it's hard for myself to think of being attached to Mainland; it's almost impossible. [I: You don't think of yourself as Chinese?] No, it's Hong Kong, basically. But not British 'cause at that time you are Chinese, is second class. Maybe my mum as well like British I wasn't speak English that well then. So I guess I perceive myself as a Hong Konger. Very much.

A similar response was offered by a female who immigrated to Canada at age 36 (P47). She described herself as a

Hong Kong person. Simply a Hong Kong person. When I was in the high school, I remember one of my classmates asked me, "What's your feeling of being a Chinese?" and I said, "I have no feeling being a Chinese." It seems that China didn't have much relation with me. I didn't have any close relatives in China. I have never been to China until I was about twenty, even for tourist. And I only have heard things like my father has some relatives there, and we always have to send some of the daily consuming goods to them. And I heard from my friends or neighbors that when they go back to China, they would wear a lot of clothings because they would not check your clothings, a lot of layers. And then when they were back home, they would take off all the clothes and leave it for them. And they are lacking of most of the things, very poor. You can simply say that I have no connection with China.

Among the 14 respondents (28%) who identified themselves as Chinese, several did so because commonly held Confucian attributes were indicative of their Chinese identity. A typically cited example was the significance attached to family relationships and filial obligations. A female who immigrated to Australia at age 29 shared this observation (P13):

I think I am still quite Chinese because I knew that values are very important, relatives are very important, the relationship is also important, family is so important. I follow my husband anywhere. I have that kind of feeling. I think it is quite Chinese if I have that sort of feeling, right?

Cognizance of the impending handover was also a determinant of participant identification with Chinese culture, but it was perceived as a complicated relationship. This is clearly illustrated in the comment by a male respondent who immigrated to Australia at age 31 (P4):

But now you are really turning your back, and we all know. So I think we have no choice, and we are Chinese; everybody knows that. Because at that time we know how China is like. They don't rule by laws; they rule by authority. Who's gaining the power, he's having the interpretation of the law. Then, you saw they can kill people in the Tiananmen Square and then what are they going to do. Like Hong Kong is being handed back, then what are we going to face, if we … Okay so, we have a protest. I mean, if people going out, are they going to suppress? What are they going to do? Do you have the freedom to speak? Nobody really knows. So, I know somehow I am going to be a China, a Chinese again. The feeling is complicated. I don't want to be, part of the, but I know I have to.

Interestingly, some respondents made the point of separating their citizenship (possession of a British passport) from their personal values, which they described as being inherently Chinese. For example, a male who immigrated to Canada at age 31 claimed (P42):

> I think Chinese. I think of myself as Chinese. Maybe British passport or, I don't think I belong to it, because seldom visit UK. There seems not too much linkage, and I am not interest in their society or political system, whatever. So I don't think I really belong to British or something. Even if it is a colony of Britain Hong Kong at that time.

Although the majority of the respondents identified themselves as Hong Kongese, one male immigrant, who immigrated to Canada when he was 51, had a unique perspective on what it meant to be a Hong Konger (P31): *"Hong Kong person is nobody. Hong Kong is only a city, so I consider myself as Chinese."*

Twenty participants (40%) identified themselves as some combination of cultural identities such as British–Hong Konger, Hong Kong–Western, Hong Kong–Chinese, or a mixture of various cultures to which they had been exposed. This idea of mingled identities was expressed by a female respondent who immigrated to Canada at age 28 (P18):

> I think it's a combination with Chinese and British. Because when we were born, you might realize that our nationality is British subject. Because we were brought up in the time when Hong Kong is still under the sovereignty of British government, so there is lot of influence on the cultural side, because we are so used to the Western culture and then so we have build up a very unique identity. We just count ourselves as Hong Kong, Hong Kongers. [I: So Hong Kongers, you see Hong Kongers as a combination of Chinese and British?] Chinese and British, yeah, right. It's like a mix.

Another female who immigrated to Canada at age 18 commented (P22):

> British–Hong Kong, because at that time we were under the British education system, everything is so British ... and then we know all the governors. We are taught the way of the British system, things that we learn in the books that we study and all, you know about British education system. And the news that you see is all British government officials speaking in front of the camera ... So very British.

A male who immigrated to Australia at age 26 had this to say (P50):

> I probably would say Hong Kong–Chinese, because I don't think I can deny the fact that I am Chinese by race but it's just the case that we happen to be born in British colony at that time, that's all.

Yet another interesting comment was made by this respondent, who immigrated to Australia at age 31 (P4):

> I think most people will treat themselves as a British or overseas British. We never really, at least I myself, I never consider myself a Chinese, I mean a Chinese Chinese. I think I am proud of a seed of China, but ... when ... all ... [I: You thought yourself as part of the British?] Yes, yes, yes.

As the emigrants prepared to embark for Canada or Australia, 40% thought of themselves as Hong Kong people and another 40% thought themselves to be a mixture of cultures. But what was their emotional state? Were they "reluctant exiles," as suggested by Ronald Skeldon, who were planning to return to Hong Kong the moment that their new citizenship was conferred? Or were they eager to embrace their international adventure with its imagined educational, economic, and security benefits?

Response to leaving Hong Kong

When asked "What was your emotional response to leaving Hong Kong?" only 8% of the respondents provided a response indicative of their emotional reaction to leaving. For those few interviewees, the emotional response was evenly split; half expressed positive emotions and half negative emotions. The following is an excerpt of a positive response to leaving Hong Kong. This respondent was 47 when she left Hong Kong for Canada (P14): *"So when I left Hong Kong, I was very excited, and really looking forward to something nice and pleasant."*

Only two interviewees expressed negative emotions upon emigrating; both were young women. An 18-year-old who left for Canada confesses that upon leaving Hong Kong (P22):

> I miss my father's side ... my paternal grandparents. Because they have been taking care of me for the past seventeen years. So it is really tough when I bid goodbye to them at the airport. Somehow that happen so you have to go anyway. Otherwise you cannot be the Canadian immigrant anymore when you reject the government offer. That is something big to the family. When I left I was not happy at all. I was very sad. I was not happy at all.

Rather than revealing their emotional response to their impending migration, a plurality of the interviewees (21, or 42%) simply indicated whether their immigration plan was a permanent or a temporary one. More than half of these respondents (14, or 67%) indicated that they planned their move to be a permanent one; 33% (7) indicated that the move would be temporary. These figures of "intention" contradict the widely held belief that all the migrants intended their moves abroad to serve as citizenship insurance; once the newly issued passport was in hand, the migrant would quickly return to Hong Kong. The actual demographic statistics, however, show that approximately 75% of immigrants returned to Hong Kong, although whether permanently or temporarily is uncertain at this time. It does appear that for the Hong Kongers, the decision to emigrate was a practical strategy to deal with an emerging situational (political) instability rather than an idea fraught with emotional baggage.

Five out of the seven who planned for their migration to be temporary indicated that they intended to return to Hong Kong immediately after citizenship. This was 10% of the total number of interviewees in the study. The moniker "boomerang," invented by the Hong Kong press, could aptly be applied to these returnees, soaring into their new countries of residence sufficiently long enough to obtain a house and a passport and then speeding back to Hong Kong in a graceful arc.

This is illustrated in the following forthright response from a female who immigrated to Australia at age 27 (P2):

> We don't really want to stay long term in Australia. Actually we don't like the other immigration people because Hong Kong people migrant. We just pack a case of clothes, and that's all. We didn't bring anything at all because we are thinking we are just going there for one or two years because two years can get citizenship. Once I get the citizenship and I will come to Hong Kong. This is political insurance.

Another female respondent, who immigrated to Australia at age 33, also expressed the desire to return to Hong Kong immediately after gaining Australian citizenship (P48): *"The purpose is after I got the visa, I got the status of citizen. And I come back because I was offer a no-pay leave for two years. So my heart was actually in Hong Kong."*

A reverse strategy was also contemplated by the emigrants. An equally practical yet unemotional comment was expressed by a male respondent who immigrated to Australia at age 32 (P33):

> I: When you went to Australia initially, were you thinking of staying there for many years?
> P: I think so.
> I: So your intention was to stay there?
> P: I intended to stay there particularly retire.

Fourteen of the respondents specifically planned to make their emigration permanent, expressing their dreams of starting businesses, buying houses, and raising their children in Sydney or Vancouver. This sentiment can be seen in the following comment by a male respondent who immigrated to Canada at age 40 (P34):

> I immigrate, the main reason I immigrate there is for my children. I want them to have a second choice when you grow up. When they grow up, probably they prefer to stay in Hong Kong. No problem. But if they want to stay there, stay in Hong Kong, probably they have another choice, they can stay in Canada. They have a choice. If I do not make this kind of decision, they don't have a choice.

Nevertheless, despite their intention to settle permanently in their chosen countries (90% of the interviewees), by virtue of their participation in this research study, 100% of the respondents had returned to Hong Kong to live, a result we will examine in more detail later in this chapter and throughout the book.

Whether planning to take temporary or permanent residence in their country of immigration, all of the study's respondents made their way to Australia or Canada sometime between 1984 and 1997. How did they respond to their new homelands, and how did their new compatriots respond to them?

Reaction to and by host country

Observations about country of settlement

The new immigrants were keen observers of their new place of residence. An overwhelming majority of the immigrants (94%) mentioned various cultural differences between Hong Kong and their host country. Values, beliefs, attitudes, the environment, work, and leisure-time pursuits were all examined and evaluated by the newcomers. For 68% of the immigrants, these observed cultural differences were to be admired and perhaps emulated, while for 32%, these differences were irritants, some mild and others profound, and served as constant reminders of how different they, as Hong Kongers, were from the local culture. For example, a male participant who immigrated to Australia at age 32 expressed a distinct appreciation for the Australian sense of neighborliness (P33):

> In Hong Kong, you even don't enjoy neighborhood. In Hong Kong, you never meet your neighbors. But I know that even for the neighborhood development, I found Australia better than Hong Kong.

I don't know why. Maybe in Hong Kong, I know the neighborhood, but for friendship, I prefer in Australia. They are easy to make friends, and in Australia, the community has not many people. So it's easy to have a neighborhood friendship in that area. But in Hong Kong, I don't feel so easy because every person is quite defensive, and they are quite busy. Every morning they go out ... We seldom have any neighborhood gathering. But in Australia, we used to have some neighborhood gathering in front of our house and their house. [I: Barbecues ...?] Yes, different culture.

The contrast between Australian and Hong Kong flexibility and adaptability struck one male participant who immigrated to Australia at age 28 (P39):

They have a very strong view on maintaining personal life style. Their respect of personal freedom. I think in Australia, everybody is a different unique individual. Unlike Hong Kong, they have their own way of seeing things ... It's quite different from Hong Kong people in a way they switch very easily. [I: Switch easily?] Sometimes they tend to see things in this way, and sometimes they tend to see things in a different way. They don't seem to have a very firm value. Unlike the Australian, they usually have a very strong way of seeing things. [I: So once they have a particular point of view, it's not easy to change their mind?] Yes, you may argue over them, but they still do the same. [I: But with Hong Kongers you can persuade people more easily?] Guess Hong Kong people are more receptive that they may actually try to do things differently and see things differently.

This keen insight underscores a basic distinction in thinking between Hong Kong and Western cultures: flexibility and situational thinking ("see things in this way, and sometimes they tend to see things in a different way ... Guess Hong Kong people are more receptive") among the former and more consistency or rigidity among the latter ("Australian, they usually have a very strong way of seeing things"). This distinction will be discussed in more detail in Chapter 10.

A common observation that the immigrants tended to evaluate negatively pertained to the Australian pace of life, which was considerably slower than the frenetic movements typical of Hong Kong pedestrians and store clerks. Reflecting these strong feelings, a male who immigrated to Australia at age 19 commented (P6):

You sometimes get annoyed and get to be angry, that is how come this sort of people can exist in the world? So it was slow. Fixing some

> simple things will make you few days. That's ridiculous. [I: So you got frustrated?] Quite, quite, quite, something like that.

Yet another example of the negative response to the slow pace of life is presented by this female respondent, who immigrated to Australia at age 27 (P2):

> They are very laid back. Because in the beginning I didn't work, and after half a year I work in a company; actually, I work at McDonald's. I just work part-time because I think I will work in McDonald's and try to make some friends. I start to know them more and seems like my life become more accomplished, accommodated by the society. I find them they are very slow, lay back; one good way to describe them is like koala bear. They are very slow, very friendly; actually, they are very simple. They not like the Hong Kong Chinese that are aggressive. My pace is very fast. I am that type of person, very fast. When I get in there, I don't really like this. The slow things, everything's so slow. And they don't used too much fast things. When I talk fast, I do things fast, even in McDonald's I do things fast. And somehow, it is the whole thing. I think it is the pace of life.

A male respondent who left Hong Kong for Australia also commented on the slow pace of the Australians (P6):

> Especially when you fixing those your home utility life, connecting electricity, getting the water meter, that sort of things. Wait for a long time queuing up, getting the contact, getting somebody entertaining you, that sort of things. It probably spend about half a day to fix your electricity and wait for a few days before you really get electricity main connected, or the accounts been transferred to use, something like that. I mean, it gets quite slow, I mean things is really quite slow. Especially when I first come Australia, there is big contrast of what Hong Kong people is doing.

Other newcomers were struck by the social liberalism they found in Canada, as against the more conservative stances on sexuality, parental rights, and family relationships espoused by Hong Kong people. A female who immigrated to Canada at age 33 was very critical of the Canadian culture, which she viewed as being embarrassingly liberal (P27):

> But afterwards, when we have our baby, we think about the education and how the culture would shape the child. And that's something we are very concern. Well, it's very liberal; everybody place out their opinion, and everybody fights for equality, fight for their human rights

to pretty much extreme case. Something we cannot go through is that we have a moral thinking and we don't think these voices should be dominant in the society. [I: Maybe too many individuals speaking up?] Yes, extreme case, the problem of homosexuality. They are speaking in the televisions. The program very much touched me. If I have a child of just about twelve or thirteen years old and she was asking whether she is a lesbian, she haven't gone through a date before ... [I: So you think that there is too much discussion on this?] Yes. And it's common. Many young people are talking about their experience with their same sex friends. We hope that Hong Kong has not yet come to that extreme. But we witnessed some voices coming out, voicing for those minority groups. But it's still a long way when it reach the American standard.

Local response to immigrants

As one might expect, local residents in Australia and Canada also expressed varied reactions to the presence of the new and fast-growing Hong Kong immigrant population. The Hong Kong Remigration Project did not interview Canadian or Australian friends, neighbors, or coworkers of the newcomers. Therefore, an important perspective is absent from the data. However, the interviewees in this study were asked to remember instances of host country national reactions to them and their behavior. Biases inherent in both their interpretations of others' behavior and their memory recall no doubt are evident in their responses. Nonetheless, participants remembered reactions ranging from acceptance to misunderstanding and resentment. According to these retrospective recollections, the predominant reactions of the locals were either acceptance (42%) or resentment (22%); only 18% of the participants reported feeling misunderstood by the locals.

Many immigrants recalled the warmth and friendliness of Australians as the migrants struggled to adjust to a new culture and environment. A female who immigrated to Australia at age 35 commented on the effusion of hospitality that she received from the Australian locals (P1):

> I got mix with the people there. The citizens there were very nice. They are kind to you. And even those in the shopping mall or even the supermarket, the people are very nice. So I feel like everybody is equal and being taken care of. So I feel the warmth there ... They welcome everybody, no matter you are Asian people, or European. They treat you on an equal base. Or maybe I work in the consul. I meet a lot of different cultural background people, so they are willing to help and willing to assist.

The friendliness and acceptance of the Australian locals was also observed by a male who immigrated to Australia at age 31 (P35):

> Actually I quite like the Australians ... I think that they are very friendly, at least with the colleagues and classmates that I met. They do not have racism; they treat Hong Kong people just like Australian people because Australia is an immigrant country. Want to help us, and they like to offer something to us.

As previously indicated, the local response was not uniformly receptive. Many of those who immigrated to Canada perceived hostility or at least aloofness from their new neighbors. A female respondent who immigrated to Canada at age 36 reported feeling misunderstood by the Canadians, whom she believed were quite "provincial" (P5):

> A lot of people in Canada, actually ... Well, I don't want to use this word, but they are quite provincial. A lot had not been out of Canada. So they are not very sure where Hong Kong is, "Hong Kong Indian" or "Hong Kong Japan"... And they sort of don't really know how to relate to you, especially somebody like me, who lived in the US and all this other things. They are not quite sure how to be comfortable with you.

Feelings of misunderstanding also stemmed from language barriers between the cultures. As this male participant, who immigrated to Canada at age 44, commented, it was sometimes difficult to get the Canadians to understand him (P24):

> Sometime, I speak, maybe my thinking is in Chinese way, then I speak in English but only in Chinese way. Then they understand. For example, "Can you help me?" Then they would say, "Give me a hand." But I was really stupid. I will say, "I have no hand." If you understand that that is a joke. That means I am busy, I can't help you. But I speak in English say, "I have no hand." And if he ask me for help, I should response, "I have no time. I am busy. I can't help you." At that time, I didn't know how I came up with this sentence. "I have no hand." And he looks at me. "What happen at you? Are you handicapped?" That's only one example. Maybe I have many examples, even I don't know. Maybe I behave in that way, the Canadian think, oh. What happen to you? Maybe that is the cultural difference, maybe that's the language barrier. But they are nice.

One male respondent was 13 years old when his family moved to Canada, and he observed the local reaction to his father's attempt to find a job (P15):

Immigration was difficult for men. They had a certain social status in Hong Kong. When they went to Canada, they had to start over again. Canada was resistant to foreigners. My dad was a chartered engineer from the UK, but couldn't get a professional designation in Canada. They told him he had to take all the tests over again. It was a tough adjustment for him ... Barriers exist, although the government says they welcome everyone, there are invisible barrier.

This female who immigrated to Canada at age 42 reported feeling that she was resented by the locals, whom she felt treated her in subtly differently ways than they treated their fellow Canadians (P12):

Yes. With that I mean I feel something in there. Suppose you go to the grocery store or supermarket, you know, we buy and then we pay and we line up, sometimes I feel their look, their face, the cashier face is different. They say hello and then they check it, check how much you have. The way they express is different from what they express when they saw a Canadian. It's kind of friendliness is not, it's in they more, to you it's just, uh, like that. It's not that sincere, which we really feel. All my friends and relatives they feel it too.

Feelings of being resented by Canadian neighbors were also expressed by this female respondent, who immigrated to Canada at age 40 (P8):

The neighbor, the developer, they bought a piece of, they bought old house, and they tear down all house and they cut all the trees, because they want to build the house to suit the new immigrant. My neighbor, one of the neighbor, he said, "I really don't like you people. You want to have a nice big house, and you don't want to have any trees." They cut all those old trees, and she cried. And she said, "I really hate to see you people." Because they like to have, they like the area, they like the environment, no change. She told me, she said, "I have been living here for thirty-five, or so many years. Now I have to move because I want to sell my house." Because she did not like the environment anymore.

This same respondent comments on the Hong Konger preference for large houses (P8):

At that time many many people immigrated to Canada. In Vancouver, I am talking about the city. And the ... "do you know the Chinese once they landed, they want to buy a very big house." They call it "monstrous" house. Monstrous, monster's house.

Canadian reactions to Hong Kongers' preference for big houses and indifference to green landscaping became a regular source of tension between the two groups. Canadians, in particular those living in Vancouver, find contentment in their leafy, verdant neighborhoods and take pride in their gardens. They defined their neighborhoods in ways in which the old trees and manicured lawns spelled material success and harmony with the environment. The Hong Kong newcomers, however, accustomed to living in cramped, overcrowded urban apartments, reveled in the large living spaces that suburban areas offered to them and their extended families. They also had no experience in the maintenance and upkeep of lawns and flower beds. Success was defined by spacious interior space. Out went the trees, up went the McMansions, and there went the neighborhood.

Adaptation strategies

In an attempt to adapt to life in a foreign culture, the immigrants adopted various strategies to reconcile sociocultural differences between Hong Kong life and life in the host country. One such strategic pattern I have labeled "Do like the Romans do," that is, adopt the local lifestyle in anticipation that this strategy will result in successful adaptation. A secondary strategy to confronting the Hong Kong–Western differences is "Stay the course," or maintain Hong Kong/Chinese family values, modes of interpersonal interaction, food and entertainment preferences, and work style behaviors. Of course, some immigrants combined these two models, drawing on adjustment tactics specific to a cultural domain or setting. For example, an immigrant could adopt the Canadian direct interaction style in the workplace ("Do like the Romans") but speak Cantonese and play mah-jong at home ("Stay the course"). Whether the setting was public or private frequently shaped the adaptation tactic.

Do like the Romans

Nearly all of the participants reported adopting some aspect of the local styles, such as family relationships, food consumption, leisure activities, or parenting methods. A large number of participants (88%) also reported adopting the same social behaviors as the locals. The following excerpts illustrate some of the ways in which the immigrants attempted to change their behavior in order to blend into the local culture.

Immigrating to Canada at age 36, a female interviewee describes the changes in her parenting style as a result of her exposure to Canadian culture (P5):

> We have already transitioned to like the Northern Americans, influence by their way they brought up children, or the way they interacted with people. [I: What examples do you think of as North American?] We were definitely more opened, less … You know the Chinese people tend to be very protective of their children, and we were also protective, but we would give them enough freedom, to make friends, expose them to variety people.

Personal finance choices and decisions (earning, saving, and spending) have significant cultural foundations, and many immigrants discovered the differences between the Hong Kong attitude about saving a portion of one's salary for future needs and the Australian emphasis on living and spending for the moment. Much of the immigrants' Hong Kong attitude was formulated when they were living in the former territory and reflected the minimal social safety net provided by the Hong Kong government. While many supported the concept of less government intervention in the economy, one worrying consequence was the need for individuals to proactively save for their retirement and old age. This female participant, who immigrated to Australia at age 35, describes her adaptation to the Australian way of budgeting (P1):

> But just psychologically, I like the Australians. They couldn't bother about saving much. Or they even don't bother to buy a house and put in a mortgage. They just earn and spend every week. They get the pay, and they spend it all out. And I feel I was not secure. Because if I don't save up, I feel insecure. Because this is my traditional way, the Chinese way. But when I get there eventually, I feel like … well, if I really have confidence in the government, they will take care of me. So [laughed] that's a way that I psychologically think that, well, if I really match it, I don't really bother anything … just get whatever and I spend whatever. And I just enjoy life.

A male respondent who immigrated to Canada at age 43 with his wife commented, with some distress, on the differences between his financial standing in Canada and in Hong Kong (P40):

> I normally have some good saving during my time in Hong Kong a year. In Canada, I do not have saving at all. How much I earn, how much I spend. In Hong Kong, in the older days, my wife do not have

to work; in Canada, she have to go to work to make a living. I did ask myself, is it worthwhile to go back to Hong Kong? I keep asking that sort of questions for years, and long last, we decided to go back.

Country of settlement provided different contexts for financial management attitudes. Immigrants to Canada perceived the local residents to be more sober and future oriented regarding personal finances than the present orientation of the Australians. In comparison, Hong Kongers were perceived as either materialistic spendthrifts (using Canada as the endpoint of a financial continuum) or conservative planners who took retirement saving seriously (when comparing their attitudes with the Australians'). One male respondent who immigrated to Canada at age 13 commented on the differences he observed between the financial practices of the local Canadians and those of the people of Hong Kong (P15):

> People in Hong Kong are "idiots" when it comes to money. They spend whatever they earn. I was more money conscious. This was a Canadian trait. Salaries are not so high in Canada. People used financial resources in a practical way, not to show off or appearances like spending money in bars and karaoke.

In other life domains, Canadian and Australian characteristics were more similar. Immigrants in both countries were often delighted with opportunities they had to enjoy outdoor leisure pursuits along with their new compatriots. Participation in these activities was equated with the adoption of a Western lifestyle and with a greater sense of belonging to their new homeland. It signaled an appreciation of the environment as well. These newly embraced leisure activities were also chosen with more spontaneity and carried out with less rigidity than the immigrants displayed when they were still living in Hong Kong.

The same male respondent who was a teenager when his family immigrated to Canada describes his newly found interest in outdoor leisure activities (P15):

> For example, outdoor activities, playing hockey, or playing baseball with them, and hanging around with them to go out and have fun, and all sorts of activities that are Canadian, young adults would do.

A similar experience is described by a female who immigrated to Canada at age 36 (P47):

> I think we did. Such as in holiday, instead of going to the restaurants only, we go cinema or shopping, we would go resort, we go for fishing,

or may be we drive a long time just go to a small city, just to walk around, without any definite things we need to do.

Engagement in and enjoyment of typically Canadian activities is also described by a male respondent who immigrated to Canada at age 23 (P11):

> Maybe go to camping, hiking, and after work, because the exceptionally long hours in Canada in Vancouver; in summertime I can still go to the park and relax and lie on the grass ... enjoy the sunshine ... really wonderful. Just go with my wife ... whatever.

Some respondents commented on their increased level of environmental awareness as a result of their sojourn. An example is provided by this comment from a male interviewee who left Hong Kong for Australia at age 28 (P39):

> Actually, even when I lived in Sydney, I finally grasped what it means to be environmental friendly, how we should love our environment. It's something that you can't understand in Hong Kong.

Similar concerns for the environment are expressed in the following comment by another male interviewee, who immigrated to Canada at age 23 (P11):

> Usually when I think about ... when I face some environmental nature, e.g., like whether you littering ... when you see people go to the beach. Because you can catch the crabs in the pier, in Vancouver, they had some law; you have to follow the law, and if the crab is not bigger than some size and you need to put it back or so. But as you know, there is some Asian people, not necessary Chinese, or some Asian or South-American people, they usually won't follow the rules. Some of them. And that's what I think they are wrong. So that's why I think I am a Canadian.

Among the interviewees, observations of Western social behaviors were frequent and the Hong Kongers, as immigrants, described their attempts to adapt. Such conduct might include dating behavior, public courtesy and manners, nonverbal behavior, making friends, social interactions, and daily life rituals.

A female interviewee who immigrated to Canada at age 18 commented on her family's observation about her now "westernized" behavior (P22):

> I think my mom once comment that I became very westernized to her; especially when I dated two guys there, one was a Canadian-born

Chinese, the second one was a French Canadian. She then feel that, "Oh, my daughter has become very westernized and very Canadian," which is something that maybe she had never expected.

A few of the respondents mentioned that it is common for Hong Kongers to cut into waiting queues. However, this male, who immigrated to Canada at age 23, commented on how that aspect of his behavior changed after being exposed to Canadian culture (P11):

I think at the very beginning I will like the Hong Kong style to cut in. Not cut in … because there are no queues, so whenever the bus come then my first reaction is to go to the door. But afterwards, because the bus in Canada is not very full, so why I need to rush? So just let the elders to go first, and … actually, I will go at the last even though I came first. I would let other people go first.

Immigrating as a teenager to Australia, one male remigrant was aware that his behavior was now very different from what would be considered typical for a Hong Kong child (P45). He describes himself as:

Probably more outgoing. I think my parents would describe it as "more direct and more outgoing than the average Hong Kong kid." Probably more independent but that may due to I left home for years … More direct I think. To do things differently. Or sometimes I did something outside the norm, they would say, "This is a character of a *gwai chai*."

Another teenaged immigrant to Canada remarked on adapting to a particularly Western activity, community volunteering (P16):

I volunteer even more when I got into university. At the beginning I help in the Chinese committee, and later on I volunteer at a Volunteer Centre. I assign the people to different volunteering opportunities. For my parents, volunteer is a waste of time. They think is, just study more. But I never thought it's a cultural different thing. I think it is my dad; he is a very practical person. So back then I didn't know it was a Canadian thing before I came back to Hong Kong and realize there are lots of people in Hong Kong who have never volunteered.

Stay the course: Act Chinese

Adapting to Western behaviors did not necessarily mean that the immigrants abandoned Hong Kong or Chinese social or leisure activities or interpersonal behaviors. Thirty-nine respondents (78%) reported maintaining some aspect of Chinese life while simultaneously attempting to adapt to the host culture. Respondents reported speaking Chinese rather than English, eating Chinese foods, engaging in Chinese entertainment (a commonly cited example was mah-jong), and maintaining a Chinese work ethic. Some even reported developing a greater sense of their Chinese identity. The following are excerpts illustrating interviewees' attempts to retain their Chinese identity.

Immigrants who continued to act Chinese in the host culture often preferred Chinese movies to the English versions, as is illustrated by this comment from a male who immigrated to Australia at age 31 (P4): *"I always watch the tape of the Chinese series, movies. And I read Chinese newspaper, I don't read the English newspaper."* And the decision to remain Chinese can also be seen in the food choices of and rituals followed by these immigrants. This male, who immigrated to Australia at age 43, comments (P41):

> Food is a good example, lots of people eat spaghetti or ... pizza or pasta ... they eat a lot of those. We find it difficult to eat these things all the time. We prefer eating rice. That is rather conservative, but it's difficult to change our diet.

Another male, who immigrated to Australia at age 28, echoed his need to maintain distinctly Hong Kong food activities (P39):

> Yes, going to *yum cha*. And once a while, a lot of friends come and visit us. And almost every month there will be one or two visitors come to Sydney, and we usually go out for *yum cha* or dinner, and sometimes they also stay in my home. So I was keeping up-to-date to what was happening in Hong Kong.

Types of cultural adjustments to the country of settlement

Adjustment and coping resources

To cope with life in the host country, respondents utilized a variety of resources. Seventy-four percent reported establishing friendships with other Chinese immigrants as a coping mechanism; 42% reported using friendships with white locals; 24% relied on family members; 12% relied on relationships with coworkers; and 10% relied on religion. The following excerpts feature the strategies interviewees used to ease their adjustment into the foreign culture.

A middle-aged female immigrant to Canada relied on the maintenance of friendships with people from Hong Kong, with whom she could reminisce (P30):

> Just usually we go out with friends from Hong Kong, so we can talk about Hong Kong because especially for the first year, and you have been here in Hong Kong for so many years and we do miss Hong Kong. So you would like to talk with friends from Hong Kong as well.

In contrast, this male, who immigrated to Australia at age 28, thought it best to rely on friendships with locals who could provide him with a better understanding of life in his new culture (P39): *"I was trying to establish my connections, trying to get myself familiar with the environment, with the people there and to know some local Australians to understand the city."*

For this female, who immigrated to Canada at age 42, the main coping strategy was staying in contact with her family (P12):

> Actually we have relatives, my sisters, my in-laws are there. So we usually, you know, communicate each other, see each other every day, that's what. Also, just like what we did in Hong Kong the same people. We have some neighbors, I mean talking about neighbors, we see each other and then we talk.

A middle-aged male who immigrated to Australia at age 43 was one of the few interviewees who found support in religious life (P41):

> I am a Catholic, and my whole family is Catholic. And I think that is how we try to merge into the Australian life. Oh yes, we did make some friends, we met the parish priest, we met some other priests, nuns. I mean that's how we started our Australian life.

Another example is provided by this comment from a male respondent who left Hong Kong for Australia at age 31 (P4):

> Yes, I think the most part is my religion belief. Because as I said after I leave I left secondary school I never go to church again. In that two and a half years, I really pick up my religious life a lot. And I see something that make your belief so strong, I want to tell you this ... So I see big thing and small things in Australia, in my life in Australia. I really see God is existing; he is helping me and guiding me. So that is the most important change I have before and after I go to Australia. And I am still having a very strong belief today.

This female, who immigrated to Canada at age 40, recalled using her newly developed Buddhist faith to cope with the pressures of life in a foreign culture (P8):

> Then I had some friends they are Buddhism. They, I mean she is a lady, she gave me those books, to read. Then I read those books. I open up my mind. No, gradually, gradually. I accept the Buddhism. So because I understand why my children have these kind of behaviors. So now I don't feel so responsible for my children's failure. If they are successful, it's their life. It's still firm, but I changed my outlook, I feel very calm. Before just little thing I will feel very upset. After, this changing process no does not happened overnight, few years, gradually, gradually. So I study I begin to read more books about Buddhism, [I: Was there a Buddhist temple in Vancouver?] Not necessary a temple you know [I: So it is a very personal religion?] Yes. So I find it very suitable for me. So I started to read the prayer and came back.

During this recent period of immigration, many Chinese churches have sprung up throughout western Canada and Australia. I anticipated that a substantial number of this study's interviewees would discuss the role of the church in smoothing away obstacles to acculturation. Yet only five remigrants (10%) mentioned organized religious involvement as an activity that facilitated their adjustment to their host country.

Postadjustment identity

For individuals who have lived in a foreign culture for some time, the Cultural Identity Model predicts shifts in cultural identity. The range of possibilities includes a stronger identification with the host culture, a deeper connection to the home culture, or some combination of the two. When asked, *"How would you identify yourself culturally prior to returning to Hong Kong?"* the majority of interviewees in the Hong Kong Remigration Project (40%) reported feeling themselves to be a mixture of their home and host cultures, 18% self-identified as Chinese, 18% self-identified as local, 16% self-identified as Hong Kongese, and a small percentage (2%) self-identified as international. Recall from the discussion of Hong Konger identity in Chapter 1 that prior to immigration, 40% of the respondents also saw themselves as having mixed identities, at that time as blending Hong Kong elements with British or Chinese identities. We will see in Chapter 5 that the additive nature of Hong Kong identity is a constant theme in their perceptions of their "cultural" selves. Not surprisingly, fewer immigrants, on the cusp of leaving their new country of residence, identify as "pure" (or unblended) Hong Kongers, dropping by more than half from a premigration high of 40%.

Identity choices

The following are excerpts illustrating the different identity choices of the respondents in this study. The widespread feeling of being a combination of the two cultures was expressed by this female, who immigrated to Canada at age 36 (P30):

> Canadian Hong Kong, yeah. I mean, I still miss Hong Kong very much and because I was in the travel business I come home almost twice a year for that thirteen years so I still have a close contacts with Hong Kong. And I still care about what Hong Kong is doing especially when that time I mean the Chek Lap Kok Airport when they first open, and the first week it was in a mess and I heard about it on the news and I feel a bit unhappy about it. I mean it's I treat myself as a Hong Kongese so I mean I don't want to see things happen in Hong Kong like this. I still have some what you call that, I do care about Hong Kong. But I enjoy the life in Canada as well, as both places have their good point.

This male respondent, who immigrated to Canada at age 23, also considered himself a combination of two cultures (P11):

> I still think ... maybe just ... Chinese Canadian something like that. Because I don't think I am one hundred percent Canadian because I am not really ... I only have a Canadian passport, but the culture ... I didn't join the community as much as other people. Because I know some of my friends who really enjoy being Canadian and then speak English day to day, and to meet some Canadian friends, but I am not that ... so I can say I am a Chinese Canadian.

Yet another example of blended identities is evident in the following comment by a male interviewee who left Hong Kong for Australia at age 33 (P37): *"I think it's a mixture. We take some of the Australian culture, but not all. We still retained our values as Chinese and our customs."*

Citizenship was not always synonymous with cultural identity. Several respondents report that although now holding a Western passport, they still identified with Hong Kong or Chinese culture. The distinction is illustrated quite clearly in this statement by a female who immigrated to Australia at age 29. She succinctly described herself as (P36): *"A Chinese holding an Australian passport."*

A male who immigrated to Canada at age 40 claimed that he felt completely Chinese despite holding a Canadian passport (P34): *"I always regard as myself regard as Chinese. Even I got the Canadian passport."* And a female, who immigrated to Canada at age 19, describes herself as being a Hong Konger (P26):

> [I: By the time you were ready to leave [Canada] in 2004, how would you describe who you are culturally?] Now? [I: Or the last year before you left.] Still very Hong Kong, style. [I: So you wouldn't say you were Canadian Hong Kong or ...?] No, I won't say.

Only 2% of the interviewees labeled themselves as international, a topic that will be explored in more depth in Chapter 7. A male who immigrated to Canada at age 44 exemplified the global perspective and reported feeling like an international person, like someone who did not necessarily identify with any one culture (P24):

> More international, I would say. I will become a more international people. [I: Did you think of yourself as an international person even before you went?] Yes, yes, yes. So I admire different culture so I told you that why I went to Canada, just for fun. A long vacation. For me it's a long vacation. [I: Right, just to see what it was like.] Yeah, you see I came back and I am a teacher now, again.

Finally, approximately 16% of the interviewees perceived themselves as fully acculturated to their country of settlement. A female who immigrated to Australia at age 30 reported feeling completely assimilated into the Australian culture (P21):

> I would call myself an Australian. [I: So you feel that you were ...] An Australian citizen. [I: And adapting there?] I felt that I have melted into the society, that's why I called myself an Australian.

This male respondent, who immigrated to Canada as a teenager, commented on feeling totally Canadian (P32):

> I start to have my own thinking, I start to have my own feelings. And after a couple of years, I actually become a Canadian. I mean by Canadian means, all my friends are Caucasian. I don't have any Chinese friends. I hang out with my friends like they are from Czechoslovakia, from Canada, they were born in Canada, Alberta. We did stuff like hanging around, movie, shopping, playing video games ...

This same respondent then went on to say:

> In 1995 before I actually come back to Hong Kong, I think myself as Canadian because I don't have a comparison of Hong Kong. Because I have lost that memory. [I: Although you have continued the ways that you live in your uncle's house. Right? So that was a little tradition in that ...] Yes, the tradition is there, but in terms of like Hong Kong, in different stages of life it's difficult. In '95 if I have to compare like after coming back to Hong Kong, then I can compare the life in Hong Kong and compare to Canada, but at that point in '95, I truly think myself as Canadian, so I don't really, I ... treat the Hong Kong style as fast, quick, they have no patient.

Citizenship choices

A commonly held assumption is that most Hong Kongers immigrated to countries like Australia and Canada for the primary purpose of obtaining citizenship. However, data obtained in this study showed that only slightly more than half of the respondents (54%) mentioned that they had been granted citizenship in their country of immigration. Of these respondents, 56% indicated that they were citizens of Australia; the remaining 44% were granted citizenship in Canada.

Returning home: Why these immigrants returned to Hong Kong

Because the Hong Kong Remigration Project (HKRP) sought to understand those Hong Kong immigrants who returned home, those who remained in their new countries of abode were not interviewed. Admittedly, they remain a sizable population and their narratives are an indispensable element to a full understanding of contemporary migration. Only the Ley and Kobayashi study reviewed in Chapter 3 compared those who remained in Canada with those who made the decision to remigrate.

Economic reasons propelled the majority of all immigrants worldwide to return to their home countries, and Hong Kong remigrants reflected that trend. By the early 1990s, specific economic conditions increased the attraction of remigration for the Hong Kong immigrants — the Hong Kong economy was heating up, jobs were abundant, and salaries were escalating — and simultaneously decreased the attractiveness of the Australian and Canadian marketplaces, where economic growth was sluggish and layoffs were common.

In 2000, the Hong Kong government conducted a survey of returnees in order to develop a profile of these individuals. Most returnees were among the top income categories and reported holding positions such as managers and administrators. Fifty percent of them held university degrees.

More than half of the respondents (68%) in the HKRP cited professional and career-related reasons for their return home, particularly their salary concerns. These issues were well founded, as there were limited employment opportunities in Canada and Australia and the salaries in those countries were indeed lower than in Hong Kong. A 2003 survey of Hong Kong immigrants living in Canada found that their incomes were low: 45% were earning less than C$1,000 per month.[2]

The discrepancy in earnings is apparent in this comment by a female who immigrated to Canada at age 40. She clearly cites financial difficulties as a primary determinant in her decision to move back to Hong Kong (P8):

> One thing is difficult to make money, that's very important. Even they tried, some of my friends' husband they tried to so some business. But all lost. I heard so many so they decided to come back to Hong Kong. Now they are doing very good.

The limited employment opportunities for Hong Kong immigrants in their destination countries are illustrated by this comment from a female who immigrated to Canada at age 33 (P27): *"It's just because we can't find any work."*

Concerns about the economic downturn in Australia and the increased prevalence of layoffs there are what motivated this female, who immigrated at age 30, to return to Hong Kong (P43):

> The reason I came back was mostly for work reason. I worked in Citibank Australia, before I immigrated to Australia, I have the interview and the boss took me, and she agreed … So before I landed Australia, I know that I have a job. The second day, I already went back to Citibank. But, of course, times no good sometimes. The business was no good in Australia and then, I remember I was an assistant vice president at that time. And starting probably 1994, '5 or '6, they started to have layoff. Within that two or three years, there was three times big rounds of layoff. Luckily, I was still there until the time I left Citibank. I wasn't being laid off. But I have the concern. Because the last time of layoff it slashes off over fifty while the company has five hundred people. Originally, when I first joined, there were around eight hundred staff and then they lay off and lay off, and the last round, with only four or five hundred people, they lay off fifty AVPs. That's quite a lot actually. I have the concern whether the next round would be my name on there.

For this male, who immigrated to Australia at age 32, the apparent unavailability of opportunities for career advancement was the impetus for moving back to Hong Kong (P33):

> And the main reason why I came back to Hong Kong is also the opportunity for my career development, for my business in Hong Kong. Because I find in Australia the potential for my development in Australia is limited so that's why … The main reason I left Australia is because I am still very young, thirty to forty; it's a period I need to have something to achieve in my career development. So that's why I came back to Hong Kong because there are more opportunity for me.

The reasons for returning to Hong Kong were not exclusively economic. Forty percent of the respondents cited personal reasons as motivators of their desire to return to Hong Kong. The male respondent just mentioned considered the move back as a return to his roots: *"Also why I come to Hong Kong. I feel I like here because the root is here in Hong Kong."*

This male, who immigrated to Canada at age 51, considered the move back to Hong Kong to be a matter of survival (P31):

> No, because I am the kind of person who really want to work. So I have been there for five or six years even though I came back here in Hong Kong every year … Not every year, all the time. And every time I come back, people say, "Hey, Richard, you look bad." Finally, I said, if I do not move back to Hong Kong, I am going to die. I would really die over there. My wife said okay. The kids are not moving back to Hong Kong because they are grown up already. So when we moved back to Hong Kong, the first one got married, no, not marry … We came back together too.

For a small percentage (8%) the move back was motivated by a desire to maintain family ties or support an ill relative. An example is this comment by a female who immigrated to Canada at age 42 (P12):

> But I realize that the condition of my father is really not good. And he has prostate cancer. And the doctor said he has six months, so to go, so terminal stage. So, and then my father actually ask me to stay, he said me to stay if possible if not going back to Canada, I think he miss me very much. So, okay, after discussing with my family, I think so I stay.

A female who immigrated to Canada at age 28 returned to Hong Kong to maintain her relationship with her husband, who at the time was commuting between Hong Kong and Canada (P28):

No, no, no. This period is very good, 1997. And then we I have separate with my husband for a long time then we find a little bit problem because if you separate for a long time then the living standard for each other I change then the communication is quite difficult. And then also at this period my company phoned, "We have job vacancy in Hong Kong. Do you interested to come back to work?" Then I think, yeah, quite good because I got my passport already. Then I don't need to stay, because if you need to get the passport you need to stay more than three years, but I live more than that. Then I think that I have nothing to do in Canada or maybe this is the good opportunity I can come back to Hong Kong to living with my husband again. That's why. And also his business is not so good at this moment. You know that we have a big expense then he need to give me money each month but later on it's quite difficult, [I: You have two households to have to sustain.] Yeah, so that I come back to help him also to not let him expense too much. That's why I come back.

Only 2% of the respondents indicated a desire to return to Hong Kong for educational reasons. This is illustrated in a comment by a female who immigrated to Canada at age 33 (P27):

And pretty much disagree with the education philosophy in schools in Toronto. We wanted to raise our child's early year with better moral education, so we came back to Hong Kong … The Canadian schools are too open, and they won't teach them what is right, what is wrong, and they let them learn by themselves. And they don't allow introduce a way of thinking to them.

Many interviewees expressed a less tangible but nevertheless important psychological rationale for coming home — they missed the excitement and fast pace of life in Hong Kong. It was common for the remigrants to disdainfully remark on the slow, quiet life in their countries of immigration, although a few found the ease of such a life a welcomed respite. One man, who immigrated to the United States thirty years ago, was interviewed in New York City. Asked to describe his adjustment to New York and his future plans, he commented that *"New York is kind of boring. There is not enough action here. Hong Kong is much more exciting. Maybe I'll return to Hong Kong when I retire."*

I confess that I was dumbfounded by his remarks. He lived in the middle of noisy and throbbing New York Chinatown, the most active and vibrant neighborhood in the city!

Emotional response to leaving country of settlement

Responses to leaving the host country varied. Twenty-four percent of the respondents reported being happy to leave the host country and return to Hong Kong, another 24% reported ambivalent feelings, 16% reported being saddened by their departure from the host country, and 12% reported no particular emotional reaction.

A female who immigrated to Australia at age 29 eagerly anticipated returning to Hong Kong, where she felt that excitement and challenges awaited her (P36):

> I was quite happy to leave because I want to have a new start. And also, apart from that, after staying there for a few years, we consider ourselves too young. We just found that the life there was a bit too boring for us, not much excitement, then we still look for excitement and challenges. We heard others say the same thing about Australia. No, at this stage, I would like going back yet!

A male who immigrated to Australia at age 39 was also happy to return to Hong Kong because he felt that it would enhance his professional life (P23):

> No, I don't feel sad. I regard myself as an international professional. When I came back to Hong Kong, I have more opportunities to attend conference, meetings around the world. That was difficult in Australia. In Australia, we don't have that much funding. Not much traveling money allowing you to travel around. But in Hong Kong, we have a very good support in attending conferences and meetings and also we go up to China quite often.

Not everyone was so happy to be returning to Hong Kong, however. One female who immigrated at age 18 recalls feeling sad to be leaving the life she had built in Canada (P22):

> Oh, I felt so sad. I felt very sad. And I missed the country, and I was very disappointed. The sadness was something that was out of my expectation too because I thought before six years ago when I went there, you know, I don't like coming here. I tell myself this is not the country I like. But then, after six years, you like it; you make so many friends, you have done so many things, you do well in school, I do well in so many other things. I like my part-time job as assistant professor in school. I like it a lot. I was the student coordinator for the MBA program with UBC (University of British Columbia). I work as a DJ and

a program host with the local Chinese radio station, so I did so many things, I like it so much, I tell myself this is something I can never do in Hong Kong.

For a male respondent who immigrated at age 44, life in Canada was much more relaxed, and he expressed regret at the thought of returning to Hong Kong (P24):

I am sad, I am sad, I am sad. [I: You were?] Yeah, because the holiday is over; yeah, I have to work again. To work like a dog. [I: Were you sad to leave Canada? Or just the holiday?] Actually, I like that place and I also like the people because they are very nice. Yeah, to be honest, they are very nice. And it's a very nice place, and it is also a beautiful place, and they have the things what I want. They have all the things that I want. They have good food, good accommodations, and beautiful place.

Not all participants viewed the move back home in unambivalently positive or negative terms. For some, including a female who immigrated to Australia at age 30, the decision to return was bittersweet (P43):

I think it's mixed. Job satisfaction-wise, I think I don't really have much in Australia, because of those kinds of reasons I first described to you, the political ... I am just an executor. I was not at a very high level, middle management, not senior ones. It's just like people give me something, and I just do it. It's not something I can manage. I didn't really have much job satisfaction. So job-wise I don't feel regret. But in terms of the living environment, it was very nice. Parents-wise I know that if I come back, my mother would definitely come with me. But I think it's okay, I can still come back and see my dad.

A male who immigrated to Australia at age 33 expressed similar feelings (P37):

It's mixed. Having been lived there for two and a half years, we miss some bit of Hong Kong and that we would be sad to leave Sydney because we love the place very much. And we have made more and more friends, so that's why I said is mixed. On the one hand, we are glad that we can go back to Hong Kong to enjoy some bit of Hong Kong things that we miss, like eating, shopping ...

Emotional response to returning home

Emotional responses to coming home to Hong Kong were affected by the amount of time that the remigrant was home. The returnee's immediate emotional response was inevitably and uniformly a reaction to the Hong Kong environment. Eighty-two percent of the participants commented on the climate, population density, noise, traffic, and size of the city. In this regard, the unequivocal response was negative. Many returnees found the Hong Kong environment unappealing in comparison to the open green spaces of Australia, the outdoor leisure pursuits available in Canada, and the low humidity and low population densities of those countries.

One female respondent who immigrated to Australia at age 35 was among the 38% of interviewees who recalled being very uncomfortable with the crowds and traffic in Hong Kong (P1): *"And I am scared to go out. There are so many people! Too much traffic and too many people around make me a bit uneasy."* Discomfort with the densely populated areas in Hong Kong was also expressed by a male who immigrated to Australia at age 26 (P50):

> I hate walking into a big shopping centre … Every second in Sunday, the whole place will go crazy with people. And I remember that when I first got back I will try to avoid the crowd by just walking just on, instead of level three, the level that actually link up with the actual railway concourse. I go one floor up and walk there because I would not be bumping into anybody. People just try to cut in front of me all the time. I still do that even now on Saturday and Sunday, I try not to walk on the busiest floor because I don't think I like the crowd that much.

A female who immigrated to Canada at age 18 recalled being saddened by her memories of Canada even as she tried to reconnect with her Hong Kong friends (P22):

> But every night when I went back home after going out with friends and stuff like that, the memories of Canada and everything came in and I felt sad. I felt very sad. Actually, I felt sad for like six months.

Once the immediate impact of the environment on the returnee was experienced and processed, there were more emotional consequences. A review of the existing research on the immigrants who return home to North America, Europe, Africa, or South America reveals one omnipresent finding: the returnees experienced long-term distress when they re-entered their home communities. Suffering from what was variously labeled as dissatisfaction, psychological distress, or reverse culture shock, nearly all felt unhappy to be back in their country of origin. This can be experienced either as general discomfort to living in their home country or as specific discomfort, for example, with their returnee jobs, their extended families, their friends, or the city of return. Research by the author has found that returnees did not expect to find themselves discontented on returning home.[3] In searching for an explanation for their distress, they frequently misattributed the source of their dissatisfaction to their jobs, spouses, or city of residence rather than, more accurately, to the repatriation adjustment process.

Hong Kong returnees also had a nearly uniform response to returning home but in the opposite direction. They either were emotionally upbeat and positive about being home or were emotionally neutral. This finding was particularly surprising in light of the data indicating that most of the returnees did not originally intend to move back to Hong Kong. In this study, the Hong Kong returnees' long-term emotional reactions to remigration were assessed in three ways: analysis of interviewee comments made during the interview and scores on two psychological scales. Asked "How did you feel when you returned home?" respondents overwhelmingly made positive remarks such as those in the excerpts that follow.

One male who immigrated to Australia at age 28 recalled having no problem readjusting to life in Hong Kong. He showed no signs of emotional distress, but instead, provided the following response (P39):

> It was kind of smooth. I guess I get back to my usual lifestyle almost the same as before I leave. Quite easily. Having lived in Hong Kong for twenty-eight years is a long time that you won't have any problem to get back to the same place.

Another male respondent who immigrated at age 49 indicated an awareness of the differences between life in Canada as compared to life in Hong Kong. Yet he expressed no negative feelings about being back in his home country (P25):

> I: What else? Any things that you saw, the sights, the smells, anything physical about Hong Kong which you have forgotten about in Canada that seems different?
>
> P: Yes, the things you mentioned are very different from Canada. But to me, it means nothing. Because I live there for many many times, so I could get used to it.
>
> I: So the first few months that you were back in Hong Kong, any problem fitting into Hong Kong life again?
>
> P: No. [I: You fit right back in? You are glad to be here?] Because at that time, it's very easy to find a job.

Similar feelings of ease and comfort are expressed by this male, who immigrated to Canada at age 51 (P31):

> [I: What about other aspects of Hong Kong life? Did you find that it is easy to fit back in after you've been away for seven years, or did you find that you had changed or Hong Kong had changed and you had trouble feeling comfortable here?] No, to me it's okay. I am that kind of person. I can fit myself into any society and any place. That's my thinking, never change the society or the world. You have to fit into it, and you make others to fit into it. You don't blame on other people give you this, give you that; it's crazy. To me, you have to do it yourself to fit into the society. That's my thinking.

In fact, respondents were often puzzled by my repeated questioning about "any difficulties in coming home" or "negative perceptions about you by family or friends." Although some respondents indicated that they had changed during the immigration period and that they retained some of those new behaviors after returning to Hong Kong, this did not cause them identity discomfort or interpersonal difficulties with family and friends.

The Hong Kong returnees' lack of repatriation distress was the most unanticipated study result in light of the unanimously negative emotional responses among Western repatriates. Interview narratives that indicated positive or neutral emotional responses were supported by the answers on two psychological scales in the survey administered after the interview. One series of questions (which were combined to form a "scale" in psychological terminology) measured general happiness and is called the Satisfaction with Life Scale (SLS). Another series of questions measured specific unhappiness related to coming back home and is called the Repatriation Distress Scale (RDS). (See Appendices A and C for details of the statistical analyses of all quantitative scales.) Looking at the SLS, the remigrants produced a high happiness score (average score was 5.1, with 7.0 being the highest happiness score possible). The second measurement of remigration emotional reaction, the RDS, indicated that the remigrants had a below average distress score to returning home (average score was 2.95, with 7.0 indicating the most distress; see Figure 4.2). Clearly, the Hong Kong returnees were not distressed but were feeling happy with their lives and satisfied with their return experience.

Happy emotions were revealed in the rekindling of relationships with family members and old friends. One male who immigrated to Canada at age 31 remarked (P42):

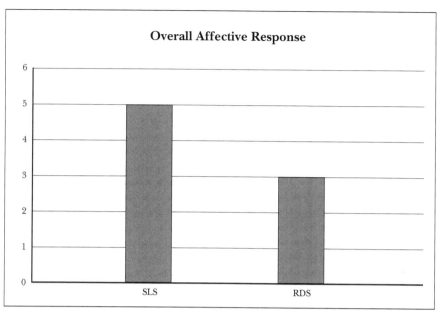

Figure 4.2 Overall average scores on the Satisfaction with Life Scale and the Repatriation Distress Scale

> Returning, it was good. Because first most of my brothers, sister already move to Canada, so my parent very lonely. So when they came, then I return so I fill the gap. It's good for my mother, now, my father die '94, my mother was alone. So I am with her for ten years. So I am very happy now because I am in Hong Kong.

The response from this male, who immigrated to Canada at age 17, was equally positive (P17):

> [I: The first few months that you were back in Hong Kong, how did you feel? What was the emotional reaction to being here?] It's great. I think I enjoy this as much as for Hong Kong has changed so much and yet you know you know something like before. It's like sort of a reunion. High school reunion always got like: I know this person very younger and so I want to know. And to myself it's like that kind of feeling. [I: Meet an old friend.] Yes, I know it, and yet I don't know it 'cause it has changed so much; so it's like every day it's an adventure.

We should note, however, that the long-term responses were not unanimously positive. While returnees felt comfortable living and working again in Hong Kong, 38% of them recalled missing aspects of the settlement country. For example, this female, who immigrated to Canada at age 42, remarked (P12):

> I still miss some part in Canada. I miss my house. I miss kind of, I mean free, freedom, I mean. [I: Not politically?] No, no, you just want to dress very casually whatever you walk into the street in Canada, nobody notice, nobody care about you. And then I miss also the supermarket, the grocery, the shopping there. [I: How was it different?] 'Cause you got a lot of choices, and the supermarket is big, and you walk very freely and then choose. It's kind of very relaxing shopping. Nobody goes after you, and then you are very free, free to shop, and there are so many choices. And that's what I really enjoy.

The literary and social pursuits were the things most missed by a female respondent who immigrated to Canada at age 36 (P5): *"But, we also got spoiled by the availability of great book stores, roadside café … all that kind of stuff. We like that kind of stuff."* However, what was most missed by another female, who immigrated to Australia at age 33, was the ability to relax (P48):

> I miss my relax. You cannot move too fast in Australia because everybody is moving in that pace. [I: So did you miss the slow pace?] Oh, yeah, I enjoy, actually, I enjoy chatting with people, and but, I think it's a value. I think chatting is good, but at the same time it's wasting your time in doing something that is more meaningful.

Other comparisons between home and immigrant country

More than half of the respondents (70%) commented on the cultural differences between Hong Kong and the host country. Another 8% made some sort of comparison between other elements of the home and host countries.

A male who immigrated to Australia at age 32 found the crowds and pressures of Hong Kong life to be unbearable (P33):

> And when you walk on the street you find it very crowded, and in Australia you work quite relaxed. But once you are in Hong Kong you get a job, you find that you are under stress and pressure again.

Differences in childrearing practices were what stood out for this male, who returned to Hong Kong after four years in Canada with his wife and two young children (P42):

> The Chinese parent have kind of expectancy, expect the children behave somewhat more controlled, like more time with them and I love them and I expect that they love me, and even when older, they will visit me

> more frequent ... I think this is more Chinese style. I talk to some *gwai lo*. They don't see their mother, every two years. But for me, every week I go back and see my mother and I expect the children to do the same to me.

And finally, a male who immigrated to Australia at age 26 commented on the cultural differences he observed in how individuals relate to figures of authority (P50):

> I don't know, I don't know. Maybe it's the way I see things, the way that I talk ... Over there you would see that maybe why I was told that I wasn't very humble. Maybe because it is an normal thing that, when you are dealing with European, you are sort of on equal footing, when you deal with them just. But in a Chinese society, especially when you dealing with more traditional Chinese who are maybe slightly older than me, they always think that you have to pay respect to the more senior citizen and people with more senior standing in organization. So it's quite a Chinese way. So maybe I was just, when I first got back from Australia, I have been too used to the way that they deal with one another, so I forget this is a Chinese society.

Hong Kongers' response to the remigrants

Returnees revealed that their behavior, thinking, customs, and identity were transformed during their immigrant residence. How did their family, friends, neighbors, and coworkers react to these changes? Their responses to the remigrants were slightly more positive than negative. Ten percent of the respondents reported feeling accepted. Another 10% reported that while the Hong Kong residents did not express positive or negative feelings toward them, they did seem to have some awareness of the remigrant sojourn experience. An even smaller proportion (6%) indicated that they felt misunderstood by the Hong Kong locals.

One male, who immigrated to Canada at age 13, credited his acceptance by the locals to his ability to speak the local language (P15): "[I: *How do you think other people here in HK view you?*] *My friends accept me as I am. Still have a perfect Cantonese accent and good English too.*" Another male, who immigrated to Australia at age 30, also reported feeling accepted by family and friends (P7):

> My mother said, "Oh, you are very good. Even if you went to Australia for five years, you still can support yourself." I can feel that she appreciate my stay in Australia ... But I can feel that some of my best friends do

think that I made a right choice to leave, to go to Australia. The case is that I have the same background with them. Some of my friends think that they didn't have that encouragement to go to another country. So I do think that they do respect my decision.

For a male respondent who immigrated to Australia at age 13, the local response was neither negative nor positive, but simply an observation of the changes in his behavior (P45):

[I: When you made new friends in university, did you look for friends who were returnees like you?] No, not really. I think it took me not too long to settle back, but a lot of my college friends would told me, "Because you done your high school ..." They would comment on my personality. [I: What did they say?] I think they said ... "*gwai lo.*" They would say that I have the personality of "*gwai chai.*" [I: What do they mean by that?] More direct I think. To do things differently. Or sometimes I did something outside the norm, they would say, "This is a character of a *gwai chai.*" [I: Did they say it good naturedly?] Probably neutral, not positive nor negative. [I: So they just commented on something different?] Yes.

A similar experience was reported by a male who immigrated to Australia at age 33 (P37):

[I: Did they say to you, "You act differently now"?] Yes, they did. [I: In what ways, what did they notice about you?] "You act differently. You act like an Australian or a Western people." They do recognize that. [I: Was there anything specific that they noticed?] Values. Just the value. Materialization. We are not as materialized as they are. [I: So that was the main thing they noticed?]

For some of the remigrants, however, the response was not so positive. One female who immigrated to Australia at age 38 reported feeling misunderstood by her friends (P10):

Because I ship the secondhand furniture back, whereas in Hong Kong nobody would do it like that. I shipped the washing machine and the refrigerator back from Australia. And then my friends always laugh at me why doing that, in Hong Kong buy new one. But I said that I have some emotional link to them, that I like. Because in Australia, it is very natural we have garage sale; it's not shameful to use secondhand thing. But in Hong Kong, once you mention it's secondhand and they will think that there must be something wrong with you. [I: So nobody wants to buy secondhand things?] I think it's slightly better now because of the financial issue. In the past they just dump; you know, they changed the furniture out every now and then and then they just dump it. But for me, I have the dining table and four chairs from garage sale, ship back, so they think that I am a bit abnormal for that.

This male, who immigrated to Australia at age 30, reported a feeling that is common to many remigrants (P7):

I seldom talk about my experience in Australia, in particular for my own feelings. Except my wife, of course. [I: Why don't you talk to them about it?] I am not sure if you understand or not. The case is when I talk to them in a positive way, people would say that, "Oh, can you not tell the truth." [I: You mean when you talk about the positive aspects of living in Australia?] Yes, I enjoy myself; I got a *degree*, I ... [I: They ask you not to tell them the truth?] Yes! They would say, "Ken, would you not ... you are just trying to justify your decision." [I: They think that you are exaggerating?] Yeah. And if I tell them I was difficult and I experienced a lot of frustrating matters in Australia, then they would probably think about that is your own decision. So it is quite difficult for people, when came back from another country, as an immigrant, to tell other people what actually he or she feels. My understanding is like that.

Remigration identity profiles

This chapter provided a portal into the thoughts of the remigrants as they reminisced about their arrival in Australia or Canada, premigration identity, emotional responses to the cultural adjustment process, observations of Australian and Canadian values and customs, decision-making process for returning home, reaction to departing their settlement country, and responses to their role as remigrant. At the time of these interviews, the returnees had been resettled in Hong Kong between one and six years.

Chapters 5 through 7 comprehensively review the identity profiles of the remigrants that are revealed in their interview narratives and questionnaire responses. Categorized by the Cultural Identity Model's four possible profiles, the chapters review behavioral, cognitive, and emotional consequences of the additive, subtractive, global, and affirmative remigration identities. Details of the classification process applied to the study respondents are found in Appendix B. Chapters 8 and 9 present the data from a different perspective. Interviews are analyzed into two important themes in the lives of the remigrants: consequences for family life and consequences for professional life, across all identity profiles. Chapter 10 investigates the historical and philosophic underpinnings of the Hong Konger identity, with a focus on Confucian teachings. Finally, Chapter 11 looks to a future for Hong Kongers that envisions continued transitions both into Western culture and deeper into Chinese culture. Employment opportunities in China will again lure Hong Kongers in search of economic gains but might result in increased psychological complexities.

5 Additive identity

A good cook blends the flavors and creates something harmonious
and delicious. No flavor is completely submerged, and the savory taste
is due to the blended but distinctive contributions of each flavor.

Zuozhan (a Confucian text)
Confucius or Kong Fuzi (Master Kong)

Albert Cheng, a prodemocracy radio personality, declared his candidacy
for the Hong Kong legislature in 2004. While stories of his open criticism
of the Hong Kong government and Beijing's meddling appeared almost
daily in the *South China Morning Post*, Cheng's exploits were also covered by
the Canadian newspapers primarily because Cheng was a Canadian citizen
and Hong Kong remigrant. As reported in Toronto's *Globe and Mail*,[1]
Cheng stated that he was fighting for the liberal values he had learned in
Canada: "I have to stand up against violence and against any evil force that
wants to shut me up ... This is a Canadian value. It's something I learned
in Canada."[2]

The major finding of the Hong Kong Remigration Project (HKRP)
is that additive identity is the most common cultural identity profile for
Hong Kong remigrants. Thirty-one out of the 50 interviewees exhibited
an additive identity, and another 7 combined additive identity with
another profile (2 with subtractive and 5 with affirmative). Their high
cultural flexibility allowed for their high adaptation when living in
Canada or Australia and an appreciation of the values and beliefs of those

cultures. Simultaneously, they could preserve their Hong Kong culture in part because of the existence of the Chinese diaspora, which figured prominently in the adaptation process. Nearly all of the remigrants in this study had settled in cities with large Hong Kong populations — Vancouver and Toronto in Canada, and Melbourne and Sydney in Australia. In addition to the apparent benefits of the diaspora social network, Hong Kong–style food, newspapers, video stores, and television encouraged immigrants to feel comfortable on arrival. Starting from a position of psychological security, the immigrants ventured into their new communities, buying houses, launching businesses, and establishing relations with their Canadian and Australian neighbors and coworkers. A male repatriate in the study who had moved to Australia alone, married another Hong Kong immigrant, and returned to Hong Kong after five years recalled the adjustment process as being very easy (P7):

> I: How would you describe your adjustment to Australia?
> P: For me, I don't think that I spent a lot of time to suit [to get used to] the Australian living environment. Simply because I am a quiet person ... For me, Australia provided me with a quiet environment. And the people, as I said, are quite nice. So that's why I didn't feel that I spent a lot of time to settle down.

Although the study respondents had in fact returned to Hong Kong to live, it was seldom due to an inability to adapt to life in their new countries of abode. In fact, the remigrants enjoyed life in the West to such a great extent that many anticipated moving back to their new passport country at a later time, perhaps during retirement. This same male repatriate commented:

> I myself want to go back to Australia. As I said, I like the environment and living there. I do think that in Hong Kong, when people become old, it is not secure ... In Australia they have a high tax system; then they can secure the social security of the people.

In this research project, no direct measure of cultural identity was devised. That is, there was no single scale that categorized the research participants into either additive, subtractive, global, or affirmative identities. Rather, their cultural identity was inferred from multiple domains and multiple indices, including their thinking styles and decisions, and their activities and behaviors. Appendix B describes the types of thinking patterns, attitudes, and behavior that were hypothesized to be represented by each of the four identities. The participants' decision-making processes and decisions were revealed in their responses to questions and free conversation during the interviews. Cultural identity preferences displayed in narratives were confirmed by psychological scales that measured how respondents saw their relationships with family and friends (called "self-construal" — how they constructed or formed their self-concepts regarding others), Chinese identity, and Western identity (see Appendix A for discussion of each of the scales).

There are many examples of how, upon their return to Hong Kong, the "additive" remigrants demonstrated their layering of Australian/Canadian identities onto their Chinese identities. These include the choices they made regarding the school in which to enroll their children, the neighborhood in which to live, and the manner in which they would refer to themselves in English (self-naming conventions).

Self-concept and self-naming

One of the most basic elements of self-identity is self-referencing: what you call yourself. Nicknames, endearments, shortened names, and name changes all reflect, in a very immediate manner, how people perceive themselves. These self-perceptions are, of course, sometimes parallel to how others perceive the individual and sometimes at odds with others' perceptions. A recent novel about Indian immigration to the United States, *The Namesake* by Jhumpa Lahiri, focuses on migration's role in and impact on the immigrant's choice of names and on the names' cultural and social connotations.

In the HKRP, an unobtrusive measure of identity was developed through a coding system that categorized the self-naming convention selected by the remigrant — that is, how the remigrants referred to themselves. Chinese speakers who interact with the West have many alternative ways to present themselves within multicultural societies. Distinctions in their approach to Anglicizing Chinese names also exist among Chinese-speaking countries. For example, in Hong Kong, given names are usually hyphenated and only the first is capitalized; in Mainland China, given names are combined and there is no hyphen or space; in Singapore, given names are treated as two separate names, both of which are capitalized, without a hyphen but with a space. Taiwan's handling of given names is most similar to the Hong Kong style.

Among the many configurations of names used by Hong Kongers are those that combine elements of name placement and national style (Chinese or Western). Four options predominate: (1) Chinese surname, followed by a Chinese given name that is either hyphenated or separated by a space (e.g., Poon Yat-yee or Poon Yat Yee); (2) English given name followed by Chinese surname and a Chinese given name (e.g., Joanne Poon Yat-yee; there is also a variant in which the Chinese surname is followed by a Chinese given name followed by an English given name, e.g., Poon Yat-yee Joanne); (3) English given name, followed by a Chinese given name (or initials), followed by a Chinese surname (e.g., Joanne Y. Y. Poon); or (4) English given name followed by a Chinese surname, an option that eliminates the Chinese given name completely (e.g., Joanne Poon).

These four options became the criteria for coding the naming preferences of each participant. Following the completion of the questionnaire, interviewees were asked to write their name in English "the way they most often wrote it." This data then became one additional source of information revealing the respondent's cultural identity. For example, option 1, the most traditional of the styles, was interpreted as representing a Chinese, or an "affirmative identity." Utilizing the traditional naming convention following an immigrant experience was seen as a clear embrace of Chinese identity. Each succeeding option was interpreted as being less Chinese and more Western. Option 4 was interpreted as demonstrating the most international or global identity.

A cognitive and behavioral manifestation of the additive identity was the predominant use of the third naming option. Here, the participant combined his or her Chinese and Western identities by positioning the English name first and moving the family name to the last position, a Western pattern. This option also preserved some of the Chinese identity, albeit in a less dominant place. Additives also used the second and fourth options, the latter clearly the most Western alternative.

Following an extensive coding process of multiple domains from the transcripts of every interviewee (see Appendix B), each participant was assigned an identity profile. These were then cross-matched with either Chinese (option 1) or Western (option 4) naming style preferences. As Figure 5.1 illustrates, those remigrants embodying "additive" or "global" cultural identities were more likely to use Western naming conventions, confirming their newly layered identity. "Affirmative" identifiers, those who adapted little while immigrants and clung to their Hong Kong identity, strongly preferred Chinese naming options. The one unexpected finding was that

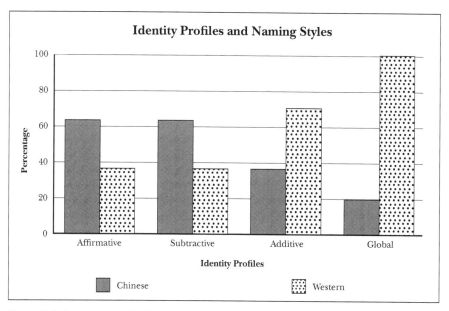

Figure 5.1 Comparison of Chinese and Western naming styles by identity profiles

the "subtractive" identifiers, those who expressed feeling less Chinese/Hong Kong on their return home, also preferred Chinese naming options.

It is not unusual for immigrants to any English-speaking country to anglicize their names upon migration. What is atypical is the use of English names in one's home country. Distinct from the citizens of Taiwan, Singapore, and China, who exclusively use their Chinese names in their home countries, Hong Kongers, who may or may not have emigrated, also combine English and Chinese naming practices, underscoring the multi-identity attributes of local residents. In the past, only those who were employed in an international workplace used an English name. But today, Hong Kong parents are selecting English names for their kindergarten-aged children. An interesting trend has emerged in Hong Kong among the teenage and college populations to choose English words as names (e.g., Apple, Ice, or Rainbow), using option 2 or 4 for name order. A recent survey of college students by the Lingnan University sociologist Annie Chan Hau-nung revealed that 93% had English names, with students often testing out several names sequentially until they found the one that most felt comfortable and best embodied their personalities.[3] The use of unconventional names sometimes reflected an attempt to find an English word that sounded similar to the Chinese name.

The use of English names reflects attempts by many Hong Kongers to appear modern, trendy, and global. Ironically, the origins lay in the practice of Catholic missionaries during the Ming Dynasty (1368–1644) who furnished converts with English names. The custom continued during British colonial rule, and for the Hong Kong workforce, it was perceived as a necessary adaptation to the increasingly global context of Hong Kong's industries.

Schooling

Hong Kongers are fortunate to have many educational possibilities for their children: public education (with instruction in Cantonese), private religious education (e.g., Catholic, Protestant, or Jewish), private nonnational schools, and private country-specific schools. This last option was developed and is utilized to provide a little bit of the home country environment to expatriates living in Hong Kong (i.e., the Korean school). No doubt this alternative traces its roots to the colonial English population who were interested in replicating the British educational environment for their children. Although founded and administered independently, many of Hong Kong's English-curriculum-based schools merged in 1967 to form the English Schools Foundation (ESF), which operates a system of elementary and secondary schools throughout the territory. The curriculum prepares students to take the English examination in advance of sitting for university entrance exams. Other nationalities have followed suit, with the creation of a Japanese school, a German-Swiss school, the Hong Kong International School (which follows a US-style curriculum), an Australian school, and a Canadian school. The language of instruction is primarily the lingua franca of the home country (e.g., Japanese, German, English) with Mandarin taught as a foreign language. One additional alternative is the private international school known as the Chinese International School, in which the curriculum is taught in both English and Mandarin.[4]

Many of the "additive" remigrants chose to send their children to Australian, Canadian, or international schools in Hong Kong as a way of preserving the children's newly acquired English language fluency and Western cultural competence. Some acknowledged that they preferred the Western values that were imbedded in the education system, including more interactive learning, less emphasis on memorization and grades, and the addition of subjects beyond the basics of mathematics, science, and history. Their clear intention was to provide their children with bilingual and bicultural expertise in preparation for a binational life. For some, the choice of a school in which the instruction was in English was a necessary one. Many immigrant children were young when they left Hong Kong or were born in their settler country. Thus, even though Cantonese was spoken at their homes in Sydney or Toronto, their Chinese-language skills (especially writing and reading Chinese characters) were inadequate for joining their age-mates in a Hong Kong public school.

One female participant who immigrated to Australia with her husband and returned to Hong Kong with their school-aged child had this to say (P1):

I: Where did you decide to have your daughter go to school?

P: She's studying at the English Schools Foundation School, and it's not a traditional way.

I: Why did you make that decision?

P: Because I don't like the Chinese kids being pushed too hard … They [ESF] have a very good way of teaching. They [students] come to explore by themselves and she read many different kinds of books to get the knowledge there by herself … The point is, I think that I was coming back [to Hong Kong] temporarily so anyway she would go back to Australia to continue her education. So I think that is psychologically to get her prepared for that kind of background or the English-speaking way of schooling. It is better for her.

A male who returned from Australia after two and a half years also made the decision to send his daughter to an ESF school (P33):

I: After you came back from Australia, that's when you had one daughter. So do you think that having lived in Australia has in any way influenced the way you are raising your daughter or any of the decisions you are making about her? … Once your daughter was born, I wonder whether having lived in Australia has influenced the way you raised your daughter.

P: Yes. That's why I put my daughter into an international school. I think of course I prefer my daughter, if possible, she can study in Hong Kong. I also have planned, maybe she need to have her education in Australia as well. So that's why I have planned my daughter's education development. I put her in an international school in Hong Kong, hope if she could get into a university in Hong Kong, okay, fine. If she cannot get into a university in Hong Kong, she also has the opportunity to study in Australia.

I: Does she go to the Australian school here?

P: No, it's not an Australian international school. It's run by the English School Foundation.

I: Did you think about the Australian school?

P: I did think about that, but the Australian International School's school fee is a bit high. So that's why for the economy, I would prefer she took the education in the EFS school.

Yet another example of this trend is provided by this male remigrant, who also spent two and a half years in Australia (P23):

P: Yes. And my kids are attending international schools. It's not because they couldn't take the local school, but we don't like putting exams and marks as a priority. Most local schools work very hard.

I: So you didn't want just an exam as the reflection of education.

P: Exactly.

I: What school do they go to?

P: My elder one studied in a local school for his primary and sec education. So after taking the Hong Kong Certificate Examinations, he's now studying in an English Foundation school. And my younger one, he attend a local primary school. And now he is studying in the Australian International School.

I: And what is it about the education styles of those schools that you like? Why was it appealing to you?

P: That kind of schools, actually, they learn lots of general knowledge. And different kind of thinking.

I: Can you describe that, different kind of thinking?

P: I think that is reflected from my children doing class projects. They read a lot of materials; they search facts and figures from different source. After that, presenting the report is also very fun.

Another male remigrant who returned from Canada viewed his daughter's enrollment in an international school as a means of easing the transition into life in Hong Kong (P38):

I: You mention that he [the son] goes to the Canadian international school. So he came back in '97. What was your thinking about where to send the children to school?

P: To minimize the impact to them as much as possible. That's why I would try to put them in Canadian school. Actually, is my son, because my daughter wasn't reach the school age yet. When she came back, she was three; when we came back she also three, wasn't at school then, so she's not a big problem. But nevertheless I still put her in international school. But for the son, because he was at grade five or grade six the time when we came back, he's a bit worry of the Chinese. He cannot read any Chinese at all. So to me, if I have to put him in a local school, it's almost impossible task. So basically I have no choice but to put him in a Canadian school. And also as I said, my original intention is that I only come back two years to stay for a few years, five, six years, that was my think at that time. So he needs to go back anyway. So I would try to minimize any destruction to his school. So that's the reason I put him in international school.

I: So where did you ultimately send your daughter?

P: First two years, I send her to a local kindergarten, which is one of the prestigious, but less demanding. So she was there two years, and then I send her to the ESF. The English School Foundation.

Housing

Of remigrants who had the choice of where to live upon their return to Hong Kong, many selected venues that echoed their former Western residences: they chose the Mid-Levels if they had the financial resources to maintain an international style of living. Another choice was the New Territories so that they could purchase larger homes with backyards and take advantage of parks and beaches that reminded them of their immigration homes. The selection of a neighborhood in which to live became another domain in which a remigrant's additive identity profile was manifest.

The same interviewee who mentioned earlier her preference for ESF schools over the local ones explained her decision regarding a choice of neighborhood in the following way (P1):

I: What about your decision of where to live when you got back to Hong Kong? Where did you go?

P: Well, I didn't decide whether ... because it is hard to pinpoint somewhere to live. The point is, we want to find a place not too crowded. Because we are used to the Australian way, not too crowded, so we want to get somewhere not too crowded. So we picked Ma On Shan, because that place is a newly developed suburb, not so crowded, not too many buildings, something like that. And there is a nice beach over there, and a park over there and it seems like I am in Australia.

Another female respondent who returned from Canada after more than eight years found comfort in the presence of her international neighbors (P47):

I: Where did you decide to live when you came back?

P: We just choose Hong Kong Island. Before we moved to Canada, we also lived in the Hong Kong Island. It's very strange, maybe our prejudice also. We found people on Hong Kong Island is more gentle, even though for the public transport.

I: And what area in the Hong Kong Island?

P: In the Mid-Levels. We just rent a flat.

I: The neighbors in your building. Are they mostly local Hong Kongers or international or ...?

P: It's quite international. The whole building is just rented out and the whole building has quite a lot expatriates.

I: Does that make you feel comfortable to have Westerners around?

P: Yes, we found that it's quite easy for us to adapt to that. Before we moved in, we don't know there are so much expatriates, or I think there is quite a lot of families like us. I know a Taiwan family, one other family who has kids in the same school with my daughter.

For this male, who returned from Canada after five years, the decision to move to the Mid-Levels was motivated primarily by the need for more living space and a desire to own property (P34):

I: Okay, well, let's talk about that now. So when you left Canada, you weren't feeling much. And then you came back. You said that you still had an apartment here, right? You moved back to here?

P: This is my dormitory. My company property. Just wait for me, just never rent out, just like I own this property. So company pay the maintenance fee and that just leave it empty.

I: And then you decided to move to Mid-Levels?

P: Because we have a lots of furniture, a lot of stuff, this area not good enough for us. And that's why we have to look for a bigger place.

I: Did you also want to live in an area that was more international?

P: In Hong Kong.

I: Or it is international here too?

P: Yeah, yeah, that's why this is international here. I don't think international, I don't think this way, I think this is Hong Kong style. This is the place I live here, I born here, I got my childhood here, and my, most of my friends here.

I: Your move to the Mid-Levels is just because you needed a bigger flat.

P: And then this is our own property, a little different from dormitory.

The lure of a rural environment was the primary determinant for this male remigrant, who returned to Hong Kong after spending more than eight years in Australia (P50):

I: Okay, when you came back here, did you decide to move to the Shatin area right away?

P: No, it was after I actually start working here. I didn't move to Shatin a few months after I start to work here the first time. I found that traveling is longer way and also it took me time to find out exactly what rental premise are available and whether I can afford that, rent it.

I: Was part of the reason that you wanted to live here because it would give you more space as you had in Perth?

P: Yes, in a way. I mean, I like to live more in the sort of rural setting instead of in the city. So here it's close to us and also in a village house; it's not like living in a flat.

I: So you actually have a house?

P: Not really. It's a three-story townhouse. We only rent one of the floor. But still is not like you have to take the lift to down.

I: Not going up to the forty-seventh floor.

P: Exactly. And we got a balcony, and we can look out.

Yet another example is provided by this female who returned from Canada after more than ten years (P26):

I: When did you and you family move back here? Did you already have a flat? Did you keep your flat?

P: Oh, we I think last year, when my mom and dad come back, they bought a new flat.

I: Is it in a neighborhood all Hong Kongers, or is it sort of an international neighborhood?

P: I think of like it's kind of quite international. It's a new building in Kowloon. And it's more, I see a lot of multicultural people living in our building.

Some remigrants had no choice as to residential venue; they returned to their former flats in Chinese neighborhoods where relatives had maintained the apartments during their absence. These repatriates often mentioned finding the small rooms and close proximity to family members uncomfortable. They expressed their wish to live elsewhere in Hong Kong, but the high cost of real estate thwarted their intentions.

This female, who returned from Australia after four years, is an example of the remigrants who went back to their former homes in Hong Kong (P2):

> I: Where did you decide to live in Hong Kong when you come back? How would you describe your neighborhood?
>
> P: Because we have a flat in Hong Kong, when we go to Australia, we rent it out. And then when we come back we ask the tenants to move out. And we move back to the flat. So the neighborhood is quite good, actually. I have a lot of good friends around that neighborhood.
>
> I: So you didn't move to a new place when you got back?
>
> P: No, no.

Another remigrant commented on her growing dissatisfaction with her Hong Kong neighborhood; she had migrated to Canada with her entire family and returned to Hong Kong after five years (P8):

> I: The neighborhood you live in now, is the same when you left for Vancouver?
>
> P: The same, right, normal … yeah.
>
> I: Would you describe the neighborhood here as international one, or mostly Chinese?
>
> P: Mostly Chinese, mostly Chinese. It's really, actually, we, I don't enjoy [the neighborhood] that much now.

A female who returned from Australia with her husband after seven years spoke of her desire to move to the New Territories. However, her desire was thwarted by rising housing prices in the region as well as by the distance from her parents (P10):

> I: Did you think, initially, about trying to find a flat that was more sort of Australian, that maybe was bigger, had a garden, or anything like that before the scheme came out?
>
> P: My husband had thought about selling this place and then have some money and live in the New Territories, have a garden, and then later on there some change in the price and things like that and is so far away and the transport in Hong Kong is a bit difficult because my mom live in the Hong Kong side, so eventually we settle. Only two of us, we don't have children, so it doesn't really matter. And is, well, we are comfortable with two of us to live in that flat.

A male remigrant who immigrated to Canada and returned after more than six years commented on his discomfort sharing the cramped living quarters of his parents' house in Hong Kong (P11):

P: When I went back my house in Hong Kong, I feel very small and uncomfortable, actually. Because I used to have an apartment in Vancouver, and my parents had went back so the apartment is actually for me.

I: You had this whole apartment?

P: But after I went back, I only have one small room, and I can't really unpack my stuffs ... very uncomfortable. And very hot, the weather, and the humidity. And I don't have a car in Hong Kong. Just inconvenient. But it's not going to that far ... It's not really I hate it. Because anyway I born here so the neighborhood, the living neighborhood, I already familiar with.

I: So you moved back to your parents' home?

P: Yes.

I: And it's a neighborhood you knew?

P: Yes.

I: Is it primarily a neighborhood that is all Hong Kongers?

P: Hong Kongers.

Interpersonal relations

Among some remigrants, a behavioral addition to their usual Chinese interpersonal behavior was a willingness to express their individual and often divergent opinions with coworkers or friends. These remigrants were aware of the slight interpersonal ripples that they would cause by forgoing the consensus behaviors that fostered harmonious relations and choosing not to muffle their disagreements with colleagues. Interviewees often remarked that because they appreciated the forthrightness that people displayed in their former Western home cities, they adopted these behaviors and have continued them after arriving in Hong Kong. Many of the examples offered by the interviewees relate to work behavior and are discussed in detail in Chapter 9.

The following are excerpts from respondents who recalled being more direct in their relations with people outside of work. This female respondent left Hong Kong at age 46 to join her husband and son in Calgary, Canada. She returned after three years and had the following to say (P9):

There are small ways. I am more open-minded. I talk about health issues, what I think. In the past, if I didn't agree with a friend, I didn't say anything others might not like it. Now, if I don't agree, I give my point of view.

Another female respondent left Hong Kong for Australia at age 30. She returned after about two and a half years with her husband and young daughter and recalled being more direct than the average Hong Konger (P21):

> Actually Jennifer's schoolmates tell her the famous word "You are very open. You do not ..." because they feel that the local people tends to be agitated very easily, regardless of the gesture, regardless of a word, they take it to heart. We are open, we are forgiving, we don't mind ... mainly they feel that we are open. We like it, we don't like it. [I: So you are direct, right? Sometimes people tell me that Hong Kong people, if others disagree with them, they won't speak out their mind. But you are more likely to do that?] But obviously, we do it tactfully.

Another female respondent, in addition to being more direct in her communication style, also felt a need for private time away from the group. She first immigrated to Australia in 1978 and returned to Hong Kong after about four years. In 1987 she returned to Australia and stayed for another five years before coming back home. She comments on her friends' perception of her as being more independent (P36):

> I do like going out at times, but I do like either way, to be alone, to have some privacy as well. So that's why they have the perception that I can have my own way. I am quite strong in their eyes.

Food choices are both an attitudinal and a behavioral reflection of identity. "Additives" often enjoyed both Western and Chinese cuisine, some with a slight preference for the Western and others with a preference toward the Chinese style.

A female remigrant who returned from Canada after three years (P12) observed:

> I will eat more European food. When I go to the grocery store, I will look for those things. Especially it's from Canada, you know, because when you talk of Canada, and then you said, "Oh, well, I have been there," and then you really, I am holding a Canadian passport. I think, then I know some part of the Canada. Oh, this is where I have been before, or something like that. Then memory is kind of you like there, you like the memory, so in your mind.

One final domain in which cultural identity might be reflected is in the respondents' future intentions about which country to live in. Additive remigrants overwhelmingly indicated their intention to return to their new country of citizenship to live, either permanently or for significant portions of the year. Many planned to return either when their children were entering university or when the respondents were ready to retire. This interviewee was only 19 when he immigrated to Australia; he returned to Hong Kong after five years (P6):

I: Do you have any intention to return to Australia sometime in the future?

P: Yep. At my age of retirement.

I: You will retire there? Okay. Why is that?

P: Good living conditions, good living environment. That's the only reason. And to the extent I should say I will move back to Australia like one or two months and move back to Hong Kong and move back again, that sort of …

I: That's what you will do?

P: Yeah, that I guess I will do at my time of retirement.

As we have seen, Hong Kong remigrants experienced both emotional and behavioral consequences when they returned home. They also experienced cognitive or attitudinal changes. The three most common attitude changes pertained to the values of materialism, the environment, and political involvement. Additive remigrants often decried the focus on wealth accumulation and display that they saw as a preoccupation of Hong Kong society. After years of living in Canada or Australia, they adopted more socially conscious attitudes that they translated into such activities as recycling, buying used furniture, and dressing casually. This antimaterialism attitude was reflected in a newfound concern about the Hong Kong environment, including the preservation of parkland and Victoria Harbor. Some returnees indicated an interest in environmental activism as well, which included signing petitions and attending rallies. This female repatriate, who had returned from Canada, expressed her enjoyment of the more casual and leisurely aspects of Canadian life (P12):

P: I still miss some part in Canada. I miss my house. I miss kind of, I mean free, freedom, I mean.

I: Not politically?

P: No, no. you just want to dress very very casually whatever you walk into the street in Canada, nobody notice, nobody care

about you. And then I miss also the supermarket, the grocery
the shopping there.

I: How was it different?

P: 'Cause you got a lot lot of choices, and the supermarket is
big, and you walk very freely and then choose. It's kind of very
relaxing shopping. Nobody goes after you, and then you are
very free, free to shop, and there are so many choices. And
that's what I really enjoy.

Another female repatriate who returned from Australia after seven years
noted how her environmental awareness had changed (P10):

> I thinking I am getting, uh, I still have the Chinese culture in myself but
> I think I have some influence [of Australia] like more environmentally
> aware of things. Now when I come back, whenever there is an empty
> bottle suddenly I will remember what day will be collect the bottle ...
> But in Hong Kong, we don't have that. Then I will think that is it the
> Australian influence on me that ...

Most notable was the respondents' positive attitude toward the
burgeoning democracy movement in Hong Kong. Consistent with the
additive identity profile, many returnees noted that they had incorporated
into their attitudinal and behavioral repertoire the Canadian/Australian
value of individual freedom, the behavior of speaking their minds, and
the habit of political activism, as Albert Cheng was quoted as saying in
the introduction to this chapter. Political activism was usually manifested
through participation in the many peaceful democracy rallies organized
in the early 2000s. With tens of thousands of migrants returning to Hong
Kong, these beliefs and behaviors could have significant consequences for
local politics and for Hong Kong's relations with Beijing. The renewed
interest in political developments is illustrated in this comment by a female
who returned from Australia after three years (P46):

I: Have you gotten interested in any of the demonstration, the
July 1st demonstration, have you participated in any?

P: Yeah, actually some of my friends also move back from Australia,
so we will celebrate the Australian Day. And the July 1st, we I
also feel I also feel I am a Hong Kong people, and I also will feel
unhappy some unreasonable policy from the government and
so concern about it.

I: I know since I've been here, that there was a demonstration on
January 1st and there is one on July 1st, and there was just one
on June 4th. Have you felt interested in participating in any of
those?

P: Yeah, yeah.
I: Did you?
P: I also like to join but got no time because I have to take care of my son.
I: Okay, but you thought about joining?
P: Yeah.

The implications of changes in the behavior and attitudes of repatriates is further illustrated in the comment by a female who returned from Canada after eight years (P47):

I: You mentioned that you are more direct now, that you say things that are on your mind. Some of the people I have talked to said that they are becoming a little bit more involved in political demonstrations, that they will go to the July 1 demonstration or the June 4th. Do you also find more interest in political life since you've lived in Canada? Do you think that has influenced you?

P: I can say I have more personal thinkings on this things. But I have not participated any activities after I came back for this year. But before we went to Canada, we went to the June 4, in the 1989, me and my husband also go on the street, before the June 4th. We supported what the students want. But this year, it seems that I am still adapting to the life in Hong Kong and a little bit more involved, not only in the politics, but I changed my style also. Before, our education is just that we are scare of saying out our idea. We are a little bit hesitate to express out ourselves before we went to Canada. But it also involve personal experience as we grow older, we have more confident and also we are not as afraid as before how people look on me. We feel free more to express more ourselves than before, combined with the reason that we've been back from Canada because Canadians are different.

A recent study of political opinions among 800 Hong Kongers corroborated our findings.[5] Collective efficacy, the citizen's belief in the capabilities of the public to achieve social and political outcomes, is, not surprisingly, highly valued among members of Hong Kong's collectivist society. However, for collective efficacy to exert an impact on political behavior high levels of internal efficacy must exist; that is, citizens must believe that individuals can understand and influence politics. Thus political opinion in contemporary Hong Kong is a combination of both individual and collective thought and action.

Quantitative data

Quantitative data derived from the questionnaires in the HKRP supported the themes revealed in the semistructured interviews. Reflective of the "additive" identity profile, remigrants rated both their behaviors and their identities as a combination of Chinese and Western styles. Study participants completed a modification of the Birman Cultural Adaptation Scale[6] that assessed participant preferences regarding three cultural domains — language competencies, behavioral activities, and identity — in regard to both the country of emigration (Canada or Australia) and Hong Kong.

Study respondents embraced both Western ($M = 2.64$) and Chinese ($M = 3.01$) identity, as was apparent from the average scores, which were similar on both the Western and Chinese subscales (see Figure 5.2). Behaviorally, the remigrants acted slightly more Chinese ($M = 3.0$) in their everyday behavior compared to Western ($M = 2.32$), as is seen by the average scores on the behavior subscales.

Two types of additive profile

A closer examination of the large number of respondents who were categorized as "additive" revealed two subtypes of additive identity. One type, referred to as a "bicultural identity," encompassed remigrants who now possessed two distinct behavioral and cognitive repertoires — Hong Kong/Chinese and Western — and had the ability to switch cultural behaviors according to the situation. Often, the remigrant behaved as a Hong Konger at home and a Westerner at work. A variant of the bicultural identity is the ability to switch behavior depending on the culture in the workplace. Here is an example of a female respondent who lived and worked in Australia. When she returned to Hong Kong, she had jobs with several different companies. Conscious of cultural differences in the workplace (Chinese vs. Western/international), she had the ability to switch her business style to fit the culture of the workplace environment (P13):

> P: At that time I had the gut feeling: I was able to do that, but now I changed a lot already. I change back to my Hong Konger's way. At that time I really did that. And I was just direct and told him my feeling, and then my colleagues thought that I am a foreigner.
>
> I: You are acting like a foreigner?

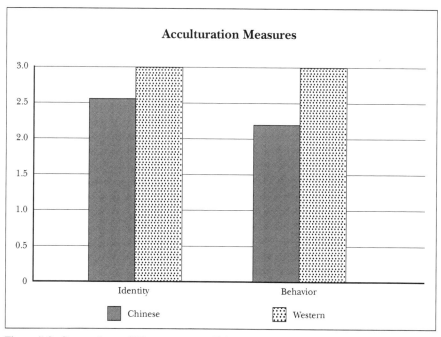

Figure 5.2 Comparison of Western versus Chinese identity and behavior scores from the Birman Acculturation Scale

P: Yes. But it also depends on which company do I work for. But in this company, this is quite Chinese. I won't do that again. I won't do that in the same way. But in that firm, because it is an international firm, I acted internationally. I found that I act according to the group. What kind of the culture is and I am sure the boss would understand me at that firm.

I: So you think that you could sort of switch back and forth now?

P: Yes. Depending on which person I am with. I would try to switch actually.

I: So you are aware enough of different styles.

P: And I know that the top boss is the foreigner. I believe that he would understand me. Not the Chinese supervisor who says she was so angry.

Another example is provided by this male, who returned from Australia after a few years (P35):

I: You mentioned that in Australia you did change your work style. How did you deal with the boss? How did you deal with the subordinates? Have you maintained that sort of Australian style in Hong Kong?

P: No. Because the working style in Hong Kong is different. I work in the Hong Kong government. In my discipline, authority is the first. We have to fit to the authority. Otherwise, if my subordinates, just like the hands, nose, mouths, if they do not follow my decision and they make their own decision, we have to bear the cost. Actually, for my subordinates, when they work at the site level, the FM meeting, they have the authority to order the contractors to do something. So that if they don't strictly follow our directions and they order the contractors in a wrong way, the contractors will claim money back from the government and in that way, the government would loss money. So they have to work strictly what we directed them to do.

I: So it's important that the subordinates follow what you do, and as you said, they are like your arms and legs?

P: Yes. So that they just give us the information and then we sit in the office to make the decisions.

A second form of additive identity can be referred to as "hybrid identity." Remigrants with a hybrid identity profile successfully merged Hong Kong and Western behaviors and thinking to form a new and unique sense of self that is more consistent and stable from one setting to another. Remigrants who possess the hybrid identity tend to be aware that their behavior does not fit Hong Kong norms but nonetheless incorporate and adapt some Western ways into their Chinese ones.

A female respondent who immigrated to Australia was interviewed twelve years after returning to Hong Kong, and she still retained strong elements of the Australian culture. She commented on her struggle to maintain her individuality in the highly collectivist Hong Kong culture and to strike a balance between her two cultures (P36):

I: So you have found that how you felt initially, which was suffocating a little bit, and you said infringement, that over the years, since then, after you have been back for more than ten years, you feel more comfortable [P: Yes.] of the Chinese culture of being with the family a lot?

P: Not a lot because I guess I can strike the balance between the two. I still maintain my individuality. I guess they come to know me. In the past, they would say, when I have a kid, my daughter, they think if I don't go back for dinner during night time and I got out with my girlfriends, they would have thought "Why?" But I guess I have my own way, and I have domestic helpers to help me as well. So I don't care much about what they say, but they don't say much nowadays. But in the beginning, they might. So I am still myself. I have my own way.

Another female, who returned to Hong Kong after three years in Canada, also commented on enjoying time alone (P9): "*I enjoy being with friends but want to be alone sometimes.*"

This sentiment was particularly revealing of her hybridity as other Hong Kong remigrants endorsed the Chinese value of avoiding social aloneness, preferring the company of family and friends as often as possible. As expressed in the interviews, the Western preference for spending less time with family and friends and being less involved with a social network matched the quantitative results of the Self-Construal Scale completed by the research participants.[7] This scale was devised to measure two interpersonal aspects of self-concept: an independent self (an "individualistic" person who prefers autonomy from other people) and an interdependent self (a "group-focused" person who prefers close relations with family, friends, and coworkers). The scale produces two scores for each respondent, an independent one and an interdependent one. In general, people from Western countries score higher on the independent subscale as compared to the interdependent subscale. For people from Asia, however, the balance is reversed. A prior study of nonmigrating Hong Kongers reported that they prefer to be interdependent and intertwined with their family and friends (reflected in a mean score of 5.67 on the interdependent subscale) rather than be separate and apart from others (reflected in a mean score of 5.0 on the independent subscale).[8]

The remigrants in the current study maintained this same balance; that is, they had a higher interdependent score (5.26) than independent score (4.90) but less of a gap between the two subscores compared to that of the nonmigrating Hong Kongers (see Figure 5.3). Presumably, as a result of immigrant experience in the West, the remigrants saw themselves as less engaged and intertwined with the group (lower interdependent score average, 5.26) compared to Hong Kongers who had not migrated (5.67). In fact, the returnees' level of involvement with the group (interdependent score) was equivalent to that of an American sample. The self-construal scores of the remigrants clearly echoed the additive identity held by the majority of the interviewees: they resembled their Hong Kong compatriots on the independent subscale and they resembled Americans on the interdependent subscale.

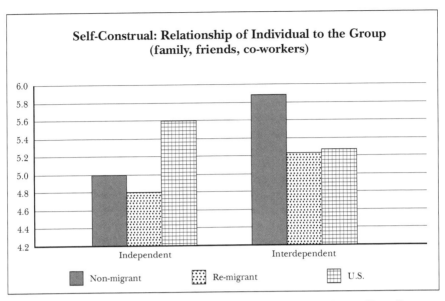

Figure 5.3 Comparison of self-construal subscale scores for nonmigrant Hong Kongers, remigrants, and Americans

In summary, for most of the remigrants, high adaptation to either Canada or Australia, combined with cultural flexibility and a complex cultural identity, resulted in one of the two types of the additive identity responses, biculturalism or hybridity.

Another major finding of the study revealed that additive identity, contrary to the prediction of the CIM, did not result in generalized repatriation distress for most returnees. As we discussed in Chapter 4, ample opportunities exist in Hong Kong for repatriates to engage in Western activities, cuisine, entertainment, and work styles when they wish. Technology and modern communication facilitate their ties to their new passport countries. One "additive" interviewee (P3), the only one indicating some distress, remarked that he regularly watched his favorite Canadian hockey team on the Internet and couldn't wait to get back to Canada. He was, however, an "astronaut," his family still resided in Toronto, and he manifested many subtractive identity elements. In contrast, the majority of the "additives" reported being comfortable with their life in Hong Kong, which now incorporated aspects of the new passport culture along with Chinese culture. For example, this respondent, who returned after spending four years in Australia, commented on actively seeking out more Western foods now that she was back in Hong Kong (P13):

> Yes, I think now, at home, I sometimes also cook Western food, although maybe in a Chinese style. But still I would like to have the lamb chops. I had a lot of lamb chops in Australia. Very nice. And now I also have it in Hong Kong. I like to go to Western restaurant instead of Chinese restaurants. I find that it is more comfortable. And Chinese restaurants are sometimes too noisy. This is a behavior change. But of course normally at home I cook Chinese food. But when there is any celebration or when I feel happy, I just prepare Western-style food.

A male who returned from Australia after five years reported that he keenly followed current events in Australia even after he returned (P6):

> After I've came back to Hong Kong I am more keen or more alert about news from Australia. Like, who's the prime minister? Why there is a great fire in Australia? And, was the, anything get change in the Chinatown? anything get change in Sydney? Trying to keep constant relations with my friends, my old connection there.

A female respondent who returned from Canada after nine years maintained her attachment to the foreign culture through her membership in various organizations (P16):

> I: I see that you joined the Canadian Chambers of Commerce?
>
> P: I join the event once in a while, yeah. So, that was another thing. What else?
>
> I: Is there a Simon Frasier Alumni Association?
>
> P: It's very small, and actually I hang out with the UBC [University of British Columbia] Alumni, because the access for alumni is … a lots of things going on around here. And actually most of my friends go to UBC anyway. So most people, and there are lots of UBC alumni here in Hong Kong, 'cause a lot of them are Chinese.
>
> I: Are most of your friends now returnees or local Hong Kongers?
>
> P: Fifty-fifty, actually more, yeah fifty-fifty about my friends.
>
> I: So you said half of your friends are returnees?
>
> P: Yeah. One thing about hang out with returnee, versus local Hong Kong people is, we talk about this among returnees. 'Cause it's funny how we like, we still like to hang out with people from here, but we find it easier to talk to people like ourselves. We got more common ground; we got more exposure. And we are more equal. We treat each other equally.

Additive identity in other Hong Kong studies

Wendy Chan found that a significant number of remigrants could be characterized as having additive identities but were paired with repatriation distress.[9] One could speculate that the reason for the negative and uncomfortable feelings expressed by these informants is that many had assumed an additive identity, that of Canadians. As Chan suggests, "I think it is clear that quite a number of my interviewees no longer identify themselves as Xianggang ren because of their experience living in Canada ... my interviewees' self-confidence or even self-righteousness, may have something to do with the high value that Canadian society places on the worth of the individual" (p. 62). Commented one of her interviewees: "Maybe I have changed too. For instance, it is without doubt that my sensitivity to things around me has sharpened because of my experience living in Canada" (p. 63). Newly acquired Canadian expectations regarding physical space, personal space, and privacy are violated regularly for the returnees as they share bedrooms, bathrooms, and common living spaces with both their returnee families and those family members who had not migrated.

Those returnees with an additive or Canadian identity found that their values and behavior were often in conflict with those of the local Hong Kongers. One remarked that her awareness of her rights as a consumer and as an individual was a direct result of her nine years living in Canada. When Hong Kong and Canadian characteristics clash, returnees face painful choices. Remarked one man, "You must compromise your character and the things you learned in Canada if you want to take advantage of the opportunities in Hong Kong. For the rules of the game are different here" (p. 75).

The returnees' emotional reactions to these conflicts can be explosive or simply an ongoing irritant: "I am always at odds with my parents in the shop. They dislike the way I do business." "My brother said the problem with me is that I don't bend ... after living in Toronto, I have learned to express my rebellion in words." "It is very hard for me to communicate with my local colleagues. When I point out their mistakes, they get offended" (p. 75).

Additive identity among remigrants to other countries

Europe. Historical references hint at the assumption of an additive identity for many nineteenth- and early twentieth-century remigrants to Europe whose changed demeanor, dress, and values disturbed the social order. Village elders, religious leaders, and the wealthy were threatened by the independence of thought and action exhibited by returnees from America. An Italian village leader, reflecting on former employees who had now returned, stated, "Then they were very humble and always came into my office with great fear, hat in hand, hardly daring to lift their eyes from the floor. When they return, they come in here and look on me as no better than themselves. They do not even take off their hats" (p. 172).[10] A wealthy woman complained that she was no longer able to find a decent servant among the returnees: "These servant girls come back with gold teeth in their mouths, and with long dresses which sweep the streets, and with unbearable manners. They do not kiss our hands when they meet us, and when they speak of their mistress in America they speak of her as if they were equals" (p. 172).[11] Local priests complained about the opposition of returnees to their edicts and rulings. Even more disturbing to the local clergy was the returnees' importation of new denominations, movements, and sects, all of which threatened the social order.

Israel. Michel Tannenbaum conducted a study of Israeli immigrants who returned to Israel. In reanalyzing her data through the lens of the Cultural Identity Model, several remigrants can be categorized as possessing additive profiles, mostly of the hybrid type.[12] One woman, who was 27 when she moved to the United Kingdom with her husband, returned to Israel with him and their three children nine years later. "When you don't live in Israel you change a lot. I went there as one person and returned a different one … England is amazing. It did wonderful things to my personality." The return home was stressful for the family. "After we came back I cried for a whole month. Not because of me. Because of my son. He cried and screamed and it just tore me apart. My husband and I also fought a lot. We didn't have a place of our own." She also exhibited some aspects of subtractive identity: "Hard to say so, but our country didn't welcome us … everything was difficult. I expected a warmer reception from my country. Really." In general, their additive identities resulted in distress and dissatisfaction for the remigrants.

Other Israeli remigrants who assumed an additive identity had a mixture of positive and negative emotional reactions. "For me, returning is a tougher immigration than the first one. The first one [emigrating to Romania] contributed much to me, and brought me to further appreciate my country and my family. I would very much want to visit again [Romania]. I would also add that when me and my friends meet, we speak Romanian and it unites us, and creates a community within a community. Overall it was very good to me there, and I feel much attached to that country." Another said, "The immigration experience has largely enriched my life, and taught me many things. I learned a lot, learned how to handle, adjust ... but returning is the most natural thing for me."

India. A study of 49 Indian graduate students and academic professionals who returned to India following sojourns in the United States that ranged from one year to 17 years was conducted by Bettina Hansel of the AFS Center for the Study of Intercultural Learning.[13] Unstructured but in-depth interviews were administered to an equal number of men and women returnees in four cities in India. This sample of interviewees had returned home for a variety of reasons, including the completion of their graduate degrees, national pride in and a wish to be of service to India, and ailing parents.

Similar to the Hong Kong participants in the HKRP, the Indian returnees exhibited primarily additive identities. One woman who received a Ph.D. from a large midwestern university in the United States and is now a university professor in India exemplifies a hybrid additive profile. She has incorporated American pedagogy into the classroom: her teaching style gives students more freedom in the classroom, and she uses open-ended questions and discussion. Her self-concept was a blend of elements of an independent self-construal and a more traditional interdependent self, separate from her instructional style.

The merging or balancing of self-construals was in evidence in the decisions she made regarding her personal life. She and her husband, another returnee, chose to live near their families but not too near so as to maintain independence, especially from her mother-in-law. She has also hired part-time (an American practice) rather than live-in, full-time domestic help (an Indian practice). Additive identities do not preclude the maintenance of some home culture behaviors; rather the nature of this identity category is to combine (bicultural or hybrid) two cultural cognitive and behavioral repertoires, home country and host country. This returnee and her husband spent all their holidays in their hometowns visiting their parents; and although she had abandoned wearing a sari while she was in the United States, she resumed wearing it in India. She also accepted, albeit grudgingly, the academic practice in India of senior professors' assuming credit for some of her (more junior) research work.

The emotional responses of the interviewees to their return to India were dichotomous. A few of the returnees found the return adjustment easy and without stress. Similar to the majority of Hong Kong returnees, these individuals took their easy adjustment for granted and "were at a loss to identify any problems they might have had" (p. 5). "It was not so difficult to return; after all, I'd lived in India for 22 years and only lived in America for two years," remarked one returnee.

The majority (35 out of 49) of the Indian returnees, however, experienced mild to severe return shock, often accompanied by depression and feelings of alienation, an emotional response in contrast to the Hong Kong sample of returnees. The Indian returnees' problems ranged from crowding to pollution to difficulty finding a job to issues with their families. Nearly 25% were already contemplating returning to the United States for work or additional studies. For example, a male engineer who had lived in the United States for nine years was frustrated in his efforts to find work in India where the equipment and infrastructure matched those available in the United States. He commented that "When you have been in a brightly lighted place, a covered place looks dark at first, but your eyes adjust after a while" (p. 7). His attempts to employ American work styles such as quick decision making were met with discomfort and employee barriers, and he was disappointed with the slow pace of change in India. His additive identity also manifested itself behaviorally in his decision to settle close to his parents' house but not in it, which was more typical for young married couples. However, he is already planning how he can return to the United States to finish his advanced degree.

A single female who returned to India with a master's degree in a liberal arts discipline found that the identity and value changes she had made while in the United States were troublesome back home. "I didn't think it would be this bad," she complained (p. 8). She experienced difficulty finding a job and chafed at the close supervision of her parents and the neighbors. She had become accustomed to living alone and somewhat anonymously in the United States, of making independent decisions and acting within her own parameters. True to additive style, though, she continued to live with her parents and did not defy the social conventions of her family and social class.

Hansel summarized the value changes experienced by her research sample, changes that exemplify the additive identity. Fifty percent cited personal changes that included being more independent, more forthright, less secretive, more confident, and more self-aware. Twenty percent cited changed patterns of work behavior and lifestyle. These included being less formal, more time conscious, more prompt in decision making, and more critical of Indian inefficiency. Many also mentioned an increased appreciation and tolerance of other groups, changed attitudes about family life, a preference for living alone, a changed pattern of male/female relationships, and a changed political outlook (some felt more conservative, but others mentioned becoming more radical or feminist).

A sizable minority of Hansel's sample experienced an affirmative identity, and this will be discussed in more detail in Chapter 7.

Japan. Another extensive study of returnees, this time Japanese, was conducted by Yasuko Kanno,[14] a Japanese native who made her home in Canada and taught at a Japanese weekend school, Hoshuko. The curriculum focused on teaching the Japanese language to the children of businessmen transferred to work in Toronto. These students were similar to each other in many ways, removed as youngsters from the warm, close-knit circle of school chums and neighborhood family they had in Japan to a cold, English-speaking environment, and compelled to attend Canadian schools during the week and Japanese school on Saturdays. Yet Kanno noticed that each student developed a unique way of interacting within Canadian society, of selecting and adopting certain Canadian values or behaviors; initially, each developed a distinctive combination of Japanese and Canadian identities. Wanting to explore these variations in more depth and over time, Kanno selected four teenaged students who represented points along the identity continuum; many of these points overlapped with the identity profiles of the CIM. She interviewed the students several times before they left Canada and four times over a two-year period in which they either were again living in Japan or were living in another country to which their fathers had been assigned. Over the entire three years, she met with the teenagers, and exchanged letters, journals, and e-mail messages with them.

The students' evolving lives and the stories they told revealed a fascinating tale. In opposition to the flexible and multilayered cultural identities held by Hong Kongers prior to immigration, Japanese adhere to a rigidly defined sense of self bounded by Japanese norms and customs. Few Japanese think of themselves as having multiple cultural identities; in fact, most readily admit to the homogeneous nature of their society and to their place within it. Exposure to the West can be disconcerting for many Japanese expatriates, cultural adjustment complicated, and returning home stressful.

Kanno found that eventually, by about a year and a half after their return to Japan as university students, all four of her interviewees had blended their Japanese and Canadian identities into an additive/hybrid identity; they felt comfortable with both English and Japanese, and had purposely selected certain values and lifestyles that reflected one or the other of their cultural histories. "Recently I have come to realize that I'm not suited to acting like one of the group so I've stopped forcing myself to pretend that I am, and try to live more individually," confessed one of the young women (p. 121). They expanded their peer memberships to encompass several different student clubs and groups and began to recognize subtle variations within Japanese society. As one young woman commented, "I eat hamburgers but I like Japanese food, too."

But their additive identities were not attained easily. They were the result of a struggle in which each returnee negotiated a path between his or her two cultures. While ultimately attaining the hybrid position, two of the students approached it from a subtractive vantage point, no longer feeling Japanese and clearly not fitting in with peers, while the other two approached their return home from an affirmative position, rejecting their Canadian "selves" and plunging into an assimilative strategy. All four students recognized that they were entering a homogenous homeland with rigid expectations, but they devised different ways to approach readjustment. The male student with an "affirmative" approach wanted to minimize any normative and social differences between himself and other Japanese. "In another two or three years in here, I think I'll become quite confident of my speech manners, my conduct in hierarchical relationships, in sum, how to play my assigned role in an organization" (p. 115). The other male student had a decidedly subtractive identity. A week after returning home, he realized that he no longer felt Japanese and regretted his decision to return to Japan; furthermore, he now derisively assessed Japanese ways of thinking and behaving. "The Japanese don't look at you in the eyes," and "In Japan, universities pretend to educate while students pretend to learn" (p. 116). He associated almost exclusively with other kikokushijo, returnee students. A female student, also exhibiting a subtractive identity, commented that while she gained information and perspective while living in Canada, "It is not as if I have the same knowledge as the people who have been in Japan all their lives. I'm not saying I'm inferior because of it, but I think it's true that there is something lacking in me" (p. 118).

Detailed descriptions of both the subtractive behaviors/identity and the affirmative will be covered in later chapters. What is unique about Kanno's Japanese study is its longitudinal nature, which allowed her to capture the transition of identities from singular to complex and from emotionally distressful to affectively calm and accepting. What is distinctive about the Japanese returnee's cultural environment compared to that in Hong Kong, however, are the unambiguous expectations of Japanese society regarding overt behavior and relationships. The multilayered Hong Kong sociocultural environment is looser in its requirements for its cultural constituents. But in Japan, whether returnee or native, all are expected to act Japanese. There is little flexibility in social behaviors — that is, at least in those shown to the outside world. Despite these cultural expectations, the four returnees Kanno studied developed additive identities, and they negotiated between their two cultural repertoires using a bicultural approach.

Kanno's qualitative study confirms what past research using psychometric scales and a quantitative approach has also revealed. Two studies examining Japanese students who were educated abroad and returned to Japan found that the students exhibited additive identities.[15] In particular, they modified their collectivist proclivities and instead were more individualistic in interpersonal situations.

Summary

Additive identities are found among returnees to other countries, frequently paired with negative emotional responses. Among Hong Kong remigrants, however, additive identities define the majority response, divided into either bicultural or hybrid categories. Interestingly, adding Australian or Canadian values, behaviors, or ways of thinking into their Hong Kong self-definitions was not stressful or unpleasant for the returnees. Few of the Hong Kong returnees found their readaptation experience to be a distressing one.

6 Subtractive identity

When I go back I know I shall be out of it; we fellows who've spent our lives out there always are.

The Gentleman in the Parlour
W. Somerset Maugham

There is a long record of both historical and fictional accounts of remigrants feeling uncomfortable on their return home. The Old Testament describes the anguish of the Jews returning to their homeland following the Babylonian exile. Cervantes, the Spanish novelist, described in 1613 the psychological and romantic difficulties of an Estramaduran, who returned to Spain after twenty years of living and prospering in South America. His psychological readjustment was complicated when he discovered his former friends were now dead.[1]

The Cultural Identity Model suggests that one common response to cultural transition is adaptation and a shift in identity away from one's home culture attitudes, beliefs, and behaviors. Labeled "subtractive" identity, this profile is adopted by individuals who experience the shift most saliently once they return to their homeland and endure great psychological distress. Emotionally, subtractive identity is characterized by depression, anxiety, and displacement. Cognitively, those with a subtractive profile perceive themselves as dissimilar from their compatriots in their essential values, beliefs, interpretation of others' behavior, and self-definition; they frequently experience isolation and bewilderment.

A Norwegian industrial and organizational psychologist, returning home after ten years abroad, found readjustment painful.[2] He suggested that re-entry becomes very difficult if the sojourner had become integrated fully in the host society. Various factors may account for this consequence: (1) the stress of severing the strong social bonds created overseas; (2) the changes one has undergone in opinions, perceptions, and development that result in returnees' feeling alienated when they go back to their own culture; (3) the loss of special and positive attention paid by host nationals to expatriates (being an object of local curiosity has its appeal); and (4) the indifferent or negative reaction from compatriots to the returnees' homecoming.

The subtractive response has been poignantly articulated by an Indian who repatriated after working for many years in Dubai. He expressed his confusion in a series of missives sent to friends and relatives. With his permission, here are some excerpts.

> **November 11.** I do not think I will be able to live in my home country ... at least I still call it that coz [*sic*] I am an Indian citizen. For the first time I am disappointed to say I got a culture shock in my own country. There are so many things about this society that I cannot tolerate ... There is a very low tolerance towards an alternative view.

> **January 12.** Life here is not getting any better, quite the contrary a bit worse and I think every time I open my mouth to reach out and have an honest conversation I get the most negative reactions. So I have decided to shut up until I leave which is gonna be by the next month. It is tragic that my time with my family is the most mentally unstimulating time I have had.

> **February 11.** Here things have took [*sic*] a turn for the worse. My brother-in-law came to our house completely pissed [drunk] ... and he hit my sister. Now I am a peaceful person by nature and do not think fighting physically fixes anything it's immature and does not improve the situation. But this was an extreme circumstance and I reacted instinctively I think. I went mad and hit him repeatedly ... Looks like my Indian fantasy is over. I dreamt of retiring in India for a long time. But there is nothing for me here.

The subtractive response is the most common response to repatriation of Europeans, Americans, and other Anglo-country citizens, although it is not uncommon among Asian returnees either. Have Hong Kongers adopted subtractive identities and felt emotional distress upon their return?

Hong Kong subtractive identity

Analyses of both quantitative and qualitative data have revealed some surprising results. First, in contrast to American and other Western returnees, only one of the 50 Hong Kong respondents (2% of the total) exhibited a pure subtractive identity profile accompanied by negative emotionality. The lack of subtractive identity was found irrespective of country of resettlement, gender, or length of time overseas. The lone "subtractive" was a male respondent who took his university degree in Scotland, returned to Hong Kong, later immigrated to Australia and then remigrated back to Hong Kong after two and a half years. Here is an excerpt from his interview (P37):

> P: When we got back to Hong Kong in December 1996, it's still like we are foreigners. We have a feeling that we are foreigners, although we are Chinese but we still feel like …
>
> I: Describe that. Why you think that you feel like a foreigner?
>
> P: The way people behave. Hong Kong is so much that people are quite rude. In Australia or in Western countries, we get used to say thank you and we do think that we appreciate the Western way. Western people keep saying thank you or excuse me but Chinese never, or seldom, I should say … Also, Hong Kong people are very materialistic. That is all they care about getting more money and things. I appreciate Westerner ways.
>
> I: How did you feel emotionally?
>
> P: I feel stressed and uncomfortable. I feel different from other people.
>
> I: How do you feel now [back in Hong Kong eight years]?
>
> P: I am still not comfortable.

The core characteristic of the subtractive identity is the feeling, on their return home, of being separate or different from their compatriots. This remigrant encapsulated this idea:

> P: Sometimes we feel a bit upset because we think different from the rest of the people. [Old friends would say] "You act differently." "You act like an Australian or a Western people." They do recognize that … [Family, brothers and sisters] they recognize that we are different.

Several remigrants demonstrated a combination of subtractive identity and additive identity — they felt less Hong Kong–Chinese and more Australian or Canadian. A male participant (P3) who returned from

Canada commented on feeling different from the average Hong Konger, a subtractive identity trait:

I: So do you feel that you don't fit into Hong Kong anymore?

P: No, no. I don't know. Sometimes I feel more comfortable to speak in English more than in Cantonese.

While displaying a subtractive identity, he combined this with additive elements. He described his work style and leisure activities as being distinctly Canadian and emphatically stated, *"I am a Canadian."* The following are some additional excerpts from his interview. In response to the interviewer's reference to Hong Kong as his home, the respondent said the following:

P: I don't consider it as a home. Just a place to work.

He continued:

P: I stay in Hong Kong just because I need to work in Hong Kong, basically. Even though I born in Hong Kong, I was raised up in Hong Kong. All Chinese newspaper I know, Cantonese ... but I don't really go into the things happen in Hong Kong. [I: So you are not following the politics in Hong Kong too much?] No, because I think that eventually I will go back to Canada.

He responded to the interviewer's question about his leisure activities in the following way:

P: I think it's more Canadian style. [I: Like what?] I don't like to go out and shop. It's just too hot and too crowd. If I have free time, I prefer to stay at home, listen to some musics, go on the net, e-mail some friends ... [I: Not the Hong Kong way to go out and shop?] Exactly. I even don't watch the Hong Kong movies. [I: Do you watch Canadian movies or American movies or ... ?] Sometimes, but not the Hong Kong movies. [I: How about Hong Kong radio stations and ...?] Yes, yes. Some of the phone-in programs. Just listen to what happens.

He also commented on the differences in his work style compared to that of the average Hong Konger:

P: I always criticize that culture in Hong Kong [referring to the Hong Kongers' refusal to challenge their employers]. Because he's not the most powerful guy ... in Hong Kong, they are too obey. They just do whatever the boss said. Right or wrong, they don't care.

I: Can you give me a situation where that happens?

P: I think that's not reasonable. Sometimes you have your own workload already. And the boss just keep on adding in and adding in ... and they just take it and take it ... endlessly. And they never say anything. I say that's wrong. You have to raise your voice. Tell them that "I am so busy. I have so many things." If you just take it, they think that the manpower is good enough. They won't say that "oh, the manpower is tight and I have to recruit more." Maybe you have to work twelve hours a day or fourteen hours a day and come back on Saturday ... I don't do that. I am sorry. But most of my colleagues they go back and work on Saturdays. And some of them leave at nine or ten at night.

I: So what do you think your boss and your coworkers think of you? Do they think that you act Canadian? Have you heard them say anything?

P: Yeah.

I: What have they said?

P: This guy is a *gwai lo* [foreigner].

I: So they think that some of the ways you behave are not like a Hong Konger.

Thus the remigrant just quoted exhibited both subtractive and additive identity features while experiencing negative emotions deriving from his sense of alienation from Hong Kong society. Several other interviewees also revealed elements of subtractive identity in their narratives.

One female respondent immigrated to Australia primarily to obtain Australian citizenship and had definite plans to return to Hong Kong. However, she remained in Australia for four and a half years before going back to Hong Kong. In the following excerpt, she described her feelings of being different from the rest of the Hong Kong population and the impact of those differences on her work life (P43):

P: Not easy, for the first year actually [referring to her readjustment to life in Hong Kong]. Because when I returned back here, I got a marketing job. Because of my few years in Australia, my sense are not as sharp as before. Pace-wise, I was at slower pace, and also the sensitivity to the environment because I was in a marketing job. I have to be very sensitive to what the market is doing and quick in thinking. I wasn't. So I wasn't like a typical Hong Kong people. I think slower than people and I still have to pick up the pace, the style of thinking and the speed of thinking with other Hong Kong people. It was very difficult for me to adjust.

I: Did you feel that you didn't fit in with other Hong Kong people? [Did] you feel different?

P: Yes. Just like the pace …

I: Some people have used these words and said that they feel different than …

P: Yes, different.

I: But it was mainly because you feel that your thinking was slower?

P: Yes, slower. Because Australian life is more relaxed. In Hong Kong, you can't relax because your boss press you for this and all the deadlines, you have to be very proactive, initiate a lot of work. But Australian is very lay back. You don't have to do it. I just have to do the job enough and that's okay, and I get my salary. But here it's different. Even though you are not at a very senior level, they expect a lot.

I: So you felt [it was] hard to get your thinking back, change back in?

P: Yes.

A female respondent who immigrated to Canada in her late teens and returned after ten years commented on feeling different from her friends and family once she was back in Hong Kong (P26):

> Especially when this time I come back to Hong Kong I found that I am different from different friends, my friends, and different thoughts with the Hong Kong people. We are Canadian. I feel I am more friendly than Hong Kong people and the way of thinking I think.

Some remigrants, however, although combining elements of subtractive and additive cultural identities, rarely experienced negative emotions. An illustration is provided by a female respondent who as a teenager migrated to Canada with her entire family. She returned to Hong Kong after nine years and clearly identified herself as "half-Canadian, half-Chinese." She described eating habits and patterns of interaction with friends and coworkers that were all indicative of an additive identity profile. For example, when asked how she behaves in a Canadian way, she replied (P16):

> P: Coffee, definitely. The way I eat, I guess. Chinese need to have rice every day. I don't. Actually I don't eat rice that often. And it's funny because when I move to Canada, I always want to have the Chinese food there, the snacks and everything. And when I came back here [to Hong Kong], I always want the *gwai lo* food, the Canadian food … And I watch foreign films, Hollywood films.

Yet she also made the following comment, in which she demonstrates a subtractive identity (P16):

> Actually, I never thought I am that Canadian until I came back to Hong Kong. Until there are people who are just couldn't quite understand the way I act or just couldn't help notice because I am older and so I can observe and realize how people react over my actions. Just small things that make me realize how I am actually not that Chinese.

This participant also exemplifies the nuanced way in which the salience of identity change emerges only on remigration.

Another example of the combined profile is a female participant whose responses were primarily additive. She left for Australia at age 27 with her husband and returned to Hong Kong four years later with her husband and a daughter who was born in Australia. Exemplars of an additive identity shift included her comments on the Western influences on her parenting (allowing her children to have more independence and freedom) and on her interactions with her colleagues. However, she also made comments that are decidedly subtractive, such as (P2): *"Yeah, when I come back to Hong Kong I feel a bit headache. I don't like Hong Kong in the beginning,"* and *"I don't like Hong Kong tricky things anymore. I like to be frank and be simple, be honest. Sometimes I find it kind of attitude I don't really like."* She also spoke of what she perceived as a lack of candor on the part of her Hong Kong friends:

> Yeah, my girlfriends, used to be my friends in HK, and I come back to have dinner with them. When we sit down, and I like this and that when we ordering the food, but it seems like there are some foods that they don't like, and they don't say it and then they don't eat it. That's the thing that I, you know ... Australians are quite frank. [I: So they will say, I don't like that, let's have another thing.]. They don't, say that, you know, that make you feel kind of, I don't know ... You are ordering something that they don't like, and they don't tell you. You know, small things like that.

She resented the close attention and keen observational skills needed to function smoothly in interpersonal situations in Hong Kong. Her comments exemplify a "high-context" style of communication whereby meaning is derived not from overt language but from subtle nonverbal behaviors, an absence of words, and social context.

This same participant made additional comments suggestive of a subtractive identity shift:

I: In what other aspects do you feel different from Hong Kongers?

P: When I come back I am really slow. I couldn't get across the traffic. When I was in Australia, it was totally different. And especially one thing is driving; I hate the people in Hong Kong the way they drive. When I drive in Australia, people are very nice, they give you ways. That's a thing. Bit by bit it reminds me of a thing that, oh, I don't really like the Hong Kong people now. The identity is very confusing actually, like down here and there. And then sometimes I think maybe it's better to stay in Australia. I used to like there already.

Yet another example of subtractive elements is provided by a male interviewee who returned to Hong Kong after four years in Canada. His responses indicated that he had adapted easily to life in Vancouver and had developed a primarily additive identity profile. However, the following comment is clearly subtractive (P24):

I: So how did, when you first came, the first week or two, how did Hong Kong look to you and feel to you?

P: Actually, I don't like and I almost, I always don't like Hong Kong and the behaviors of Hong Kong people. And even I went to Canada at that time I don't like Hong Kong this place and Hong Kong people.

Among those respondents with combined additive and subtractive profiles, the most common means of expressing the subtractive identity profile was through their negative comments about the Hong Kong environment and the Hong Kong people's focus on materialism. Similarly, P37, who was categorized earlier as "pure subtractive," remarked on the aggressiveness and focus on materialism that he believed to be characteristic of the Hong Kong people:

I: Are there other ways that you felt different from Hong Kongers?

P: Value.

I: Are there values that you and your wife hold different than people here?

P: That is the major difference. We are aggressive, but we are not as aggressive as other Hong Kongers … Values. Just the value. Materialization. We are not as materialized as they [the Hong Kongers] are.

He also reported his distaste for the Hong Kong people's emphasis on accumulating material possessions:

I: I am very interested in what you said about coming back and feeling as a foreigner and after eight years still not feeling comfortable. Sometimes people have described a feeling of not fitting in back to Hong Kong, not being like other Hong Kongers. Did you have that feeling?

P: Yes, to a certain extent, I have that kind of feeling. Although we consider environment is very important, we were not as materialized as other Hong Kong people who have never lived in another Western countries. We need money, but we are not as desperate as other Hong Kong people. They will try every means to earn money as quickly as possible and as easy as possible.

P37 also highlighted the dissatisfaction with environmental conditions in Hong Kong that was common among respondents with subtractive and combined additive and subtractive profiles:

I: You mentioned that you felt like a foreigner. Was there anything about Hong Kong that made you feel uncomfortable?

P: The environment in terms of the air quality, crowdedness of the city.

I: The crowdedness?

P: Yes, very crowded. We should have get used to this place because we were born here. But having been absent in Hong Kong for two and a half years, we get used to have more space on your own and not many people on the street. But when you get out, there are so many people on the street. We still think that we don't want to go out in crowded place. When we were young, we like to go to crowded places; we like to see a lot of people there. But since we've been living in Australia for two and a half years, we don't like to go to places where there are so many people there.

Dissatisfaction with the Hong Kong environmental condition was also expressed by this male respondent, who lived in Sydney with his wife for two and a half years (P33): *"One thing, when I back to Hong Kong, I was not suit to the environment is that I found it very noisy and also the air was not good."*

Another male respondent immigrated with his wife and daughter with the intention of living permanently in Australia. However, he returned to Hong Kong after only two years for job-related reasons. He had this to say about the quality of the air in Hong Kong (P20): *"And the weather is so bad, and even the air is poor. You don't have such a refreshing feeling as in Australia. You feel very stuff, stuffy, very stuffy."* The negative response to the Hong

Kong environment is also illustrated in the following comment by a female respondent who returned from Canada after three years (P12):

> You don't really feel like, you feel Hong Kong is filthy, the environment, you know busy, so many traffic ... Because in Canada is quiet, the traffic is, the pollution is not bad. I think everybody when they live in outside Hong Kong, sometime they come back they think, first they won't like it, humid.

When asked to reflect on their place in Hong Kong society and on the emotional aspects of returning home, the majority of respondents were puzzled by the question. Why *should* they have difficulty returning to Hong Kong, to friends and family, and to be speaking their native language? This attitude is clearly illustrated in the following excerpt from a male interviewee who returned to Hong Kong after spending two years in Australia (P49):

> I: So really you have to get readjusted to Hong Kong a few times, after three years in China coming back, then after two years in Sydney, and then after Shanghai. So was it ever difficult to adjust back?
> P: No. Because I born here. Why would it be difficult? You just feel Hong Kong change so quick in terms of the development here.

A similar sentiment is expressed in the following excerpt by a male respondent who immigrated to Australia and returned to Hong Kong after two years (P35):

> I: Did you find at all that you didn't fit in back to Hong Kong?
> P: No.
> I: So you felt comfortable.
> P: You just count the years. When I came back to Hong Kong I was thirty-three. I just left for two years, less the one-fifteenth of my life. Not too much difference.

What explanatory factors will help us understand why so few remigrants felt alienated from Hong Kong culture and society and therefore incorporated few subtractive identity elements? Chapter 10 delves into historical and philosophical explanations to account for the Chinese response to cultural transitions. Here, I offer two more proximal ideas.

First, the Hong Kong identity is, at its core, a complex, flexible, and practical one. It is also a collectivist and group-oriented one, sensitive to the mores and values of the wider community. This has been demonstrated in the nature of the immigrants' successful adaptation to life in Canada or Australia. In a number of the questionnaires that they completed, study respondents scored high in both the Western Behavior and the Identity Acculturation subscales, and their self-concepts were less relational (Twenty Statement Test [TST] results) and less interdependent (Self-Construal Scale comparisons). That is, they integrated Western notions into their sense of self by altering their work behaviors, family rituals, and ways of obtaining entertainment and using leisure time to match those of surrounding communities. Returning to Hong Kong, they utilized the same contextual matching processes by paying close attention to situational constraints. In this way, the returnees recognized the effective means through which to relate harmoniously to their extended family, their friends, and their coworkers. Western behaviors and attitudes were merged (additive) with Hong Kong ones; they did not supplant them. Thus, Hong Kong culture was psychologically accessible to the respondents once they returned home.

It should be noted that while integrating Western ideas into their cultural repertoire, the returnees utilized the Chinese diaspora community as a resource to aid in their relatively smooth adjustment. Even among American expatriates returning to the US, those with the highest level of interdependence between themselves and their family and friends, adjusted better overseas and on returning home.[3]

Second, the social network and environment of the remigrants was substantially international. Among the middle class, a large percentage of the Hong Kong population had lived overseas, as sojourners if not as immigrants. Until recently, for example, the Hong Kong government provided all civil servants (including the children of teachers and professors) with an overseas education allowance (to the UK) for their children, a remnant of the British colonial days in which British workers in Hong Kong were provided with this education perquisite. The demographer Ronald Skeldon estimates that 20,000 visas were issued yearly for students attending either secondary school or university overseas.[4] The remigrant's overseas experience and adaptation may not have differed in substance from that of a returned sojourner. Rather than being different from their compatriots, the remigrant experience echoed those of the returned Hong Kong student or worker. This resulted in an external environment, that is, a social and workplace network, that was flexible in its expectations of the remigrant. In contrast to Japanese culture, for example, Hong Kong culture allows a broader range of acceptable behavior and thought from its residents. Thus returnees' various interpersonal networks did not look askance when remigrants behaved in direct or individualistic ways.

Subtractive identity in other Hong Kong studies

While the HKRP found few subtractive identities among its participant sample, Wendy Chan's study of Hong Kong remigrants determined that they most frequently described themselves as different from other *Xianggang ren* (Hong Kong people), or subtractive.[5] Their anecdotes of life back in Hong Kong were full of disparaging characterizations of the residents, which also distanced the respondents from the "man on the street."

"I really don't like the materialistic side of Hong Kong. My children are asking me to hold birthday parties in function rooms of five-star hotels, like many of their classmates do but I refuse." Another commented: "People here don't like to think about philosophical issues, e.g., about the meaning of life. They are too busy making money." Yet another remarked: "*Xianggang ren* are *jigongjinli* [obsessed with fast results]. My boss will phone me as soon as I am not reporting any results and will ask me sarcastically whether I am enjoying life so much that I forget to do my job." Still a fourth respondent sputtered, "I had people jumping right in front of me for the cash dispenser and when I protested, I was told that I was not putting my card into the machine fast enough!"

Other remigrants considered *Xianggang ren* to be impolite, rude, and lacking both a sense of fair play and consideration for others in public:

> I was the first on the street waiting for a taxi then a young guy appeared and stood in front of me; then a family of four stood in front of him. And when the family got onto a taxi, the young guy protested. I found myself wondering whether I should join the protest. I did not. What's the use? This is Hong Kong.

Subtractive identity in Taiwan

Nora Chiang and Sunny Liao investigated the return to Taiwan of young adults whose families had migrated to Australia.[6] Opportunities for careers drew most of these adults back home after 10 to 20 years of living abroad. Similar to the Hong Kong remigrants, many of these returnees commented on the difficult physical environment in Taiwanese cities: "The air is polluted." "Living space is small. Too many people." "Pace of life in Taiwan is much faster than Australia's." "Taiwanese are crazy about politics here." "It's hard to get along with people." Regarding identity issues, again there is a striking similarity with Hong Kong. The majority of the respondents were additive/bicultural, "I am Australian when I live there; and Taiwanese when I live here." But several expressed subtractive identities, as did a 29-year-old woman who had lived eight years in Australia: "I have spoken with many friends who are of similar ages — their feelings are similar to mine — we are neither Australian nor Taiwanese, and we are perturbed by our social distance with either." Another commented, "When we are in Australia, we felt like aliens. When we are back in Taiwan, we are regarded as different because we are from overseas."

Subtractive identity among Westerners

The most common remigrant response to returning home to the West is the subtractive profile. Repatriates feel they are less a part of their home cultures, different from their compatriots. In other words, their home culture has been subtracted from their identity. Emotionally, the subtractive identity is frequently accompanied by psychological distress, depression, and anxiety.

The majority of returnee citizens in the West have experienced repatriation as returned sojourners rather than as remigrants owing to low emigration from the United States, Canada, and Europe. These sojourners lived overseas as expatriates because of job assignments, educational opportunities, diplomatic or military assignments, or missionary work. When the assignments were completed, they returned home. Among these populations of repatriates, the majority of research studies have been conducted with American or European returnees.

Italy. Daniela Grisi's personal experience sparked her empirical research.[7] After returning home to Italy following a year's study program in Sweden, she "experienced the feeling that I no longer fit into my home country, and talking with other students that had an experience similar to mine I found the same feeling, the same distress." She then began to work with an Italian program offering technical assistance in Latin America. There she "met some returned volunteers and I noticed the same distress but accentuated. They had this common feeling of not being able anymore to live in their country [Italy] and a lot of them went through a really bad time, frequently ending with a new departure."

In a subsequent qualitative study, she interviewed Italian repatriates from a technical assistance program (MLAL, Movimento Laici America Latina).[8] Sara, one of the interviewees, had been working on a project in

Peru and spent two years there. She had a deep and significant adaptation: "I really felt at my ease. I felt better there than here [Italy], for the quality of life. I loved their food, I loved their way of being, etc. The population is always so cheerful." In fact, she felt so comfortable with Peruvian culture and the way of life that she married a local man.

However, as suggested by the Cultural Identity Model, Sara's self-concept changes and adaptation to Peru presaged a "subtractive" identity shift and re-entry distress. "My return has been more difficult than my arrival [in Peru] ... I've lived very badly since my return." She no longer identified with Italy. "I feel something, it's like my place isn't really here [Italy]." Later, she again remarks: "Here I don't, here I feel that I'm not in the right place."

Israel. One exception to the Western repatriation reaction is the remigrant response to Israel, which, in several ways, is similar to that of remigrants to Hong Kong. Both Israel and Hong Kong are recipients of immigrants, senders of emigrants, and recipients of returned migrants. In other respects, however, Israel possesses unique migratory characteristics. The rationale behind outgoing immigration differs: Israeli immigrants leave for love, adventure, and financial security; they frequently return for relational reasons, because of attachment to the nation and people, or to ensure that their children speak Hebrew and understand the culture. In the past decade, Hong Kongers left for political reasons and returned for financial or family reasons, but also to ensure that their children were fluent in Cantonese and Mandarin. The latter cause was less for transmission of culture and history and more for strategic reasons, to position their children for future employment as multilingual, international employees.

The important role that incoming and outgoing citizens play in Israeli society is captured in the specific Hebrew terminology used to convey these distinctions. Newly arrived immigrants are called *olim*, translated as "those going up" (a biblical reference to the importance to Jews of a return to Israel from the diaspora). Outgoing emigrants were stigmatized until recently with the term *yordim*, translated as "those going down," a clear reference to the sense of betrayal and the ideological threat that Israelis felt from those who left the country. Today, the term *yordim* is rarely used, and Israeli attitudes toward emigrants are less critical.[9]

Despite subtle dissuasion not to emigrate from Israel, nearly 1% of the Israeli Jewish population is living overseas.[10] However, personal circumstances have led many to return, some after living for as long as 20 years in another country; it is estimated that 12,000 Israelis return each year.[11] Michel Tannenbaum recently studied Israeli remigrants, most of whom left Israel not anticipating a return.[12] She found that many experienced subtractive identities. Rami, a 61-year-old man, moved to the United States with his American wife. After eight years, at Rami's insistence, they returned to Israel with their children. He wanted his children to live in Israel, speak Hebrew, and enjoy all the advantages of the country. "But the minute we landed it [anticipatory elation] all ended. Although I am a sixth-generation Israeli, I felt entirely as a new immigrant. My expectations were tremendous and so was my disappointment. The return to my homeland was one of the greatest disappointments of my life ... I felt a new immigrant in my own country."

Oded emigrated to the United States at the age of 26 and returned to Israel ten years later. "Most of all, I'd lost my Israeli-ness, which sort of disappeared, and sometimes I did not feel I belonged to either place ... no doubt returning was like another immigration ... On the one hand, I returned to something familiar, but this familiar thing is different ... I too have changed a lot."

Tannenbaum reports that many negative emotions were experienced by the research participants. "It was very hard for me when I came back. I had gotten used to my independence and suddenly I needed to consider the feelings and opinions of others. Coming back was harder for me than going away in the first place." Another said, "I felt really depressed after we returned. Not in first few weeks. Then I was still rather euphoric. But after the first period I was deeply depressed. I felt I'd made the wrong decision, felt alienated from things around me, felt they were not mine." And yet another said, "To return was like immigrating again. Having to adjust to a new place. I felt strange."

Ireland. For more than 150 years, Ireland has been a net emigration country because of drastic economic downturns and agriculture droughts; it is estimated that between 1845 and 1900, 2.8 million Irish migrated to the United States alone.[13] But as the twentieth century closed, the Irish migrants began to return home in record numbers. In referring to the population of one Irish county, Marese McDonagh, a reporter for the *Irish Times*, remarked, "After 150 years of poverty and forced emigration, the tide has turned and the people of Leitrim are coming home. Others are coming too of course. The biggest factor in the population surge is that native sons and daughters of Leitrim are returning not just from London and New York ... lured by the easier lifestyle, cheaper property and a more hopeful economic output."[14] Government statistics confirm these estimates, as the 2005 figure indicated that approximately 18,000 people emigrated from

Ireland while nearly 70,000 immigrants arrived, a sizable portion of which were returning nationals and their dependents.[15]

Michael Curran, an Irish researcher, recently investigated the social and psychological ramifications of returning to Ireland.[16] His multimethod approach included qualitative techniques (structured interviews and focus groups) and quantitative ones (questionnaires administered in person and on the internet). He sampled a total of 105 returnees or those contemplating return. Participants were recruited either from Counties May and Donegal or from a dedicated web site. A huge range of ages (20 to 76 years old), years abroad (6 months to 59 years), education, and occupations was represented in the sample, but it was divided primarily by the method of data collection. Online responders were younger, better educated, and more professional, and had been abroad for fewer years (average of 11.5 years) compared to those who completed the questionnaires or participated in the focus groups. They also differed significantly in their reasons for returning to Ireland. The younger cohort (45 years and younger) was drawn back for familial reasons (the desire to raise their families in Ireland or the needs of aging parents), economic reasons (desire to participate in the "Celtic Tiger" economy), and environmental ones (quality of life in Ireland). For the older cohort, quality of life was overwhelmingly the most important reason as many were nearing retirement age. The technological divide continued for the younger cohort, as the Internet was the primary source of re-entry information for those considering a return to Ireland, whereas government "advice centers" located in many countries served the older cohort.

Most respondents indicated that they had adjusted well to living abroad and their anticipation of the return to Ireland was tinged with anxiety. Several respondents reflected that their spouses and children were not "really Irish," and they were concerned about how their families would "fit in" to rural Irish life. For those who returned, the actual homecoming was often fraught with even more problems than they had expected. One remigrant maintained that coming home was "like emigrating for the second time," and another claimed to have been "conned" by the government's appeals to emigrants to return home. A number of older returnees felt so unwelcome back in Ireland that they quickly returned to their place of emigration, often England. So many have experienced feeling "ripped off" or "different" from their Irish neighbors that the terms *blow ins* and *blow backs* have been coined to describe this revolving remigration. Even among those older remigrants who have remained in Ireland, many admit that "it had been a mistake to return to Ireland in the first place." Subtractive identities clearly describe many of the remigrants in Curran's study.

7 Global and affirmative identities

Global identity

The Cultural Identity Model (CIM) suggests a third possible identity profile that develops following a cultural transition. The global identity commences from a novel point of departure. Individuals with this profile are multiple sojourners prior to their immigration; that is, over time they have moved in and out of their home countries, primarily for work assignments, and consequently have a keen sense of themselves as cultural beings. Thus, they begin their migration journey with an awareness of how their values, beliefs, customs, and preferences are shaped by their home culture.

Global identity among Hong Kong remigrants

Among Hong Kong multiple sojourners, cultural salience starts at a high point. We have noted earlier that the average Hong Konger possesses an awareness of the multiplicity of cultural influences on his or her identity. For the frequent cultural mover, this awareness is heightened and articulately described.

The CIM predicts that few migrants will experience a global identity, and the Hong Kong Remigration Project confirms the prediction. Five of the 50 respondents (10%) in the study appeared to have a purely global identity. They bore the hallmark elements of global identifiers. They had moved in and out of Hong Kong often, raising their children in different, mostly Western countries. Their naming configuration was always the least traditionally Chinese — English given name followed by Chinese surname. Their scores on the self-concept scales also matched the global identity: they had the highest individualistic self-descriptions on the Twenty Statement Test (TST) and identically high independent/interdependent scores. They were neutral (had midpoint scores) in both the Satisfaction with Life Scale and the Repatriation Distress Scale. Through their narratives, these remigrants unequivocally indicated that their stay in Hong Kong would be temporary, and while in Hong Kong, they chose to live in international neighborhoods, join international clubs, and send their children to international schools. Here is a response by one such remigrant (P5):

I: Before you left, if I would have asked you to describe yourself culturally, that is: who are you inside? How would you describe yourself? What values and traditions do you have?

P: I think my background is a little bit different from the "stereotyped" Hong Kong immigrant going to Canada because I had made a few international moves because my husband was transferred many times. We lived in Singapore for three years. I have lived and worked in Australia, [and] we had gone to University of Michigan … So it's like departure and re-entry, many times before we did this. So, I think that would have affected the question you asked about how much impact it had on me culturally. It was actually a series of moves rather than a single move. So I think when I left, I was pretty international, culturally I guess. There may be some ingrained Chinese values, but I was more cosmopolitan because of all the contacts that I've made, and all the experiences I had for all my routes.

This same respondent also commented on her desire to expose her children to a wide range of cultural experiences and activities while traveling outside of Hong Kong:

I: Did you find after a while that you think of yourself as Canadian? Can you think of an example or a situation where you said to yourself: I am acting like a Canadian?

P: Interesting question … [I: The way you raised your daughters? Leisure activities? Or where you are interacting with friends … ?] Definitely when I was raising my daughters. I took them to ice-skating classes. When we went down toboggan, it was definitely Canadian. But actually I have gone through this transition early on, like when we lived in Walnut Creek [California], I have already transitioned to like the Northern Americans, influenced by their way they brought up children, or the way they interacted with people.

I: What examples do you think of as North American way?

P: We were definitely more opened, less ... you know, the Chinese people tend to be very protective of their children, and we were also protective, but we would give them enough freedom, to make friends, expose them to variety people. A lot of people newly immigrated to some place, especially from Hong Kong, tends to like to stick together with Chinese people because they feel comfortable. And we just deliberately didn't do that. 'Cause we wanted our children to have exposure to different cultures, and it sort of impact on them even till today because they are very international people. We exposed them to different kinds of schools; we didn't always just live in Chinatown, so they actually eat everything.

This respondent actively maintained a Western style of parenting even after she returned to Hong Kong:

I: Is there a different way in how you relate to your children?

P: We are definitely more open-minded and westernized. Both my daughters have American boyfriends, and endless people have asked me that "Don't you mind?" And I was thinking: my daughters don't see the colors in people; they just see "Joe" or "Bill" or whoever. And I feel the same way. But I know a lot of people don't. And I let them take more responsibilities for their lives. My daughters are very well traveled anyway. And they have lived, expose to a lot of things. I think they probably ... We let them make a lot of decisions. [I: Like what? Did you help shape their career plans?]

P: When my daughters went to college, we told them that they have to find their own passion because if you don't, you will be like boring. And they did. In their second year of college, they found what they wanted to do and they went for it. I never told them: I want you to major this or that; it was for them. But having said that, I have exposed them to a lot of different things. At the very young age, they volunteered in different organizations. They done the normal things that a lot of kids do. Activities or so. I guess they were exposed to enough that it was quite obvious what they really liked. And it was just natural for them to go from there.

She also observed a difference between people like herself, who had traveled, and the rest of the Hong Kong population:

> P: I think there is difference between those who have lived overseas a great deal and those who haven't because the mind-set is different. The perspective is not as wide, it tends to be a little bit narrow, and the things they talk about is not as varied. But most of the people in Hong Kong are quite well traveled, especially if they could afford it, like professionals, and they would usually take some trips a year, but they have not have the experience of actually going overseas. But quite a large percentage I would say of professional people here you would find they have made that trek to Australia and Canada at some point. Because people either don't have the resources to do it or don't have the capacity to do it because they are not qualified. So most of the people, though I have to say I have some friends here who have their own business who would not be able to make the same thing overseas, they have not make the loop. They are well traveled, but there is a little bit of a difference. And actually when I get back to Hong Kong, I think the people who had done what we had are the people we relate to more.

She summed up the foundation of her global identity as follows:

> P: Actually, I may not be a very good subject for your study because I am so not Hong Kong. Because somewhere along the way of all the various ... Well, first of all, I was brought up to be very westernized, because my mother is not from here. My mother was born in Surinam in Dutch Guyana. She came back to Hong Kong when she was sixteen and she does not even read Chinese, she speaks Dutch.
>
> I: Is she ethnically Chinese?
>
> P: Yes, but she was born and educated in Surinam. So I was always very westernized. And then, on top of that, with all the international moves that I made, I am actually not a typical Hong Kong person that you could interview.

The pattern of multiple country moves was also the life path followed by a male respondent who was 51 when he immigrated to Canada. However, he had a long history of sojourns prior to his emigration to Canada. He began as a college student studying for a few years in New York. He then moved to Miami because he liked the weather there better. However, after three years he moved to Thailand and stayed there for about five years before finally returning to Hong Kong. He reported adjusting very easily to life in each of the places that he had visited, and provided the following explanation (P31):

> No, to me it's okay. I am that kind of person. I can fit myself into any society and any place. That's my thinking, never change the society or the world. You have to fit into it, and you make others to fit into it. You don't blame on other people give you this, give you that; it's crazy. To me, you have to do it yourself to fit into the society. That's my thinking.

Another exemplar of the global identity is a male respondent whose travel experience was rather extensive. In 1985 he moved with his wife to Singapore and stayed for five years. They then moved to Canada because they felt the need to experience life in a different culture. However, it was difficult for him to find employment so he moved to London, where he stayed for another three years. He then moved back to Hong Kong, stayed for about a year, and then returned to Canada. In response to the interviewer's comment on his considerable travel activity, he readily admitted that he felt no strong ties to Hong Kong but, instead, felt the need to experience life elsewhere (P38):

> I: And was it the lure of another country that you are interested in? What is it like to live in another country, or is it because you wanted to leave Hong Kong? Or some combination?
>
> P: I guess is a combination. First of all, frankly, I don't really like the, what we use to call, the quality of living in Hong Kong. Although even nowadays you earn more than what I could earn anywhere else. But the living standard, compare to other places, the general environment is not as pleasant as the most of the places I visit. Basically, it is always in my desire to live somewhere else and not take Hong Kong as long as my permanent home. Okay, we always in there. Nineteen ninety-seven maybe have a very small effect. But I don't think it is a major factor because personally I don't believe there will be any significant changes, as soon as the takeover happen. So that has never been my concern. It is really my personal desire just to go somewhere else. And, in fact, even today I am still thinking of going somewhere else. I really, after so many years, I really enjoy, even my wife enjoy it. Living in different country, meeting different people, try to have a taste of different culture. We enjoy that.

This same respondent described himself as a "Hong Konger ... modified by exposure to a different culture," and he provided the following response, which is characteristic of persons with a global identity profile:

I think I'm more an international person, I must say. Although as I said earlier, I still have the desire to take Canada as my permanent home, but still I have the desire to move around to the few more places in the near future. So I don't see myself as a person who would like to stay at one place forever. I really like to go to different places. So that's I would say. I rather choose myself as a international person, if you like. And also because of my past experience, I think I can fit in every different culture or different environment quite easily without much problem.

He described his future plans in the following way:

It's time to move, don't know where. There's some thinking, we might go back to Canada, we might go to the States, or we even consider going to Australia. So there's quite a few things on the table at the moment. So again we were thinking the date what should be done at this point. Of course, original one idea is go back to Toronto, since my son is going back after summer anyway.

Several of the study's respondents exhibited blended global and additive identities; that is, they have added Canadian or Australian values and ways of behaving and thinking to their self-concepts. This broadening of their cultural identity led them to ascribe "globalness" to their self-descriptors.

One female respondent is an example of this blended identity. She was born in Hong Kong to Malaysian parents, so as a child she spent time going back and forth between these two territories. As a teenager she sojourned in the United Kingdom, where she received her college education. After about eight years, she returned to Hong Kong. She then left for Australia and stayed there for about two and a half years. This extensive travel contributed to her developing some elements of a global identity. Similar to the "pure" global respondents, she claimed to possess the ability to adapt very easily to any environment. In the following excerpt she explains (P21):

I: How about in terms of raising your children? Do you think that there were Australian influences in your decisions you made about raising your children? Some people would say: "In Australia, children are much independent. They allow them to make their own choices." Do you think you raised them with any of those Australian values or traditional Chinese values?

P: I won't say it's traditional Chinese or Australian, but the parent's value sort of changed a little bit with the ... Because I would think it doesn't matter whether your child is raised traditional way or the Australian way; nowadays, you have to communicate with your children, you have to respect them, but to a certain degree, there still require control in their needs. Actually, regardless wherever you are, I would say that parents should guide and lead their children as they would like their children to grow up to be.

I: So you think that child rearing is more universal, not Australian way or Chinese way?

P: It should be. I can allow them to have certain freedom, but under control. It's not whether the Chinese ways: girls cannot go out but boys can at the same age, but the matter of security … [I: Do you believe that?] No, I don't agree with that. It's based on communication, whether the child is secured, based on trust, and as a parent, you should allow the child to have certain degree of personal life as well. It was very different from when I was younger; my father had a different degree. Boys at twelve could go out, but girls at twelve, no. Stay in. Not even until I was twenty-one.

The following comments by this same respondent are a poignant expression of the global aspect of her identity:

I: How do you think of yourself now? You have been back for ten years. Do you still think of yourself as Australian?

P: That's what I write down in the nationality.

I: But in terms of what values or beliefs that influence how you live your life?

P: In fact, ever since I have sense, I always turn myself: I am a nobody. And I would introduce myself as a Hong Kong–born Malaysian. I have no sense of belonging as such. I don't know if I am a local Hong Kong or I am a Malaysian. It's the same now. Although I write down Australian in nationality, but I feel that I am a local, regardless it is Hong Kong, Australian, China, or Malaysia. I am a resident and I accustom. I get around, I enjoy the culture, I learn to enjoy. I am adaptive. I would say that. I mix in.

Toward the end of the interview, she again reflected on the complexity of her identity:

P: I have not actually put down in black and white of my identity. But I had always … but I go to Australia. After I came back from Australia, I have kept my identity that I am a nobody.

I: Or … somebody with a very complex identity?

P: That's correct. And one of the reason why I adapt to Hong
Kong well is because it's so cosmopolitan. If I was sent back to
Mainland China, I would be very difficult.

Another example of the blended global and additive identity is a
female respondent who returned to Hong Kong after 13 years in Canada.
She worked in the travel industry so she traveled extensively. She expressed
her desire to "see the world" as the primary motivator of her decision to
move to Canada. She adapted easily to life in Canada and admitted to
adopting behaviors that were distinctly Canadian (P30):

I: So while you were doing all this were you feeling glad to be back
in Hong Kong, or was it hard to be here?

P: It was okay. I think I made the right decision. I prefer to come
here. Even though I am quite adapted to the Canadian style
of living, but I still find that it is more easy for me to stay here.
Except that the living standard is not as good as in Canada.

She also expressed a distinct preference for Chinese cuisine:

I: When you cook, do you cook at home now? [P: Yes, I do.] Do
you cook Chinese or Western?

P: Chinese. I really don't enjoy the *gwai lo* very much. Some of
my friends took me to a French restaurant, very expensive. And
I thought that maybe we should use the money to have a long
day of shopping or [eat] at a Chinese restaurant; then maybe it
would be a bit more enjoyable.

Yet another remigrant from Canada spent nine years there as a youth, and
his additive identity now included a global perspective (P15):

I am not attached to one place. The world is globalizing. I am
interested in working in other places. I have a global sense, more than
other Hong Kongers. They don't want to leave, but I wouldn't mind. If
I adjusted to life in Canada, I can adapt to others. I don't care where
I would go, just want good work. Every place has its advantages and
disadvantages. Definitely would consider Canada but other places too.

Another example of a blended identity is that of a male respondent
who immigrated to Australia at age 32. Unlike the other respondents, his
sojourn in Australia was his first travel experience. However, he adapted well
to Australian life, becoming more environmentally aware and interacting
with his Australian friends. He commented (P33):

> I think I brought up my daughter quite the similar way for the parents in Hong Kong. I think I emphasized on the language because I understand that in the future, with the globalization, international people, so I hope my daughter, at least, bilingual: Chinese, Mandarin, Cantonese, and also English. So that's why I prefer her to take her education in an international school because in the grammar schools, although quite tough, like DGS, they are also quite good, but the competition is very high. I think that my daughter can never go into that school. So that's why I select a more easy way and put her into an international school. I prefer my daughter to at least know the language, both English and Chinese. For my accents, are quite difficult for me ... I can write English very well, but speaking, quite difficult for me to have an English speaking accent. I want that my daughter, when she grow up, she can easily communicate with the English and some Western culture and also Chinese culture. That's what I expect my daughter. [I: A good combination.] Yes, a good combination.

When this same respondent was asked to describe who he thinks he is culturally, he gave the following response:

> Yes, primarily Chinese. But I think I have some Western style. I would say I am quite an international man. I think in the future, because of globalization, there is no country barriers. So I think future man, the next generation or the next next generation. I think all the people need to have a globalization mind. There are some international norm there. So that's why I think language is very important, particularly Chinese and English. These two language, you can go everywhere.

These Hong Kong remigrants express in their statements, in their ideas about their identities, and in their actions a cultural narrative that is international and expansive. They are the exemplars of the global identity, finding their psychological home in whichever country they are geographically residing. They develop new friendships and establish professional ties, yet they are always prepared to move on to another country and to begin anew.

Other studies reporting global identities

Although the CIM has not been explicitly tested among remigrants in other countries, characteristics of the global identity can be found in the accounts of returnees captured by other researchers.

Taiwan. In the Chiang and Liao study of returned Taiwanese,[1] 3 out of the 22 respondents described themselves as global citizens or world citizens. They characterized themselves as being able to adapt anywhere and indicated that their friendship networks were diverse in nationality and race. These individuals have been referred to as intercultural or international. Sociologists have used "transcultural identities" to refer to persons who attempt to maintain a cultural attachment to both their home country and their immigration country. This term is similar to "transnationalism" in definition. However, people with global identities transcend home and settlement country. They embrace a vision of self that is borderless.

Japan. A Japanese researcher describes a cultural identity she calls transculturation, which she defines as "a state in which individuals feel less loyal to and less constrained by any of their affiliated cultures."[2] This closely resembles the global identity category in the CIM. She describes one respondent in her study, a Japanese physician in his mid-30s who, accompanied by his wife, was a postdoctoral fellow in the United States. Following their lengthy identity negotiation between Japan and the United States, swinging between an additive and a subtractive identity, he and his wife described themselves as global, or transcultural. After two years in the United States, "Takashi thought that there was 'no heaven or no hell,' and as long as he and his wife could base their core identity as Japanese, they could go into any culture and get by [transculturation]."

Other researchers describe a global identity in terms of a personality trait known as cosmopolitanism, which is defined as "a belief that several cultures, including one's own culture can possess valuable elements; it is an open and at the same time a detached attitude towards several cultures."[3] Cosmopolitanism has been positively associated with open-mindedness, cultural empathy, and social empathy (a belief that there are multiple ways to achieve a given outcome). But it is not clear whether cosmopolitanism develops as a consequence of multiple cultural transitions and adaptations (as the CIM would suggest) or is the outcome of child-rearing practices, of home culture beliefs, or of some other precedent and then motivates individuals toward cultural wanderings.

Hong Kong. Admittedly not all research supports the finding that a small segment of Hong Kongers acquire global identities. Chan's study of 18 remigrants refutes the notion that Hong Kong returnees from Canada are global identifiers.[4] Chan uses Skeldon's terminology, "modern sojourners" (1995), and she defines people with this profile as individuals who ostensibly are willing to move around the world to avail themselves of economic opportunities and who are expected to feel at home anywhere.

In summarizing her respondents, she states, "They do not feel at home anywhere and everywhere and are not prepared to make home anywhere" (p.109). However, her informants were often reluctant returnees to Hong Kong and, simultaneously, "reluctant exiles" in Canada. Chan eventually admits that some of her remigrants *do* report that they are prepared to "make home anywhere," but she dismisses their narratives as naïve and misplaced. After all, she claims, their sense of belongingness in Canada rested on their being able to find "islands of home," or an active Hong Kong diaspora, that would support their adjustment.

Chan's conclusions to the contrary, a few of her respondents do appear to hold global identities. This identity profile does not stipulate overseas adjustment methods — if Hong Kong remigrants describe themselves as being able to live anywhere in the world and if that is accomplished by their establishing strong links with the diaspora community, that is considered a positive coping strategy and the outcome may be a global identity.

Affirmative identity

For a small but significant group of immigrants, the cultural transition to a new country results in the strengthening of their identification with their home country. For them, the entrance into a new culture highlights and explains the values, ways of thinking, interpersonal relations, preferences, and attitudes of their country of origin. They are suddenly aware of themselves as cultural beings and understand their own cultural framework with a new clarity. As we have seen, cultural identity salience is an initial step for identity change for many immigrants. But for a minority, the transition process ends here, with recognition of their home country identity and pride in those values. Psychologists speak of collective self-esteem, of being proud of one's cultural or ethnic group. Those immigrants who experience this cultural identity are referred to as having affirmative cultural identities — the transition experience affirms their existing but unconscious cultural identity and heightens their collective self-esteem.

Hong Kong affirmative identities

To this point in the book, we have discussed three major findings from the Hong Kong Remigration Project. First, the most common identity profile for remigrants is additive, either bicultural or hybrid. Second, the general emotional response to returning to Hong Kong is positive or neutral.

Third, a small portion of returnees experience either subtractive or global identity, and there are specific individual variables that account for those identity responses.

Let us now discuss a fourth, more limited identity result. The affirmative identity profile is predominantly influenced by the age at which migration took place: these individuals migrated either as teenagers or when they were over 40 years old; the latter group was mostly men. The former group was more likely to find repatriation emotionally distressing than did other age groups. Their discomfort may have been due in part to the depth of their immigrant adaptation and to their combined additive/subtractive identity profile.

However, for those who immigrated in middle-age the cultural shifts resulted almost uniformly in affirmative identities — low overseas adaptation, high motivation to return to Hong Kong, and strong desire to remain in Hong Kong. In the HKRP, 6 of the 50 participants (12%) were classified as pure affirmative identifiers as a consequence of their interview responses. The narrative data were confirmed by the psychological scales. Compared to the other identity categories, affirmatives acculturated least to their countries of settlement. They scored the lowest on Western identity and behavior and the lowest on speaking and understanding English and on the amount of English spoken. Affirmatives also had the lowest score on independent self-construal, the second highest score on interdependent self-construal, the highest percentage of relational responses on the TST, and the lowest number of dispositional (or individualistic) responses. Together, these scores indicate low adaptation to the West and a "self" that is perceived as highly group-oriented (Chinese values) and low on individualism (Western values). (See Appendix C for average scores.) Behaviorally, the affirmative identifiers often chose the naming option that was most traditional — Chinese surname followed by Chinese given name. Nearly 50% of the study respondents who chose the traditional naming convention were affirmative identifiers.

The Cultural Identity Model outlines the effects of an identity awareness that emerges during cultural transitions for some immigrants. One consequence is a heightened sense of cultural identity with their homeland.

One returnee, who expressed a strengthening of her Chinese roots during her one year in Canada, became a Buddhist when she returned to Hong Kong (P14). A 46-year-old male "astronaut" who commuted between Canada and Hong Kong for four years before remigrating permanently also claimed that his Chinese identity had intensified (P19):

I: So when you came back here [Hong Kong], you still felt very "Chinese"? You didn't feel like a Canadian person?

P: No. In fact, after that [returning to Hong Kong] I went back to [visit] China more frequently.

Even before he immigrated this same respondent had had a very strong sense of his Chinese identity:

For me, it's just natural. They are not taught in school of Chinese. In my family, I have just told you, my father was very fear of the Communist. So he will go anyway. He didn't told us that we are Chinese. But we just grow up and accept that we are Chinese.

When he was asked about his future plans, his response was characteristic of someone with an affirmative profile:

I: Do you ever think about moving away from Hong Kong anymore? Moving back to Canada?

P: Not for me.

I: You are going to stay in Hong Kong?

P: Yes. When I become older, maybe I move back to China. [I: Why is that?] Because the living standard there is not that high. You can spend less money and still keep your living.

Another male respondent left Hong Kong at age 31 because he was concerned about the political situation and also because he wanted to obtain Australian citizenship. He adapted quite well to life in Australia but maintained his ties to Hong Kong culture. He also reported that his sense of being Chinese got stronger during his Australian sojourn (P35):

P: A big change already. When I left Australia after two years, actually, my sense of belonging to be a Chinese is more than when I live in Hong Kong.

I: So you felt more Chinese?

P: Yes.

I: Explain a little bit to me about that.

P: The same thing in my wife and some of my friends. When we are in Hong Kong, our living style is Hong Kong and we see so many Chinese people. But when we go to Australia, Western living style, we begin to be interested in the Chinese things and also in Australia. There are many Chinese coming from the Mainland China. At that time, it's about 1980, there is about eighteen thousand students studying in Australia, especially in Sydney. And there are also some Chinese people from Australia,

Singapore, South Korea, et cetera. So that, for these people, the link is our race. We are students, and we are Chinese. [I: So you felt this link to all the Mainland Chinese people who were there and the Taiwanese ...?] We associated us together; we have the same living style, same thinking. One thing is that at that time Polly Hanson in 1996, in Queensland, and there started to be some cases of racism in western part of Sydney. So we started to think that we are Chinese. So we think we are more Chinese than in Hong Kong. And one interesting thing is that in Hong Kong we seldom sing the national song of People's Republic of China. But in Australia, when we saw the Olympic Games, et cetera, when the Chinese athletics win the game and the national song sing up, we have a feeling that we belong to China.

That sense of a stronger Chinese identity is evident years after he returned to Hong Kong:

I: Now that you are back from Australia for seven or eight years, how would you describe your cultural identity?

P: I would start to think that I am more Chinese.

A female interviewee left for Canada at age 40 and returned after five years. During those five years, however, she returned to Hong Kong with her family for annual vacations. Even though she admitted to slight changes in her behavior as a result of her sojourn, she still considered herself primarily Chinese (P8):

I: So when you left Canada, you didn't think of yourself as Canadian?

P: Only the passport as Canadian. [I: But inside Hong Kongers?] That's right?

I: And today, you still feel like a Hong Konger when people say who are you? Hong Kong?

P: Yes. It is difficult to change, I think.

Another example of the affirmative profile is in the following comment by a female who immigrated to Canada at age 47 after a divorce. She returned to Hong Kong after one year because she could not find a job and her savings were quickly dwindling. She also reported her dislike of Canadian weather and her feelings of loneliness. Interestingly, she considered herself quite westernized prior to her sojourn to Canada, but once in Canada she discovered that perhaps she was not so westernized after all (P14):

P: I just Hong Kong; I just stay Hong Kong ... [I: Hong Kong person, okay?] Hong Kong. Deep inside me that I don't realize. I thought I was very westernize. But maybe in I still have the Chinese in me. So I don't know. [I: Sometimes you don't discover that till you go to another country.] Yeah, I don't know. I really, while in Hong Kong I thought I really like very westernize. And then until I went there. So I begin to, began to realize that I have something tradition Chinese deep inside me.

She was grateful to have experienced life in another culture, but she also found that the experience made her realize that she belonged in Hong Kong:

I said, well it's good for me in a way I went and I knew the experience. If I never go, and I never might I always have that yearning to go there. Oh, I want to go there; I don't want to stay in Hong Kong. I never realize that I belong here. So now, that close, close, my make up the decision for me, where I belong, what I should do. In a way, it's a good thing. It give me some experience, although it's a bad experience. But it really taught me something.

For a male respondent, who immigrated when he was 31 years old, the plan was simply to move to Australia to gain citizenship and immediately return to Hong Kong. He did not attempt to become integrated into Australian society. His friends were primarily Hong Kongers, and he continued to maintain his usual Hong Kongese lifestyle (P4):

I cannot really interest or affect many ways by the Australian culture, because, as I say, all the friends I met, all the people except work, are really Chinese Hong Kong people. And I don't really watch a lot of Australian TV. I always watch the tape of the Chinese series, movies. And I read Chinese newspaper. I don't read the English newspaper. Except working in a Australia, my life is very much like ... [I: Very Chinese?] Right, yes, very Chinese.

A female respondent left Hong Kong because she believed Canada to be a better place in which to raise her children. However, she quickly became disenchanted with Canada and expressed objections to the Canadian educational system and to the liberal values espoused in the Canadian culture. She found it difficult to adjust to the Canadian pace of life, and she maintained a Hong Kong way of life even as she tried to adapt to Canada. The following is an excerpt from her transcript (P27):

> I: At the point that you decided to leave Canada, how would you have described yourself culturally then?
>
> P: I think I have not much change during the four years.
>
> I: So you would still say "Hong Kong person," not Canadian Hong Kong?
>
> P: I am not a Canadian. Actually, our neighbors living in Canada, they are still carrying their own culture. British is British. Their way of living is British. They would tell us about their native even though they have lived in Canada for many years. Canada is a very lovely place. They allow the cultures to remain there. It's really a multicultural nation. And we love it.

This same respondent's living arrangements once she returned to Hong Kong are also typical of the affirmative profile:

> I: Describe a little bit about that readjustment. Did you feel stress or anxiety when coming back? What was it like emotionally during these first few weeks or months?
>
> P: I was just too busy to think about it. Because we have a lot of things to do. We've got to settle down, carrying my daughter who is two year old then. It is a big struggle, so we don't have time to think that we cannot adjust the changes. But it's a home place; it's feeling get back home.
>
> I: So it felt good? Where did you decide to live when you came back? Did you think of what kind of neighborhood do you want to live in?
>
> P: Just near to my mother-in-law because she would take care of my daughter.

Affirmative identifiers are described by the Cultural Identity Model as being "grateful repatriates," happy to return to their home country, to be surrounded once again by family and compatriots. Quantitative data confirmed this emotional response among the Hong Kong affirmatives identifiers. They scored the lowest on the Repatriation Distress Scale and the second highest on the Satisfaction with Life Scale. In other words, as a group, the affirmative identifiers were happy to be back home in Hong Kong. A male interviewee aptly described this emotion (P4):

> I am happy to be back. I mean, first of all my family is here. My wife, my mother, my father, my sister, everyone is here. And, this, the feeling you have in Australia is really ... I am not sad by really feel lonely because anytime I go into my house, it's me alone. No one there.

Immigrating to Australia at age 28 and returning after three years, another male returnee mentioned that he had not quite fit into Australian society and was happy to return to Hong Kong. Like many of the other respondents with affirmative profiles he commented on feeling more Chinese after his overseas sojourn (P39):

> The Chinese culture, the tie become stronger and stronger because now that I live in Hong Kong, with the proximity with China, with the media, more and more Chinese news, I get to understand Chinese a bit more. I guess I have become even more Chinese. I would still describe myself as Hong Kong people, but I would probably say I am a Hong Kong Chinese.

This same respondent went on to say:

> P: I guess a bit more differently is my thinking of myself of being more a Chinese person of a Chinese heritage. In that three years, one thing that caught me by surprise is that I find myself asking the question "Who am I?" quite often. And I start asking myself, Where is my root? The more I know I won't be very happy staying in Australian forever, that I more wanted to come back to Hong Kong to be more myself. I can't explain it in an logical way, but it's just the search for who am I.
>
> I: That's very interesting. Tell me more about that. What did you discover about your Chineseness, your Chinese roots? What parts of you were Chinese?
>
> P: I guess the experience living in Sydney actually satisfied my curiosity of how it is like living aboard and what is mean by foreign culture. The more I stay in Sydney, the more I found the importance of friends and family. My family are all in Hong Kong. My friends, most of them have migrated to Canada, Australia, Singapore … There are still a lot of friends in Hong Kong. And I still have a lot of friends in Hong Kong.

A female reacted similarly to returning home (P14): *"I felt so happy [to return to Hong Kong]. I ate wonton soup you know, quite happy. Relief."*

Many affirmative identifiers found the migrant experience uncomfortable and disturbing. Thus one female respondent who immigrated to Canada at age 19 found the experience was not entirely positive. She spent ten years in Vancouver, during which time she attended university and worked for a year. She had high praise for the Canadian education system but found the Canadian work ethic and pace of life intolerable. She also claimed that it was difficult to make friends with the locals; thus, her friends were mostly Hong Kong immigrants. The following are a few excerpts from her interview (P26):

> P: I think that, after nine years, I am still very Hong Kong style. [I: Like what?] Like habits, like eating, the food that I eat. I still like Chinese food more than Western food. The lifestyle. I still watch Hong Kong TV more than Canadian TV. The clothing style still …
>
> I: So by the time you were ready to leave Canada in 2004, if I would have met you a few months ago, now how would you describe who you are culturally?
>
> P: Now, [I: Or the last year before you left?] still very Hong Kong style. [I: So you wouldn't say you were Canadian Hong Kong or …] No, I won't say. [I: So you still feel very Hong Kong?]

She also commented about being bored with the Canadian work style and that she was very excited to be returning to Hong Kong. Once she was back in Hong Kong, she stated that she felt very comfortable and felt as though she was finally home:

> I found that I am very Hong Kong, Hong Kongese. [I: So you feel like you're home?] Yes. [I: That this is the place you belong?] Yes, I feel very comfortable here. Especially for communications. Because it is easier for communicate in Cantonese for me than in English, so … [I: Even though your English is quite good?] But I still found that my English is not good enough. I move in Vancouver when my age is like nineteen, so and I don't have a lot of English. I don't have, don't even got English friends in Canada, so I don't think my English is good enough to have even social talk or good communication or speaking deeper things. So speaking Cantonese, I am very comfortable, easy for me to express myself. It's good, easier. [I: It feels good to be back.] Yeah. It feels good.

Affirmative/additive combination

An unexpected finding of the HKRP was that 10% of the respondents seemed to have a blend of affirmative and additive profiles. These respondents typically said that although they enjoyed living in Canada or in Australia, that they often engaged in leisure activities typical of that culture, and that they had adjusted to some degree to life in a foreign country, they still found their Hong Kong–Chinese identity strengthened by the experience. The following is an excerpt from one of the respondents with a combined identity profile. He immigrated to Canada at age 43 with his wife and two children. He lived there for about four years and seemed to adjust quite well. He even maintained some aspects of Canadian life after returning to Hong Kong. However, when asked about his identity he said (P40): *"As what I see, we are Chinese, always Chinese. We were born to have some sort of Chinese thinking. That's what I believe."* This same respondent also claimed to be *"One hundred percent Hong Kongese."*

Another example of the blended profile is a female interviewee who returned from Australia after three years there with her husband. She admitted to feeling like she had been discriminated against on occasion but still found elements of the Australian culture that she enjoyed. She eventually obtained citizenship and commented that she was *"happy to be Australian."* However, some aspects of her life indicated that she had developed an affirmative identity (P46):

I: Now that you've been back eight years, how do you think of yourself now from a cultural point of view?

P: Hong Kong people. [I: So not like an Australian?] Not like an Australian.

I: Do you think any friends or family or coworkers think that you act Australian now?

P: No.

I: So nobody said you act like a *gwai lo?*

P: Yeah, no, no, no. Because I have been there just three years. Maybe thirty years I will, they will say that.

Yet another example is a female who immigrated to Australia at age 33. Prior to this, however, she had spent some time in Toronto pursuing a college degree. She reported enjoying life in Australia, but her intent was to eventually return to Hong Kong. She explicitly stated that although she became familiar with the Australian culture, she had no intention of blending in (P48):

I: So in 1995, before you came back, right? You and I meet again, and at that point how would you have describe who you were culturally?

P: In '95? ... Oh, yeah. I thought I believed that I know the way the people there, how they live. But I at that period of time, I didn't prepare for, I didn't prepare to mix.

I: So you think of yourself as Chinese or Hong Kongers? Or? Which or some combination, Hong Kong–Chinese?

P: I think I, because today I definitely know that I am still Chinese. But at that time I know that I got a passport, and I know the

> I: lifestyle there. And but, because my I think my life value is still
> moving forward, moving forward. So I think going to Australia
> only give me a passport.
>
> I: Okay, so it didn't change the way you, what culture influence
> your everyday. You still acted and thought Chinese? Right?
>
> P: Yeah. I would say, yeah. I would say that Hong Kong.

This same respondent commented on her friends' awareness of the changes in her attitudes; however, she claimed that inside she continued to feel Chinese:

> P: I like being so exploring and positive in life attitude, and I quite
> like it. But when I come back, well most of my friends say that
> I'm quite Western, in terms of I think appearance. But inside
> me I am a Chinese. I definitely know …
>
> I: But when you say appearance, the way that you act?
>
> P: Yes, the way I act. But I gradually find that I am a totally, one
> hundred percent Chinese.

Affirmative identity responses from other returnees

Taiwan. In Chiang and Liao's study of Taiwanese returnees, the majority of the 22 respondents described themselves in additive terms.[5] However, one articulate woman, who lived for 13 years in Australia, embodied the affirmative identity:

> Being in Taiwan give me a sense of belonging … I missed Taiwan the
> first year I arrived in Australia [at the age of 10]. I always think that
> Taiwan is my home. I return to Taiwan every Christmas, to keep up
> with what is going on here and experience the sense of fulfillment.
> Memory of childhood stays back in Taiwan. Right from the beginning,
> I said that I will come back after graduation. I just cannot find my sense
> of belonging in Australia.

India. Hansel's study of Indian returnees, discussed in Chapter 5, reported that most of her sample experienced an additive identity in which American and Indian values either were blended or resulted in bicultural individuals.[6] However, a minority found their Indian identity confirmed through the cultural transition process. Some students returned home when they realized that they belonged and felt comfortable in India. "I suddenly realized that I like India," explained one returnee. Many reported that they did not have to apologize for living in India as they had often felt compelled to do when they were living in the United States. One female returnee realized that the Indian values of family support and group interdependence were very important to her. She had felt isolated living in California and described herself as having "values sickness." In India, she explained, "Even when you buy vegetables you talk to the person. So even living alone you can have all these levels of human interaction, which I wasn't getting there [in the U.S.]. I felt like I was living in a sort of vacuum, where even if I wanted to meet with what I would call in those terms a close friend, I'd have to make an appointment for lunch. You can't drop in at people's places … Here I am happy [back in India]. I'm more relaxed. I just like being an Indian in India" (p. 14).

Other returnees in the Hansel study were not as articulate about their Indian cultural affirmation but subtly revealed it through their comments. Many were delighted to return to the warmth and security of their extended families after living alone and isolated in the United States. Despite spending years in an individualistic, self-reliant society, these returnees did not hesitate to accept Indian values and norms: to move in with their families, accede to their parents' wishes regarding arranged marriages, or follow parental career advice. Most of the returnees expressed psychological comfort in and embraced the mutual dependence of the Indian family.

The affirmative identity among many Indian returnees was not simply a time-sensitive reflection of the 1980s. A recent case study underscores the enduring affirmative experience. Harsh Manglik was a senior executive of an American high-tech consulting company who, after 35 years of education and career building, returned to live and work in India.[7] His father's dying prediction was that his son, Harsh, would one day recognize that his roots and soul were in India and would return. Soon after his father's death, Manglik accepted the top position at a US firm's Indian operation and he and his wife made the move back to India. Affirmation of their Indian heritage began immediately, as Manglik's wife, long referred to as Sally, resurrected her Indian name, Madhuri.

Israel. A recent study interviewed 30 Israeli remigrants who had lived abroad for at least four years.[8] These well-educated, professionally employed returnees, who generally had school-aged children, were similar in many ways to the Hong Kong remigrants. Whereas several reasons for the Israelis' return surfaced (including aging parents and enticing job offers), a primary motivation was the need to ensure that their children developed an Israeli identity. This is a concrete manifestation of the affirmative identity developed by many of the respondents. Living overseas "had the effect of reinforcing their identification with the country of origin [Israel]." In particular, Israelis living in the United States were more religiously observant than they were when living in Israel. They lit Sabbath candles, attended synagogue, fasted on Yom Kippur, and celebrated Chanukah. Their conversation topics tended toward Israeli politics and social issues. Their immigrant or sojourn experiences abroad highlighted for them and made salient their Israeli identity. Upon remigration, their emotional response was positive for the most part. The remigrants embraced the closeness of family and friends, although job satisfaction served as a moderating variable. If they found their job to be fulfilling and rewarding, their re-entry adjustment was easy and they achieved a sense of belonging to the society. If the remigrants had employment problems, their psychological adjustment was affected in several ways. These issues are discussed in more detail in Chapter 9, on remigrants' professional life.

Japan. Research investigating Japanese student returnees suggests that a "strategic affirmative" cultural identity may be pursued; one might call it an additive identity in affirmative clothing.[9] Students who studied in countries that valued individualism and separation from the social network returned to Japan exhibiting higher collectivist (or regard for the social group) thinking than students who never left Japan. It was suggested that because they were keenly aware of the rigid norms in Japan for collectivist social behavior, the returnees may have manifested overly collectivist or affirmative thinking and behavior as a tactic to fit back into Japanese society.

A similar adjustment and identity response occurred during a study I conducted in Japan in 1985.[10] A Japanese corporate repatriate relayed this tale to me. While living in Los Angeles, he came to enjoy reading *Newsweek* magazine. He wanted to continue reading this weekly periodical when he returned to Tokyo, but he knew that those who observed him reading the magazine would judge him negatively as being too Western. He imagined that they would interpret his choice of reading material as boastful in either flaunting his English fluency or subtly indicating his international background and therefore underscoring the domestic and limited perspectives of his coworkers. His concern carried over to the imagined attributions of complete strangers who might observe him reading *Newsweek* in the crowded subway car during his commute. His solution? He folded the English-language magazine into the center of a typical Japanese adult comic book, thus conforming to social expectations of a "strategic affirmative" identity but maintaining a hybrid additive identity privately.

8 Remigrants and family life

Just as migration can change the social landscape of a country in the domains of social structure, religion, language, and politics,[1] so can return migration. Macro-level shifts will invariably occur in Hong Kong as a result of the unprecedented number of returnees. However, micro-level, individual transformations are the source of the larger societal changes. In particular, remigrants have altered their values and their beliefs about family life and relationships between spouses, parents and children, and siblings — the core relationships in traditional Chinese culture.

For example, one might speculate that social institutions such as marriage can be shattered through the experience of migration and then return to Hong Kong. One study of women and divorce in Hong Kong found that the divorce rate, which was 0.76 per 1,000 in 1984, jumped to 2.0 per 1,000 by 1999.[2] Although the investigators suggest many possible explanations, one that they did not discuss is the fact that this was the exact time period of the largest return migration to Hong Kong. While divorce surely has multiple causes, the changes in expectations and individual aspirations, and the altered geographic arrangements (astronaut phenomenon) of married couples returning to Hong Kong no doubt contributed to the escalation in the divorce rate.

Nuclear and extended family relationships

Traditional Chinese culture endows family relationships with the highest importance. A key relation is the husband-wife dyad, for it represents not only the start of a new family but also the continuity of two extended family lines. The woman's central roles were to bear children, serve her husband's family, maintain the household, and sustain loyalty; the husband's role was to provide sustenance. Thus marriage combined reproduction and economics. Preserving the stability and harmony of the newest families was a priority, especially for the husband's family.[3]

In the 150 years of British rule in Hong Kong, Western ideas of romantic love and gender equality were introduced into husband-wife relationships. The turn of the twenty-first century saw vast changes in the roles both partners played within a marriage. These changes coincided with the other societal upheavals, including the large-scale immigration and remigration of Hong Kongers.

Often, prior to their remigration to Hong Kong, immigrant families led a boomerang type lifestyle. Husbands flew between their country of resettlement and Hong Kong throughout the year, with their wives and children joining them in Hong Kong during summer holidays and at the Lunar New Year. Eventually, as an initially temporary work situation became permanent, the families would choose to reunite in Hong Kong to preserve their relationships. But time together soon proved to be as difficult for them as time apart.

One female who immigrated to Canada described her strained relationship with her husband once she returned to Hong Kong. He had gone back to Hong Kong some time earlier, while she had remained in Canada (P28):

> My relationship with my husband is quite difficult to adjust. We separate for a long time that he live his own life and I live with my own life. When I come back, I am not so happy because he usually go out mostly of the time. When I come back I want to have somebody to talk; it's quite different for a few months. But after it I just back, then it's okay.

Other respondents found the Western model of marriage appealing. They particularly liked that it encouraged spouses to spend their leisure time together. The differences between the Western model and the Hong Kong style were stark, as highlighted by a male interviewee who immigrated to Australia with his wife. Now that they were both back in Hong Kong, and living what he called a "stressful life," he remembered their more enjoyable times spent in Australia (P33):

> I quite miss the relationship with my wife when we both stayed in Australia. We have only two person there. We enjoyed the life, and we don't have any working pressure. When we were in Australia, everything was new to us, and every Saturdays and Sundays we have visit every place, and we enjoy the life.

A female interviewee who returned from Canada with her husband and children described the changes in her relationship with her husband now that they were together again in Hong Kong (P47):

> Especially when my husband was jobless, we have all the time staying together. We go together to pick up the kids, and sometimes we go to market together, even though he also has his own time around the computer. But still we have a lot of time staying with the family. Or the night time, it's not so tired; then we can watch a movie. We can sleep late because if we are tired, we can have some rest during the day. But in Hong Kong, you are very tired, but you still have to go out everyday to do something. That is the different way of life. That's why I found the Hong Kong way of life stressful. Even though on holiday, you are filled up with functions and activities, you would fully utilize your time.

Traditional aspects of marriage again became relevant, and those returnees who had been changed by the migration experience chafed at the expectations. One female respondent who returned with her husband from Australia after five years expressed her discomfort with her role in her extended family (P36):

> I: When you first came back, once you felt emotionally better, in terms of your personal life, did you then sort of [make] any cultural adjustment to being back? Are there any ways in which you discover you are more Australian than you thought, or there are certain Australian behaviors that you either have to change or didn't want to change?
>
> P: Not interference. But sometime I thought there's an infringement on my freedom and individuality, when I was back to Hong Kong, just like my in-laws' family, as they are quite wealthy in a way, so they take good care of the kids, they buy them flats, say; for example, my in-law even cook the breakfast and put it in front of our flat so that my husband could have breakfasts. She has a good intention, but at that time, I thought, "What is that mean? Does it mean that I won't cook breakfast for him?!" But she takes care of everything, trying to be helpful. She has a good intention, but in a way … I still, but you don't go back there for dinner, or even during the weekends, usually

> they have gatherings together. Sometimes I strike over that and not happy about that and say, "I just don't want to be together all the time." But the Chinese culture, the family want to be together. The togetherness sometimes suffocate me. But with age, nowadays, I don't quite mind. I find the way in between. And also, when I grow older, especially with kids, sometimes I become more mature, and I try to appreciate their helpfulness. They help a lot. So I come to see that it's not so black and white. But in reality, individualism and collectivism sometimes you have to make a balance.

Another example is this female respondent, who returned with her two daughters from Canada after four years. She described the relationship between her children and their "very Chinese" grandparents (P5):

> I think that the immediate family is very close, but the extended family is not. Simply because we have much time to spend together. My daughters actually don't have very good relationship with their grandmother on my husband side, mainly because she is very, very traditional Chinese. And my daughters are very westernized. When in fact most of my husband's family are all very traditional Chinese. Very, very Chinese …

She described the Chinese grandparents in the following way:

> They were more conservative … [I: About moral standards?] Not very accepting of things that are different. When my daughters have family gatherings when they are back, unfortunately they feel very uncomfortable with that … They [the children] feel they are like outsiders.

A female respondent who returned from Australia after four and a half years described her guilt over her lack of time to spend with her parents now that she was back in Hong Kong (P43):

> When I return back to Hong Kong, I would try to, even though timewise I cannot do so; but when I cannot do so, I feel guilty. I try to have more time with them. But in Hong Kong you don't have a lot of places to go. People only go out for dinner. There's not much countryside for you to go to. But right now, if I have time in a year, I usually would go one or two trips with my parents, long or short. But in Australia, it's easy. Friday night, drive the car, and go to some suburb and stay there for one or two days, have some resort somewhere. So I often go out with my parents when I was in Australia. That kind of tradition, you can say that. When come back and I don't have time, I feel guilty.

A female respondent who left Hong Kong at age 18 for Canada spoke of her struggle both to assert her independence and to please her parents (P22):

> It's like an internal struggle, because at that time I kind of had an arrangement that I would like to get married with my French-Canadian boyfriend. And his whole family they met me in Quebec, in Montreal, in Toronto, and I knew all his family, his parents, brothers sisters; everybody they all accept me and love me a lot. But then my mother, my mother side, she could not accept anything. I even suggest that, oh, mom, let's come out with my boyfriend for lunch or for dinner. My mom reject, so I try so many different things for them to get together. But my mother she just couldn't accept any of the suggestions.

Because of her mother's refusal to accept her relationship with her boyfriend, the interviewee eventually ended it.

Relationships between parents and children

Another critical traditional family relationship is that between a parent and a child. Historically, Chinese parents received the utmost of respect from their children, a way of behaving known as filial piety. Parents also had near complete authority over children's decision making, whether in selecting a mate or a career. Both the British influence and modernity have modified these customs, but Hong Kong parents still have more control over their children than do Western parents. The life of this young woman, who emigrated at age 14 to Canada and lived there for nine years, exemplified Chinese parents' involvement with their children (P16):

> I think I behave most, like most teenagers, rebellion, just don't want to follow rules. But I do seek their [her parents'] advice. Like even I apply university, even though they couldn't really give me a lot of advice, I still keep them up to date. I have them consent about what faculty I want to go into, what university I want to choose. I guess that's considered to be very Chinese.

A male interviewee who also emigrated to Canada as a teenager explained why he had returned to Hong Kong (P32):

> I finish my degree and that when I have to make another big decision. Whether I want to work in Canada or in Hong Kong. And that decision I have, actually my parents kind of helped me. I was thinking about going to Hong Kong for the reason that now I finish my degree,

basically complete my mission to Canada. And my parents in Hong Kong and I want to spend more time with parents. So I decided to come back to Hong Kong ... My dad helped me because he actually got me a job.

Many Hong Kong emigrants to Canada and Australia made cultural adjustments that included substantial changes in their parenting patterns. Return migration highlighted these shifts and in some instances caused distress. Yet although returnees reverted to a more Hong Kong style of spousal roles and relations, they resisted a return to traditional parenting styles, choosing to maintain Western-style relationships with their children. One factor that no doubt influenced this decision was the extent to which their children had embraced the Western model of adolescent behavior.

One male who had lived in Canada for four years (P42) remarked:

I try to be friend with my children. Not like, "I am your father, you have to listen to me." Always try to always try tell them I love them. "I love you." Like I think people, Chinese, sometimes never say they love their children, very shy, or whatever. I try change in child rearing two or three times per year, just try to enjoy my life with them and I know even I want to stick with them but when they get older they may go away.

A female interviewee left Hong Kong for Australia and returned after four years (P2):

I: So your husband is involved in raising the children?
P: Yeah, we have lots of discussion with the kids, of what they wanted, try to talk to them. You know, not like the ordinary way, the traditional Chinese, "You got to do this or that," you know.
I: So, for instance, when it comes to the children thinking about their careers, would you say, "I like you to do this, like become a doctor"?
P: No. You should tell them [do] whatever you like, as long as you think it makes you happy. It can be a chef, even a chef, or whatever you like. It's quite open. And my daughter, she is talking about her boyfriend with me. She's only fourteen anyway. I am just scared when she talks about it. She talk about her boyfriends. And my younger son, he's nine years old. He talk about his girlfriend. [I: They start very young.] Yeah. It's quite open actually.

She also described her nonmigrating Hong Kong friends' astonishment at the open relationship she has with her teenage daughter:

I think we are more Western because of my experience, a bit open. Like, for example, I can see one things is there is an occasion we have barbecue party at home. And my daughter ask me if it's possible to bring my friends, that means her boyfriend, home? That's her boyfriends. That's fine. Bring him home. I want to talk to him as well. And then at that moment we have other family as well, the relatives, this and that. I can tell when they see that I allow my daughter to bring her boyfriend home, they are a bit astonished. But they can't say "Out." To me, I think it's okay; actually, I want to talk to him to see how he's like. Seems like they're astonished how come you are so open and let her bring the boyfriend home.

A third female interviewee immigrated to Canada at age 33 and returned after four years. She reminisced about the activities she could engage in with her daughter while they lived in Canada (P27):

I am quite sorry about that, because I didn't have enough time spending with her. If we were in Canada, we might have some time to spend with other families. We go outing. We go to other places. We let her run around. Things like that. But we just don't have enough time. Talking about the Easter holiday, I enjoyed very much because I have some time spending with her. Not much during other days.

She also described how, now that she was back in Hong Kong, she tried as much as possible to recreate that atmosphere, including allowing her daughter to go to parks and playgrounds. She expressed regret that she and her husband no longer had as much time to spend with their child as they had while in Canada:

I: But how about your husband's spending time with your daughter and with you. Has that changed?

P: Yes, both of us are too busy, so ... Yeah, that's a big change. My daughter has to spend time with her grandmother all by herself.

I: Do you ever feel that you don't want to work so hard?

P: Definitely. That's what I look for.

A male respondent who returned to Hong Kong from Australia after two years described how he now believed that he should respect his children and allow them to make their own decisions (P49):

We just give them advice. When they grow up, just like Hong Kong Chinese just try to control everything of their children. But we learn from Australia that we should respect our children. But we can guide them, just as you said.

Another male remigrant from Australia (P37) also commented on allowing his children to make their own decisions:

> Hong Kong Chinese will ask the kid to do a lot of extra curricular activities which the kid may not want to go or do. But we pretty much adopt a kind of laissez-faire approach and we would not ask the kid to do something which apparently they don't like to do. Just like my sister [who didn't immigrate], she keep asking her daughter to practice piano, dancing, choir singing ... You never know whether the kid think this kind of things. I don't think I would take that approach. I think I would adopt a laissez-faire policy: if my son wants to learn piano, I will get him a teacher to teach him how to do piano. If he want to do sports, I can play with you and get a coach to teach you how to do it.

A male respondent returned to Hong Kong after four years in Canada. He described his experience parenting his "Canadian" son (P38):

> In terms of family, I think is quite different, especially in terms of parenting. In fact, very different, because my son went to Canada when he was three. When we went back he was ten, so basically he has received seven years of Canadian education. So I guess deep in his heart, he is more a Canadian than a Chinese. And obviously he would not accept the Chinese way of parenting, which I was brought up. Unfortunately, initially, I was still trying to institute those kind of Chinese teaching, thinking, Chinese moral standard to him. [I: Even in Canada, or when you got back?] In Canada and when I got back, both. But I guess it is more so when I got back here. But, unfortunately, it didn't work out. So actually, I have one point in mind. I have quite sore relationship with my son, because of this conflicting. So I guess in the past two years I decide I got a Canadian son, I had to do the Canadian way. [I: So what is the Canadian way? How was that?] Basically, you treat the children as equal, rather than like the traditional Chinese way of father-son relationship.

Another male interviewee who had immigrated to Canada also commented on his parenting style and on changes in his children (P31):

> They [his children] have their own privacy at home. And they have their own car and everything. Actually, we spoiled them. Gradually, they became too Canadianized because it's hard to tell them the Chinese way of thinking. They have their own thinking there. They have their way for school. [I: So what was that Canadian way of thinking?] They still respect us as their parents. And, of course, they don't bother tell you what they want to do, and they don't bother just like the Canadians and Americans. They have their own way of life.

Another male who returned from Australia after three years also described his changed relationship with his children (P39):

> I became more appreciative of the importance of having their ... individualism. They have their own strength. They have their own style and future. So it become more important not to just train them to have technical skills, but to develop them in a all-round manner, to let them think and be more creative and have more exposure so that they can find their way.

School decisions

Hong Kongers have a variety of schooling options for their children: private or public, religious or secular, international or country-specific. Although many returnees choose to return to Hong Kong in part to ensure that their children will maintain Cantonese linguistic fluency, they also want them to preserve their English skills and to learn Mandarin. Parents strategically plan to raise global children. To achieve this goal, the majority of parents choose either international schools (e.g., the English Schools Foundation or the Chinese International School) or Western-curriculum-based schools oriented toward a specific country (e.g., the Canadian School; the Australian School; or the Hong-Kong International School, which follows an American curriculum). Linguistic competence was not the only rationale for parents' educational choices. Following years of living in the West, Hong Kong parents enthusiastically accepted a model of education that highlighted Western values. Most prominent were pedagogical techniques that reinforced independence of action, critical thinking, the challenging of authority (the teacher), and self-reliance. Rote memorization, exam-based curriculum, reserved demeanor, and obedience to teachers were nearly absent from the Canadian and Australian classrooms.

The decision regarding choice of school was explained by this female respondent who returned from Australia after five years (P36):

> P: Because, in the long run, we do think that we would move back to Australia, so I want her English to be polished, and also because I don't quite like the Hong Kong education system.
>
> I: What is that you don't like, and what is that you like about EFS system?
>
> P: The system [Hong Kong education system] now is even worse than when I was in before. Even like the product, the education system here, university students, like in this university, I didn't

think that they are quite up to par but, of course, there's related to ... In the past Hong Kong, there are only two universities, so it's quite a elite system, but now ... [I: Democratization of education, meaning more people in the past would not have gone to university are going now.] That's true. But it's just that I think the government and the education department now changes their policies too often. I guess the teachers, and also it's too exam-oriented, I don't quite like that. Because a lot of kids lose their motivation to study, and in my opinion, I think that if you don't kill their motivation, then they might believe that they are able to learn in the long way as much as possible. I think that's very important, and as far as I can see, a lot of the students in the local education system in the local school, they don't like study at all. They hate going to school, and I don't want my kid to hate going to school. And they don't like reading books, so I think that really horrible.

One male interviewee, returning from Australia after two and a half years, explained his decision to send his daughter to an international school in the following way (P33):

Yes. That's why I put my daughter into an international school. I think, of course, I prefer my daughter, if possible, she can study in Hong Kong. I also have planned, may be she need to have her education in Australia as well. So that's why I have planned my daughter's education development. I put her in an international school in Hong Kong, hope if she could get into a university in Hong Kong, okay, fine. If she cannot get into a university in Hong Kong, she also has the opportunity to study in Australia.

A female respondent who returned from Australia after two years explained her struggle to navigate between her traditional Chinese ways of behaving and Australian influences (P48):

P: I think I try to learn, make myself to learn the meaning, the meanings of life. Enjoy the process everyday. Not really aiming at the result. But it's, of course, it's worry. My heart will be worry and trouble because, oh, is that way can be okay, is that being irresponsible? Because what I am doing. [I: Am I being a good parent by doing this?] Yeah, all the way I bought up is different. Because every Hong Kong people bought up is like the same. Very objective oriented, and so this sort of value will be like a change relationship. Carry for every generation, every generation, every generation ...

I: But you made a decision, for instance, to send your children to a ESF school? Why did you do that?

P: I think I am a part of it from, westernize person. I tried every different way to, I really want to explore, is this okay? This way can be okay? This way better than this way or? I always want to try so my kids are my experiment.

Another remigrant from Australia explained his decision to send his children to an international school (P23):

P: I have a good relationship with my parents. And also my wife's parents. But I realize that we have cultural gap with our children. [I: Could you describe that?] Probably, as I said, my heart is Chinese. Our activities, our behavior are not that Chinese. Like we don't give too much constraint to our kids. We let them do what they want unless they cross the boundary. So this is the way we grow our kids.

I: So you think that is some more Western style?

P: Yes. And my kids are attending international schools. It's not because they couldn't take the local school, but we don't like putting exams and marks as a priority. Most local schools work very hard.

I: So you didn't want just an exam as the reflection of education?

P: Exactly.

In the excerpt that follows, he described what he saw as the difference between traditional Chinese education and the education offered by the international school:

I: And what is it about the education styles of those schools that you like? Why was it appealing to you?

P: That kind of schools, actually, they learn lots of general knowledge. And different kind of thinking. [I: Can you describe that different kind of thinking?] I think that is reflected from my children doing class projects. They read a lot of materials; they search facts and figures from different source. After that, presenting the report is also very fun.

Another example is an interviewee who returned to Hong Kong with his wife and children after four years in Canada. He explained his decision to send his son to an international school in the following way (P38):

To minimize the impact to them as much as possible. That's why I would try to put them in Canadian school. Actually, is my son, because

my daughter wasn't reach the school age yet. When she came back, she
was three; when we came back she also three, wasn't at school then. So
she's not a big problem. But nevertheless I still put her in international
school. But for the son, because he was at grade five or grade six the
time when we came back, he's a bit worry of the Chinese. He cannot
read any Chinese at all. So to me, if I have to put him in a local school,
it's almost impossible task. So, basically, I have no choice but to put
him in a Canadian school. And also, as I said, my original intention is
that I only come back two years to stay for a few years, five, six years.
That was my think at that time, so he needs to go back anyway. So
I would try to minimize any destruction to his school. So that's the
reason I put him in international school.

A male respondent who returned to Hong Kong with his wife and
kids set out the difference between the Canadian and Hong Kong
education system (P42):

I want them to know the outside world, first things is. Second things is
to me Canadian education is more creative. Hong Kong education is
very, you know, that's reading, reading, reading. I can tell my daughter's
quite creative; my son is, like me, very stubborn, not too creative. So
I want them to look at particular system. And to me Canada is a good
place for study. I know, good quality of teacher, people friendly, a lot of
space, more practical learning, rather than Hong Kong just textbook,
textbook, textbook.

Residential choices: Apartments and neighborhoods

Returned migrants faced other major decisions besides where to educate
their children. One that affected the entire family was where to live? Hong
Kong is composed of geographic areas, some of which are distinctively
different — Hong Kong Island, Kowloon, New Territories, Lantau Island
— and some of which are more subtly dissimilar — Wan Chai or Happy
Valley. One constant was the high price of real estate. Hong Kongers who
emigrated in the early 1990s left a depressed housing market, whereas
returnees who sold in Canada or Australia in the late 1990s and early 2000s
found real estate prices low in those countries and a rebounding housing
market in Hong Kong.

For some returnees, there was no choice of residence despite any
preference they might have to live somewhere else. These were the families
who had maintained an apartment in Hong Kong throughout their
immigration. In their absence, a relative or friend may have been living

there. In rare cases, the apartment remained vacant and was used by the family during its Hong Kong holidays and vacations. Some remigrants, while no longer homeowners, felt compelled to choose a flat located near an elderly parent. But these were in the minority. The majority of the returnees viewed the housing choice with one clear objective: Where can I duplicate the living experience I enjoyed in Sydney or Toronto? This translated into flats with larger rooms in a quiet neighborhood and with access to green space, parks, and outside leisure activities. For some, this goal also meant a neighborhood with an international presence, by virtue of either its residents or its shops and services.

Returning from Canada after eight and a half years, a female interviewee described her choice of neighborhood in the following excerpt (P29):

I: So is your apartment, is it very international, or is it primarily Chinese who lived there?

P: Right now, as I moved back to Happy Valley. We used to live in that building before, and my husband like the place, quiet and the view is good. So we bought a house in Happy Valley. The same house before we moved. But it was higher in the thirtieth floor.

I: So you lived in the Mid-Levels initially. Was that an international environment?

P: Yes. There are a lot of English people. It's very convenient because of the walk. The escalator. That's why.

I: But then you moved to Happy Valley because it was more green?

P: Not too crowded. More space in that area.

I: How about that? Is it also sort of an international neighborhood?

P: Yes. There are a lot of international people. But most of them are rented out. Some of them are rented out to the overseas people.

This female respondent immigrated to Canada at age 36 and returned with her husband and children (P47):

The big difference is, while we are in Canada, we have a peaceful time. More spacious, even though in the house. In Hong Kong, we have less space, even the kids. Sometimes they already adopt the habit to eat in front of the TV. But in Canada, we usually eat in the kitchen, and we don't have a TV in the kitchen. So it's good, we talk. And now I would say, "I would stop the TV because we have no time over the dinnertime we can talk about what's happening in school." And in Canada we drive them and pick them from school ourselves. So there's a lot of time that we are together. But it seems that back to Hong Kong everyone is much more busier. But not because of their homework. They have their own corners. They play on their games. They are attracted by the TV ... It's not so peaceful as before. I really feel more stressful. Even though I am not working now, but I find that once I go out on the street, I take the transport and I give into the MTR, I want to get something from the shop ... all are stressful. Much more stressful than in Canada. It's much more peaceful there. You can have space, not like in Hong Kong. That's why our whole family is still looking forward to go back.

She also explained her family's decision to move to Hong Kong Island. The neighborhood was quite international, and, she claimed:

> We found that it's quite easy for us to adapt to that. Before we moved in, we don't know there are so much expatriates, or I think there is quite a lot of families like us. I know a Taiwan family, one other family who has kids in the same school with my daughter.

One male respondent returned to Hong Kong after four years in Canada with his wife and children. Prior to his sojourn in Canada, he traveled to the United Kingdom and the United States. His choice of a neighborhood was motivated by the desire to replicate what he called "Canadian style" (P40):

> P: But in Hong Kong there are some other place, like the Peak, Mid-Levels, and then Yau Yat Chuen area, Kowloon Tong, quite nice. Where the sort of overseas type of environment.
> I: So you decide to live in a place that wasn't so crowded?
> P: That's right. [I: So that's why you move to Kowloon Tong?] Yes. Select the Yau Yat Chuen so you can drive your car to the car park and then go up stairs. It's all under cover, very Canadian style.

Another example is provided by a female respondent who returned from Australia after two and a half years (P1):

> I: What about your decision of where to live when you get back to Hong Kong? Where did you go? Did you say that you wanted to be with your family in a very Hong Kong neighborhood, or an international neighborhood, or ...?
> P: Well, I didn't decide whether ... because it is hard to pinpoint somewhere to live. The point is, we want to find a place not too crowded. Because we are used to the Australian way, not too crowded. So we want to get somewhere not too crowded. So we picked Ma On Shan, because that place is a newly developed

suburb, not so crowded, not too many buildings, something like that. And there is a nice beach over there, and a park over there, and it seems like I am in Australia.

I: Are there many of your neighbors who've lived in other countries?

P: Yes. Some Japanese, Koreans, and even some Western; I think they are expatriates. [I: And even some Chinese who came back from other countries like you?] Uh, yes.

Balancing family and work

The behavior of some repatriates remained more Hong Kong than Western — not an unexpected finding in that an additive identity profile does not supplant home identity but adds to it. One example is the area of work–life balance, that is, how people balance their time between work commitments and family life. This issue will continue to be explored from the vantage point of career and workplace in Chapter 9. Owing to the Confucian tradition of hard work, Hong Kongers tend to put in long hours, often six days a week, at their jobs, dramatically tipping the scales to the work side. Once they immigrated, however, many Hong Kongers appreciated the opportunity to spend more time with their families. They often traveled with their children, went hiking and biking, and enjoyed the natural beauty of Canada or Australia. They shifted the balance toward family life while living in their new countries. But the scales tipped back again when they remigrated. The interviewees commented that hard work and long hours was "the right way" to approach work. Despite many years of living in the West, these remigrants, sometimes regretfully, resumed this lifestyle upon their return to Hong Kong. This tendency is illustrated quite clearly in a comment from a male repatriate who returned from Canada after four years (P38):

> And for myself, I spend more time at work. So a lot of time I don't finish at eight or nine in evening. And sometimes I work like, most of the time I work in weekend as well. So we see each other less than before. And a lot of time she really have a impact on me, because sometimes my wife come to and say, "Do you have time to talk to me?" And that really impact me a lot. I must be leaving my family behind for quite a long time. Although we see each other every evening, we sleep in the same bed every evening, but it seems that we don't have kind of intimate or close dialogues as often as we would have in Canada.

A similar observation is made by this male repatriate, who moved back to Hong Kong after two years in Australia (P49):

P: Before we have children, my wife also worked. We are just busy with our own work. We seldom talked to each other in Hong Kong. In Australia, no such problem because you always have a long weekend day and my wife was not working. She was studying there, and you still have a lot of leisure time. When we came back in Hong Kong, the working time is so long, and my wife always need to work until eight or nine. Sometimes it's overnight, just before we publish of annual report.

I: So is it frustrating after you lived in Australia and you know that one can have a life which has more leisure?

P: We don't think so because you can't compare. The salary you get here, and what you got in Australia, is quite a big difference. When you get more, you have to pay more, in terms of your effort and time.

I: So the salary compensates for having less time together, and people all feel comfortable with the trade off having more money but less time?

P: Because we need to get the saving and in the future we can retire earlier.

The experience of migration transformed the most central values in the minds and lives of Hong Kongers. Core Chinese values of filial piety and obedience to parents, interdependence on the family, focus on the material, and learning through repetition receded in prominence and were replaced by Western values of independence of thought, freedom of action, individuality, focus on nature and leisure, and creativity. A select few traditional values survived, although in modified form: flexibility of thought and behavior, long-term strategic planning for the family, and an emphasis on hard work.

9 Remigrants and professional life

Earlier chapters have focused on the identity profiles of return migrants. Hong Kongers have overwhelmingly adopted an additive identity, superimposing their newly learned Canadian or Australian values and customs onto their layered Chinese/British/Hong Kong self-concepts. As we have seen, identity profiles influence a wide range of remigrants' thinking, acting, and decision making — the choice of naming practices, of the neighborhood in which to live, of how to conduct extended family relationships, of where to educated one's children's education, and of parenting style.

The immigrant experience also has a profound influence over workplace behavior, relationships between employees and employers, and productivity. Culture and identity influence attitudes toward work hours, compensation and rewards, privacy boundaries, and notions of organizational loyalty. These cultural workplace attitudes are factors used in assessing employee performance, judging who is a "good" worker and who is "lazy and disinterested," and in evaluating whether a company is an exciting workplace or an unacceptable one.

Hong Kongers had mixed and nuanced reactions to Western work attitudes and behaviors. They found some refreshing and incorporated them into their personal styles. Even when they returned to Hong Kong, they maintained those Western styles. They adopted other work behaviors only temporarily — "When in Sydney, do as the Australians do" — and on returning to Hong Kong eagerly readopted the local customs. Still other Western ideas about work were diametrically opposed to Hong Kong attitudes, and the immigrants never felt comfortable adopting them.

Work environment

Remigrants uniformly contrasted the relaxed, easy atmosphere of the workplace in Canada and Australia with the more pressured and demanding work environment in Hong Kong. The differences were manifest in many ways. Westerners worked fewer hours each day and at a more leisurely pace, which surprised most immigrants, although they perceived it in a positive light.

Several immigrants to Australia articulated their work experiences. One male respondent immigrated, at age 32, to Australia with his wife. He returned after two and a half years because he felt that there were more opportunities for career advancement in Hong Kong. He had worked for a local company in Australia and made the following observation (P33):

> Yes, you would say the big difference than in Hong Kong is the management … But I would say in the Australian company, the pressure is a bit relaxed. When I was working in an Australian company, more relax, not many work, easy to handle, and the culture for the Australian company, they seldom have OT [overtime]; at five o'clock everyone would leave the company. There is no overtime in Australian company. [I: No one does that?] No, even the boss. At five o'clock, they all go. Sometimes I was the only one still working. So I think maybe I love working in Australia because there is not much pressure.

This female respondent left Hong Kong at age 30 for Australia and returned after four and a half years. In the following excerpt she described what she saw as the main difference between Australian and Hong Kong work life (P43):

> Because Australian life is more relaxed. In Hong Kong, you can't relax because your boss press you for this and all the deadlines; you have to be very proactive, initiate a lot of work. But Australian is very lay back. You don't have to do it. I just have to do the job enough, and that's okay, and I get my salary. But here it's different. Even though you are not at a very senior level, they expect a lot.

A male who immigrated to Australia at age 39 described his experience working in Australia and provided a clear example of how he adjusted his behavior to the local work environment (P23):

I have no problem with my colleagues. In the university, our school, has a common room, I worked in common room. So every morning, we have tea at around ten thirty. And then lunch break. Many colleagues, they brought their lunch and after having their lunch they play bridge. And in the afternoon you see how relax in Australia? At around three or three thirty, we have another round of tea. So I went with them as much as possible. When I have time, I spent ten or fifteen minutes chatting with my colleagues. And sometimes when we have a short lunch, I went upstairs and watch my colleagues play bridge. So I didn't have any problem mixing with my colleagues.

Another male respondent left for Australia with his wife and daughter. He spent some time working there, and his interpretation of the relaxed workplace was not a positive one, perhaps because he was a supervisor rather than an employee (P20):

[The Australian workers are] not as dedicated as the Hong Kongers. They expect a big live life after work, and they expect a lot of time as well. Not very, not quite willing to work overtime even though you pay them double. And I have difficulty finding some helpers after all these time.

One male interviewee hypothesized on why Australians did not work so hard (P4):

In Australia, first of all, the people don't work so hard. And later I find out why they don't want to work so hard because the tax was so heavy. If I work hard, half of my income goes to the government, why work so hard? Just relax and enjoy your life ... To me they are slow, not everything will, most people are slow. Slow mean, when they go to the bank, first of all, they will ask how's the day? They will ask about the weather before they ask what you want from the bank. In Hong Kong, it never. You go, please tell me what you want. Finish. Another one.

Immigrants to Canada experienced similarly relaxed working conditions. One young woman immigrated to Canada at age 18 with her parents and her younger brother. She returned to Hong Kong after six years (P22):

Canadian work style is that they are very friendly; they are more relaxed. People do things, I think, step by step, open to discussion ... The Hong Kong style is very stringent, very strict, I think very political, I think very fast, very efficient, multitask. You have to like ten people's work at one time. Very demanding, very performance-based.

A male respondent migrated to Canada at age 33 and returned to Hong Kong after approximately ten years. He resented the long work hours and retained his Canadian attitude toward work (P3):

> [In Hong Kong] maybe you have to work twelve hours a day or fourteen hours a day and come back on Saturday … I don't do that. I am sorry [laughs]. But most of my colleagues, they go back and work on Saturdays. And some of them leave at nine or ten at night.

Relationship between supervisor and employee

Hong Kong bosses were often described as demanding of employee time and attention. One remigrant from Australia complained that local bosses (P6):

> Squeeze you even though you have finished your job. They'll think of something new for you, to make, full utilize your time, always get you busy and keep you stay late for your work, stay late from home … Local boss is more tough, require more than expect. And yell to get the things done, quick, cheap, fast, good, good quality, high quality. But the US boss, they do not bother me, as long as you get the things done, that's okay. Not trying to get extra things from you.

Paternal relationship

In the traditional Chinese workplace, subordinates have an obligation to obey their supervisor, to loyally and effectively work long hours. As in other essential relationships, though, responsibilities are two-sided. The supervisor also has obligations, which include caring for the employee in a holistic way: ensuring a productive work environment, inquiring into the employee's extended family life, and assisting the employee with personal problems. One can characterize the role of the boss as paternal and personal; he is a workplace father who looks after his large family. One of the five essential Confucian relationships (*wu lun*) includes boss-subordinate and is modeled on the father-son dyad.

In the following excerpt, a remigrant describes her current experience working for a Chinese boss (P2):

> My fourth boss is typically Chinese, I can't stand him at all. I got almost crazy in those two years, because he is so typical Chinese. [I: So what does that mean? Tell me something he did that is hard for you.] Very

parenting. He is like a parent. He never leave free hand for me to handle things. He tell me exactly what he wanted this and that. But sometime I find that I don't agree with him all the time. He is a very parenthood type. [I: Do you feel very uncomfortable? Were you able to say to him "I don't agree with you"?] Yeah, I tell him straight. I don't like it. And actually I fight with him all the time. I fell on the table and talk to him. He is very surprise how come I am like this. Because he really get into my nerve.

One female interviewee migrated to Canada with her parents as a teenager. She returned to Hong Kong after nine years and spoke of her perception of the differences in management style in the following excerpt (P16):

> In Chinese company, you are more bond with your boss. Like in a personal level, because you might depends on different instance that but during different festival the boss will have dinner with the employees, and you are more tied with the employees. And there is one, I don't know the right word in English, but they have a certain word that describe how, even in bad times, the boss who is Chinese, the boss would still take care of the employees ... Even when they are close to the age of retirement, even though the employee is not performing that well. The boss will keep him, because he has been around for so long. And he knows his family; he knows his situation he is in. But in big company, in foreign company, that might not be the case. When you don't perform well, so that's the major difference, you can say in foreign company the employers might be more logical, it's just work, I don't need to be emotional about having you around. But in, and it's more fair to everyone, performance counts. But in a Chinese company, it's the relationship you have with the boss that matters. And that's why sometimes some of the boss may be very emotional. After all, I have heard of bosses, Chinese boss, that will throw things in the conference room in the meetings.

She described her relationship with her boss, in which she retained some Western work elements. In general, she related to him in a less formal way than is typical in Hong Kong:

> Just being here with the coworker, they are mostly local. They tell me when times that they think I am acting like more like a Western girl. [I: When is that?] I can't think of any particular, maybe I chat with my boss more often, just over coffee or just over anything. [I: Just informal conversation? You feel more comfortable with him?] Yeah. Well, first because of the language. I don't have much language barrier, and the culture because things that he talk about I would know, things that I talk about he would know.

Status differentials

Traditional Chinese culture is delineated by unequal relationships: parent-child, older brother-younger brother, teacher-student. Workplace relationships mirror familial ones. Inequality and status differences typify relations between the boss and employees or between older workers and younger workers. Most remigrants found these situations of inequality intolerable in light of the relatively egalitarian work environments in Canada and Australia to which they had become accustomed.

One male respondent immigrated to Australia at age 26 and returned after eight years (P50):

> I don't know. I don't know. Maybe it's the way I see things, the way that I talk ... Over there you would see that maybe why I was told that I wasn't very humble. Maybe because it is an normal thing that, when you are dealing with European, you are sort of on equal footing, when you deal with them just. But in a Chinese society, especially when you dealing with more traditional Chinese who are maybe slightly older than me, they always think that you have to pay respect to the more senior citizen and people with more senior standing in organization. So it's quite a Chinese way. So maybe I was just, when I first got back from Australia, I have been too used to the way that they deal with one another. So I forget this is a Chinese society. [I: Right. So you weren't showing enough respect or so forth to a older?] Yeah, I think maybe that was the reason.

Another male interviewee was a teenager when he left Hong Kong for Canada. He returned to Hong Kong after 14 years and was quite critical of the Hong Kong work style. Like many of the other respondents, he noticed the more relaxed pace of the Canadian work life. He also commented on the importance of *face* in the Hong Kong workplace (P17):

> Face ... I think in here everything is giving face first; they really want to do some stupid things that just want to show they are more superior than you are ... They got their own set of culture, and that's the way it is when you are a junior, you have to be tortured by the senior. It's just ridiculous, and you really have to say the right thing to people, make sure you hang out the right source group, making good friends with this kind of people so that they give you all the convenience ... It's Chinese way. It's in the blood someway ... It's been well recognized in business world that Chinese people love to play those *guanxi* or relationship

games. They still want to play around that I am a good friend of such and such.

After a brief sojourn to Singapore, this male respondent migrated to Canada at age 33 and returned to Hong Kong after approximately ten years. He was very critical of the Hong Kong work style (P3):

> P: And that's a very bad culture. I always criticize that culture in Hong Kong. Because he's not the most powerful guy … In Hong Kong, they are too obey. They just do whatever the boss said. Right or wrong, they don't care.
>
> I: Can you give me a situation where that happens?
>
> P: I think that's not reasonable. Sometimes you have your own workload already. And the boss just keep on adding in and adding in … And they just take it and take it … endlessly. And they never say anything. I say that's wrong. You have to raise your voice.

He also commented on the extreme and immutable status differences between supervisors and employees manifested in both compliance and salary:

> The Chinese people in Hong Kong, they still have the vertical; if you are in a different level, then the higher level always have the right. They (the subordinates) are just too obedient. They still rank people. You can't see it in Canada or in the States. They treat everybody fair. I don't care whether you are a manager or you are just a guy working as an electrician, they treat everybody fair. After tax income is more or less the same. But over here, if you are a manager, or if you are a clerical clerk, the salary difference may be 20 times.

Another interviewee confirmed the authority of the boss in Hong Kong workplace:

> I worked in a hotel here as hotel management; my boss she was local Hong Konger, very, very traditional, parental kind of management style. I could not work well with her and with other management at all because they do not listen to your point of view. They want you to do what they want … It's too authoritative, too absolute; it's not democratic, and it's something like the CEO says that the CEO … push the idea to the senior management, the senior management then push the idea to me as a manager — you have to do this. When you share your ideas with her, she says, "I don't know, I don't care, don't ask me, if you ask me why don't you give your salary to me, I do your job?"

Communication

Status inequities are often played out in interpersonal workplace communications. In the Hong Kong office, higher status means there is no obligation to explain decisions or policies to staff or to consult with employees. Opinions of staff are not encouraged nor sought. Senior executives can harshly rebuke junior staff with impunity and tolerance. Self-restraint and passivity is expected from the object of the scorn.[1] But immigrants were able to adjust to a workplace in which communication was more open and direct, and most remigrants relished the opportunity to offer their opinions and ideas once they were back in the Hong Kong setting. These behaviors, however, often led to frustration for the returnees and critical responses from their supervisors and senior coworkers.

Two remigrants found strategies in which they could retain open communication. Now back in Hong Kong, one described the differences he observed in the relationships between bosses and their employees in Hong Kong and in the West (P33):

> I: What about the relationship between a boss and an employee, is that different?
>
> P: Maybe the Western-style management. Because the Chinese-style management, boss always on the higher side; they never communicate with his subordinates. But I think I would not do that even before I migrated to Australia because that's what I studied from the Western style. They quite emphasize the management. They emphasize on the communication. So I will put human to be a treasure. So in my company, I am a boss in my company. I have very good communications with my subordinates, and our firm is a progressive firm. When I come to Hong Kong, I have only twelve staff and now it become twenty-five staff. So even so tight economy in Hong Kong, we are a progressive firm. That's why I quite emphasize on the, you can say the Western style of management, and mixed up with some Chinese style of management, and put in an effective way.

Another male respondent migrated to Canada at age 23 and returned to Hong Kong after six years. In the following excerpt, he showed his willingness to directly approach his boss (P11):

> But in my case, I would talk to my boss … It's more bidirectional. But in Hong Kong, they usually feel: he is my boss so what he says is right. [I: So you would negotiate with your boss?] Yes. I mean … I think it's

a teamwork. He is not the one who own the company. He is just my coworker and doing different job duty. Yeah, I can think of this way.

Lack of privacy for workers

In the Hong Kong workplace, high status differentials gave supervisors unfettered access to their employees and their employees' personal lives. Few topics were considered off-limits for a boss to ask an employee about. Immigrants found a completely different system in the West, where individual rights superseded employer prerogatives and polite yet restrained conversation between boss and employee was essential. Remigrants brought these notions about privacy and politeness back to Hong Kong and attempted to implement them, although this style was easier to put into effect when the remigrant was the supervisor rather than the subordinate.

Note the comment by a female respondent who had studied in Canada and then immigrated to Australia, where she lived for four and a half years prior to remigrating to Hong Kong (P43):

> I: What is your work style like?
> P: In Australia, they are very respectful to staff. [I: What do you mean?]. They respect staff's privacy. Now I am back in Hong Kong, I respect their privacy.
> I: Can you give me an example?
> P: If they [a staff person] call and say, "I can't come to work today," I don't ask why. This is an infringement into their personal life. This is a right.

She provided another example of differences in coworker relationships:

> One of the ways I have pick up and probably I still carry on right now is that I have to be very respectful and courteous when interacting with my colleagues. Because the Australians are very egoistic. [I: What you mean by that?] If you want to get something done, you couldn't be authoritative. You have to say "Could you do this for me?" et cetera. And also one of the things I picked up is you really have to respect their own privacy.

Work performance and relationships

The emphasis on prescribed relationships in the office underscores the importance of relationships in general within the Chinese and Hong

Kong cultures. Since loyalty and trust are crucial elements to the success of any enterprise in Hong Kong, the linchpin is working with individuals in whom one has this trust. Familial relationships form the core of trust but are also the core of obligation. Business owners and office supervisors feel a special obligation to employ, reward, and retain family members. In part, this is because of the expectations of their extended clans. But it is also due to the essential trust that a boss can have in a worker who is kin. Decisions regarding hiring, performance evaluations and promotions are thus subjective and ambiguous allowing relationships to dominate.

The familial system is at odds with the Western emphasis on objectivity, meritocracy, and unemotional relationships among workers. In fact, hiring relatives is labeled "nepotism" and banned in most Western workplaces. Job performance evaluation seeks objective measures; standardized rewards are given for exceptional work and uniform punishments for subpar results. Decisions are supposed to be rule-based and clear.

Following a two-and-a-half year residence in Australia, a male interviewee summarized his perspective on how a Western work style differed from a Hong Kong style (P33):

> What I say is when I work for the Western people, they quite emphasize on the right and wrong. But the Chinese, we would have a middle, maybe some quite ... Say my subordinates, he or she did something wrong. For the Western style, you did wrong and you have get fired or some punishment or penalty. But Chinese style, we would find out why they did it wrong. Maybe something what we call the reason. Why I have such consideration because of the relationship. Chinese style quite emphasize on the relationship. [I: Relationship between employee and the boss.] And also the year people working so long, maybe you know him or her for a long time. Maybe the trust. But the Western, they are very clear: if you do it right or wrong, they never emphasize on the relationship or the trust. [I: So the personal should get into it?] I don't know, I interrupt it right or wrong, because Chinese is a little bit, they will use those person if they trust, the first priority.

He illustrated the importance of relationships and connections with the following anecdote about employment in Hong Kong:

> One of my subordinate is an office assistant. He is a son of my sister. His performance is not very good, like the punctuality and stained his hair golden. I don't like it. If you are not the son of my sister, I suppose I would get you off. But Chinese style, because you have some relationship with that guy, I want him to be good. He is working okay,

but he is a young guy. Particularly in winter, he did not wake up, so the punctuality. I get a lot of complain from my other subordinate. His performance is not so good because he is always late. But I checked it; he only have this problem, but generally his performance in work is okay. But for the Western style, I think this guy should go home. But the Chinese style, we also emphasize it, because my relationship with that guy, some relative relationship, and that's why I also try to give him more opportunity.

Harmony vs. confrontation in the workplace

Remigrants in this study emphasized one particular cultural difference in the workplace: the emphasis on harmony and agreement with coworkers and supervisors in Hong Kong compared with the encouragement of disagreement and the articulation of one's own opinion in the Western workplace. Interestingly, the Hong Kongers often interpreted these disagreements as particularly negative and described them as "confrontations." Hong Kong researchers experimentally demonstrated that the norm for group harmony is so strong that personal insults in the presence of a group member elicit less of a response than an insult directed privately.[2]

One female respondent who immigrated to Canada at age 28 described how she maintained a core Chinese work dynamic between boss and employee despite working for a Western company (P18):

> When I have that conflict with my superior in the American company, I don't want to defend. I just thought that the job didn't suit me, and I didn't want to make a scene. So I prefer to quit. I didn't … [I: You didn't want to fight?] Fight that, yeah, no, no. Because I also explain to her that I didn't want the job and actually I am looking for a different, a job which suit my capability. Because I don't that kind of confrontation, because I also want to make clear that I have no interest in her post. [I: So one of the Chinese values is not to confront people and maybe not be direct in other's feeling?] Yeah, we are more constraint.

The change in interpersonal interactions is illustrated in this comment by a female who returned from Canada after six years (P22):

> I: Let me ask you about work style. I know that you didn't work in Canada, but if you compare the way that you interact with your bosses compared to friends who've never left Hong Kong, do you see a difference in work style? Do you think you have a Western work style or … ? '

P: I have a Western work style. I worked in Canada as a part-time financial analyst for Merrill, Lynch and Royal Bank of Canada. I also worked for the school, assistant professor is to help them mark papers, read essays, attend examination sessions. Those are easy jobs.

I: So how would you compare Canadian work style and Hong Kong style?

P: Canadian work style is that they are very friendly; they are more relaxed. People do things, I think, step by step, open to discussion.

I: If you disagree with something your boss says, how do you respond to that?

P: I think I would just share my point with the boss; "Oh, I see your point but then I have another suggestion that this may be better," or "I don't agree with that point." You can actually state it out that you don't agree and people won't get angry too much. They will kind of listen and try to understand your point, and I see that Western working style is that they are not too stringent about rules.

Work communication styles were influenced by the cultural norms of encouraging or prohibiting direct conversation. Western office discourse was more direct, with less concern about saving face and preserving harmony. Hong Kong office conversations constrained the voicing of dissenting opinions. If disagreement needed to be expressed, great care was taken to be subtle and tactful in the utterances.

One female interviewee immigrated to Canada with her husband and returned after two and a half years. She commented that she was more direct after she came back to Hong Kong but was aware that she would have to be more "tactful" now. She also had insight into the differences that culture brings to the interpretation of behavior, such as whether an expression of opinion is seen as honesty or as rudeness (P18):

P: Yeah. I also find some changes in the way you have just describe. I become more direct. If I find something wrong, I will speak up. But before I migrated to Canada, I am more passive. Even though I have some complain, normally I won't say it.

I: Now that you are back to Hong Kong, how do you maintain those work style changes? Are you still more direct and ... ?

P: Yes. I believe once you build up that kind of attitude very difficult to get rid of it or go back. But in Hong Kong you have to be more tactful, I believe. Because people are more sensitive, they didn't like to be irritated. But in Canada, probably they consider it as directness, but in Hong Kong, they will consider you to be rude. Probably this is different culture.

Another female, who immigrated to Australia at age 27, described the changes in her work behavior. She spent four years in Australia and returned to Hong Kong with her husband and a daughter who was born in Australia (P2):

> P: My style is quite westernized actually.
>
> I: And what does that mean to you in terms of the work, the settings?
>
> P: For example, when we go for the meeting to discuss something, common thing, because all the EO [executive officers of each department] go to the same meeting. They don't like to express their ideas, and I am the one always asking this and that, and requesting this and that. Maybe they found me a bit troublesome. Yeah, that's like that. This is the difference I can see.
>
> I: So the Hong Kong staff might not speak up?
>
> P: More subtle. They are more subtle. Even they don't like the things, they won't tell you. The[y all say the] same thing.

Here is an additional example of her direct communication with her boss and coworkers. She admitted to being frank and outspoken rather than using subtle nonverbal gestures as most of her Chinese colleagues did. She described their response to her candor:

> P: Yeah, I will say it out and tell them frankly what I am thinking.
>
> I: Can you think of a time when it happened recently? A specific example?
>
> P: Yeah! Because recently we are doing the postgraduate program; we have a master international business. And it becomes self-finance. And somehow under the faculty of business, under the department there are six programs. Each of us has our postgraduate program. And I think the faculty is trying to unify the policy, you know, the fee and the admission process. And somehow we held quite a lot of meeting, and we got these. And when we have meeting, because I express something, I think something wrong with their arrangement, this and that. Well, the other have nothing to say; they follow whatever the faculty say. And they will find that, oh, why do you ask this kind of question? I don't know. I don't know. Sometimes I find that's funny. Those EO, AO (administrative officer), sometimes when they refer to me, they say this *gwai mui*. You know what is *gwai mui*? It means it is quite a Caucasian.

I: Is it like *gwai lo?*

P: Yeah. *Gwai mui* means women; *mui* means women. *Gwai lo* means men. *Gwai* means foreigners. *Lo* means men. *Mui* means women. This *gwai mui* is saying something ... you know. Yeah, they'll say things like that. I can tell the difference.

A similar response was elicited in coworkers by the behavior of a male respondent who returned from Canada after nine years (P15):

> Sometimes my coworkers think that I am an alien. I am more direct than others. If I saw an issue, I spoke up and others were uncomfortable. They saw me as aggressive. They spoke in more indirect ways.

Harmonious and interdependent relationships among Hong Kong workers were demonstrated in another domain — the blurring of lines between job responsibilities and the need to assist each other. Migrants to the West found the clear demarcation of job duties there and the lack of cohesion puzzling. A male respondent related this anecdote about his work in Australia (P4):

> I am the one that take care of all the garment, merchandising work. The other is one reception, one accountant, and one guy who is really taking care of the warehouse. And to me ... You cannot ask them something they are not suppose to do. They won't do it. But in Hong Kong, you do everything. Even is not your job. You know it is going to make your work easier. If I can, I would rather do it and get the job done.

Adaptation to Western style

Thirty-eight percent of the HKRP participants reported adopting a Canadian or Australian style of work. Included are workplace behaviors such as closer contact between boss and employee, type of relationship with coworkers, and general work ethic.

One male interviewee who had immigrated to Canada decided to adapt a more Western style of management once he returned to Hong Kong (P42):

> I treat my staff equal. I always want to talk to them, because to me everybody just performing their own duty. And each duty so important. So I am working, on those paperwork, but I did step outside to make sure they work to the point. So to me I treasure everyone and try to make them everyone perform. This is my way, try to lead. But

sometimes like I was in a construction site before and everybody under me have a good team. And up to here, it is more complicated, because I get less supporting staff and more bosses. So I can feel like you say, that's a gap. The boss want to act like a boss. [I: So do your bosses here act like a boss?] Yeah, I have boss. To me, I was, I don't know, maybe people think I act like a boss. But when I talk to them, they just say, "What is your opinion? Shall we do it this way?" I don't say, "You have to do that, you have to do that." I just say, "Open a question. Is it this way better? And you have better suggestion?" But they come up with a problem, and then I share with them the problem, but eventually I will ask them to solve the problem. Then try to build up their confidence.

Another male remigrant from Canada was very vocal about his workplace disagreements and earned a reputation as the resident *gwai lo* (P3):

I: So what do you think your boss and your coworkers think of you? Do they think that you act Canadian? Have you heard them say anything? [P: Yeah.] What have they said?

P: This guy is a *gwai lo* [foreigner].

I: So they think that in some of your ways in which you behave are not Hong Kong style?

P: Sometimes when I see something which is not fair I raise my voice, angrily. And the Chinese people in Hong Kong, they still have the vertical. If you are in a different level, then the higher level always have the right. They are just too obedient.

Some remigrants adopted aspects of a Western communication style. One male respondent who was 46 when he moved to Canada remarked that he was more polite now (P19):

[Canadians] speak very open and polite. Not like Hong Kong people. They talk very straight. Maybe they ask you for something, they may not say "thank you." They talk straight. But in Canada, the meaning is just one thing: decorative.

We have seen that there are several Western workplace styles that the remigrants have retained: direct conversation, a lessening of status differences between superiors and subordinates, respect for employee privacy, and a preference for objective performance standards. However, Hong Kong identity is distinguished by its flexibility. The additive identity, in particular, combines both Western and local cultures. There are many examples of immigrant job-related adjustments that were subsequently abandoned by the remigrants, who reverted to a Hong Kong work style once they returned home. One male respondent who returned to Hong Kong after four years in Toronto immediately went back to working longer hours and with more focus (P42):

> Like Canada, just working thirty-seven hours a week. Here, I think, is more than fifty. It's a big difference. Also the work load and the timing, deadline more deadline here ... Canada, you know, talk to them we just like friends and chat. But here, very careful.

Balancing family and work

Most Hong Kongers consciously adjusted to the Australian and Canadian style of family/work balance — less work time and more family time. An illustrative example is one female who immigrated to Canada at age 28 with her future husband. At first, she continued to work long hours as she had done in Hong Kong, but eventually she began to appreciate the Canadians' separation of work and family life (P18):

> They [the Canadians] ... stick to their working hours. They don't want to work overtime. They ... actually, they refuse to work overtime, right. [I: Was that frustrating to you?] I am not used to it yet, when I first, at the beginning. But after a while, I when I think about their working style, I thought their quality of life is actually better than Hong Kong. Because they separate their working life with their personal life. And they have a, I mean, they have more leisure time for themselves. So I really appreciate that kind of living style.

A male immigrant to Australia commented on how he adjusted to the local work schedule and its effect on his family life (P37):

> [Working in Australia] affect me in a way that I would prefer to finish all my work during work days, and I don't want to come back on weekend ... because Sunday is family day. I think most of the Western people would regard Sunday or weekend as a family day. Before I was migrated to Australia sometimes I do have to come back on Saturday and Sunday. Since then [migrating], I tried to avoid doing so. They [Australians] play hard during the weekend. And we enjoy it very much, and we do the same thing.

As a result of this adaptation, one experience common to remigrants who reverted to Hong Kong style was the re-emphasis on work life. This resulted in their working long work hours followed by a lengthy commute home; thus the scales tipped back to work over family. In part, long hours were equated with pride in work, in the company, and in the very definition of a good worker. In fact, many immigrants had felt lazy and guilty when they adapted to Western hours, so resuming a Hong Kong work schedule made them feel secure and positive.

One male respondent commented on the differences in the work–family balance between Hong Kongers and Australians (P33):

> And I would say the efficiency of Hong Kong people when they work in Australia, more efficiency than those local people. [I: Because they work longer or they are more efficient?] I think for Hong Kong people, especially during the 1980s, most of the people put working and career as first priority. Even today, most of the Hong Kong people put working and career as their first priority. But in Sydney, people are different. Of course, working and the job is important, but they also put a lot of priority into family and hockey ... So I think the culture is a little bit different. But I don't think that it is only mainly the place difference. Hong Kong people prefer working.

Other remigrants made similar observations. Hong Kong work life was characterized as six days a week, 10 to 12 hours a day. Immigrant work life was five days a week, 8-hour days, and an easy automobile commute. Some respondents remarked that work in Canada or Australia seemed like a vacation. For many of them, the truncated Western work schedule did not match their conceptions of employee excellence or of what a company expected of its employees. The response of some of the immigrants was to maintain the Hong Kong schedule that they were accustomed to, putting in longer hours than their coworkers and supervisors. These efforts, however, were appreciated by neither their coworkers, who interpreted their hard work as an attempt to influence the supervisor, nor their bosses. Some remigrants reported that their bosses had told them to go home and stop working so hard!

When the immigrants returned to Hong Kong, nearly all of the men reverted to long work days and work weeks; consequently, they spent less time with their wives and children. They finally felt as though they were "really working," and their guilt over the shorter hours they worked in Canada or Australia lessened. Rarely did respondents indicate angst about or resentment of the Hong Kong work ethic. Rather, they took pride in their hard work and comfortably readjusted to Hong Kong's cultural pattern.

10 Confucius and Socrates: Ancient philosophies, migration, and cultural identity

Balance is the great schema of the cosmos;
   Harmony is the universal path of life as a whole.

Adapted from *Zhuangzi*

There was an old farmer whose only horse ran away. Knowing that the horse was the mainstay of his livelihood, his neighbors came to commiserate with him. "Who knows what's bad or good?" said the old man, refusing their sympathy. Indeed, a few days later his horse returned, bringing with it a wild horse. The old man's friends came to congratulate him. Rejecting their congratulations, the old man said, "Who knows what's bad or good?" As it happened, a few days later when the old man's son was attempting to ride the wild horse, he was thrown and broke his leg. The friends came to express their sadness about the son's misfortune. "Who knows what's good or bad?" said the old man. As it happened, the army came to the village to conscript all the able-bodied men to fight a war against a neighboring province, but the old man's son was not fit to ride and was spared. And so on ...

Ancient Chinese story

Geography, history, politics, economics, and psychology intersect with any investigation of Hong Kong identity. When cultural transitions are added to the mix, the outcome is understandably complex. Flexibility and pragmatism, hallmarks of Hong Kong society, set the tone for overseas adaptations and for repatriation accommodations. The resultant additive identity allows Hong Kongers to feel comfortable whether in the Western diaspora or back home in Hong Kong. In both large and small decisions, the behavioral consequences of the additive identity were enacted. This investigation predicts that in the future Hong Kongers will continue to be both geographically and psychologically mobile, returning to their countries of immigration to fulfill strategically developed family decisions and plans.

What accounts for the pragmatism and ease with which the Hong Kongers adjusted to their return? And, conversely, why is repatriation so stressful for Westerners? One likely explanation is in the opposing foundational cultural philosophies of the East and West regarding psychological consistency, compromise, and stability. Chinese philosophy has a 2,500-year tradition of accepting contradiction and complexity through compromise. Daoism and Confucianism both extol the virtues of the dialectic and of the importance of finding the middle way. The ancient name of China itself, the Middle Kingdom, underscores these notions.

An equally long tradition stemming from ancient Greek philosophy teaches the opposite lesson — that logic and its corollary, the "either-or" principle, are preeminent. Contradictory ideas or behaviors must be resolved to support one idea or the other, and, once the contradictions are resolved, consistency must be maintained. Changing responses whenever contexts change must be avoided in favor of unswerving stability.

Cultural identity appears to be influenced by these divergent, yet fundamental philosophical foundations. Throughout the immigration cycle, the Chinese response to identity complexity shows flexibility and additivity. Individuals activate one identity or another in response to situational and contextual prompts. This reaction occurs without stress or angst; it is a pragmatic solution to an ever-changing cultural and geographic landscape. Identity consistency is not paramount in this psychological universe, but harmonious and sensible compromise is. Pragmatism also supports the rationale for Hong Kong remigration, in this case, economic pragmatism. The majority of returnees found the higher salaries that Hong Kong employment would pay them irresistible (although some questioned whether their standard of living actually improved).

The Western response to cultural transition is highly emotional, partly because of the felt inconsistency of holding dual identities. The response is to resolve the duality by choosing "either-or" — that is, choosing either one cultural identity or the other. An American returning to the United States from a well-adapted sojourn in France cannot be both French and

American culturally. If the individual "feels" more French, then he or she must "feel" less American, hence the preponderance of subtractive identity profiles among Western repatriates following a cultural transition. The changeover period is filled with uncertainty, the need to adjust, and a search for the correct and sole cultural identity, resulting in significant distress and discomfort for the individual. The classic psychological theory of cognitive dissonance, in which tension arises within individuals who hold conflicting attitudes, also predicts an either-or response from the individual, followed by a lessening of distress.

The remainder of this chapter seeks to expand on these ideas by exploring how the musings and teachings of philosophers twenty-five centuries ago and around the world from each other have shaped the psychological landscape of today's global traveler.

The teachings of Confucius and Laozi

The political world of China in the sixth century BCE was torn by instability, as various warlords and kingdoms vied for superiority in the face of ineffectual emperors. Kong Qiu was born amid this turmoil and developed his ethical teachings in response to his environment and as a salve for the uncertainty of the times. As the tale of the old farmer in the epigraph at the beginning of this chapter reveals, the world is full of uncertainty and change. Finding paths to social harmony dominated Kong's thoughts and writings. In his lifetime, in recognition of his brilliant insights as a scholar and civil servant, he was called Kong Fuzi, or Master Kong. Two thousand years later, Jesuit missionaries translated his name as Confucius and called his philosophy, then adhered to by China's intellectual and political elite, Confucianism. Described as the Confucian Classics, his writings were not the beginnings of a religion that focused on explanations for suffering, life after death, and Truth but were an ethical guide that focused on the daily, here-and-now concerns of human interaction, good government, and friendship. These basic works consist of the *Five Classics* (*Wu Jing*) and the *Four Books* (*Si Shu*; the first book being the famous *Dialogues* or *Analects*), plus commentary, interpretation, and expansion by his disciples.

Five hundred years after the birth of Confucius, a Han dynasty emperor set up the semblance of a state university system with five colleges, each one devoted to the study of one of the *Five Classics*. The brightest students in the country were assigned to these colleges, and those who excelled at their studies and passed a rigorous examination would be selected to join the cadre of administrators running the vast empire (considered the forerunner of the modern civil service system). It was not the devotion of the Emperor Wu Di alone that ensured the continuance of Confucian thinking. Because the philosopher's works grew out of the very ecology of China and addressed the daily dilemmas of the people, millions of peasants accepted them as guides for living. Plagued by famine and flood, the natural environment also was unstable, and life was unpredictable. Confucius counseled people to exercise restraint over their desires and to distribute limited resources equally among family members. The family, not the individual, then was the core of social organization, and children were counseled to respect the dignity of all and to exercise restraint over their individual wishes in order to maintain family harmony.

By situating his dictums within nature and the agrarian economic system, Confucius developed a viable code that revived an older and orderly social system based on virtue, truth, harmony, and flexibility. Chinese schoolchildren have, for the past 2,000 years, studied those same texts, aided by the continuity of the Chinese culture and language. Subsequently, Confucian dictates have formed the foundation for the social life and thinking processes of more than 2 billion Chinese within China and the diaspora.[1]

The turbulent times of 500 BCE China produced another great scholar and teacher, Laozi, the founder of Daoism (Taoism), "The Way." Daoism offered another path to harmony. Laozi advocated meditation over action, coexistence with nature, and retreat from the world. He also recognized the ever-changing nature of life, its balances and counterbalances. These he symbolized in *yin-yang* swirls of black and white, solid and circle. Returning, moving in endless cycles, is the basic pattern of movement of the Dao (Tao).[2] Laozi's philosophy also provided practical advice for achieving balance and calmness of body and spirit through the free flow of *qi* (energy) and the balance of the Five Elements (*feng shui*).

While Confucianism focuses on education and economic well-being, and Daoism stresses calm and harmony, both philosophies offer a way to live in a chaotic and unpredictable world. Their tenets allowed the Chinese to see the world as a whole despite its variability, to see a middle way despite extremes. Harmony with nature or with other human beings was elemental. Chinese social life was interconnected, and the fibers formed a supportive cushion for its members.

Consequences of the ancient philosophies for values, emotions, and cultural transitions

In the famous opening lines of the *Analects*, Confucius states: "Isn't it a pleasure when you can make practical use of the things you have studied?" An emphasis on the practical application of ideas reverberated in the Confucian and Daoist texts. Many themes in the writings of the *Classics* focused on ways to achieve smooth social relationships, and on ideal leadership qualities. Those themes help us understand the ease of the cultural adjustment of Hong Kong remigrants, who tended to have complex, additive identities and to make transitions relatively free of anxiety, distress, and emotionality.

This discussion necessarily begins with one of the basic Confucian principles: humans exist in relationship to others. Five relationships are preeminent; each is hierarchical, and each has clearly defined rules of correct behavior. Harmony (*he*) reigns if every member of the relationship acts in the prescribed manner of proper social behavior (*li*). However, each person holds membership in many relationships (one can be a parent to one's child, yet a child to one's own parents; a younger brother to an elder, yet a boss to an employee). In some relationships the person has the superior role, in others the subordinate. Learning how to reconcile these various, sometimes conflicting roles and the appropriate rituals for each is the key to growth. Adaptability, not consistency, becomes the hallmark of maturity and good character.[3] The highest ethical goal of every person is to achieve *ren* (defined as humanity or benevolence). The Chinese character for *ren* is composed of two parts, one meaning "man" and the other meaning "many" or "society." The best interests of both the individual and the group require attention to balance and to the adjustments needed to achieve the highest levels of humanity.[4]

Much of Chinese social behavior and the Chinese response to migration, remigration, and sojourner experiences can be traced to these ideas. There is a fundamental acceptance of duality, of what has been summarized as the principle of "both/and"; a tolerance for multiplicity. The Chinese can embrace multiple religions; they can engage in Buddhist and Christian rituals and follow Confucian ethics. It is interesting to note that religious wars, in which adherents of one religion attempt to dominate the adherents of another and demonstrate that they alone know the Truth, have rarely erupted in China's long history.

Make no mistake — harmony did not imply conformity or a lack of creativity. Throughout China's four millennial history, innovations that have had worldwide repercussions have abounded — the introduction of ink, porcelain, nautical instruments, astronomical techniques, and medical methods. But these creative inspirations were practical solutions to real-world problems, and the development process frequently involved group discussion rather than individual thought.

Two links connect Confucian precepts and an explanation for the unique transitional behaviors of the Hong Kong immigrant and remigrant. The first connection involves understanding how Confucian teachings, through formal methods (education) and informal means (observation of family members), shape the life priorities of the people. We often refer to these concepts, which are held in high regard by a culture and are evaluated as crucial to life, as societal values. The second consideration in understanding the Hong Kong behavioral and identity response to remigration is the connection between Confucian values and a particular way of thinking about and viewing the world. This is referred to by psychologists as cognitive style.

The values held by contemporary Chinese people, whether the people are within the national borders of China; in other Asian countries with Confucian traditions, such as Taiwan, Korea, or Japan; or in countries having significant Chinese populations through immigration, such as Singapore, Vietnam, and Thailand, derive directly from Confucian and Daoist teachings. What are those values, and how can they be identified? One method for examining the multitude of human values is to use a model created by the Dutch psychologist Geert Hofstede.[5] In this model, hundreds of possible values were categorized into five superordinate dimensions. Scores on each of the five dimensions aid in mapping out the cultural contours of a country. Two dimensions are particularly relevant to the discussions here, Uncertainty Avoidance and Long-term Orientation.

Uncertainty Avoidance is a constellation of values encompassing ways of handling the inevitable uncertainties in life. Some cultures have developed an intricate system of rules, regulations, laws, technology, and religion to shield their members from the anxiety of the unknown and the threat of ambiguous situations. Techniques abound to reduce ambiguity. These countries score high on the Uncertainty Avoidance Scale; out of 74 countries, at the highest end of the 100-point scale are Greece, Portugal, Guatemala, Belgium, and several Eastern European nations. In other countries and cultures, people are less concerned about the inconsistencies and ambiguities of daily life, and their anxiety levels tend to be low. They are emotionally calm and disapprove of aggression. These citizens score on the low end of the Uncertainty Avoidance scale. Of the ten countries at the lowest end of the scale, five are Asian, including China and Hong Kong. In these countries, rules are more flexible, and the world is perceived as basically benevolent; uncertainty is considered a part of life. Lenient rules, easy toilet training for toddlers, and relaxed family life and workplace environments are typical. Problems can be solved without formal rules and on a case-by-case basis by examining each unique situation.

A second value dimension relevant to our discussion is Long-term versus Short-term Orientation. This category was developed by a team of Chinese psychologists and adapted by Hofstede.[6] Specific values embedded in Long-term Orientation (LTO) include perseverance, thrift (being sparing with resources), willingness to subordinate oneself for a purpose, and personal adaptiveness. While Confucian values appear at both poles of this time dimension, the countries that scored highest on Long-term Orientation were China, Hong Kong, Taiwan, Japan, and Vietnam. High LTO countries have low divorce rates and consider humility to be a general human virtue. And what is virtuous depends on circumstances and not on any absolute criteria for good or evil. People learn these values by example. Work values are similar to those pertaining to the family and include learning, adaptiveness, accountability, and self-discipline; the development of lifelong personal networks (*guanxi*); and a focus on work life rather than leisure pursuits.

The research of Hofstede and other cultural psychologists has enabled us to identify, measure, and compare values in different countries. Within a country, however, the importance placed on some values rather than on others, or the prominence given to one value over another, helped shape the development of the national culture, which encompasses not only values but also attitudes, emotions, thinking style, and actions.

Confucius teaches that the superior (or virtuous) person is quiet and calm. Daoist ideals are also reflected in contemporary emotional responses to cultural transitions. As already discussed, recent social science investigations have found a general lack of anxiety and stress among Chinese sojourners or migrants. The Hong Kong Remigration Project found similarly low levels of reported distress among returnees. Hong Kong remigrants scored low on the Repatriation Distress Scale and high on the Satisfaction with Life Scale.

The second explanatory link between the ancient philosophers and contemporary transitions is to understand how the Confucian values of low uncertainty avoidance and long-term orientation, coupled with a preference for calm, have shaped the thinking style of Hong Kongers. For this we can turn to a series of ingenious psychological experiments that compared Western (primarily American and Canadian) college students with East Asian ones (primarily Chinese, Hong Kong, Japanese, and Korean).[7] What did these studies reveal about the connection between values and cognitive style and about how Chinese thinking is conceptualized?

In the first series of studies, researchers demonstrated that the "middle way," the path to holding opposing viewpoints that resulted in reasonableness, operated in everyday thinking. In one study, college students in the United States and China were asked to rate how much they liked common American and Chinese proverbs. The Chinese students preferred proverbs that contained contradictory statements (e.g., Too humble is half-proud; Beware of your friends, not your enemies), and the American students preferred proverbs without such inconsistencies. Perhaps the students were reacting to familiarity, with the Chinese preferring Chinese proverbs and the Americans liking theirs. The study was repeated using proverbs from Yiddish (a language of Eastern-European Jews, and based on the assumption that neither group of students would be familiar with these adages. Again, the Chinese rated the proverbs that expressed contradictions as more to their liking than did the Americans.[8] Dialectical thinking prevailed, as the Chinese students preferred to focus on contradictions and resolve them.

Another study asked American and Chinese graduate students at an American university to read stories about conflict: one disagreement was between a mother and daughter, and one was between the conflicting desires of a single individual. The participants were asked to analyze these conflicts. The investigators coded the responses as either dialectical resolutions (seeking a compromise or middle way) or nondialectical resolutions. For the mother-daughter conflict, 72% of the Chinese answers were dialectical as opposed to 26% of the American ones. The Chinese responses often suggested compromise solutions. In the scenario involving conflicting desires, 50% of the Chinese responses endorsed compromise but only 12% of the American responses did; the Americans' responses suggested change in only one direction.

One final empirical example of the dialectic: East Asians can simultaneously hold opposing emotions, as well as opposing thoughts.

Chinese, Korean, and American student participants were asked to rate their emotional states at the moment of the investigation, and, in general, American participants reported either uniformly positive or uniformly negative emotions. But Chinese and Korean students reported having both strong positive and strong negative emotions at the same time.[9] Again, we can trace the foundations of dialectical emotions to Confucius, who stated, "When a person feels happiest, he will inevitably feel sad at the same time."[10]

A second series of research studies confirmed that the Chinese embrace a holistic approach to life and to the relationships between objects within an environment. In other words, the situation in which events take place influences the events themselves and their interpretation. Korean and Americans college students were given a "holism" questionnaire that included statements like "Everything in the universe is somehow related to everything else." Results revealed that Koreans had a more holistic worldview than Americans. In another study, Korean and Americans were given a news account of a Chinese graduate student in the United States who tragically shot and killed his adviser and several other students. The research participants were given 100 pieces of information about the student, the professor, the school, and so on, and were asked which items would not be relevant in determining the motive for the shooting. The Koreans thought that only 37% of the information would not be relevant, whereas the Americans thought that 55% would not be useful.[11]

In 1991, when the abovementioned Chinese graduate student Gang Lu killed his adviser and fellow students, the story was covered widely in the press. Two psychology graduate students wondered whether the US and Chinese press would attribute similar explanations for this tragedy.[12] They coded newspaper articles from both the *New York Times* and the Chinese-language US newspaper the *World Journal* for the type of explanation. The Chinese reporters focused on situational or contextual explanations for the killing rampage — for example, the availability of guns in the United States, the pressures on Chinese students, and the killer's relationships with his adviser and fellow students. The stories in the *New York Times* focused on the unique qualities and character of Lu — he had a bad temper, he had a sinister personality, and so on — and his personal beliefs and attitudes. Subsequent studies examined explanations for the mass killings by a non-Chinese worker, and similar results were found. Yet another related study found that Chinese students thought that the murders might not have taken place had the contexts been different, whereas American students, whose perspective assumes that behavior is driven by stable, individual characteristics, thought that the murders would still have taken place despite situational changes. The Chinese perspective was holistic and situational; the American view was that causes of behavior are individualistic and stable.

A third series of studies inadvertently confirmed the Confucian values of adaptability and change. Although the study set out to examine the type of interpretations that Hong Kongers give to the causes of behavior, the findings relate directly to the flexibility of identity. Hong Kong students were shown animated cartoons in which one fish was swimming in front of other fish. They were asked why that fish was in front of the others. First, however, the students had either their Western or Chinese identities "primed" by showing some of the subjects pictures of a dragon or a temple or of men writing Chinese characters using a calligraphy brush; other subjects were shown Western icons, such as Mickey Mouse or a cowboy on horseback. Flexibility of cultural identities were such that when their Western identities were primed, the Hong Kong students focused on the motivation of the individual fish, similar to the reaction of Western students. Those Hong Kong students who had had their Chinese identity primed gave a greater number of explanations that dealt with the other fish and the context.[13]

In summary, the flexible and additive identity, behavioral decisions, and emotional calm of the Hong Kong remigrants can be traced directly to Confucian and Daoist teachings that emphasize situationalism, compromise amid contradictions, harmony in interpersonal relations, and tranquility of emotion. These ancient philosophers prepared the Chinese well for twenty-first-century global transitions. However, Western sojourners are not as fortunate.

The teachings of the ancient Greek philosophers

What did the ancient Greek philosophers espouse that led to the development of Western values, and how did they differ from the Chinese approach? Historically, Confucius and Socrates were contemporaries, with Socrates being born 80 years later. Socrates, Aristotle, and Plato were Western counterparts to Confucius and Laozi. Their teachings, and those of their disciples, provided the philosophical foundations for Western culture in the fourth, fifth, and sixth centuries BCE. But the similarities with Chinese philosophers end there.

These ancient Greeks developed their ideas in response to a natural environment that encompassed both maritime activities and solitary farming and herding in mountainous regions. Food was available to those who expended great effort, and those individuals, by dint of their hard work, could influence their own lives. Additionally, individual effort could be combined with a political system and leadership style that allowed citizens freedom of movement and thought. Travel throughout the countryside expanded, and public debate of the ideas of individuals took root. This sense of personal agency or control became one of the dominant themes in Greek life. The individual, rather than the group, was the central unit of life. It is not surprising that the Olympics Games, in which individuals, not groups, competed against each other, were created by the Greeks some two thousand years ago. The Games were a celebration of individual training, strength, and spirit, and the competition, held among nude athletes, glorified the human body and elevated the winners to the level of demigods. Individual effort and individual honor were hallmarks of the Games.

Western concern was with Truth, belief, and exclusivity, as opposed to the Way, action, and harmony. The Greek preoccupation with certainty and curiosity about the natural world led Aristotle, considered by some to be the father of biology, to classify flora and fauna. He created categories and defined the shared attributes of the members of those categories; each object could then belong only to one group, either-or. Curiosity about the world also led to the development of abstract theories and models by which natural processes could be explained and predicted.

Categorization and mutual exclusivity gave rise to the philosophical Law of the Excluded Middle. When confronted with contradictory propositions, the ancient Greeks tended to polarize their beliefs — to hold one or the other. The Chinese, however, moved toward equal acceptance of the two propositions.[14] Logic, a cornerstone of Western thought as a paradigm to evaluate arguments, dictates that a statement excludes its opposite: if A is true, then B (the opposite of A) must be false. Rationality is abstract, analytical, and extreme. As one scholar has said, the "Western tendency [is] to think in terms of 'either/or' such that the fine lines of distinction and exclusiveness so typical of Western life … are not common to the Chinese mind" (p. 6).[15] Confucian thought is specific and practical, and allows that both A and B may be true at different times and in different circumstances.

Another important element of Greek thinking was the emphasis on examining objects in isolation from their surroundings. Although the Greeks studied both human "objects" and physical objects, their focus was increasingly on the physical and less on human attributes and relationships. Further, they considered the objects and the world around them to be static. Parmenides, another fifth-century BCE philosopher who strongly influenced Plato, suggested that the universe is an indivisible, unchanging entity and that all reference to change is self-contradictory. In his poem *Way of Truth*, he claimed that change is impossible.

Extrapolating from the Greek teachings, Western psychological theory assumes that humans need and demand consistency, that they act in stable ways and search for universal laws by focusing on discrete attributes and elements in both the psychological and physical world. Even the presentation of Western philosophy and thought since Aristotle has become compartmentalized and analytic, dividing experience and life into separate aspects of knowledge and separating the mind and body for study or treatment by psychologists or physicians. Eastern thinking, however, focuses on wholeness and practical applications. Chinese philosophers looked at life and knowledge in its totality, not in its parts.[16] Witness Chinese traditional medicine, which treats the mind and body as parts of a whole.

Western philosophies and contemporary cultural identity

Greek writings provided the blueprint for the development of Western values, thought, and behavior. The inhabitants of the continent, who subsequently became the nations of Europe and the Anglophone world, had Romance languages at its core and were heirs to the Roman Empire. The Roman legacy provided a system of laws that promoted consistency, the reduction of ambiguity, and universal application rather than case-by-case adjudication. Consistency within their lives could be amplified by keeping foreign elements away from the society and by minimizing contact with those who were different.[17] Thus in the *Laws*, Plato warns that the Utopian state must be insulated from the outside world as much as possible. In terms of foreign visitors, "good care" needs to be taken lest any "of this category of visitor introduces any novel custom." Contact with strangers is to be kept "down to the unavoidable minimum." Plato implores citizens not to stray from their homeland. "No young person under forty is even to be allowed to travel abroad under any circumstances; nor is anyone to be allowed to go for private reasons, but only on some public business, as a herald or ambassador or as an observer of one sort or another." If citizens do go abroad, they are obligated when they return to "tell the younger generation that the social and political customs of the rest of the world don't measure up to their own."[18] Thus the Greeks developed a categorical and ethnocentric worldview, a word whose very roots are Greek.

What, then, were the links between early Greek thought, the development of Western societal values, and contemporary cognitive style? They follow a clear, linear path just as the teachings of the Chinese philosophers led to current Chinese thought.

Western countries are emphatically individualistic in their orientation to the group. The relevant Hofstede dimension in this regard is Individualism–Collectivism (introduced in Chapter 1). On the Hofstede Scale of Individualism (ranging from 0 to 100), every single country scoring 70 or above (15 countries) was Western; the United States ranked first, with a score of 91. Confucian countries, valuing family and group relationships above the self, scored in the lowest quadrant. Hong Kong scored 25; Singapore and China, 20. Proclivity toward the self among Westerners is the antithesis of the group harmony that Easterners value. Cultural adaptation, both overseas and return, is an individual struggle for the Western identity.

A corollary value, that of interpersonal equality versus hierarchy, again distinguishes Western cultures from Confucian ones. Scores on power distance, the value dimension created by Hofstede that captures these behaviors, reveal China, Singapore, and Hong Kong to be significantly more accepting of inequality and hierarchy than the United States and other Anglo and European countries are. Because they value equality, Westerners also feel less compelled to adjust their behavior in a context that may include a superior or higher-status individual. In the West, norms are looser, and cultural imperatives are less clear; as an alternative, personality-driven behavior propels the individual.

Self-emphasis overshadows other values, although the West and East differ on other Hofstede value dimensions as we have seen. The United States and other Anglo countries have a moderate score on Uncertainty Avoidance; they are more concerned about avoiding ambiguity than most Asian countries, but there is not as large a gap as with the other value dimensions. To shield themselves from uncertainty, Westerners express pride in being "governments of laws" rather than "governments of man," as the Chinese described themselves. Western cultures have more linguistic rules. They consider what is different to be dangerous. Having less tolerance for ambiguity also generates more anxiety for the Westerner, an emotion that surfaces during cultural adaptation and repatriation.

The United States, Great Britain, and other Western countries value

Short-term Orientation (STO) compared to the Confucian countries that score the highest on Long-term Orientation. One prominent characteristic of the STO dimension is a concern with personal stability and a wish to discourage change. Another is a focus on beliefs that convey the "Truth" as embodied in "the Book" among some world religions (the Old and New Testaments, the Qu'ran) and in the legal systems. These concepts lead to sharp distinctions between good and evil, right and wrong, one identity and another. Applied to cultural transitions, these values lead to the development of permanent or clearly described identities and work against the easy cultural identity flexibility and behavioral switching of the Chinese. However, "Truth," stability, and cognitive consistency may prove to be liabilities in the fast-changing global world of the twenty-first century.

The empirical link between Western values and cognitive style has been demonstrated in many psychological studies. Do Westerners have a narrow, single-focused perspective while Easterners focus on the wider situation (the context)? Japanese and US college students were shown a short animation of rapidly moving, centrally located fish against a background of rocks, plant life, and fish that were not moving. The students were asked what they saw. While both groups mentioned the moving fish, the Japanese made 60% more references to other elements in the clip, such as the water, bubbles, and plants. The Americans were also more likely to start their narratives by describing the large, moving fish, while the Japanese tended to provide context first: "This looks like a pond." The American students were not influenced by the environments in other recognition tasks either, as their focus was on the central objects, and they perceived fewer relationships between objects and the environment.[19]

In a series of studies, Richard Nisbett and his students demonstrated that, consonant with the early philosophers, Americans today are more likely to see stability in a wide number of situations compared to Chinese.[20] Shown various statistical graphs about how likely it was that a dating couple would continue to date, about whether a trend in global economic rates would continue to rise, or about whether world cancer rate trends would continue to accelerate, the Americans thought change was much less likely to occur than did the Chinese.

In general, Westerners saw fewer objects in their field of vision and fewer relationships among objects. They were also more likely to assume that the behavior of an individual was caused by stable personality traits rather than by the situation in which the behavior took place. This reliance on personal characteristics rather than on contextual elements was demonstrated in the analysis, described earlier, of the studies on the campus shooting by Gang Lu. Psychologists have labeled this Western cognitive bias as the fundamental attribution error (FAE). Other studies have demonstrated FAE by asking research participants to read an essay that expressed a particular political point of view written by another student. Some participants were told that the students were paid to write about that particular point of view; other participants were told that the student-writers could choose their own point of view. In other words, the conditions under which the students wrote their essays were said to vary. However, this made no difference to the US participants. When asked what they thought was the actual point of view of the student whose essay they read, they indicated that they believed that all the students wrote about their own personal points of view. The notion of stable traits and beliefs overwhelmed the situational explanations.

Westerners' anxiety-laden subtractive identity response to cultural transitions follow from the values and cognitive style laid out for them 2,500 years ago by the Greeks. A proclivity to categorize the world and make either-or decisions, to believe in one Truth, to perceive stability rather than change, to endow the individual with control, to separate the individual from the group, to ignore the situational context, and to feel distress in uncertain and ambiguous cultural situations all formed the Western sense of who they should be throughout the cultural transition cycle.

Descendants of Confucius and Laozi, Socrates and Aristotle have had their basic life values and ways of thinking shaped by the teachings of these ancient philosophers. Perhaps it should not surprise us that these values and cognitive styles also influence people's day-to-day behavior and the decisions people make during the migration and remigration experience.

11   The new Hong Kong boomerang

The Hong Kong Remigration Project estimates that 500,000 people have returned to live and work in Hong Kong. Speculation, however, is that a portion of these remigrants are not permanent residents but rather belong to a growing global group of transnationals. Participants in this investigation confirm that they have strategic plans for the future regarding their place of residence. But now, in light of Hong Kong's tranquil political scenario and stable and growing economic outlook, one may well ask why all Hong Kong immigrants do not return to their homeland, prepared to settle in through retirement.

Why don't more Hong Kongers return and stay?

There are multiple reasons why all Hong Kong migrants have not returned to Hong Kong, either temporarily or permanently. The background against which all return decisions are made is the still uneasy relationship between Hong Kong and China. Hong Kong is formally designated as a Special Administrative Region of China, giving it considerable independence in the financial sector. However, continuing political uncertainty remains regarding the effects of Chinese sovereignty over the territory. Small cycles of relief are followed by anxiety, as when the Beijing government three times postponed the general election for Hong Kong's chief executive, first to 2007, then 2012, and now scheduled for 2017. Doubts about the effectiveness of the national authorities also ripple into Hong Kong from China as evidence mounts about governmental cover-ups in the food industry following scandals about tainted dairy products and in the construction industry following revelations of shoddy school construction in the aftermath of the 2008 earthquake in Sichuan Province.

Against nagging queasiness about living permanently under Chinese rule were a host of other, more practical issues that formed decision-making barriers to the immigrants' returning home. Chief among these were quality-of-life concerns. Post-1997, Hong Kong apartments remained small, crowded, and expensive. These housing constraints have become exaggerated in comparison to the migrants' residential options in Canada or Australia, where large apartments with balconies, or private homes surrounded by greenery and parks, were now within the financial reach of most migrants. The Hong Kong equivalent in housing was priced for only the wealthiest. In addition to housing, the cost of living in Hong Kong remained high in comparison to the costs of their immigrant lifestyles. Schooling, clothing, and entertainment all exceeded the costs of their equivalents in the Hong Kongers' new homelands. The immigrants also became accustomed to blue, pollution-free skies in Australia or Canada, and they considered the visual and olfactory pollutants, drifting down through the Pearl River Delta from Guangdong factories, not only as an everyday annoyance but with alarm for its long-term health consequences as their awareness of environmental issues had been raised while they were living overseas. Moreover, the heat and humidity of the Hong Kong summer became oppressive to many returnees after their acclimation to the cooler temperatures of Vancouver and moderate climes of Sydney and Melbourne. Finally, Hong Kong's traffic congestion and narrow roadways were more troublesome for and less tolerated by the returnees, although the efficiency of the MTR subways was gratefully appreciated.

Another concern expressed by potential returnees was the pressure to revert to the idiosyncratic Hong Kong balance between work and family life. Although most returnees interviewed in this study made the transition to a longer, more time-consuming work life and less involvement in family life, it was not accomplished easily or willingly. Migrants reported that in their countries of settlement they reveled in participating in regular family dinners, attending children's plays and sporting events, and taking weekend trips with their family. Although working parents regretted the rebalancing process, they acknowledged that the hard work ethic of Hong Kong companies was an immutable element of the society, and they showed little interest in countering the normative expectations of the workplace culture.

For many immigrants contemplation of a move back to Hong Kong centered on their children. After several years of living in their country of migration, their young children spoke fluent English, and because their parents determinedly spoke Cantonese at home, they achieved fluency in that dialect as well. But the children were sadly lacking in knowledge of Chinese characters, either for writing or reading. Competence in this area would require the hours of memorization and drills that were a crucial aspect of the Hong Kong educational curriculum. Furthermore, few of the immigrant children were familiar with Mandarin (Putonghua). Since the handover, the Beijing government has insisted that Mandarin be taught in the Hong Kong schools, be displayed on public signage, and be utilized in public address systems in the transportation system. Parents shuddered to contemplate the difficulties of returning their children to the local schools without the requisite linguistic skills.

The children of immigrants also lacked cultural knowledge of Hong Kong's popular culture, games, sports, and adolescent mores and attitudes. In schools, play yards and classrooms, where social cliques provided small group comfort but also exclusion, parents were concerned that their remigrated children would be easy targets for bullies. Parents were also aware of the high number of adolescent suicides in Hong Kong and were terrified that their sons or daughters would fall prey to teen depression.

As we examined in previous chapters, a wide range of schooling options were available to the remigrants. Parents could enroll their children in private international schools where the curriculum was more flexible and was geared in part to returning students. Elementary Mandarin would be introduced, English fluency could be maintained, and ignorance of the local culture would be the norm rather than the exception. But these schools were expensive and had limited seating for the growing number of returnees. Less expensive local schools were an obvious alternative, but their students were expected to know thousands of characters, have moderate Mandarin fluency, and be able to adjust to a teaching style based on rote memorization and acquiescence to the authority of the teacher.

Family-related issues were the source of further apprehension for potential returnees: for some remigrants, few family members remained in Hong Kong. Entire extended families had migrated in the years leading up to the handover. Despite the allure of a high-paying job back in Hong Kong, what would life be like back in there without the comforting presence and interconnectedness of the extended family?

One additional chink in the armor of life's security back in Hong Kong was the absence of a pension for retirement. In Hong Kong, saving for retirement is a private pursuit without significant public or employer assistance. Families begin accumulating retirement savings when they are young. However, much of those savings were exhausted by the migrants during their early adjustment years in Canada or Australia. They had not grown new nest eggs as large because the national governments in both of those countries provided retirement relief for their citizens. A return to Hong Kong signaled a return to retirement anxiety.

A final obstacle to returning and staying was more psychological in nature. Some migrants, in moments of self-reflection, were aware that they had changed since settling into their new homelands. They had adapted to the lifestyle of Melbourne or thought like their Toronto neighbors, and they enjoyed local leisure pursuits like hiking or hockey. How comfortable would they be living again in Hong Kong? And how would they be perceived by their families and new coworkers and neighbors? Would they be seen as too Western and lacking in Hong Kong manners and behaviors?

How to lure Hong Kong immigrants back home

The return of migrants was crucial to the functioning of both the Hong Kong government and the private sector. Immediately following the large-scale emigration of the late 1980s and early 1990s, government officials and political pundits decried the dire economic effects on Hong Kong of losing its best and brightest in so many fields. Attempts began to lure the migrants home.

First efforts focused on offering high-paying jobs to the newly migrated. However, these workers, primarily men, were reluctant to move their families again after the initial settling-in process in their new homelands. Hong Kong employers countered by offering work flexibility, which allowed husbands to return alone to Hong Kong but frequently fly back to their new settlement countries and to their families.

Second attempts focused on families and children. Educational policy makers in Hong Kong were aware of the linguistic barriers faced by returning children. They proposed establishing special bilingual programs where the children could simultaneously maintain their fluency in English and receive intensive instruction in Cantonese and Mandarin. Much could also be learned from the example of other countries that encouraged migration or return migration. Israel, for example, has long encouraged both its own citizens living abroad and Jews living in the diaspora to return. To accommodate the need to learn fluent and colloquial Hebrew, Israel developed intensive language programs (*ulpan*) and offered them on a regular basis and at low or no cost at multiple sites (cities, suburban areas, *kibbutizim*) throughout the country. Similar programs could be developed throughout Hong Kong.

Additional policies can be implemented to bolster and accelerate the return of entire families. I would make the following recommendations. Language proficiency programs should begin in host countries. Hong Kong government-funded language schools could be established in Canada, Australia, England, and the United States. Programs could be extracurricular, with course offerings after school and on the weekends, as well as embedded in the regular curriculum. The Chinese government has begun these efforts through the establishment of Confucius Institutes throughout the United States. These organizations are based at universities; they fund the offering of Mandarin-language courses and hold national competitions and award prizes to recognize the excellence of US high school and university students who are studying Mandarin. Although these organizations are not specifically focused on the Chinese migrant, immigrant children no doubt benefit from the increasing richness and depth of Mandarin instruction available in American schools.

A second policy to encourage family return would focus on the remigrated schoolchildren. Once children have returned to Hong Kong, a range of language courses could be offered them in the public schools. Advanced English language courses would enable remigrant children to maintain their English fluency, an ardent goal of their parents and of international employers in Hong Kong. A separate Mandarin curriculum would enable them to catch up to their age mates in reading and writing. As an adjunct to the linguistic support, psychological assistance in the form of counseling and tutoring should be offered. Academic and personal counseling would ensure a smoother adjustment and provide students with transition coping skills that will serve the peripatetic Hong Kongers well.

Another recommendation is to provide special housing subsidies and resettlement money to the returnees. As was mentioned early, housing is a negative quality-of-life issue for returnees. Funding so that remigrants could rent larger apartments or small homes in the New Territories would improve their readjustment to Hong Kong. Again, by way of comparison, Israel's housing policy for returnees could be used as a model. *Aliyah* (meaning, "to go up") programs provide a wide range of subsidies to assist both newcomers and repatriates.

Although many migrants have secured employment prior to their return, some return to Hong Kong for other reasons and become job-seekers. They would benefit from employment assistance and remigrant adjustment workshops. Life in Hong Kong has changed during the decade that some of the immigrants have been residents elsewhere. Learning in more detail about Hong Kong's political, economic, social, and educational life under Chinese sovereignty would assuage anxieties and worries.

Financial assistance would be most welcomed by returnees. Start-up funding for new businesses plus strategic planning would enable entrepreneurs to enter the new markets of and better understand the new policies regarding trade with China. Similarly, alleviating retirement trepidation could be met with programs that subsidize or assist the development of retirement benefits.

How to maintain and retain remigrants

Once families have returned to Hong Kong and employment has been secured, the task shifts to maintaining the family residence in the city. Surely, full employment with high salaries and retirement benefits would be the most direct route to retention. But research has shown that happy spouses and children are also a key to the retention of these bilingual, bicultural returnees.

Recreation and leisure opportunities play a role in retention attempts. Fortunately, more than 30% of Hong Kong territory is made up of country parks and nature preserves that are embedded with hiking trails and picnic areas. While I do not advocate building ice hockey rinks (for the impassioned Canadian remigrants), I do suggest building golf courses and increasing the number of tennis courts, indoor badminton courts, and similar leisure facilities with which remigrants had become accustomed in their countries of resettlement.

A most audacious suggestion, but one that remigrants most cherish in their decision to remain in Hong Kong, is to maintain a stable government that is on the path to democratic rule. Elections need to be scheduled and held on a regular basis. The chief executive and Legco (Legislative Council) must be able to operate independent of Beijing's control and be prepared to focus on solving Hong Kong's social, educational, and fiscal problems.

If Confucius is correct ...

Confucian teachings and their relevance to migrants and remigrants were discussed in Chapter 10. Flexibility of cultural identity and practicality in geographic movements have been the essential characteristics of Hong Kongers for the past 200 years. If Confucius' ideas predict future behavior as well as past, we would expect continued movement on the part of these peripatetic residents. Sociologists have incorporated these concepts into the notion of the transnational citizen.

If Confucius is correct, remigrated Hong Kongers will return to Canada and Australia, most likely to retire. In another decade, they will have reaccumulated considerable savings that they will take with them back to their passport countries — consumer spending that is advantageous to the economies of those countries. Hong Kongers' return to their countries of immigration is not without fiscal and social consequences. It will be a burden on the Canadian and Australian governments as they must provide retirement benefits to their newest citizens who most recently contributed little in the way of taxable income. Regrettably, the Hong Kong economy will be the biggest loser: in the accumulated savings of the returnees that are not spent on Hong Kong real estate or consumer goods, in the multilingual and multicultural employees who depart yet again, and in the politically and socially active citizens who are no longer present.

Yet from a wider perspective, Hong Kong might also be seen as a big winner in the global movement of peoples. Remigrants have not only carried with them attitudes about environmental conservation and laissez-faire parenting, but they have also imported democratic values and ideas. Historically and culturally, Hong Kongers have been reluctant to publicly express their opinions. Maintaining interpersonal harmony took precedence over proclaiming one's personal, and possibly contradictory, point of view. But years of living in Australia or Canada released those personal opinions for the remigrants. Public protests in Hong Kong have been one consequence. "June 4" has become a rallying cry for a growing number of residents and remigrants. Nominally, the date symbolizes the anniversary of the 1989 Tiananmen Square crackdown by Mainland soldiers on prodemocracy students. But many in the growing crowds of protestors come to demonstrate against Beijing-imposed restrictions on democratic developments in Hong Kong. Similar protests coincide with the anniversary of the handover to Chinese sovereignty on July 1, 1997. By 2003, nearly one-tenth of the territory's population participated in the July 1 events.[1]

These political attitudes may be the most durable and widespread import attributed to the remigrants.

The new boomerang: Hong Kongers in China

While the boomerang between Hong Kong and countries of resettlement continues, a new boomerang trajectory has also emerged, this one between Hong Kong and Mainland China. In 2005, it was estimated that out of 6.9 million Hong Kongers, more than 500,000 were living and working in China,[2] approximately 60,000 having moved there in 2003 alone. These may be remigrants from the West or a new cohort of sojourners who are taking advantage of the employment opportunities that life in China can offer. It has been estimated that 70% moved for job-related reasons, and an increasing number of Hong Kong companies have relocated to Southern China. In fact, Hong Kong is among the biggest investors in the Mainland and is ranked as China's fourth largest source of direct foreign investment.[3]

Other reasons for Hong Kongers to move to China include retirement (11%) and to be reunited with their families (8%). A survey by the Hong Kong Planning Department found that an additional 161,000 planned to move to the Mainland in the next ten years,[4] although the 2008–09 economic recession will surely interrupt or slow down this movement.

Metropolitan Hong Kong can now be considered to encompass the Pearl River Delta and Shenzhen. An increasing number of Hong Kongers either commute daily to work in Guangzhou (a 45-minute train ride on the newly planned high-speed train) or live in China during the week and return to Hong Kong on weekends.

This new cycle of migration and remigration (or sojourn/repatriation) is one that traces its roots not back to political fear of China but to the economic embrace of China. The new Hong Kong immigrant is likely to be a manager whose work takes him or her to Shenzhen or Dongguan or Shanghai for a week or a month at a time and whose family remains in Hong Kong. His or her coworkers or boss or subordinates are Mainlanders, as are his temporary neighbors. Will these Hong Kongers prove to be equally adaptive and additive in this new cultural environment? How will families and the society at large in Hong Kong be influenced by the eventual return of thousands from the Mainland? At this time, it is unclear what the identity, behavioral, and attitudinal consequences are for these new migrants and for the two cultural end points of their transition, but it is the opportune time to begin longitudinal investigations into this newest layer of the Hong Kong identity.

Chinese in Hong Kong

Hong Kongers move or commute to the Mainland, but the relocation is bidirectional. Some Mainlanders are choosing to move, without government intervention, to Hong Kong for the freedoms that it affords, such as the reproductive freedom to have more than one child. In 2005, nearly 20,000 Mainland women crossed the border into Hong Kong to have a second child, a more than 150% increase from 2001. In addition to skirting the Mainland policy of one child per family, these women knew that choosing to have their babies in Hong Kong would ensure that the newborns would possess a Hong Kong residency card and passport, still considered documents that lead to special privileges.[5] The strain on the medical and hospital systems in Hong Kong is already being felt, and policies are being enacted to stem the maternity tide.

Since 1997, when the border with China opened, more than half a million Mainlanders have moved to Hong Kong, and 13.6 million visit each year. Nearly 500,000 live on one side of the border but work on the other.[6] The economic consequences have been dismal for Hong Kongers, including lowered wages for everyone because Mainlanders are willing to work for less and there is no set minimum wage. Work life in Hong Kong can be dreary for the Mainlanders, who are often discriminated against in hiring even if they speak Cantonese. Once hired, they are paid at less than the prevailing wages. The social consequences have been equally grim: increases in crime, disease, lowered employment opportunities — all blamed on the influx of Mainlanders.

Nonetheless, cultural understanding between the Mainlanders and Hong Kongers is growing, cultural conflicts are lessening, and distinctions between the two groups blurring. Friendships are being established, and dating and marriage has become more common.[7] It has been reported that one-third of all Hong Kong marriages in 2003 (11,613 out of 34,439) were between Hong Kongers and Mainlanders, primarily between Hong Kong men and Mainland women.

Educational interactions are increasing, as Hong Kongers are studying on the Mainland and Mainlanders are studying in Hong Kong universities. There is increased interest in Mainland media, especially television soap operas like *My Fair Princess*, which has entranced Hong Kongers. With the scope and depth of interactions increasing, old stereotypes of Mainlanders as country bumpkins have been modified, aided by the fact that more of the newcomers have been professionals and urban dwellers, some of whom lived in the West. Lastly, because the *yuan* has strengthened in value, it has become eagerly accepted by Hong Kong merchants.

Some scholars believe that these two cultural groups are forming a hybrid culture, bilingual but one culture, distinct from the bicultural identities in which immigrants switch from one set of behaviors to another. Fluency in accentless Cantonese is an important part of the hybrid identity, but Hong Kongers also need to have mastered Mandarin. One interviewee commented (P42):

> I learn Putonghua (Mandarin) starting in 1997. And now I can make a speech in Putonghua. I like to learn, that is why I watch the Putonghua TV, for news and the, because I need it for working. One of my contractors is Putonghua-speaking guy. And his English is not good. And he doesn't speak Cantonese. Then I try to improve myself, and I know Putonghua will be getting more important in the future. And I can tell Putonghua is important for my children, if they really need to go back to work in China.

Despite increased knowledge and acceptance, numerous cultural distinctions remain. Hong Kongers' entertainment preferences lean toward popular culture, movies, music, cartoons, and video games; Mainlanders focus on news, politics, and world history. Echoing their British traditions, Hong Kongers queue up for buses, relinquish their seats for the elderly, and, now, are adhering to the ban on public smoking; one will rarely observe these behaviors on the Mainland or among the new residents. Psychological studies comparing Hong Kong/Mainland biculturals have yet to be done, but it is now possible to contrast their cognitive, social, emotional, and self-concept components.

A future of increased economic and social assimilation seems inevitable. Even though nearby Shenzhen has eclipsed Hong Kong in population (9 million compared to 6.9 million) and land mass (780 square miles vs. 426 square miles), it is the Hong Kong government that is encouraging closer integration. A plan is being considered that would allow 2 million Shenzhen residents to enter Hong Kong freely. Also under this plan, transportation to the South China region would be improved by building a new high-speed railway from Hong Kong to both Shenzhen and Guangzhou.[8]

Another identity layer to the cultural complexity of Hong Kongers

Worldwide, a growing trend has revealed that millions of people are returning to their homelands following residences in countries of settlement that ranged from short-term to decades long. The displacement of these individuals has the potential for both disruptive and beneficial consequences for the social, economic, and political fabric of all the regions involved. Social scientists are only beginning to understand the psychological effects of return migration on the individuals and their families. Preliminary findings indicate that returning home can have wide-ranging emotional, familial, and social consequences, the result being, on the one hand, a cohort of discontented multicultural global nomads and, on the other, culturally adaptable, sophisticated transnational world citizens.

In this book, we have examined with sharper scrutiny the case of Hong Kong return migration of the late twentieth and early twenty-first centuries due to massive "handover"-related migration between 1984 and 1997. Utilizing multiple methodologies, the quantitative and qualitative sources corroborated each other in a process known as triangulation, thereby increasing the confidence in the results. The Hong Kong Remigration Project found that Hong Kongers have a complex and multilayered cultural identity not unlike the nacred layers of the pearl to which Hong Kong is often compared: a traditional Chinese and Confucian core, covered by layers stimulated by war, typhoons, political crises, discrimination, irritation, economic recessions, health epidemics, and geographic mobility. Major psychological layers of British, Hong Kong, and the newly acquired migration identity (Canadian, Australian, etc.) have been added over the past 200 years. Now another layer is being created, the modern Chinese layer that has Hong Kongers speaking Mandarin and immersed in contemporary Chinese culture. Comparing herself to her Hong Kong friends and coworkers who did not emigrate, one interviewee observed, with keen self-insight (P16):

> We have a different experience. We have more exposure. It doesn't make us a smarter person, but it's just make life easier for us to move around and be more flexible. Just be more open to world of different kind of people. I have learned to become more observant just being able to hang out with different people. And, in turn, being more observant toward myself, being to see how people react over my actions, and improve myself … In different occasions being able to communicate to local people … If you are never left one country, you would never be able to see the world and being to realize how much more you can be improved. So I am looking forward to just moving around, and probably, I don't know, Singapore or Shanghai, go to different cities in the world.

These identities are flexible and dynamic; they change based on political, social, and workplace contexts. Behavioral consequences of cultural identity are far-reaching: residential choices, educational curriculum, friendship networks, workplace selections, cuisine preferences, and naming conventions. Communication styles are more direct with superiors and coworkers and more respectful with subordinates. Styles of thinking too have been influenced. Most remigrants have developed self-concepts that are equal parts independent and interdependent; therefore, they exhibit a decrease in family and group orientation compared to nonmigrating Hong Kongers, and pay increased attention to individual needs and desires. New attitudes have developed as well. After years living in Western democracies, many remigrants have returned to Hong Kong with a heightened political consciousness and an awakened activism. They have also become aware of environmental issues (air and water pollution, global warming, etc.). Emotionally, Hong Kong remigrants have emerged from their global wanderings as relatively stable, calm, and positive individuals. As one remigrant stated (P17):

> I am totally in it [back to Hong Kong]. I am a survivor. Let me put it this way. If I am a Hong Kong Chinese, local young boy, who totally adapt to this northern [Canadian] lifestyle and enjoy it. As a matter of fact, I lived in Saskatoon [city in Canada] for about eight years and really enjoy it. Got sort of a career ... working relationship with people and almost like stay there. Now moving back ... I had seventeen years in this city, no way I am not going to get used to it ... You never get it if you never make the move. So focus on that, and every day you would be happier.

There are some negative social indicators (e.g., increased divorce rate) that may be associated with cultural transitions, but a causal relationship is not clear. Anxieties that plague most Western repatriates are noticeably absent among the Hong Kongers. The operative Hong Kong immigrant characteristic is pragmatism about the events at hand and strategic planning for themselves and their children. Additive or global identities are the desired objective, and in most cases they have been obtained, producing multilingual, multicultural citizens well prepared for an interconnected future world.

Conclusion: The Cultural Identity Model re-examined

In Chapter 3, a summary of the Cultural Identity Model of Cultural Transitions described postremigration psychological consequences including four identity profiles and profile-specific emotional outcomes. The Hong Kong Remigration Project was designed to test the generalizability of the CIM to a remigrant population and to a Hong Kong sample. The primary confirmation of this research project was the discovery of all four pure identity profiles (additive, subtractive, affirmative, global) among the Hong Kong remigrants, as well as two blended identities (subtractive/additive and affirmative/additive) and the bifurcation of the additive profile (additive/hybrid and additive/bicultural). Both qualitative and quantitative data supported the notion of identity changes as a consequence of transitions.

However, the data also revealed culturally distinctive results, chief among those being the distribution of identity profiles. Research among European, US, and, to some extent, Japanese repatriates indicated a strong preference for subtractive identities. Returnees consistently remarked that they felt less a part of their home culture, dissimilar from their compatriots, and alienation from their home country. Hong Kong remigrants, however, overwhelmingly experienced additive identities. The consequence of this additive identity profile resulted in either a unique personal hybridity of home and immigrant culture (additive/hybrid) or a bicultural identity in which ways of behaving and thinking varied according to the cultural situation within various domains (family, workplace, school, social setting). Because the CIM does not specify the distribution of the identity profiles, this finding in and of itself does not necessitate a major reconceptualizing of the model. However, as these findings are radically different from those for Westerners, it does suggest that the external variable of the culture of the immigrant be added to the model.

A second contradictory finding strengthens the need to add a cultural factor to the model. The CIM does predict the emotional reaction of people with the various identity profiles. Both subtractive and additive profiles were predicted to be accompanied by emotional distress and discomfort. Research findings among US, European, and Japanese repatriates confirm these predictions of the model. Hong Kong remigrants do not. They display near uniform positive or neutral affective reactions to returning home and their identity changes. Most startling is the lack of distress among the additive identifiers. Chapter 10 developed in some detail the philosophical and historical explanations for these empirical findings. Thus, culture will be added as an explanatory variable in the model.

Which cultures might lead to flexible (additive) adaptations to cultural sojourns and which to more rigid and difficult adjustments? One might conclude that individuals from cultures that have a Confucian perspective (East and Southeast Asian countries, for example) would experience additive identity and lack of emotional distress to remigration. Evidence is accumulating from disparate research studies that highlight the adaptability and flexibility of East-Asian peoples. One study of negotiation styles and conflict resolution among American and Japanese participants found that the Japanese were more likely to adapt to a US negotiation style than the opposite. Furthermore, Japanese participants accepted the need to compromise.[9] Additional evidence of flexibility and high-context communication was found in a study of East-Asians. When they were divided into groups that had to work together on a consensus task, participants adopted the other party's norms in order to maintain harmony. The authors noted that when Asians worked with New Zealanders, they often adopted the New Zealand communication style.[10] However, one may assume that there is a range of adherence to Confucian principles among Asian countries. Currently, there are no scales that measure adherence to Confucianism. The development of such a scale would be a beneficial addition to the research area.

I suggest that yet another factor be added to the CIM as an external predictor of remigration identity and affect, that of level of cultural homogeneity. It appears that the multilayered Hong Kong identity, created through sustained contact with China and Britain and the continuous flow of immigrants across its borders, resulted in cultural heterogeneity and predisposed Hong Kongers to a cultural flexibility and pragmatism that resulted in their lack of distress. A revised CIM would predict that those cultures high in heterogeneity would be more aware of their cultural identity, be better prepared for cultural adjustments, would be more likely to adopt an additive identity, and would experience low levels of remigration distress. Conversely, cultures high in homogeneity would be more likely to experience subtractive identity and negative emotional reactions to returning home.

Research testing the predictive power of these additional variables to the model needs to be designed and implemented. In light of the growing remigration population among many countries, data collection among this population will have fewer barriers and availability will be increased. Vast numbers of remigrants worldwide also amplify the significance of understanding the psychological terrain of these binational migrants and the consequences for home and settlement countries.

Appendix A
Hong Kong Remigration Project questionnaire and psychological scales

Interview protocol

1. First, I want to ask you a few questions about the dates on your time living overseas — what year did you leave Hong Kong? _____ How old were you? _____ How long did you live in _____ ? ____ years. When did you return to Hong Kong? _____ Did any family members return with you? _____

2. Before you emigrated, how did you think of yourself culturally?

3. Think about your feelings about living in _____. Describe an experience in which you were happy or glad to be living there. Describe an experience that was confusing. Describe an experience that was unpleasant or made you wish you were back in Hong Kong.

4. Describe where you lived — the neighborhood, your friends, coworkers?

5. Describe some particular situation that shows the extent to which you thought like an _____ (country). Describe a specific situation in which you could have acted in either an _____ way or a Chinese way.

6. How would you describe yourself on forms and documents when you were asked about nationality/ethnicity?

7. Please describe your thoughts about returning to Hong Kong — why did you decide to return? Describe your emotions — how did you feel about leaving _____ (host country)?

8. Think about your first day back in Hong Kong after _____ years. Describe how the city looked ... smelled ... felt. Where did you go? Who did you see?

9. Describe your emotional reaction to returning home. Happy? Confused? Relieved? Stressed? Did your emotional reaction change during the past

_____ years since you have returned (that is, do you feel the same way about being back in Hong Kong today as you did when you first returned).

10. Describe the ways that you may still act or think like an _____ (host country) regarding family practices. For example, think about the goals you have for your children versus what goals they have.

11. Describe your neighborhood, where you live now. Think about your neighbors. Describe one way in which you feel similar to them or have a lot in common. Describe one way in which you feel different.

12. Where do your children attend school? Why this choice?

13. Describe your relationship with your spouse and how it has changed after returning home.

14. Describe food preferences — seafood? Chinese food? Western food?

15. Describe work style — Western? HK style?

16. The answer to the next question may be a little difficult to put into words but I would like you to describe to me how you think about who you are culturally. Chinese? Hong Kong Chinese? _____ (host country)? Combination? Different than both _____ and Chinese. Depends on the situation? Walk me through a specific situation you experienced which is an example of how you feel about yourself culturally.

17. How do you think other people here in Hong Kong view you?

18. Now that you have been back in Hong Kong, what advice would you give a Chinese immigrant in the US who is thinking about coming back to Hong Kong?

19. What are your future plans? Do you intend to stay/retire in Hong Kong?

I would like to have a little more information about you and your background.

How many years of formal education did you have? _____

What was your occupation in Hong Kong prior to your departure? _____

What was your occupation in _____ (host country)?

What is your occupation now? _____

How would you rate your ability to speak English? Please use the following scale:

Very good   Good   Somewhat good   Not very good   Hard to communicate
                                                      in English

Please complete this form which asks questions about being both a Hong Konger and an _____ (attachment 1).

Please complete these questions which relate to your experience of returning to Hong Kong (attachment 2). The other side has some general questions about your life.

Please complete these last questions which ask about yourself (attachment 3).

We have now covered many topics that deal with your experience in the _____ (host country) and now back in Hong Kong. Any other questions I should ask you to think about regarding this idea of returning home and your "cultural" self?

Modified Birman Acculturation Scale

Please read each question and circle the number that corresponds to your opinion.

		Not at all			Very well, like a native
1.	How would you rate your ability to speak English:				
	(a) with colleagues at work	1	2	3	4
	(b) with Western friends	1	2	3	4
	(c) on the phone	1	2	3	4
	(d) with strangers	1	2	3	4
	(e) overall	1	2	3	4
2.	How would you rate your ability to speak Cantonese:	1	2	3	4
3.	How well do you understand English:				
	(a) on TV or at the movies	1	2	3	4
	(b) in newspapers or magazines	1	2	3	4
	(c) on the phone	1	2	3	4
	(d) overall	1	2	3	4
4.	How well do you understand Cantonese:	1	2	3	4

I. Please indicate to what extent are the following statements true of you. In using the term "Hong Konger" I am referring to someone who spent most of their growing-up years in Hong Kong.

		Not at all			Very much
1.	I think of myself as being Australian	1	2	3	4
2.	I feel good about being Australian	1	2	3	4
3.	I have a strong sense of being Australian	1	2	3	4

4.	I am proud of being Australian	1	2	3	4
5.	I think of myself as being a Hong Konger	1	2	3	4
6.	I feel good about being a Hong Konger	1	2	3	4
7.	I have a strong sense of being a Hong Konger	1	2	3	4
8.	I am proud that I am a Hong Konger	1	2	3	4

9. How do you think of yourself?

_____ (a) I consider myself more Hong Konger than Australian overall.

_____ (b) I consider myself more Australian than Hong Konger overall.

_____ (c) I feel Hong Konger and Australian about equally.

_____ (d) I feel I don't really belong to either Hong Konger or Australian culture.

_____ (e) None of the above (Please explain) _____

10. When you think of yourself, what culture is deep inside — Chinese, Hong Konger, Australian, Westerner?

_____

_____

_____

_____

II. To what extent are the following statements true about the things that you do? Again, we use the term "Hong Konger" to refer to the culture shared by residents of Hong Kong.

	Not at all			Very much
How much do you speak English:				
1. at home?	1	2	3	4
2. with your neighbors?	1	2	3	4
3. with friends?	1	2	3	4
4. with coworkers?	1	2	3	4

How much do you:

5. read Australian books, newspapers, or magazines	1	2	3	4
6. eat at Western restaurants?	1	2	3	4
7. watch Western/Australian movies on VCR or in the movie theatre?	1	2	3	4
8. eat Western food?	1	2	3	4
9. attend Western concerts, exhibits, etc.?	1	2	3	4
10. buy groceries in international stores?	1	2	3	4
11. go to English-speaking doctors?	1	2	3	4
12. socialize with Australian friends?	1	2	3	4
13. participate in Australian clubs or events?	1	2	3	4

How much do you speak Cantonese:

1. at home?	1	2	3	4
2. with neighbors?	1	2	3	4
3. with friends?	1	2	3	4
4. with coworkers?	1	2	3	4

How much do you?

5. read Cantonese books, newspapers, or magazines?	1	2	3	4
6. eat at Chinese restaurants?	1	2	3	4
7. watch Cantonese movies on VCR or in the movie theatre?	1	2	3	4
8. eat Cantonese food?	1	2	3	4
9. attend Chinese concerts, exhibits, etc.?	1	2	3	4
10. shop at Chinese/local grocery stores?	1	2	3	4
11. go to Cantonese-speaking doctors?	1	2	3	4
12. socialize with Cantonese friends?	1	2	3	4
13. participate in Cantonese clubs or events?	1	2	3	4

Modified Twenty-Statement Test

Please use any words to describe yourself.

I am:

1. _____

2. _____

3. _____

4. _____

5. _____

6. _____

7. _____

8. _____

9. _____

10. _____

Print Name

Satisfaction with Life Scale

For each of the following please indicate (circle) the number that best describes how you feel.

		Strongly Disagree						Strongly Agree
1.	In most ways my life is close to my ideal.	1	2	3	4	5	6	7
2.	The conditions of my life are excellent.	1	2	3	4	5	6	7
3.	I am satisfied with my life.	1	2	3	4	5	6	7
4.	So far I have gotten the important things I want in life.	1	2	3	4	5	6	7
5.	If I could live my life over, I would change almost nothing.	1	2	3	4	5	6	7

Repatriation Distress Scale

These statements refer to your life and work since you returned to Hong Kong after living abroad.

Using the 1 to 7 scale, indicate your agreement with each item by circling the appropriate number.

		Strongly Disagree						Strongly Agree
1.	I feel lonely or have homesick feelings for _____.	1	2	3	4	5	6	7
2.	I have trouble concentrating at work.	1	2	3	4	5	6	7
3.	I am more anxious and irritable since I returned home.	1	2	3	4	5	6	7
4.	It is difficult being back in Hong Kong.	1	2	3	4	5	6	7
5.	I fit back in with my extended family in Hong Kong.	1	2	3	4	5	6	7
6.	I feel comfortable with my old friends.	1	2	3	4	5	6	7
7.	I feel as though I never left Hong Kong.	1	2	3	4	5	6	7

Self-Construal Scale

Please rate the extent to which you agree or disagree with each of the following statements.

		Strongly Disagree		Neither agree nor disagree			Strongly Agree	
1.	I have respect for the authority figures with whom I interact.	1	2	3	4	5	6	7
2.	I'd rather say "no" directly, than risk being misunderstood.	1	2	3	4	5	6	7
3.	If my brother or sister fails, I feel responsible.	1	2	3	4	5	6	7
4.	It is important for me to maintain harmony within my group.	1	2	3	4	5	6	7
5.	Having a lively imagination is important to me.	1	2	3	4	5	6	7
6.	My happiness depends on the happiness of those around me.	1	2	3	4	5	6	7
7.	I am comfortable with being singled out for praise or rewards.	1	2	3	4	5	6	7
8.	I value being in good health above everything.	1	2	3	4	5	6	7
9.	I act the same way no matter who I am with.	1	2	3	4	5	6	7
10.	I respect people who are modest about themselves.	1	2	3	4	5	6	7
11.	I will sacrifice my self-interest for the benefit of the group I am in.	1	2	3	4	5	6	7
12.	Being able to take care of myself is a primary concern for me.	1	2	3	4	5	6	7
13.	I am the same person at home that I am at school.	1	2	3	4	5	6	7
14.	I often have the feeling that my relationships with others are more important than my own accomplishments.	1	2	3	4	5	6	7
15.	I feel comfortable using someone's first name soon after I meet them, even when they are much older than I am.	1	2	3	4	5	6	7
16.	I should take into consideration my parents' advice when making education/career plans.	1	2	3	4	5	6	7

	Strongly Disagree		Neither agree nor disagree			Strongly Agree	
17. I prefer to be direct and forthright when dealing with people I've just met.	1	2	3	4	5	6	7
18. It is important to me to respect decisions made by the group.	1	2	3	4	5	6	7
19. I enjoy being unique and different from others in many respects.	1	2	3	4	5	6	7
20. My personal identity independent of others is very important to me.	1	2	3	4	5	6	7
21. I will stay in a group if they need me, even when I'm not happy with the group.	1	2	3	4	5	6	7
22. Speaking up during class is not a problem for me.	1	2	3	4	5	6	7
23. I would offer my seat in a bus for my professor.	1	2	3	4	5	6	7
24. Even when I strongly disagree with group members, I avoid an argument.	1	2	3	4	5	6	7

(Chinese version of the research questionnaire)

請用任何字／詞語形容你自己。

我是：
1. _____

2. _____

3. _____

4. _____

5. _____

6. _____

7. _____

8. _____

9. _____

10. _____

你的名字

_____

一．請閱讀以下每條問題並按你的意見在適當的數字上打圈。

	完全不能		非常好，與當地人一樣	
1. 你會如何評定你説英語的能力：				
(a) 與同事在工作中	1	2	3	4
(b) 與西方朋友	1	2	3	4
(c) 在電話中	1	2	3	4

(d) 與陌生人	1	2	3	4
(e) 整體上	1	2	3	4
2. 你會如何評定你說廣東話的能力：	1	2	3	4
3. 你有多了解英語：				
(a) 在電視電影中	1	2	3	4
(b) 在報紙雜誌中	1	2	3	4
(c) 在電話中	1	2	3	4
(d) 整體上	1	2	3	4
4. 你會如何評定你了解廣東話的能力：	1	2	3	4

二．請表示以下句子對你而言有多正確。以下「香港人」一詞是指大部份時間在香港長大的人。

	完全不正確			非常正確
1. 我認為自己是加拿大人。	1	2	3	4
2. 我為自己作為加拿大人感覺很好。	1	2	3	4
3. 我對於自己是加拿大人有很強的意識。	1	2	3	4
4. 我為自己作為加拿大人感到驕傲。	1	2	3	4
5. 我認為自己是香港人。	1	2	3	4
6. 我為自己作為香港人感覺很好。	1	2	3	4
7. 我對於自己是香港人，有很強的意識。	1	2	3	4
8. 我為自己作為香港人感到驕傲。	1	2	3	4

9. 你如何理解自己？
_____ (a) 我認為在整體上，我是一個香港人多於加拿大人。
_____ (b) 我認為在整體上，我是一個加拿大人多於香港人。
_____ (c) 我認為自己是香港人，也同時是加拿大人。
_____ (d) 我認為自己既不屬於香港的文化也不屬於加拿大的文化。
_____ (e) 以上皆非（請解釋）_____

10. 當你想一想自己，在你心深處你認為自己屬於那一種文化呢？舉例説：中國、香港、加拿大、西方或是其他的組合？

三．請表示以下句子有多正確地形容你所做的事。以下「香港」一詞是指在香港居民的共同文化。

	完全沒有			非常多
你有多經常說英語：				
1. 在家中	1	2	3	4
2. 與鄰居	1	2	3	4
3. 與朋友	1	2	3	4
4. 與同事	1	2	3	4
你有多經常：				
5. 閱讀加拿大的書、報紙或雜誌？	1	2	3	4
6. 在西式餐廳用膳？	1	2	3	4
7. 在影碟中、或到電影院看西方／加拿大的影片？	1	2	3	4
8. 吃西式食品？	1	2	3	4
9. 去西式的演唱會或展覽等？	1	2	3	4
10. 在國際式的商店購買雜貨／日用品？	1	2	3	4
11. 看說英文的醫生？	1	2	3	4
12. 參加加拿大的協會（如同鄉會／俱樂部）或活動？	1	2	3	4
你有多經常說廣東話：				
1. 在家中	1	2	3	4
2. 與鄰居	1	2	3	4
3. 與朋友	1	2	3	4
4. 與同事	1	2	3	4
你有多經常：				
5. 閱讀中文／香港的書、報紙或雜誌？	1	2	3	4
6. 在中式餐廳用膳？	1	2	3	4

7.	在影碟中、或到電影院看香港的影片？	1	2	3	4
8.	吃中式食品？	1	2	3	4
9.	去中式的演唱會、大戲或展覽等？	1	2	3	4
10.	在中式／本地的商店購買雜貨／日用品？	1	2	3	4
11.	看說廣東話的醫生？	1	2	3	4
12.	與香港的朋友交際？	1	2	3	4
13.	參加中國／香港的協會（如同鄉會／俱樂部）或活動？	1	2	3	4

以下句子關於你從外地回港以後的生活和工作。請以1–7表示你有多同意下列句子，並在適當的數字上打圈。

		非常不同意						非常同意
1.	我想到加拿大時，我會感到孤獨或有思鄉的感覺。	1	2	3	4	5	6	7
2.	我在工作中難以集中。	1	2	3	4	5	6	7
3.	我覺得我回港後比較焦慮和易怒。	1	2	3	4	5	6	7
4.	回到了香港是一件很困難的事。	1	2	3	4	5	6	7
5.	在香港，我能夠重新融入我的親戚當中。	1	2	3	4	5	6	7
6.	在我的舊朋友當中我感到很自在。	1	2	3	4	5	6	7
7.	我覺得我好像從來沒有離開過香港一樣。	1	2	3	4	5	6	7

請在下列各句子中最能形容你的感覺的數字上打圈。

1. 我的生活各方面大部分都接近我的理想。

1	2	3	4	5	6	7
非常不同意	不同意	偏向不同意	既不贊同也不反對	偏向同意	同意	非常同意

2. 我的生活條件非常好。

1	2	3	4	5	6	7
非常不同意	不同意	偏向不同意	既不贊同也不反對	偏向同意	同意	非常同意

3. 我對我的生活感到滿意。

1	2	3	4	5	6	7
非常不同意	不同意	偏向不同意	既不贊同也不反對	偏向同意	同意	非常同意

4. 直到現在為止，我已得到我生命中最重要、最想得到的事物。

1	2	3	4	5	6	7
非常不同意	不同意	偏向不同意	既不贊同也不反對	偏向同意	同意	非常同意

5. 如果我可以重新活過，我不會對我的人生作些什麼改變。

1	2	3	4	5	6	7
非常不同意	不同意	偏向不同意	既不贊同也不反對	偏向同意	同意	非常同意

請評定你有多同意／不同意以下各句子。

		非常 不同意			既不贊同 也不反對			非常同意
1.	我尊重與我有交往的掌權者。	1	2	3	4	5	6	7
2.	我寧願直接説「不」，也不願被人誤會。	1	2	3	4	5	6	7
3.	如果我的孩子失敗了，我會覺得我要負上責任。	1	2	3	4	5	6	7
4.	與我群體中的人維持和諧的關係對我而言很重要。	1	2	3	4	5	6	7
5.	擁有生動的想像力對我而言很重要。	1	2	3	4	5	6	7
6.	我的快樂建築在我身邊的人的快樂之上。	1	2	3	4	5	6	7
7.	我對自己在眾人面前被單獨地挑選出來讚賞或獎賞感到自在。	1	2	3	4	5	6	7
8.	健康於我而言比其他一切更有價值。	1	2	3	4	5	6	7
9.	我總以一貫作風處事，不管面對任何人。	1	2	3	4	5	6	7
10.	我尊重謙虛的人。	1	2	3	4	5	6	7
11.	我會犧牲我個人的利益以令我身處的群體得益。	1	2	3	4	5	6	7
12.	能夠照顧自己是我的首要考慮。	1	2	3	4	5	6	7
13.	我在家裡的行為和在工作上的一樣。	1	2	3	4	5	6	7
14.	我時常覺得我與別人的關係比我自己的成就更為重要。	1	2	3	4	5	6	7
15.	我覺得以名字稱呼剛相識的人是自然的，即使對方的年紀比我年長很多。	1	2	3	4	5	6	7

		非常 不同意			既不贊同 也不反對			非常同意
16.	我覺得孩子在決定升學或就業計 劃時應考慮父母的意見。	1	2	3	4	5	6	7
17.	我較喜歡直接和坦白地與初相識 的人交往。	1	2	3	4	5	6	7
18.	尊重我團體所作的決定對我而言 很重要。	1	2	3	4	5	6	7
19.	在很多方面，我享受自己的獨特 性和與眾不同。	1	2	3	4	5	6	7
20.	我覺得表現為一個獨立的人對我 是重要的。	1	2	3	4	5	6	7
21.	即使我在一個團體中感到不愉 快，我仍會因他們需要我而留下 來。	1	2	3	4	5	6	7
22.	在會議中發言對我來說沒有困 難。	1	2	3	4	5	6	7
23.	在巴士上，我會讓座予我的老 板。	1	2	3	4	5	6	7
24.	即使我非常不同意我組員的看 法，我會避免與他們辯論。	1	2	3	4	5	6	7

Appendix B
Methods, sample, and qualitative analysis

Method

The methodology for the Hong Kong Remigration Project combined qualitative interviews with quantitative psychological scales measuring overseas adaptation, repatriation stress, life satisfaction, and self-concept. Interviews each lasted approximately two hours and consisted of participant responses to a semistructured interview schedule followed by the completion of a questionnaire packet. The interview explored the nature of the immigration experience, reasons for returning home, and the remigration experience, including questions about changes in behavior and thinking; perceptions of the remigrant by family, friends, and coworkers; and future plans. During the scheduling of interview sessions, if a participant's English fluency appeared questionable, a bilingual research assistant accompanied the interviewer. However, once the interviews began, the "interpreter" was rarely needed.

The questionnaire included the Satisfaction with Life Scale (Diener, Emmons, Larsen, and Griffin, 1985), the Repatriation Distress Scale (Sussman, 2001), a modified version of the Birman Cultural Adaptation Scale (Birman and Trickett, 2001), the Self-Construal Scale (Singelis, 1994), the Twenty Statement Test (Kuhn and McPartland, 1954), and demographic items. The participants were offered an English or a Chinese version of the questionnaire. All participants requested the English version.

Four cultural identities and psychological domains

The Cultural Identity Model posited that those experiencing a subtractive identity could be characterized as having a moderate home country identity, being culturally flexible, and adapting well to the country of resettlement. Those individuals with an additive identity were similar but possessed a stronger home identity. It was hypothesized that neither subtractive nor additive identities were salient to migrants prior to their immigration. Those individuals with affirmative identities were suggested to have strong home culture identity, cultural inflexibility, and low adaptation to the resettlement country. Once their home country identity was highlighted upon emigration, it was embraced. Global identities were characterized by an awareness of cultural identity formed in part from frequent cultural sojourns. People with global identities had high cultural flexibility and high adaptability.

Measures of the identities and the remigration experience were developed to tap three essential psychological domains: cognition (thinking), behavior, and emotion. Examples of cognitive probes were self-construal, self-concept, self-described cultural identities, linguistic choice, beliefs about family structure and relationships, attitudes about Hong Kong government and institutions and the government of the People's Republic of China, and attitudes about the environment. Behavioral measures included choices of naming convention, residence neighborhood, children's schooling, friendship network, religious affiliation, food preferences, and leisure pursuits. Emotion was probed through questions and scales of anxiety, distress, irritability, relief, pleasure, satisfaction, concern about the future, and economic well-being.

Sample

Using "snowball sampling" methods (each respondent assisting in the recruitment of others), 50 interviews of both male and female returnees took place in 2004. The majority of interviews were conducted in the conference room in an office located in Central, the business district of Hong Kong Island. Occasionally, interviews were held in the respondent's workplace following normal work hours, in the interviewer's apartment, and in a few cases, the interviews took place at cafes or coffee shops. These were rare, as the background noise interfered with the audio recordings.

Research participants were selected if they met certain criteria. They departed from Hong Kong no earlier than the mid-1980s and returned to Hong Kong after living at least one year in either Canada or Australia. Some respondents returned to Hong Kong as early as 1986 (as soon as they qualified for citizenship in their new country of abode) and some not until 2003. The age range at the time of immigration was 13 to 51 years. All but one participant immigrated because of "handover anxiety" — concern about the aftermath of the PRC's assuming sovereignty over Hong Kong. Reasons for remigration were slightly more diverse — the majority returned for economic reasons, a smaller minority were concerned about the education of their children (the need to learn Cantonese and Mandarin), and the fewest came back because of extended family obligations.

Interviews

All interviews were audiotaped. The audio was then transferred to a computer program (Power Voice II) that facilitated the transcription of the interviews by two bilingual Hong Kong research assistants. After the transcription was complete, all interviews were edited and revised by two native English-speaking assistants.

Qualitative coding

Analysis of the data involved identification of specific themes in participants' responses (coding). A coding book, which included an a priori list of possible emergent themes, was created and was used to guide the coding process. Subsequent revisions were made in the coding book as coders encountered new themes. Each interview was individually coded, and on completion of coding, all coders met and reviewed copies of the coded interviews to ensure that there was high interrater reliability. Disagreements were discussed, and the classification of remigrants into profiles was resolved.

The CIM predicted four identity profiles. Coding of interview responses revealed seven: three main profiles (subtractive, affirmative, and global), one bifurcated identity profile (additive/bicultural and additive/hybrid), and two combined identities (subtractive/additive and affirmative/additive). Those interviewees whose responses indicated high immigrant adaptation and maintenance of Western values, behaviors, and thinking as remigrants were labeled additive and displayed two differentiated subtypes, bicultural or hybrid. Bicultural remigrants ($n = 10$) frequently commented on developing two cultural frameworks (Hong Kong and Western) and on their ability to switch their behaviors according to the situational context (work vs. home; Chinese workplace vs. international workplace; Hong Kong vs. Australia). They often described their identity as being both Hong Kong and Western. Hybrid remigrants (n = 21) spoke of merging Chinese, Hong Kong, and Western behaviors, values, and thinking into a unique blended identity that was consistent across situations. Emotional reactions to remigration were either neutral or positive.

Participants categorized as subtractive (n = 1) and subtractive/additive (n = 2) mentioned unequivocally feeling less Chinese or no longer fitting into Hong Kong society. This was the key identity characteristic of these remigrants. They also reported distress or negative emotional response to being home. Those who were classified as subtractive/additive additionally mentioned incorporating Western traits into their identity. If not for the reported sense of feeling less "Hong Konger," these remigrants might have been classified as additive/bicultural.

Affirmative remigrants (n = 6) were primarily characterized by statements of poor adjustment to their settlement country, poor English skills, and positive emotional reaction to returning to Hong Kong. They often described themselves as Chinese both before migration and after remigration. Affirmative/additive remigrants (n = 5) were an unexpected identity classification in that they had often had difficult immigrant adaptation and revealed positive emotions about their return to Hong Kong, yet they also indicated that they had incorporated some Western values and behaviors into their repertoire. One respondent commented that while she was a Hong Konger and felt comfortable being home she also recognized that she was now different from her friends who had not emigrated.

Remigrants who were classified as global (n = 5) routinely had a life history of multiple international experiences. They may have studied overseas in high school and then again in college, prior to immigrating. Some had relocated internationally for job assignments. Nearly all explicitly used the terms "global citizen" or "international person" when describing themselves in the interviews, yet on identity scales they often checked off feeling their Hong Kong and Western identities equally. Some indicated feeling as though they were foreigners being back in Hong Kong, and many described their friends as being Western expatriates or Hong Kong remigrants.

Classification of identity types via qualitative analysis were triangulated and confirmed through the use of quantitative measures such as cultural behavior and identity measures, self-construal, naming conventions, choice of school for their children, or choice of residential neighborhood.

Table B.1   Coding Book

CODE	ABBREVIATION
Reasons for leaving Hong Kong	LEAVHK
– escape	LEAVHKESC
– instability	LEAVHKINS
– political	POL
– economic	ECO
– work pressure	WKPRES
– density/crowds	DENS
– personal	PERS
Pre-migration identity	PREMIGID
– Hong Kongese	HKESE
– Chinese	CHIN
– mixture	MIXT
– international	INT
– Hong Kong Chinese	HKCHIN
– British Hong Kong	BRITHK
Emotional/Behavioral Response to leaving HK	LEAVRES
– delighted to leave	DEL
– permanent	DELPERM
– temporary	DELTEMP
– regretful/sorry	SOR
– permanent	SORPERM
– temporary	SORTEMP
– no emotional response	NERESP
– permanent	NERESPPERM
– temporary	NERESPTEMP
Hong Kong/Chinese Differences	HKCHINDIFF
Hong Kong/Chinese Similarities	HKCHINSIM
#1 Response to immigration	RTI
A. Adaptation Strategies	ADAPSTRAT
A1. General Adaptation	GENADAPT
A2. "Do Like Romans"	DLR
a. *workplace*	WP

– work family balance	WFB
– work ethic	WE
– boss/employee relationship	B-ERSHIP
– work style communication	WCCOMM
– coworker relationship	CWORKERR

b. *family*

– food	FOOD
– Western	WEST
– Chinese	CHIN
– combination	COMBO
– leisure	LEIS
– outdoor	OUTDR
– indoor	INDR
– parenting	PARING
– laissez-faire	LAIS
– allows kids to be independent	IND
– financial	FIN
– spend	SPD
– save	SAV
– entertainment	ENT
– housing	HOUS
– family togetherness	FAMT
– spousal equality	SPOUEQUAL

c. *social behavior*	SOCB
– pace of life	PAL
– slower walking	SLOWW
– slower talking	SLOWT
– slower service	SLOWS
– communication	COMM
– direct	DIR
– opinionated	OPIN
– nonverbal	NONV
– more gestures	MOREG
– more touch	MORET
– more smiling	MORES

– male/female relationships	M/F REL
– more freedom	MOREF
– more equitable	MOREEQ
– group relations	GROUPR
– doing activities independently	ACTIND
– neighborliness	NEIG
– household activities	HOUACT
– less judgmental	LESSJUDGE

d. *cultural activities*	CULACT
– holiday celebration	HOLCEL

e. *laws/legal system*	LLS
– don't accept	NOACC
– accept	ACC

f. *political awareness*	POLAWR

g. *community service*	COMMSERV

h. *emotional reaction*	EMOREAC
– calm	CLM

A3. Act Chinese	ACTCHIN
– Chinese friendships	CHINF
– eating Chinese foods	EATCHINF
– Chinese entertainment	CHINENT
– greater Chinese identity/sense of belonging	MORECHINI
– work	WRK
– religion	REL
– speak Chinese	SPKCHIN
– moral values	MOREVAL
– Chinese furniture	CHINFURN
– driving	DRIV

A4. Resisting Local Culture	RESLOCULT
– I don't want to adapt	DWNTAPT
– not adapting	NTADT

A5. Wait it Out	WAITOUT
– immediate plans to return to HK	IMMRET
B. Resources	RES
– religious	REL
– family	FAM
– friends	FRNDS
– Hong Kongese	HKS
– Chinese immigrants	CHINIMM
– White locals	WHTLOC
– Chinese locals	CHINLOC
– self	SELF
– coworkers	COWKER

C. Postmigration Identity	PMIGID
– local	LOC
– mixture	MIX
– Hong Kong	HK
– Chinese	CHIN
– International	INT

D. Affective Response to Immigration	AFFRESIMM
– alienation/discrimination	ALIEN/DIS
– workplace	WPLAC
– community	COMMY
– desire to belong	DES2BEL
– psychological well-being	PSYCHWB +/–

E. Response to local culture	RESLCULT
– admire	ADM
– dislike	DSLK

F. Type of adjustment	TYPOFAD
– difficult	DIFF
– easy	EASY

G. Local response to immigrants	LCLRESPIM
– resentment	RESNTMT
– misunderstanding	MSUNDER

– acceptance	ACCP
– professional	PRSL

H. Observation of culture	OBSCUL
– similarities	SIM
– differences	DIFF

I. Observation of cultural differences (Workplace)	OBSCULDIFFWP

J. Behavioral Outcome	BEHOUT
– staying	STAY
– going	GO

K. Emotional response to leaving	EMORESLEAV
– positive	EMOPOS
– negative	EMONEG
– neutral	EMONEU
– mixed emotions	EMOMIX

L. Citizenship	CITZ

M. Flexibility	FLEX

#2 Response to Remigration	REMIGRESP
A. Reasons for remigration	RFR
– escape	ESC
– better/poor economy	BET/PORECO
– better/poor values	BET/PORVAL
– better/poor education	BET/POREDU
– personal	PERS
– maintain family ties	MFAMTI
– professional	PRFSL

B. Environmental response	ENVRESP
– positive	POS
– negative	NEG
– crowded	NEGCRD
– polluted	NEGPOL
– noisy	NEGNOI
☐small	NEGSML

C. Remigration identity
- – Affirmative   AFF
  - – cognitive   AFFCOG
  - – behavioral   AFFBEH
  - – emotional   AFFEMO
- – Subtractive   SUB
  - – cognitive   SUBCOG
  - – behavioral   SUBBEH
  - – emotional   SUBEMO
- – Additive hybrid/bicultural   ADDHYB/ADDBIC
  - – cognitive   ADDCOG
  - – behavioral   ADDBEH
  - – emotional   ADDEMO
- – Global   GLO
  - – cognitive   GLOCOG
  - – behavioral   GLOBEH
  - – emotional   GLOEMO
- – Marginal   MRGNL

D. Immediate/initial affect   IMMAFF
- – positive   IMMAFFP
- – negative   IMMAFFN
- – neutral   IMMNEU

E. Subsequent affect   SUBAFF
- – positive   SUBAFFP
- – negative   SUBAFFN
- – neutral   SUBNEU

F. Future plans   FPLAN
- – certain to leave Hong Kong   FPLANCERT
- – perhaps will leave Hong Kong   FPLANPERH
- – unsure   FPLANUNS
- – will not leave   FPLANSTAY
- – will alternate between HK and host   FPALT

G. Cultural response	CULTRESP
– cultural response positive	CULTRESPPOS
– cultural response negative	CULTRESPNEG
H. Observation of cultural differences	OBSCULDIF
Observation of cultural similarities	OBSCULSIM
I. Observation of cultural differences (workplace)	OBSCULDIFFWRK
J. Compare remigrants to locals	COMPARE
K. Local response to remigrants	LCLRESPREM
– acceptance	ACCP
– misunderstanding	MSUNDER
– resentment	RSNT
– awareness	AWARENESS
L. Missing	MISS
M. Difference in housing	DIFFHOUS
N. Type of readjustment	TYPOFREAD
– difficult	DIFF
– easy	EASY
O. Flexibility in behavior	FLEXHK

NVivo

NVivo is a qualitative data analysis software program designed by QSR International. Version NVivo 7 was employed for data analysis in this project. NVivo 7 is a versatile analytical tool that allows researchers to analyze data from multiple media. It allows for the importation of data (e.g., interviews, field notes, case studies) from other software applications (e.g., Microsoft Word) that can then be coded for specific content. Once data has been imported into NVivo, it is possible to begin coding. To code in NVivo, it is necessary to create a hierarchy of nodes (which are simply the themes identified in the coding book) and then attach all relevant exemplars to the specific node(s). On completion of coding, NVivo's search and query tools allow the researcher to ask and answer an array of research questions.

Appendix C
Quantitative analysis

A total of 50 Hong Kong repatriates participated in this study. Twenty-six (52%) participants were male and 24 (48%) were female. Their ages, at the time of the interview, ranged from 26 to 76 years old. Twenty-seven (54%) participants immigrated to Canada, and 23 (46%) immigrated to Australia. Their age at immigration to Canada or Australia ranged from 13 to 51 years old, from which 10 (20%) immigrated below age 26 and 40 (80%) above age 26. Among the Canadian immigrants, 13 (48%) were male and 14 (52%) were female. The Australian immigrants consisted of 13 (57%) males and 10 (43%) females. The cultural identity profiles consisted of seven groups: subtractive, subtractive additive, additive bicultural, additive hybrid, affirmative, affirmative additive, and global (see Table C.1). Among the total sample of participants, 1 (2%) was identified as subtractive, 2 (4%) were identified as subtractive additive, 10 (20%) as additive bicultural, 21 (42%) as additive hybrid, 6 (12%) as affirmative, 5 (10%) as affirmative additive, and 5 (10%) as global. It is worth highlighting that 62% of the participants were additive/bicultural or hybrid plus another 14% included additive features (subtractive/additive and affirmative/additive), which strongly suggests that the culture in Hong Kong embraces integration of cultural features from other countries and enables Hong Kongers to combine cultural elements from their host and home countries into their cultural identity.

The main outcome measures that were used in the study analyses included three adaptation scales and two self-concept scales. The adaptation scales were the 5-item Satisfaction with Life Scale (7-point Likert Scale), 7-item Repatriation Distress Scale (7-point Likert Scale), and Birman's 8 acculturation subscales (4-point Likert Scale). The self-concept measures were the 12-item Independent and 12-item Interdependent Self-Construal Subscales (7-point Likert Scale), and

Percentage Dispositional and Relational Response based on the researcher's 10-statement modified version of the Twenty Statement Test (TST). See Chapter 5 for an explanation of the Singelis Self-Construal Scale.

Table C.1   Frequencies of the seven cultural identity profiles

Cultural Identity Profile	N (%)
Subtractive	1 (2)
Subtractive Additive	2 (4)
Additive Bicultural	10 (20)
Additive Hybrid	21 (42)
Affirmative	6 (12)
Affirmative Additive	5 (10)
Global	5 (10)

The researcher shortened the Twenty Statement Test to ten statements because the pilot test for the TST showed that Hong Kongers had difficulty describing themselves twenty ways. In the modified Ten Statements Test, participants were instructed to describe themselves in 10 ways, starting with "I am _____." The researcher coded the statements into two categories of responses, dispositional and relational. In the TST scoring guide, Kuhn and McPartland (1954) defines dispositional responses to be "personal qualities, attitudes, beliefs, states and traits that DO NOT relate to other people." Examples may be "I am honest" and "I am intelligent." Relational responses are defined as "statements about group membership, demographic characteristics, and groups with which people experience a common fate." Some examples are "I am a daughter" and "I am a student." For each of the two categories, the total number of responses was multiplied by 100 to obtain the percentage dispositional response and percentage relational response.

Acceptable to high reliability have been found in previous studies on the Satisfaction with Life Scale, Repatriation Distress Scale, Birman's Acculturation Subscales, and Self-Construal Subscales, with Cronbach alphas ranging from $\alpha = .69$ to $\alpha = .95$ (Diener et al., 1985; Sussman, 2001; Birman, Trickett, and Vinokurov, 2002; Singelis, 1994). For the sample in the present study, the reliabilities were also acceptable to high, with Cronbach alpha coefficients ranging from $\alpha = .66$ to $\alpha = .92$. Reliability coefficients for the TST were not available in Kuhn and McPartland's (1954) Twenty Statement Test and in the present study's modified Ten Statement Test.

Means and standard deviations were computed for the adaptation measures (see Table C.2). On average, participants were highly satisfied with their lives (Mean = 5.10; SD = 0.86), and experienced little re-entry distress (Mean = 2.95, SD = 0.93). For Table C.2, three of Birman's Acculturation Subscales — ability to speak English, ability to understand English, and amount of spoken English — were collapsed into one subscale called English Language by taking the average of the three subscales. Similarly, the three Chinese-language subscales were collapsed to one. Therefore, Birman's subscales were reduced from a total of eight to six. Overall, participants had moderate Western acculturation and high Hong Kong acculturation. They displayed lower average scores on Western identity acculturation (Mean = 2.64, SD = 0.75), Western behavioral acculturation (Mean = 2.32, SD = 0.46), and English language (Mean = 2.66, SD = 0.41) than Hong Kong acculturation (Mean = 3.01, SD = 0.67; Mean = 3.00, SD = 0.45; and Mean = 3.59, SD = 0.52, respectively).

Table C.2   Mean and standard deviation scores of adaptation measures by participant demographics

Measures	Mean (SD) for Total	Mean (SD) for Males	Mean (SD) for Females	Mean (SD) for Canadians	Mean (SD) for Australian	Mean (SD) for Can-Male	Mean (SD) for Can-Fem	Mean (SD) for Aus-Male	Mean (SD) for Aus-Fem	Mean (SD) for Age imm below 26	Mean (SD) for Age imm above 26
Life Satis-faction	5.10 (0.86)	5.05 (0.86)	5.17 (0.88)	5.08 (0.92)	5.13 (0.81)	5.06 (0.83)	5.10 (1.03)	5.03 (0.93)	5.26 (0.67)	5.10 (0.73)	5.11 (0.90)
Repa-triation Distress Scale	2.95 (0.93)	2.82 (0.82)	3.10 (1.03)	2.99 (0.92)	2.91 (0.95)	2.74 (0.67)	3.23 (1.07)	2.90 (0.96)	2.91 (0.99)	3.26 (0.96)	2.88 (0.91)
Western identity	2.64 (0.75)	2.65 (0.78)	2.61 (0.73)	2.76 (0.82)	2.49 (0.64)	2.88 (0.81)	2.64 (0.83)	2.42 (0.70)	2.58 (0.59)	3.10 (0.64)	2.52 (0.73)
Western behavior	2.32 (0.46)	2.33 (0.43)	2.32 (0.49)	2.41 (0.49)	2.22 (0.39)	2.40 (0.44)	2.42 (0.56)	2.26 (0.43)	2.17 (0.35)	2.64 (0.53)	2.24 (0.40)
English language	2.66 (0.41)	2.66 (0.34)	2.65 (0.49)	2.63 (0.46)	2.68 (0.36)	2.64 (0.36)	2.62 (0.56)	2.68 (0.34)	2.68 (0.40)	2.95 (0.42)	2.58 (0.38)
Hong Kong identity	3.01 (0.67)	2.94 (0.68)	3.07 (0.67)	3.02 (0.66)	2.99 (0.70)	3.02 (0.67)	3.02 (0.68)	2.87 (0.71)	3.15 (0.68)	3.23 (0.46)	2.95 (0.71)
Hong Kong behavior	3.00 (0.45)	2.99 (0.42)	3.01 (0.49)	2.99 (0.52)	3.01 (0.37)	3.03 (0.49)	2.95 (0.57)	2.94 (0.36)	3.10 (0.37)	3.20 (0.41)	2.95 (0.45)
Chinese language	3.59 (0.52)	3.47 (0.62)	3.72 (0.36)	3.47 (0.62)	3.73 (0.33)	3.31 (0.77)	3.62 (0.41)	3.63 (0.38)	3.85 (0.21)	3.68 (0.47)	3.57 (0.53)

Table C.3 Mean and standard deviation scores of self-concept measures by participant demographics

Measures	Mean (SD) for Total	Mean (SD) for Males	Mean (SD) for Females	Mean (SD) for Canadians	Mean (SD) for Australian	Mean (SD) for Can-Male	Mean (SD) for Can-Fem	Mean (SD) for Aus-Male	Mean (SD) for Aus-Fem	Mean (SD) for Age imm below 26	Mean (SD) for Age imm above 26
Independent Self-Construal	4.90 (0.63)	4.80 (0.61)	5.00 (0.64)	5.03 (0.64)	4.75 (0.59)	4.99 (0.64)	5.07 (0.65)	4.62 (0.54)	4.91 (0.65)	4.91 (0.83)	4.90 (0.58)
Interdependent Self-Construal	5.26 (0.67)	5.25 (0.55)	5.27 (0.79)	5.29 (0.77)	5.22 (0.55)	5.11 (0.55)	5.46 (0.91)	5.39 (0.53)	4.99 (0.51)	5.27 (0.63)	5.25 (0.68)
Percentage Dispositional Responses	49.00 (31.48)	45.82 (30.70)	52.45 (32.61)	58.80ᵃ (27.97)	37.50 (32.04)	49.91 (27.74)	67.05 (26.50)	41.73 (34.02)	32.00 (30.11)	62.00 (20.98)	45.75 (33.01)
Percentage Relational Responses	18.89 (17.28)	16.95 (16.36)	21.00 (18.33)	19.06 (18.91)	18.69 (15.56)	20.07 (20.55)	18.13 (17.99)	13.83 (10.70)	25.00 (19.00)	13.00 (9.49)	20.36 (18.53)

Note:

ᵃAn independent samples t-test for place of immigration on mean percentage of dispositional responses revealed that dispositional responses for Canadian–Hong Kongers were higher than for Australian–Hong Kongers ($t(48) = 2.51$, $p = 0.016$).

Means and standard deviations were also computed for the self-concept measures (see Table C.3). In general, all participants scored high on both independent and interdependent self-construal, but slightly higher on interdependent self-construal (Mean = 5.26, SD = 0.67 vs. Mean = 4.90, SD = 0.63); that is, their self-concepts included certain domains or times when they were involved with family and friends and other domains or times when they acted more independently. The self-construal results matched the cultural identity profile of the sample in that most were additive. With regard to the modified TST, the average percentage of dispositional responses (Mean = 49.00, SD = 31.48) was higher than the relational responses (Mean = 18.89, SD = 17.28).

The following analyses involve comparisons between groups and correlational analyses. The study's sample size was insufficient for analyzing most group differences, thus limiting the inferential statistics to differences in the variables "gender" and "country of immigration" on the main outcome measures. Descriptive statistics were employed for other group comparison analyses.

Participant demographics, which included gender, place immigrated, place immigrated by gender, and age at immigration categorized as below age 26 and above age 26, were also examined in relation to life satisfaction, self-construal, and repatriation distress. In terms of adaptation for each demographic grouping, participants were highly satisfied with life and had low re-entry distress, moderate levels of Western acculturation, and moderate to high levels of Hong Kong acculturation (see Table C.2). With self-concept for each demographic grouping, participants had fairly high independent and interdependent self-construal scores, moderate to moderately high percentages of dispositional responses, and low percentages of relational responses (see Table C.3). Independent samples t-tests were performed to test differences in "gender" and "country of immigration" on life satisfaction, repatriation distress, Western acculturation, home country acculturation, self-construal, and percentage dispositional and relational responses. With respect to gender, males were statistically no different from females on all of the measures ($p > .05$). When examining the country from which the participants immigrated, Canadian–Hong Kongers had significantly higher percentage dispositional responses than Australian–Hong Kongers ($t(48) = 2.51$, $p = 0.016$). This confirms the qualitative results, which suggest that Canadians think of themselves as more individualistic and thus Hong Kong–Canadians perceive themselves as more individualistic compared to Hong Kong–Australians (see Chapter 5). Descriptive statistical analysis of "age at immigration" comparisons indicated that although distress was low for both groups, participants who immigrated at a younger age (13–26 years) experienced more distress than those who were older than 26 (Mean = 3.26, SD = 0.96 vs. Mean = 2.88, SD = 0.91).

Closer examination of comparisons between "gender" and "place immigrated," and with "age at immigration," using the descriptive statistics revealed several nuances, although the small sample size precluded any meaningful significance testing. There was an interesting pattern regarding the effect of "country of immigration" in terms of within-sex comparisons (see Table C.2), although none of the comparisons was statistically different. Females who had immigrated to Australia appeared happier (Mean = 5.26, SD = 0.67) and less distressed (Mean = 2.91, SD = 0.99) during remigration than females from Canada (Mean = 5.10, SD = 1.03 and Mean = 3.23, SD = 1.07, respectively). However, the reverse was true for males. Canadian male remigrants were happier (Mean = 5.06, SD = 0.83) and less distressed (Mean = 2.74, SD = 0.67) than were males who remigrated from Australia (Mean = 5.03, SD = 0.93 and Mean = 2.90, SD = 0.96). There were also some interesting patterns regarding country of immigration in relation to between-sex effects. Australian females were most satisfied with their life and had a greater mean difference relative to Australian males than compared to the Canadian males and females (Mean diff = 0.23 vs.

Mean diff = 0.04). Canadian females were most distressed with re-entry and had a greater mean difference relative to Canadian males compared to the Australians (Mean diff = 0.49 vs. Mean diff = 0.01). With respect to age at immigration, participants who immigrated to Canada or Australia before age 26 were found to show higher levels of Western identity acculturation (Mean = 3.10, SD = 0.64), Western behavioral acculturation (Mean = 2.64, SD = 0.53), and English language acculturation (Mean = 2.95, SD = 0.42) compared to those who immigrated after age 26 (Mean = 2.52, SD = 0.73; Mean = 2.24, SD = 0.40; and Mean = 2.58, SD = 0.38, respectively).

With regard to self-concept (see Table C.3), Canadian females showed the highest independent self-construal score, but the Australian females indicated a greater mean difference with Australian males than compared to their Canadian counterparts (Mean diff = 0.29 vs. Mean diff = 0.08). Canadian females also displayed the highest percentage dispositional responses (Mean = 67.05, SD = 26.50) and a greater mean difference with Canadian males than compared to their Australian counterparts (Mean diff = 17.14 vs. Mean diff = 9.73). With relational responses, Canadian females exhibited lower percentage relational responses (Mean = 18.13, SD = 17.99) than the Canadian males (Mean = 20.07, SD = 20.55). However, the opposite was true for the Australians — Australian females displayed higher percentage relational responses (Mean = 25.00, SD = 19.00) than Australian males (Mean = 13.83, SD = 10.70). In terms of age at immigration and TST, participants who immigrated to Canada or Australia before age 26 showed a higher percentage of dispositional responses and lower relational responses than those who immigrated after age 26. This is consistent with the earlier finding that participants who immigrated before age 26 displayed higher levels of Western acculturation than those who immigrated after age 26. It is logical that participants who immigrated before age 26 also described themselves more so in Western individualistic terms and less so in Chinese relational terms than those who immigrated when they were older (after age 26).

Pearson's Product Moment Correlations were computed for age at immigration, life satisfaction, self-construal, repatriation distress, percentage relational and dispositional response, and Birman's eight acculturation subscales (see Table C.4). Age at immigration was negatively correlated with ability to speak English ($r = -.31$, $p = .029$) and to understand English ($r = -.41$, $p = .003$), such that the younger the partcipants were when they immigrated to Canada or Australia, the greater their ability now to speak English, and the greater their ability to understand English. Independent self-construal was positively correlated with ability to understand English ($r = .35$, $p = .013$), Western identity acculturation ($r = .36$, $p = .009$), amount of English spoken ($r = .41$, $p = .003$),

Table C.4   Bivariate intercorrelations between age at immigration, life satisfaction, self-construal, repatriation distress, percentage relational and dispositional response, and Birman's eight acculturation subscales

	1	2	3	4	5	6	7	8	9	10	11
1. Age at immigration	—										
2. Life satisfaction	−0.3	—									
3. Independent self-construal	.003	−0.1	—								
4. Interdependent self-construal	.01	.01	.17	—							
5. Repatriation distress	−.26	.10	.18	.14	—						
6. Percentage relational	.07	−.07	−.09	.002	−.10	—					
7. Percentage dispositional	−.10	.14	.16	.08	.03	−.57***	—				
8. Ability to speak English	−.31*	−.16	.21	−.17	.19	−.24	.25	—			
9. Ability to understand English	−.41**	−.12	.35*	−.25	.08	−.12	.04	.70***	—		
10. Western identity	−.17	.14	.36**	.32*	.41**	−.14	.14	.17	.08	—	
11. Home country identity	.01	.14	.26	.18	−.22	−.17	.15	.08	.11	.24	—
12. Amount of spoken English	−0.1	−.10	.41**	−0.6	.12	−.18	.18	.35*	.31*	.20	.23
13. Western behavior	−.28	−.08	.38**	−.12	−.44**	−.33*	−.31*	.43**	.60***	.35*	.06
14. Amount of Cantonese spoken	−.22	−.02	−.03	−.24	−.02	−.03	−.07	−.02	.02	−.06	.26
15. Cantonese behavior	−.14	−.02	−.02	−.25	−.17	−.001	−.04	−.04	.03	.20	.51***

$* p < .05$; $** p < .01$; $*** p < .001$

and Western acculturation behavior ($r = .38$, $p = .006$), whereby the higher their independent self-construal, the higher their ability to understand English, the higher their Western identity acculturation, the greater their amount of English spoken, and the higher their Western acculturation behavior. Interdependent self-construal was positively correlated with Western identity acculturation ($r = .32$, $p = .026$), indicating that the higher their interdependent self-construal, the higher their Western identity acculturation.

Repatriation distress was positively correlated with Western identity acculturation ($r = .41$, $p = .003$) and Western behavioral acculturation ($r = .44$, $p = .002$), such that the higher their Western identity and behavioral acculturation, the greater their re-entry distress. Percentage dispositional response was also positively correlated with Western behavioral acculturation ($r = .31$, $p = .028$), whereby the higher their Western behavioral acculturation, the higher their dispositional responses. Percentage relational response was negatively correlated with Western behavioral acculturation ($r = -.33$, $p = .021$), such that the lower their Western behavioral acculturation, the higher their relational responses.

Given that percentage dispositional and relational responses are opposite conceptual categories in the modified TST, as expected the two types of responses were negatively correlated with each other ($r = -.57$, $p < .001$), such that the higher their dispositional responses, the lower their relational responses. Similarly with Birman's acculturation subscales, as expected several were positively associated with each other, where correlation coefficients ranged between $r = .35$ and $r = .70$ (all at $p < .05$). These associations were consistent in that the Western acculturation variables — ability to speak English, ability to understand English, amount of spoken English, Western behavioral acculturation, and Western identity acculturation — showed positive correlations, and the home country acculturation variables — Cantonese behavior, home country identity, and amount of Cantonese spoken — indicated positive correlations.

Associations between the main variables were found in several cases. High acculturation to Australia or Canada (West), in either behavior or identity, were linked to several variables. The more one acted (behaved) Western, the higher the independent self-construal and the higher the repatriation distress. Similarly, the more one's identity was Western, the higher the distress when remigrating home. High Western behavior was also correlated with making more dispositional (personal) self-descriptors in the TST task, and using fewer relational descriptors. Finally, age at immigration was associated with several variables, as was seen with some of the mean comparisons. The older one is at the time of immigration, the less the acculturation to the West and the less distressing is the return migration. This finding supports the ones mentioned earlier that indicates that Western acculturation is linked to increased remigration distress.

All of the associations except for one were consistent with the idea that the more acculturated the Hong Kongers were to the Western host countries, the more they adopted the cultural elements of their host country. The single discrepancy was that higher interdependent self-construal was related to higher Western identity acculturation. The most important finding, however, was that Hong Kongers' Western acculturation of their identity and behavior was related to greater re-entry distress.

The final set of descriptive statistical analyses employed the researcher's model of cultural identity shifts. For the following analyses, the researcher collapsed the subtractive and subtractive additive groups into subtractive, and the affirmative and affirmative additive into affirmative. Therefore the cultural identity groups utilized for the following analyses were a total of five groups: 3 (6%) subtractive, 10 (20%) additive bicultural, 21 (42%) additive hybrid, 11 (22%) affirmative, and 5 (10%) global. The mean and standard deviations of life satisfaction, repatriation distress, and self-construal, and the percentage dispositional and percentage relational responses were computed for each of the five cultural identity groups (see Table C.5). Overall, the five cultural identity groups were high in life satisfaction, independent and interdependent self-construal, and dispositional responses, and low in repatriation distress and relational responses. In all the groups, their life satisfaction scores were higher than their repatriation distress (see Figure C.1). The affirmative cultural identity group, also known as the "grateful repatriates," had the lowest repatriation distress, followed by the additive bicultural group. For these groups, a flexible way of behaving is free of negative effects. In countries where Confucian teachings are prevalent in everyday living, people tend to show less re-entry distress during remigration compared to people who return to the United States or to European countries (see Chapter 5). Given that Hong Kong is a country where Confucianism is prevalent, Hong Kongers are able to cross national boundaries with little distress.

Table C.5   Means and standard deviations of life satisfaction, self-construal, repatriation distress, and percentage dispositional and percentage relational responses by cultural identity group

Measures	Mean (SD) for Subtractive Group (n=3)	Mean (SD) for Additive Bicultural Group (n=10)	Mean (SD) for Additive Hybrid Group (n=21)	Mean (SD) for Affirmative Group (n=11)	Mean (SD) for Global Group (n=5)
Life Satisfaction	5.47 (0.31)	4.98 (1.03)	5.22 (0.77)	5.23 (0.75)	4.36 (1.14)
Independent Self-Construal	5.22 (0.65)	4.76 (0.57)	5.01 (0.63)	4.61 (0.60)	5.15 (0.70)
Interdependent Self-Construal	5.67 (0.36)	5.17 (0.78)	5.21 (0.58)	5.36 (0.86)	5.18 (0.51)
Repatriation Distress	4.00 (0.87)	2.71 (0.60)	3.27 (0.87)	2.22 (0.81)	3.09 (0.94)
Percentage Dispositional Responses	35.83 (45.85)	45.75 (33.38)	53.58 (31.42)	38.27 (32.14)	67.78 (6.30)
Percentage Relational Responses	21.93 (10.53)	19.25 (15.09)	16.20 (14.61)	24.69 (25.87)	14.86 (13.81)

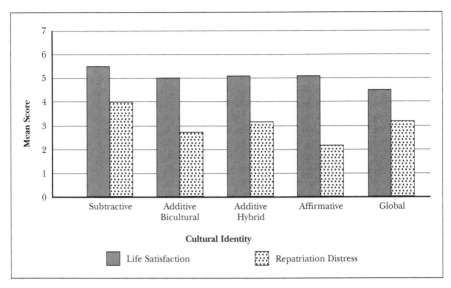

Figure C.1 Mean life satisfaction and repatriation distress scores among the five cultural identity groups

When comparing cultural identity groups, several differences are worth noting (see Figure C.2). First, with regard to self-construal, the subtractive, additive bicultural, and affirmative groups had much higher interdependent self-construal average scores than their independent self-construal scores. However, the two self-construal scores for the additive hybrid and global cultural groups were relatively equal. This is consistent with the Cultural Identity Model. Hong Kongers with an additive hybrid cultural identity combine cultural elements from their home country and from their host country, and therefore they have somewhat equal levels of interdependent and independent self-construal (Mean = 5.21 and Mean = 5.01, respectively). Similarly, Hong Kongers with a global cultural identity consider themselves to be part of the global community, and therefore they were expected to show the most balance in their interdependent and independent self-construal scores (Mean = 5.18 and Mean = 5.15, respectively). Second, the affirmative cultural identity group was found to have the greatest mean difference between their interdependent and independent scores (Mean diff = 0.75). This finding is also consistent with the Cultural Identity Model, where these Hong Kongers share a common bond with their home country, and affirm their home country identity. Therefore their interdependent self-construal score was expected to deviate the most and be the highest from their independent self-construal score out of the five cultural

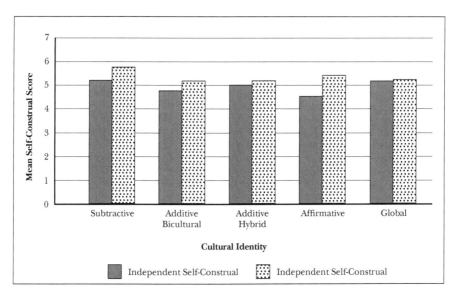

Figure C.2 A comparison of cultural identity groups on mean independent and interdependent self-construal scores

identity groups. This reflects the Hong Kong culture, where an interdependent self-concept is higher than an independent self-concept.

One final outcome focuses on the percentage dispositional responses. A high dispositional individualistic self-concept is the hallmark of Western self-description. As mentioned, the average percentage of dispositional responses was higher than the relational responses. The lower mean percentage in relational responses was most likely a result of respondents having recently returned to Hong Kong from their Western host country. Adapting to the Western culture suppressed their relational self-concept. However, the subtractive and affirmative cultural identity groups showed the lowest dispositional responses compared to the other three groups (see Figure C.3). This suggests that Hong Kongers with a subtractive or an affirmative cultural identity do not adopt a Western mentality of individuality as much as those do with additive or global cultural identities. Perhaps for the subtractive group, the negative affect from their experiences of immigrating to the host country led them to have lower dispositional responses. For the affirmative group, having a strong home country identity may have prevented them from adopting a Western mentality of individuality.

All research has its limitations, concerns, and cautions. Three will be discussed here. First, an American of European descent served as the research interviewer. It is uncertain if respondents altered their comments in light of

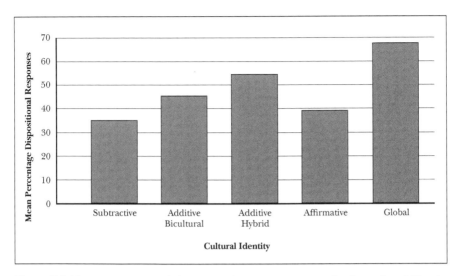

Figure C.3 Mean percentage of dispositional responses among the five cultural identity groups

some perceived cultural dissimilarity. For example, might the interviewees have intentionally or unintentionally withheld revealing symptoms of remigrant distress? Psychologists label as "social desirability responses" (SDR) the tendency to give responses that make oneself look good. SDR can be subdivided into two types — self-deceptive enhancement (seeing oneself in a positive light) and impression management (manipulating the ideas of the self by other people). Research comparing Americans, Singaporeans, and Korean-Americans (Lalwani, Shavitt and Johnson, 2006) found that the Americans scored higher on self-deceptive management but that both Asian samples scored higher on impression management. Might the interviewees in the Hong Kong Remigration Project have minimized their repatriation distress as an impression management technique? Two other studies examining Hong Kongers who return home (described in Chapters 5 and 6) found more distress voiced in interviews by remigrants than did this current study. The interviewers were Hong Kong remigrants themselves, and the respondents may have felt more comfortable and less inclined to portray a smooth and stress-free return process.

Conversely, there is data to suggest that if Hong Kong respondents actually experience repatriation distress, they are more likely to express those negative emotions to a Caucasian, American researcher. In a large cross-cultural study of emotions and display rules, Matsumoto et al. (2008) found that individuals from collectivist cultures were more apt to express negative emotions to an outgroup person; negative emotions would be suppressed and positive emotions displayed to an ingroup member, to preserve ingroup harmony. Given that the interviewees in the Remigration Project did not report distress to an outgroup individual (the interviewer), we might assume the accuracy of the reported neutral or positive emotions. According to Hofstede and Hofstede (2005) data, despite its historical linkage to the United Kingdom, Hong Kong is considered a collectivist culture and thus is subject to greater ingroup-outgroup distinctions.

This concern about social desirability overlaps with a second issue of possible response bias, in this case, linguistic. Attempts were made to minimize language barriers. While English was the language of the interviews, a bilingual assistant was present during them to provide interpretation if needed. Further, the questionnaire packet was available in both Chinese and English. None of the respondents chose the Chinese version. Finally, all respondents had been immigrants to English-speaking countries and had lived in their host country a minimum of one year.

A final methodological concern regards the oft-used psychological technique of collecting data retroactively. There is justifiable concern as to the validity of oral and written responses concerning immigration experiences, some of which took place up to ten years in the past, and remigration narratives that may have taken place several years prior to the data collection. However, over the course of more than 100 hours of interviewing I found that both the immigrant and remigrant experiences were vividly recalled by the respondents. They demonstrated no difficulty in providing clear examples of family, interpersonal, and work situations. In fact, the similarity of most of the narratives was remarkable and revealed that the interviews were indeed uncovering the remigrants' lived experiences. Furthermore, the interviews primed the recall of the respondents, which increased the reliability and validity of using the psychological scales in the questionnaire packets.

Appendix D

Demographic characteristics of research participants

Participant	At Departure from Hong Kong						In Country			At Return to Hong Kong		
	Gender	Age	Marital Status	Child(ren)	Occupation	Resettlement Country	Occupation	Time There	Age	Time Back in Hong Kong	Occupation	Cultural Identity Profile*
1	Female	35	Married	No	Secretary	Australia	Secretary	2.5 yrs	37	11 yrs	Student Business Management	AD/H
2	Female	27	Married	Yes; 1	Secretary	Australia	Secretary	4 yrs	31	12 yrs	Administrator	AD/H
3	Male	31 — 33	Married	Yes	Electrical Engineer	Singapore — Canada	Electrician	2 yrs — 10 yrs	33 — 43	4 yrs	Electrical Engineer	S & AD/H
4	Male	31	Married but went alone	No	Garment Industry	Australia	Garment Industry	2.5 yrs	34	9 yrs	Garment Industry	AF
5	Female	36	Married	Yes; 2	Finished Working	Canada	Worked for IBM	4 yrs	40	12 yrs	Marriage Counselor	G
6	Male	19	Single	No	Student	Australia	Student	5 yrs	24	9 yrs	Accountant	AD/B
7	Male	30	Single married in Australia	No	Surveyor	Australia	Surveyor	5 yrs	35	7 yrs	Land Surveyor	AD/H
8	Female	40	Married	Yes	Government Administrator	Canada	Did Not Work	5 yrs	45	14 yrs	Did Not Work	AF/AD

Participant	At Departure from Hong Kong						In Country		At Return to Hong Kong			
	Gender	Age	Marital Status	Child(ren)	Occupation	Resettlement Country	Occupation	Time There	Age	Time Back in Hong Kong	Occupation	Cultural Identity Profile*
9	Female	46	Married	Yes	Nurse	Canada	Nurse	3 yrs	49	11 yrs	Nurse	AD/H
10	Female	25 — 38	Single — Married	No — No	Nurse — Nurse	UK — Australia	Nurse — Speech Therapist	3 yrs — 7 yrs	28 — 44	3 yrs	Speech Therapist	AD/B
11	Male	23	Single	No	Student	Canada	Retail IT	6 yrs	29	4 yrs	IT	AD/H
12	Female	42	Married	Yes; 2	Secretary	Canada	Secretary	3 yrs	45	7 yrs	Secretary	AD/H
13	Female	29	Married	No	Law Clerk Paralegal	Australia	Law Clerk Paralegal	4 yrs	33	12 yrs	Law Clerk Paralegal	AD/B
14	Female	47	Divorced	No	Hotel Administrator	Canada	None (No Work)	1.5 yrs	49	11 yrs	Hotel Admin / Teacher English	AF
15	Male	13	Went with parents	No	Student	Canada	Student	9 yrs	22	7 yrs	European Bank	AD/H
16	Female	14	Went with parents	No	Student	Canada	Job in Immigration	9 yrs	24	4 yrs	Canadian Firm	AD/H
17	Male	17	Single	No	Student	Canada	Bank Work	14 yrs	31	3 yrs	Banking	AD/B
18	Female	28	Single went with future husband	No	Secretary	Canada	American Company Simple Work	2.5 yrs	30	13 yrs	Tourism	AD/B
19	Male	46	Married	Yes	Worked in Government	Canada	None (No Work)	4 mo/ 1 yr	46	9 yrs	Worked in Government	AF
20	Male	38	Married	Yes	Electrical Engineer	Australia	Grocery Shop	2 yrs	40	11 yrs	Engineer	AD/B
21	Female	30	Married	Yes	Food Quality Control	Australia	Had a Business	2.5 yrs	33	11 yrs	Bank Manager	G

Participant	At Departure from Hong Kong					In Country				At Return to Hong Kong		
	Gender	Age	Marital Status	Child(ren)	Occupation	Resettlement Country	Occupation	Time There	Age	Time Back in Hong Kong	Occupation	Cultural Identity Profile*
22	Female	18	Single	No	Student	Canada	Student	6 yrs	24	4 yrs	Asst. Professor/Local DJ	AD/H
23	Male	39	Married	Yes; 2	Professor	Australia	Consultant/Teacher	2.5 yrs	41	12 yrs	Professor	AD/H
24	Male	44	Single	No	Teacher	Canada	Student	4 yrs	48	8 yrs	Teacher	AD/H
25	Male	49	Married	Yes; 1	Teacher	Canada	Could Not Work	4 yrs	53	10 yrs	Teacher	AF
26	Female	19	Single	No	Student	Canada	Student in Fashion and Make-up	10 yrs	29	Just back	Wants to Open Business	AF/AD
27	Female	33	Married	Yes; 1	Accountant	Canada	No Work	4 yrs	37	2 yrs	Accountant	AF
28	Female	28	Single/Married	Yes; 1	Sales	Canada	Garment Industry	8 yrs	36	6 yrs	Merchandising	AD/H
29	Female	40	Married	Yes; 2	Travel	Canada	None	8.5 yrs	49	2 yrs		AD/B
30	Female	36	Single	No	Exec. Secretary in Bank	Canada	Travel Agent	13 yrs	49	3 yrs	President of Travel Agency	G
31	Male	51	Married	Yes; 2	Factory Business	Canada	Factory	7 yrs	58	18 yrs	Real Estate Developer	G
32	Male	15	Single	No	Student	Canada	Student	9 yrs	24	9 yrs	Tele-communications Manager	AD/H
33	Male	32	Married	No	Quality Surveyor	Australia	Surveyor	2.5 yrs	34	11 yrs	Surveyor	AD/H
34	Male	40	Married	Yes; 2	Ran Company	Canada	Retired	5 yrs	45	3 yrs	Ran Company	AD/H
35	Male	31	Married	Infant	Engineer	Australia	Engineer	2 yrs	33	8 yrs	Engineer	AF

Participant	Gender	Age	Marital Status	Child(ren)	Occupation	Resettlement Country	Occupation	Time There	Age	Time Back in Hong Kong	Occupation	Cultural Identity Profile*
					At Departure from Hong Kong		**In Country**			**At Return to Hong Kong**		
36	Female	20 / 29	Single / Married	No / No	Student / Occupational Psychologist	Australia / Australia	Student / Counselor	4 yrs / 5 yrs	34	12 yrs	Counselor	AD/H
37	Male	23 / 33	Single / Married	No / No	Student / Did Not Say	UK / Australia	Student / International Company	4 yrs / 2.5 yrs	27 / 35	8 yrs	Surveyor	S
38	Male	27 / 35	Married / Married	Yes; 2	Transportation Planner / Transportation Planner	Singapore / Canada	Transportation Planner / Transportation Planner	5 yrs / 4 yrs	32 / 39	7 yrs	Transportation Planner / Transportation Planner	G
39	Male	28	Single	No	IT Field	Australia	IT field	3 yrs	31	9 yrs	IT	AF/AD
40	Male	43	Married	Yes; 2	Construction Industry Power Company	Canada	Construction	4 yrs	47	13 yrs	Construction Industry Power Company	AF/AD
41	Male	43	Married	Yes; 2	Engineer	Australia	Engineer	6 yrs	49	12 yrs	Engineer	AD/B
42	Male	31	Married	Yes; 2; both born in Canada	Engineer	Canada	Engineer	4 yrs	35	11 yrs	Engineer	AD/H
43	Female	20 / 30	Single / Single	No / No	Student / Banking (CitiBank)	Canada / Australia	Student / Banking (CitiBank)	2 yrs / 4.5 yrs	22 / 35	7 yrs	CitiBank Manager	S & AD/H
44	Female	30	Single	No	IT Field	Australia	IT Field	3 yrs	33	15 yrs	IT Field	AD/B
45	Male	13	Single	No	Student	Australia	Student	5 yrs	18	4 yrs	Student	AD/H
46	Female	35	Married	No	Secretary	Australia	Student & Temp Jobs	3 yrs	38	8 yrs	Secretary	AF/AD

Participant	At Departure from Hong Kong					In Country			At Return to Hong Kong			
	Gender	Age	Marital Status	Child(ren)	Occupation	Resettlement Country	Occupation	Time There	Age	Time Back in Hong Kong	Occupation	Cultural Identity Profile*
47	Female	36	Married	Yes; 2	Government Work	Canada	Housewife	8 yrs	44	1 yr	Housewife	AD/H
48	Female	19 — 33	Married	No	Student — Hotel Industry	Canada — Australia	Graduate Student	3 yrs — 2 yrs	23 — 35	9 yrs	Hotel Industry	AD/H
49	Male	32	Married	No	Engineer	Australia	Engineer	2 yrs	34	11 yrs	Engineer	AD/B
50	Male	26	Married	No	Building	Australia	Building Estate Agency	8 yrs	34	10 yrs	Estate Surveyor	AD/H

* Identity Profiles

AD/H = Additive/Hybrid

AD/B = Additive/Bicultural

AF   = Affirmative

S   = Subtractive

G   = Global

Notes

Introduction

1. Cinel, 1991.
2. British Broadcasting Corporation, 2007.
3. Meredith, 2007.
4. Carney, 2008.
5. Day and Hope, 2008.

Chapter 1

1. Diamond, 1997.
2. DeGolyer, 2007, p. 21.
3. Morris, 1989.
4. Chiu and Hong, 1997; Nisbett, 2003.
5. Lau, 1981.
6. Bond and Hewstone, 1988.
7. Hall, 1976.
8. Chiu and Hong, 1999.
9. Ho, 1986; Sung, 1985; Yang, 1986.
10. MacFarquhar, 1980.
11. Hofstede and Hofstede, 2005; Chinese Culture Connection, 1987.
12. Chiu, Morris, Hong, and Menon, 2000.
13. Peng and Nisbett, 1999.
14. Kuah and Wong, 2001.
15. Skeldon, 1994.
16. Sinn, 1995.
17. Skeldon, 1994.
18. Sinn, 1995.
19. Sinn, 1995, p. 50.
20. Skeldon, 1994.
21. Shweder and Miller, 1985.
22. Triandis, 1995.

23. Nisbett, 2003.
24. Nisbett, 2003.
25. Bond and King, 1985, pp. 29–45.
26. Bond and Hewstone, 1988, p. 153.
27. Lin and Fu, 1990; Yang, 1986.
28. Siu, 1999, p. 111.
29. Cheng and Ng, 1995, p. 218.
30. Government of Hong Kong, 2003.
31. Ralston, et al., 1992.
32. Wong, 1991.
33. Bond, 1993.
34. Brewer, 1999.
35. Hong, Chiu, Fu, and Tong, 1996.
36. Bond and Hewstone, 1988.
37. Siu, 1999.
38. Lau and Kuan, 1988.
39. Lau, Lee, Wan, and Wong, 1991.
40. Wong, 1999.
41. DeGolyer, 2007; Hong Kong Transition detailed reports are available at www.hkbu.edu.hk/~hktp.
42. Hong, Liao, et al., 2006.
43. Salaff and Wong, 2000.
44. Hamilton, 1999, p. 8.
45. Wong, 1999.
46. Skeldon, 1994.
47. Skeldon, 1994.
48. Ho and Farmer, 1994.
49. Skeldon, 1994.
50. Kang, 1997.
51. Data from UN Population Division, 2004.
52. Johnson and Lary, 1994.
53. Johnson and Lary, 1994.
54. Costigan and Dokis, 2006.
55. Van Oudenhoven, 2006.
56. Ghuman, 2000.
57. Chan, 2004, p. 236.
58. Chan, 2004, p. 241.
59. Olds, 1998.
60. Pookong and Skeldon, 1994.
61. Pookong and Skeldon, 1994.
62. Wu, Ip, Inglis, Kawakami, and Duivenvoorden, 1998.
63. Mak, 2001.
64. Hofstede and Hofstede, 2005.
65. Soh, 2003.
66. Shih, 2001.
67. Kwan, 1997.
68. Ong, 1999.
69. Ho and Farmer, 1994.
70. Hughes and Chu, 1993.
71. Ley and Kobayashi, 2005, p. 122.

72. *South China Morning Post*, April 1990.
73. Wu, *The Standard*, July 2000.
74. Wyman, 1993.
75. Cinel, 1991
76. Guo and De Voretz, 2006.
77. McKenzie, 1994.
78. Wallis, 2004.
79. Kee and Skeldon, 1994.
80. Skeldon, 1994, p. 64.
81. Government of Hong Kong, 2000.
82. Ley and Kobayashi, 2005.
83. Sussman, 2000; Sussman, 2007.
84. Wong, 1988, pp. 111–112.

Chapter 2

1. Wilford, 2008.
2. Chen, 1999.
3. Faxon, 1999.
4. Wu, 2002, p. 64.
5. Wu, 2002.
6. Karetzky, 2001.
7. Lin, 2004.
8. Lui, 2004.
9. Heartney, 2002.
10. Hart, 2003, p. 618.
11. Gu, personal website.
12. Clarke, 2000.
13. Steiner and Hass, 1995, p. 9.
14. Cover, *Idea Magazine*, 1980 in Steiner and Hass, 1995, p. 10.
15. Steiner and Haas, 1995, p. 9.
16. Chow, 1992; Huppatz, 2006.
17. Simal, 2004.
18. Zhang, 1998.
19. Koh, 1991, p. 2.
20. Wyman, 1993.
21. Hawthorne, 1990, p. 461.
22. Desai, 2006.
23. Mishra, 2006.
24. Ishiguro, 2000.
25. Grinberg, Grinberg, and Festinger, 1989.
26. Berry, 1997; Ward, Bochner, and Furnham, 2001.
27. Kim, 1988.
28. Argyle, 1982.
29. Hall, 1966.
30. Furnham and Bochner, 1982.
31. Ward and Kennedy, 1999.
32. Tafjel, 1978, pp. 61–76.
33. Turner, Hogg, Oakes, Reicher and Wetherell, 1987.
34. Ashmore, Deaux, and McLaughlin-Volpe, 2004.

35. Deaux, 1996.
36. Ashmore, Deaux, and McLaughlin-Volpe, 2004.
37. Baumeister, 1986.
38. Berry, 1995.
39. LaFromboise, Coleman, and Gerton, 1993.
40. Rudmin, 2003.
41. Hermans and Kempen, 1998.
42. Oyserman, 1993.
43. Benet-Martinez, Leu, Lee, and Morris, 2002; Hong, et al., 2001.
44. Baumeister, Shapiro and Tice, 1985; Baumeister, 1986.
45. Leong and Ward, 2000.
46. Dion and Dion, 1996.
47. Ong, 1999.
48. Chan, 2005.
49. Chan, 2005, p. 126.
50. Sussman, 2000.
51. Wang, L. L., 1991.
52. Dion and Toner, 1988.
53. Dyal and Chan, 1985.
54. Chataway and Berry, 1989.
55. Zheng and Berry, 1991.
56. Rosenthal and Feldman, 1996.
57. Rosenthal and Feldman, 1996.
58. Bourne, 1975.
59. Kang, 1972.
60. Graham, 1983.
61. Iwamasa and Kooreman, 1995.
62. Sussman, Truong, and Lim, 2007.
63. Lieber, Chin, Nihira, and Mink, 2001.
64. Phinney, 1995.
65. Benet-Martinez, Leu, Lee, and Morris, 2002.
66. Ward and Kennedy, 1999.

Chapter 3

1. Sachse, 1948.
2. Handlin, 1956.
3. Ghosh, 2000.
4. Virtanen, 1979.
5. Wyman, 1993, p. 4.
6. Wyman, 1993, p. 150.
7. Cinel, 1991.
8. Glick-Schiller, Basch, and Szanton-Blanc, 1992, p. 48.
9. Foner, 1997.
10. Pedraza, 2006.
11. Kasinitz, Waters, Mollenkopf, and Anil, 2002.
12. Laguerre, 1998.
13. Pedraza, 2006.
14. Kasinitz, Waters, Mollenkopf, and Anil, 2002.
15. Wyman, 1993.

16. Skeldon, 1995.
17. Sussman, 1985.
18. Kanno, 2003; White, 1992.
19. Monbukagakusho, 2001, as cited in Kanno, 2003.
20. Wang, G. W., 1991.
21. Wang, 1998.
22. Iredale, Guo, and Rozario, 2003; Liu and Hewitt, 2008.
23. As reported in Chan, 1996, and the *Chinese Entertainment Weekly*, 1993.
24. Chan, 1996.
25. Chan, 1997.
26. Virtanen, 1979.
27. Curran, 2007.
28. Gmelch, 1980; King, Strachan, and Martimer, 1985; Petras and Kousis, 1988.
29. Cerase, 1974.
30. Olesen, 2002.
31. Iredale, Guo, and Rozario, 2003.
32. Schmiedeck, 1973.
33. Dustmann, 2003.
34. Waldorf, 1995.
35. Day and Hope, 2008.
36. Gorman, 2008.
37. Matza, 2008.
38. Heenan, 2005.
39. Olesen, 2002.
40. International Organization for Migration, 2004.
41. Curran, 2007.
42. Tsay, 2003.
43. Luo, Guo, and Huang, 2003.
44. Iredale, Guo, and Rozario, 2003.
45. Mindlin, 2007.
46. Dougherty, 2008.
47. Chaudhary, 2007.
48. Schmiedeck, 1973.
49. Hatzichristou and Hopf, 1995.
50. Guarnizo, 1997.
51. Iredale, Guo, and Rozario, 2003.
52. Deaux, 2006; Phinney, 2003.
53. Adler, 1981; Brein and David, 1971; Ward and Rana-Deuba, 1999.
54. Berry, 1980.
55. Tan, Hartel, Panipucci, and Strybosch, 2005.
56. Sussman, 2001.
57. Hertz, 1984.
58. Sussman, 1985.
59. Sussman, 2000.
60. Higgins, 1996.
61. Shweder, 1991.
62. Chan, 1996, p. 3.
63. Suda, 1999.
64. Alatas, 1972.
65. Sussman, 2002.

66. Storti, 2001, p. xvii.
67. Sussman, 2001.
68. Storti, 2001, p. 21.
69. Grisi, 2004.
70. Gregerson and Stroh, 1997.
71. Sahin, 1990.
72. Kyntaja, 1998.
73. Sussman, 1985.
74. Kidder, 1992.
75. Minoura, 1988.
76. Suda, 1999.
77. Roth, 2002; Tsuda, 2003.
78. Larmer, 2000; Wilhelm and Biers, 2000.
79. Zweig, 1997.
80. Li and Liu, 1999.
81. Chan, 1996, p. 2.
82. Ley and Kobayashi, 2005.
83. Salaff, Shik and Greve, 2008, p. 17.
84. Diener, Emmons, Larsen, and Griffin, 1985.
85. Sussman, 2001.
86. Birman and Trickett, 2001.
87. Singelis, 1994.
88. Kuhn and McPartland, 1954.
89. Kanno, 2003, p. 9.
90. Hull, 1987; Dinges and Hull, 1992.
91. Governnment of Hong Kong, 2000.

Chapter 4

1. DeGolyer, 2007.
2. Devoretz, Ma, and Zhang, 2003.
3. Sussman, 2001.

Chapter 5

1. York, 2004.
2. Anecdote referenced in Ley and Kobayashi, 2005.
3. Angel, May 17, 2004.
4. Bray and Koo, 2005, for a detailed discussion of the Hong Kong educational system.
5. Lee, 2006.
6. Birman and Trickett, 2001.
7. Singelis, 1994.
8. Singelis, Bond, Sharkey, and Lai, 1999. Also see Ng and Zhu, 2001, for similar nonmigrant Hong Kong self-construal ratings.
9. Chan, 1996.
10. Wyman, 1993.
11. Wyman, 1993.
12. Tannenbaum, 2007. The quotations from this study are excerpted from several

of the interviewee transcripts translated by Tannenbaum and provided to the author.
13. Hansel, 1993.
14. Kanno, 2003.
15. Minoura, 1988; Nagao, 1998.

Chapter 6

1. Cervantes, [1613], 2006.
2. Eikeland, personal communication, 2007.
3. Sussman and Sanzari, 2007.
4. Skeldon, 1995.
5. Chan, 1996.
6. Chiang and Liao, 2005.
7. Grisi, personal communication, 2004.
8. Grisi, 2004.
9. Attias and Benbassa, 2003.
10. Gold, 2002.
11. Chabin, 1997.
12. Tannenbaum, 2007.
13. Facts about Irish immigration, 2009.
14. McDonagh, 2006.
15. Government of Ireland, 2006.
16. Curran, 2007.

Chapter 7

1. Chiang and Liao, 2005.
2. Sakamoto, 2006.
3. Van Oudenhoven, 2006.
4. Chan, 1996.
5. Chiang and Liao, 2005.
6. Hansel, 1993.
7. Meredith, 2007.
8. Gold, 2002.
9. Sasagawa, Toyoda, and Sakano, 2006.
10. Sussman, 1985.

Chapter 8

1. Ong, Chan, and Chew, 1995.
2. Kung, Hung, and Chan, 2004.
3. Kung, Hung, and Chan, 2004.

Chapter 9

1. Bond, Wan, Leung, and Giacalone, 1985.
2. Bond and Chung, 1991.

Chapter 10

1.   Reid, 1999.
2.   Nisbett, 2003.
3.   Bond and Hwang, 1986
4.   Moore, 1967.
5.   Hofstede and Hofstede, 2005.
6.   Chinese Culture Connection, 1987.
7.   Nisbett, 2003.
8.   Peng and Nisbett, 1999.
9.   Bagozzi, Wong, and Yi, 1999.
10. Nisbett, 2003.
11. Choi, Dalal, and Kim-Prieto, 2000.
12. Morris and Peng, 1994.
13. Hong, Chiu, and Kung, 1997.
14. Nisbett, 2003.
15. Moore, 1967.
16. Moore, 1967.
17. LaBrack, personal communication, 2007.
18. Kauppi and Viotti, 1992.
19. Masuda and Nisbett, 2001.
20. Nisbett, 2003.

Chapter 11

1.   Bradsher, 2004.
2.   DeGolyer, 2007.
3.   Graham and Wada, 1992.
4.   Cheung and Wu, 2004.
5.   Fowler and Qin, 2007.
6.   Lau, 2007.
7.   Angel, May 24, 2004.
8.   Cheung and Wu, 2004.
9.   Gelfand, et al., 2001.
10. Pekerti and Thomas, 2003.

References

Adler, N. (1981). Re-entry: Managing cross-cultural transitions. *Group and Organizational Studies, 6*, 341–356.

Alatas, S. H. (1972). The captive mind in development studies: Some neglected problems and the need for an autonomous social science tradition in Asia. *International Social Science Journal, 24*, 9–25.

Angel, K. (May 17, 2004). Game names. *South China Morning Post*, C5.

Angel, K. (May 24, 2004). Relativity. *South China Morning Post*, C5.

Argyle, M. (1982). Intercultural communication. In S. Bochner (ed.), *Cultures in contact: Studies in cross-cultural interaction* (pp. 61–80). Oxford: Pergamon.

Ashmore, R. D., Deaux, K., and McLaughlin-Volpe, T. (2004). An organizing framework collective identity: Articulation and significance of multidimensionality. *Psychological Bulletin, 130*, 80–114.

Attias, J. C., and Benbassa, E. (2003). *Israel: The impossible land.* Stanford, CA: Stanford University Press.

Bagozzi, R. P., Wong, N., and Yi, Y. (1999). The role of culture and gender in the relationship between positive and negative affect. *Cognition and Emotion, 13*, 641–672.

Basch, L., Schiller, N. G., and Blanc, C. S. (1994). *Nations unbound: Transnational projects, post-colonial predicaments, and deterritorialized nation states.* Langhorne, PA: Gordon and Breach.

Baumeister, R. F. (1986). *Identity: Cultural change and the struggle for self.* Oxford: Oxford University Press.

Baumeister, R. F., Shapiro, J. P., and Tice D. M. (1985). Two kinds of identity crisis. *Journal of Personality, 53*, 407–424.

Benet-Martinez, V., Leu, J., Lee, F., and Morris, M. W. (2002). Negotiating biculturalism: Cultural frame switching in biculturals with oppositional versus compatible identities. *Journal of Cross-Cultural Psychology, 33*, 492–516.

Berry, J. W. (1980). Acculturation as variations of adaptation. In A. Padilla (ed.), *Acculturation, theory, models and some new findings* (pp. 9–25). Boulder, CO: Westview Press.

Berry, J. W. (1986). Multiculturalism and psychology in plural societies. In L. H. Ekstand (ed.), *Ethnic minorities and immigrants in a cross-cultural perspective.* (pp. 35–51). Lisse, The Netherlands: Swets and Zeitlinger.

Berry, J. W. (1995). Psychology of acculturation. In N. R. Goldberger and J. B. Veroff (eds.), *The culture and psychology reader* (pp. 457–488). New York: New York University Press.

Berry, J. W. (1997). Immigration, acculturation and adaptation. *Applied Psychology: An International Review, 46,* 1–30.

Birman, D., and Trickett, E. J. (2001). Cultural transitions in first-generation immigrants: Acculturation of Soviet Jewish refugee adolescents and parents. *Journal of Cross-Cultural Psychology, 32*(4), 456–477.

Birman, D., Trickett, E. J., and Vinokurov, A. (2002). Acculturation and adaptation of Soviet Jewish refugee adolescents: Predictors of adjustment across life domains. *American Journal of Community Psychology, 30,* 585–607.

Bond, M. H. (1993). *Between the yin and the yang: The identity of the Hong Kong Chinese.* The Chinese University of Hong Kong, Professorial Inaugural Lecture Series 19. Chinese University Bulletin (Suppl. 31).

Bond, M. H. (1996). Chinese values. In M. H. Bond (ed.), *The handbook of Chinese psychology* (pp. 208–226). Hong Kong: Oxford University Press.

Bond, M. H., and Chung, K. V. (1991). Resistance to group or personal insults in an ingroup or outgroup context. *International Journal of Psychology, 26,* 83–94.

Bond, M. H., and Hewstone, M. (1988). Social identity theory and the perception of intergroup relations in Hong Kong. *International Journal of Intercultural Relations, 12,* 153–170.

Bond, M. H., and Hwang, K. K. (1986). The social psychology of Chinese people. In M. H. Bond (ed.), *The psychology of the Chinese people* (pp. 213–266). New York: Oxford University Press.

Bond, M. H., and King, A. Y. C. (1985). Coping with the threat of westernization in Hong Kong. *International Journal of Intercultural Relations, 9,* 351–364.

Bond, M. H., Wan, K. C., Leung, K., and Giacalone, R. A. (1985). How are responses to verbal insult related to cultural collectivism and power distance? *Journal of Cross-Cultural Psychology, 16,* 111–127.

Bourne, P. G. (1975). The Chinese student: Acculturation and mental illness. *Psychiatry, 38,* 269–277.

Bradsher, K. (May 31, 2004). Democracy supporters march in Hong Kong. *The New York Times.*

Bray, M., and Koo, R. (2005). *Education and society in Hong Kong and Macao: Comparative perspectives on continuity and change* (2nd ed.). Dordrecht, The Netherlands: Springer.

Brein, M., and David, K. (1971). Intercultural communication and the adjustment of the sojourner. *Psychological Bulletin, 76,* 215–230.

Brewer, M. B. (1999). Multiple identities and identity transition: Implications for Hong Kong. *International Journal of Intercultural Relations, 23,* 187–197.

British Broadcasting Corporation (May 12, 2007). Official says many Chinese returnees cannot find jobs. *BBC Worldwide Monitoring.*

Carney, S. (March 4, 2008). India beckons Indian-Americans back with jobs. http://www.npr.org/templates/sstory/story.php?storyId=87884391.

Cerase, F. P. (1974). Expectations and reality: A case study of return migration from the United States to southern Italy. *International Migration Review, 8*, 245–262.

Cervantes, Miguel de. ([1613]2006). The jealous Estramaduran. In *The exemplary novels of Cervantes* (pp. 335–367). London: BiblioBazaar.

Chabin, M. (March 2, 1997). Behind the headlines: Israelis living abroad wooed to return by government firms. *Jewish Telegraphic Agency Online.*

Chan, K. B. (1997). A family affair: Migration, dispersal and the emergent identity of the Chinese cosmopolitan. *Diaspora, 6*, 195–214.

Chan, K. B. (2004). From multiculturalism to hybridity: The Chinese in Canada. In J. Rex and G. Singh (eds.), *Governance in multicultural societies* (pp. 227–244). Aldershot, England: Ashgate.

Chan, K. B. (2005). *Chinese identities, ethnicity, and cosmopolitanism.* London: Routledge.

Chan, W. W. Y. (1996). Home but not home: A case study of some Canadian returnees in Hong Kong. Thesis, Division of Social Science, Hong Kong University of Science and Technology.

Chataway, C. J., and Berry, J. W. (1989). Acculturation experiences, appraisal, coping, and adaptation: A comparison of Hong Kong Chinese, French, and English students in Canada. *Canadian Journal of Behavioural Science, 21*, 295–309.

Chaudhary, V. (December 16, 2007). Take the money and run — Illegal migrants go "home" on handouts. *The Sunday Times* (London), News, p. 10.

Chen, R. Y. (November 18, 1999). Masami Teraoka's work — A multiplicity of themes. *Asian Week, 21*(13), 1–3.

Cheng, J. (August 9, 2007). Hong Kong aims to embrace nearby Shenzhen. *The Wall Street Journal.*

Cheng, S. M., and Ng, S. H. (1995). The Chinese migrant ethos and Hong Kong's brain drain. In J. H. Ong, K. B. Chan, and K. C. Ho (eds.), *Crossing borders: Transmigration in the Asia Pacific.* Singapore: Prentice-Hall.

Cheung, G., and Wu, E. (May 15, 2004). Hongkongers look to the mainland for a better life. *South China Morning Post.*

Chiang, N., and Liao S. (2005). Back to base: Adaptation and self-identity of young Taiwanese transnationals. Paper presented at "People on the move: The transnational flow of Chinese human capital," Hong Kong University of Science and Technology, October 20–22.

Chinese Culture Connection (1987). Chinese values and the search for culture-free dimensions of culture. *Journal of Cross-Cultural Psychology, 8*, 143–164.

Chinese Entertainment Weekly, The (October 8, 1993). Toronto, Canada.

Chiu, C., and Hong, Y. (1997). Justice in Chinese societies: A Chinese perspective. In H. S. R. Kao and D. Sinha (eds.), *Asian perspective on psychology* (pp. 164–184). Thousand Oaks, CA: Sage.

Chiu, C., and Hong, Y. (1999). Social identification in a political transition: The role of implicit beliefs. *International Journal of Intercultural Relations, 2*, 297–318.

Chiu, C., Morris, M. W., Hong, Y., and Menon, T. (2000). Motivated cultural cognition: The impact of implicit cultural theories on dispositional attribution varies as a function of need for closure. *Journal of Personality and Social Psychology, 78*, 297–318.

Choi, I., Dalal, R., and Kim-Prieto, C. (2000). Information search in causal attribution: Analytic vs. holistic. Unpublished manuscript, Seoul National University.

Chow, R. (1992). Between colonizers: Hong Kong post-colonial self-writing in the 1990's. *Diaspora: A Journal of Transnational Studies, 2,* 57.

Cinel, D. (1991). *The national integration of Italian return migration, 1870–1929.* Cambridge: Cambridge University Press.

Clarke, D. (2000). The culture of a border within: Hong Kong art and China. *Art Journal, 59,* 88–101.

Costigan, C. L., and Dokis, D. P. (2006). Similarities and differences in acculturation among mothers, fathers, and children in immigrant Chinese families. *Journal of Cross-Cultural Psychology, 37,* 723–741.

Curran, M. (2007). Returning to Ireland. Paper presented at the American Conference for Irish Studies. New York, April 18–21.

Day, M., and Hope, C. (October 23, 2008). A third of Poles are heading home. *The Daily Telegraph,* p. 1.

Deaux, K. (1996). Social identification. In E. T. Higgins and A. W. Kruglanski (eds.), *Social psychology: Handbook of basic principles* (pp. 777–798). New York: Guilford Press.

Deaux, K. (2006). *To be an immigrant.* New York: Russell Sage Foundation.

DeGolyer, M. E. (2007). Identity in the politics of transition: The case of Hong Kong, "Asia's World City." In K. B. Chan, J. Walls, and D. Hayward (eds.), *East-West identities: Globalization, localization, and hybridization* (pp. 21–54). Leiden: Brill Academic Publishers.

Desai, K. (2006). *The inheritance of loss.* New York: Grove.

Devoretz, D., Ma, J., and Zhang, M. (2003). Triangular human capital flows: Empirical evidence from Hong Kong and Canada. In J. Reitz (ed.), *Host societies and the reception of immigrants* (pp. 469–492). LaJolla, CA: Center for Comparative Immigration Studies, University of California, San Diego.

Diamond, J. (1997). *Guns, germs, and steel: The fate of human societies.* New York: Norton.

Diener, E., Emmons, R. A., Larsen., R. J., and Griffin, S. (1985). The satisfaction with life scale. *Journal of Personality Assessment, 49,* 71–75.

Dinges, N. G., and Hull, P. (1992). Personality, culture, and international studies. In D. Lieberman and M. Gurtov (ed.), *Revealing the world: An interdisciplinary reader for international studies* (pp. 133–162). Dubuque, IA: Kendall-Hunt.

Dion, K. L., and Dion, K. K. (1996). Chinese adaptation to foreign cultures. In M. H. Bond (ed.), *The handbook of Chinese psychology* (pp. 457–478). Hong Kong: Oxford University Press.

Dion, K. L., and Toner, B. B. (1988). Ethnic differences in test anxiety. *Journal of Social Psychology, 128,* 165–172.

Dougherty, C. (June 26, 2008). Strong economy and labor shortages are luring Polish immigrants back home. *The New York Times,* A6.

Dustmann, C. (2003). Children and migration. *Journal of Population Economics, 16,* 815–830.

Dyal, J. A., and Chan, C. (1985). Stress and distress: A study of Hong Kong Chinese and Euro-Canadian students. *Journal of Cross-Cultural Psychology, 16,* 447–466.

Facts about Irish immigration. (2009). http://www.udel.edu/soe/deal/IrishImmigrationFacts.html.

Faxon, A. (1999). Masami Teraoka: From tradition to technology, the floating world comes of age. *Art New England, 20*(4), 56.

Foner N. (1997). What's new about transnationalism? New York immigrants today and at the turn of the century. *Diaspora, 6*, 355–376.

Fowler, G. A., and Qin, J. (February 5, 2007). Hong Kong's baby boom. *The Wall Street Journal*.

Furnham, A., and Bochner, S. (1982). Social difficulty in a foreign culture: An empirical analysis of culture shock. In S. Bochner (ed.), *Cultures in contact: Studies in cross-cultural interactions* (pp. 161–198). Oxford: Pergamon.

Gelfand, M. J., Nishii, L. H., Holcombe, K. M., Dyer, N., Ohbuchi, K. I., and Fukuno, M. (2001). Cultural influences on cognitive episodes in the United States and Japan. *Journal of Applied Psychology, 86*, 1059–1074.

Ghosh, B. (2000). *Return migration: Journey of hope or despair*. Geneva: IOM and United Nations.

Ghuman, P. A. S. (2000). Acculturation of South Asian adolescents in Australia. *British Journal of Educational Psychology, 70*, 305–316.

Glick-Schiller, N., Basch, L., and Szanton-Blanc, C. (eds.) (1992). *Towards a transnational perspective on migration: Race, class, ethnicity, and nationalism reconsidered* (Vol. 645). New York: New York Academy of Sciences.

Gmelch, G. (1980). Return migration. *Annual Review of Anthropology, 9*, 135–159.

Gold, S. (2002). *The Israeli diaspora*. Seattle: University of Washington Press.

Gorman, A. (September 1, 2008). A darker state economy sends day laborers packing. *The Los Angeles Times*, Metro, p. 1.

Government of Hong Kong (2000). *Returnees to Hong Kong*. Census and Statistics Department, Special Topics Report No. 25.

Government of Hong Kong (2003). *Survey of returnees*.

Government of Ireland Central Statistics Office (2006). Dublin population and migration estimates.

Graham, E. M., and Wada, E. (1992). Foreign direct investment in China: Effects on growth and economic performance. Peterson Institute Working Paper Series, http://www.petersoninstitute.org/publications/wp/01-3.pdf

Graham, M. A. (1983). Acculturative stress among Polynesian, Asian and American students on the Brigham Young University–Hawaii campus. *International Journal of Intercultural Relations, 7*, 79–103.

Gregersen, H., and Stroh, L. (1997). Coming home to the artic cold: Antecedents to Finnish expatriate and spouse repatriation adjustment. *Personnel Psychology, 50*, 635–654.

Grinberg, L., Grinberg, R., and Festinger, N. (1989). *Psychoanalytic perspectives on migration and exile*. New Haven, CT: Yale University Press.

Grisi, D. (2004). Cultural transition and change in social identity: MLAL's returned volunteers. Master's thesis, Faculty of Education, University of Verona, Italy.

Guarnizo, L. E. (1997). The emergence of a transnational social formation and the mirage of return migration among Dominican transmigrants. *Identities: Global Studies in Culture and Power, 4*, 281–322.

Gu, X. http://dianeferrisgallery.com/artist/xiong.

Guo, S., and DeVoretz, D. J. (2006). The changing face of Chinese immigrants in Canada. *Journal of Immigration and Integration, 7*, 425–447.

Hall, E. T. (1966). *The hidden dimension*. Garden City, NY: Doubleday.

Hall, E. T. (1976). *Beyond culture*. New York: Anchor Books.

Hamilton, G. (1999). *Cosmopolitan capitalists*. Seattle: University of Washington Press.

Handlin, O. (July 1956). Immigrants who go back. *Atlantic*, 70.

Hansel, B. (1993). An investigation of the re-entry adjustment of Indians who studied in the U.S. *Occasional Papers in Intercultural Learning, 17*, 1–28. New York: AFS Center for the Study of Intercultural Learning.

Hart, D. (2003). Looking for home. *Art and Australia, 40*, 618–625.

Hatzichristou, C., and Hopf, D. (1995). School adaptation of Greek children after remigration: Age differences in multiple domains. *Journal of Cross-Cultural Psychology, 26*, 505–522.

Hawthorne, N. ([1860] 1990). *The marble faun*. New York: Penguin Books.

Heartney, E. (2002). Cai Guo-Qiang: Illuminating the new China. *Art in America, 90*(5), 92–97.

Heenan, D. (September 19, 2005). High-powered immigrants going home. *US News and World Report*.

Hermans, H. J. M., and Kempen, H. J. G. (1998). Moving cultures: The perilous problems of cultural dichotomies in a globalizing society. *American Psychologist, 53*, 1111–1120.

Hertz, D. G. (1984). Psychological and psychiatric aspects of remigration. *Israel Journal of Psychiatry and Related Sciences, 21*, 57–68.

Higgins, E. T. (1996). The "self-digest": Self-knowledge serving self-regulatory functions. *Journal of Personality and Social Psychology, 71*, 1062–1083.

Ho, D. Y. F. (1986). Chinese patterns of socialization: A critical review. In M. H. Bond (ed.), *The psychology of the Chinese people* (pp. 1–37). Hong Kong: Oxford University Press.

Ho, E. S., and Farmer, R. (1994). The Hong Kong Chinese in Auckland. In R. Skeldon (ed.), *Reluctant exiles? Migration from Hong Kong and the new overseas Chinese* (pp. 215–234). New York: M. E. Sharpe, and Hong Kong: Hong Kong University Press.

Hofstede, G., and Hofstede, G. J. (2005). *Cultures and organizations: Software of the mind*. New York: McGraw-Hill.

Hong, Y., Chiu, C., and Kung, T. (1997). Bringing culture out in front: Effects of cultural meaning system activation on social cognition. In K. Leung, Y. Kashima, U. Kim, and S. Yamaguichi (eds.), *Progress in Asian social psychology* (pp. 135–146). Singapore: Wiley.

Hong, Y., Chiu, C., Fu, H., and Tong, Y. (1996). Effects of self-categorization on intergroup perceptions: The case of Hong Kong facing 1997. Presentation at the Annual Convention of the American Psychological Society. San Francisco, CA.

Hong, Y., Ip, G., Chiu, C., Morris, M. W., and Menon, T. (2001). Cultural identity and dynamic construction of the self: Collective duties and individual rights in Chinese and American students. *Social Cognition, 19*, 251–268.

Hong, Y., Liao, H., Chan, G., Wong, R. Y. M., Chie, C., Ip, G. W., Fu, H., and Hansen, I. G. (2006). Temporal causal links between outgroup attitudes and social categorization: The case of Hong Kong 1997 transition. *Group Processes and Intergroup Relations, 9*, 265–288.

Hughes, M., and Chu, D. (November 6, 1993). Disillusioned migrants seek jobs at home. *South China Morning Post*.

Hull, P. V. (1987). *Bilingualism: Two languages, two personalities? Resources in education.* Educational Resources Clearinghouse on Education. Ann Arbor: University of Michigan Press.

Huppatz, D. J. (2006). The chameleon and the pearl of the orient. *Design Issues, 22,* 64–76.

International Organization for Migration. (2004). *Return migration: Policies and practices in Europe.* Geneva: International Organization for Migration.

Iredale, R., Guo, F., and Rozario, S. (2003). *Return migration in the Asia Pacific.* Cheltenham, UK: Edward Elgar Publishing.

Ishiguro, K. (2000). *When we were orphans.* New York: Knopf.

Iwamasa, G.Y., and Kooreman, H. (1995). Brief Symptom Inventory scores of Asian, Asian-American, and European-American college students. *Cultural Diversity and Mental Health, 1,* 149–157.

Japanese children overseas. *Dissertation Abstracts International:* Section B.

Johnson, G. E., and Lary, D. (1994). Hong Kong migration to Canada: The background. In R. Skeldon (ed.), *Reluctant exiles? Migration from Hong Kong and the new overseas Chinese* (pp. 87–97). New York: M. E. Sharpe, and Hong Kong: Hong Kong University Press.

Kang, K. C. (June 29, 1997). Chinese in the Southlands: A changing picture. *Los Angeles Times.*

Kang, T. S. (1972). Name and group identification. *Journal of Social Psychology, 86,* 159–160.

Kanno, Y. (2003). *Negotiating bilingual and bicultural identities: Japanese returnees between two worlds.* Mahwah, NJ: Lawrence Erlbaum Associates.

Karetzky, P. (2001). A modern literati: The art of Xu Bing. *Oriental Art, 47,* 47–62.

Kasinitz, P., Waters, M. C., Mollenkopf, J. H., and Anil, M. (2002). Transnationalism and the children of immigrants in contemporary New York. In P. Levitt and M. Waters (eds.), *The changing face of home: The transnational lives of the second generation* (pp. 96–122). New York: Russell Sage Foundation.

Kauppi, M. V., and Viotti, P. (1992). *The global philosophers: World politics in Western thought.* Issues in World Politics series. New York: Lexington Books.

Kee, P. K., and Skeldon, R. (1994). The migration and settlement of Hong Kong Chinese in Australia. In R. Skeldon (ed.), *Reluctant exiles? Migration from Hong Kong and the new overseas Chinese* (pp. 183–196). New York: M. E. Sharpe, and Hong Kong: Hong Kong University Press.

Kidder, L. H. (1992). Requirements for being "Japanese." *International Journal of Intercultural Relations, 16,* 383–393.

Kim, Y.Y. (1988). *Communication and cross-cultural adaptation: An integrative theory.* Clevedon, UK: Multilingual Matters.

King, A. Y. C., and Bond, M. H. (1985). The Confucian paradigm of man: A sociological view. In W. S. Teng and D. Y. H. We (eds.), *Chinese culture and mental health: Overview* (pp. 29–45). New York: Academic Press.

King, R., Strachan, A., and Martimer, J. (1985). The urban dimension of European return migration: The case of Bari, Southern Italy. *Urban Studies, 22,* 214–235.

Koh, T. A. (1991). Summary report on workshop on perceptions of migrants in literature. Paper presented at the International Conference on Migration, Centre for Advanced Studies, National University of Singapore, February 7–9.

Kuah, K. E., and Wong, S. L. (2001). Dialect and territory-based associations: Cultural and identity brokers in Hong Kong. In P. T. Lee (ed.), *Hong Kong reintegrating with China: Political, cultural and social dimensions* (pp. 203–217). Hong Kong: Hong Kong University Press.

Kuhn, M., and McPartland, T. (1954). An empirical investigation of self-attitudes. *American Sociological Review, 19,* 68–76.

Kung, W. W., Hung, S. L., and Chan, C. L. (2004). How the socio-cultural context shapes women's divorce experience in Hong Kong. *Journal of Comparative Family Studies, 35*(1), 33–50.

Kwan, K. L. K. (1997). Ethnic identity and cultural adjustment difficulties of Chinese-Americans. *Dissertation Abstracts International:* Section B: The Sciences and Engineering, 57(7-B), 4784.

Kyntaja, E. (1998). Ethnic remigration from the former Soviet Union to Finland: Patterns of ethnic identity and acculturation among the Ingrian Finns. *Yearbook of Population Research in Finland, 34,* 102–113.

LaFromboise, T., Coleman, H. K., and Gerton, J. (1993). Psychological impact of biculturalism: Evidence and theory. *Psychological Bulletin, 114,* 395–412.

Laguerre, M. (1998). *Diasporic citizenship: Haitian Americans in transnational America.* New York: St. Martin's Press.

Lalwani, A. K., Shavitt, S., and Johnson, T. (2006). What is the relation between cultural orientation and socially desirable responding? *Journal of Personality and Social Psychology, 90,* 165–178.

Larmer, B. (July 31, 2000). Home at last. *Newsweek International,* 32.

Lau, J. H. C. (June 24, 2007). Drawn by vibrant city, Mainlanders reshape Hong Kong. *The New York Times.*

Lau, S. (1981). Utilitarianistic familialism: The basis of political stability. In A. Y. C. King and R. L. P. Lee (eds.), *Social life and development in Hong Kong* (pp. 195–216). Hong Kong: The Chinese University Press.

Lau, S. K., and Kuan, H. C. (1988). *The ethos of Hong Kong Chinese.* Hong Kong: The Chinese University of Hong Kong.

Lau, S. K., Lee, M. K., Wan, P. S., and Wong, S. L. (eds.) (1991). *Indicators of social development: Hong Kong, 1988.* Hong Kong: Institute of Asia-Pacific Studies, the Chinese University of Hong Kong.

Lee, F. L. F. (2006). Collective efficacy, support for democratization, and political participation in Hong Kong. *International Journal of Public Opinion, 18,* 297–317.

Leong, C., and Ward, C. (2000). Identity conflict in sojourners. *International Journal of Intercultural Relations, 24,* 763–776.

Ley, D., and Kobayashi, A. (2005). Back to Hong Kong: Return migration or transnational sojourn? *Global Networks, 5,* 111–127.

Li, J., and Liu, D. (1999). Analysis of demand for foreign education in China. *Consumer Demands and Economy, 5,* 20–28.

Li, P. S. (2005). The rise and fall of Chinese immigration to Canada: Newcomers from Hong Kong Special Administrative Region of China and Mainland China, 1980–2000. *International Migration, 43,* 9–32.

Lieber, E., Chin, S., Nihira, K., and Mink, I. T. (2001). Holding on and letting go: Identity and acculturation among Chinese immigrants. *Cultural Diversity and Ethnic Minority Psychology, 7,* 247–261.

Lin, C. C., and Fu, V. R. (1990). A comparison of child-rearing practices among Chinese, immigrant Chinese, and Caucasian-American parents. *Child Development, 61,* 429–433.

Lin, X. (2004). Globalism or nationalism? Cai Guoqiang, Zhang Huan, and Xu Bing in New York. *Third Text, 18*(4), 279–295.

Liu, M., and Hewitt, D. (August 18/25, 2008). Rise of the sea turtles. *Newsweek,* 28–31.

Lui, C. (2004). Being and nothingness. *Print, 58*(2), 90–95.

Luo, K., Guo, F., and Huang, P. (2003). China: Government policies and emerging trends of reversal of the brain drain. In R. Iredale, F. Guo, and S. Rozario (eds.), *Return migration in the Asia Pacific* (pp. 88–111). Cheltenham, UK: Edward Elgar Publishing.

MacFarquhar, R. (February 9, 1980). The post-Confucian challenge. *The Economist,* 67–72.

Mak, A. (2001). *Relocating careers: Hong Kong professionals and managers in Australia.* Hong Kong: Centre of Asian Studies, The University of Hong Kong.

Markus, H. R., and Kunda, Z. (1986). Stability and malleability of the self-concept. *Journal of Personality and Social Psychology, 51,* 858–866.

Masuda, T., and Nisbett, R. E. (2001). Attending holistically vs. analytically: Comparing the context sensitivity of Japanese and Americans. *Journal of Personality and Social Psychology, 81,* 922–934.

Matsumoto, D., Yoo, S. H., Anguas-Wong, A. M., Arriola, M., Ataca, B., Bond, M. H., et al. (2008). Mapping expressive differences around the world: The relationship between emotional display rules and individualism versus collectivism. *Journal of Cross-Cultural Psychology, 39,* 55–74.

Matza, M. (November 16, 2008). As US economy sours, immigrants head home. *The Philadelphia Inquirer,* A01.

McDonagh, M. (July 20, 2006). The tide has turned for county plagued by poverty and forced emigration. *The Irish Times.*

McKenzie, S. (May 24, 1994). Emigrants' return sparks fears. *South China Morning Post.*

Meredith, R. (July 23, 2007). Back to India. *Forbes,* 86–95.

Miller, E. (January 1973). Return and nonreturn in-migration. *Growth and Change,* 3–9.

Mindlin, A. (November 11, 2007). A homeland beckons. *The New York Times,* section 14CY, p. 4.

Ming Pao (April 7, 1994). Vancouver's astronaut families. p. A11.

Minoura, Y. (1988). The psychological reorganization of overseas experience after returning to Japan: A symbolic interactionist approach to returnees. *Shakai Shinrigaku Kenkyuu, 32,* 3–11.

Mishra, P. (February 12, 2006). Wounded by the West: The inheritance of loss. *The New York Times.*

Moore, C. A. (1967). Introduction: The humanistic Chinese mind. In C. A. Moore, *The Chinese mind: Essentials of Chinese philosophy and culture* (pp. 1–10). Honolulu: University of Hawaii Press.

Morris, J. (1989). *Hong Kong.* New York: Vintage Books.

Morris, M. W., and Peng, K. (1994). Culture and cause: American and Chinese attributions for social and physical events. *Journal of Personality and Social Psychology, 67,* 949–971.

Nagao, C. T. (1998). Where to belong? An empirical study of the cultural identity of Japanese children overseas. *Dissertation Abstracts International: Section B: The Sciences and Engineering*, 58(12-B), 6848.

Ng, S. H., and Zhu, Y. (2001). Attributing causality and remembering events in individual- and group-acting situations: A Beijing, Hong Kong, and Wellington comparison. *Asian Journal of Social Psychology*, 4, 39–52.

Ng, W. C. (1998). Becoming "Chinese Canadian": The genesis of a cultural category. In E. Sinn (ed.), *The last half century of Chinese overseas* (pp. 206–218). Hong Kong: Hong Kong University Press.

Nisbett, R. E. (2003). *The geography of thought: How Asians and Westerners think differently and why.* New York: Simon and Schuster.

Olds, K. (1998). Globalization and urban change: Tales from Vancouver via Hong Kong. *Urban Geography*, 19, 360–385.

Olesen, H. (2002). Migration, return, and development: An institutional perspective. *International Migration*, 40, 125–149.

Ong, A. (1999). *Flexible citizenship: The cultural logics of transnationality.* Durham, NC: Duke University Press.

Ong, J. H., Chan, K. B., and Chew, S. B. (eds.) (1995). *Crossing borders: Transmigration in Asia Pacific.* New York: Prentice-Hall.

Oyserman, D. (1993). The lens of personhood: Viewing the self, others, and conflict in a multicultural society. *Journal of Personality and Social Psychology*, 6, 993–1009.

Pedraza, S. (2006). Assimilation or transnationalism? Conceptual models of the immigrant experience in America. In R. Mahalingam (ed.), *Cultural psychology of immigrants* (pp. 33–54). Mahwah, NJ: Lawrence Erlbaum.

Pekerti, A., and Thomas, D. C. (2003). Communication in intercultural interaction: An empirical investigation of idiocentric and sociocentric communication styles. *Journal of Cross-Cultural Psychology*, 34, 139–154.

Peng, K., and Nisbett, R. E. (1999). Culture, dialectics, and reasoning about contradiction. *American Psychologist*, 54, 741–754.

Pe-Pua, R., Mitchell, C., Castles, S., and Iredale, R. (1998). Astronaut families and parachute children. In E. Sinn (ed.), *The last half century of Chinese overseas* (pp. 279–298). Hong Kong: Hong Kong University Press.

Petras, E., and Kousis, M. (1988). Returning migrant characteristics and labor market demand in Greece. *International Migration Review*, 22, 586–608.

Phinney, J. (1995). Ethnic identity and self-esteem: A review and integration. In A. Padilla (ed.), *Hispanic psychology* (pp. 57–70). Thousand Oaks, CA: Sage.

Phinney, J.(2003). Ethnic identity and acculturation. In K. Chun, P. Organista, and G. Marin (eds.), *Acculturation: Advances in theory. Measurement and applied research* (pp. 63–81). Washington, DC: American Psychological Association.

Pookong, K., and Skeldon, R. (1994). The migration and settlement of Hong Kong Chinese in Australia. In R. Skeldon (ed.), *Reluctant exiles? Migration from Hong Kong and the new overseas Chinese* (pp. 183–196). New York: M. E. Sharpe, and Hong Kong: Hong Kong University Press.

Ralston, D. A., Gustafson, D. J., Elsass, P. M., Cheung, F., and Terpstra. R. H. (1992). Eastern values: A comparison of managers in the United States, Hong Kong and the People's Republic of China. *Journal of Applied Psychology*, 77, 664–671.

Reid, T. R. (1999). *Confucius lives next door.* New York: Vintage Books.

Rosenthal, D. A., and Feldman, S. S. (1996). Crossing the border: Chinese adolescents in the West. In L. Sing (ed.), *Growing up the Chinese way: Chinese child and adolescent development* (pp. 287–320). Hong Kong: The Chinese University Press.

Roth, J. (2002). *Brokered homeland: Japanese Brazilian migrants in Japan.* Ithaca, NY: Cornell University Press.

Rudmin, F. W. (2003). Critical history of the acculturation psychology of assimilation, separation, integration, and marginalization. *Review of General Psychology, 7,* 3–37.

Sachse, W. L. (1948). The migration of New Englanders to England, 1640–60. *American Historical Review, 53,* 252–254.

Sahin, N. (1990). Re-entry and the academic and psychological problems of the second generation. *Psychology and Developing Societies, 2,* 165–182.

Sakamoto, I. (2006). When family enters the picture: The model of cultural negotiation and gendered experiences of Japanese academic sojourners in the United States. *Cultural Diversity and Ethnic Minority Psychology, 12*(3), 558–577.

Salaff, J. W., and Wong, S. L. (2000). Migration and identities in Hong Kong's transition. In F. Ash, B. Hook, and R. Porter (eds.), *Hong Kong in transition: The handover years* (pp. 247–268). London: Macmillan.

Salaff, J. W., Shik, A., and Greve, A. (2008). Like sons and daughters of Hong Kong: The return of the young generation. *The China Review: An Interdisciplinary Journal on Greater China, 8,* 31–58.

Sasagawa, S., Toyoda, H., and Sakano, Y. (2006). The acquisition of cultural values in Japanese returnee students. *International Journal of Intercultural Relations, 30,* 333–343.

Schmiedeck, R. A. (1973). Motives for emigration and remigration in Austrian scientists. *Koelner Zeitschrift fur Soziologie und Sozialpsychologie, 25,* 594–605.

Shih, S. F. (2001). The relations among acculturation, cultural values, and counseling expectations among three Chinese American groups. *Dissertation Abstracts International:* Section A: Humanities and Social Sciences, 62(1-A), 91.

Shweder, R. A. (1991). *Thinking through cultures: Expeditions with cultural psychology.* Cambridge, MA: Harvard University Press.

Shweder, R. A., and Miller, J. G. (1985). The social construction of the person: How is it possible? In K. J. Gergen and K. E. Davis (eds.), *The social construction of the persons* (pp. 41–69). New York: Springer-Verlag.

Simal, B. (2004). "Moving selves": Immigration and transnationalism in Gish Jen and Chitra Divakaruni. In B. Simal and E. Marino, *Transnational, national, and personal voices: New perspectives on Asian American and Asian diasporic women writers* (pp. 151–173). Piscataway, NJ: Transaction.

Singelis, T. (1994). The measurement of independence self-construals. *Personality and Social Psychology Bulletin, 20,* 580–591.

Singelis, T. M., Bond, M. H., Sharkey, W.F., and Lai, C. S. (1999). Unpackaging culture's influence on self-esteem and embarrassability: The role of self-construal. *Journal of Cross-Cultural Psychology, 30,* 315–341.

Sinn, E. (1995). Emigration from Hong Kong before 1941: Organization and impact. In R. Skeldon (ed.), *Emigration from Hong Kong: Tendencies and impacts* (pp. 35–50). Hong Kong: The Chinese University Press.

Siu, H. F. (1999). Hong Kong: Cultural kaleidoscope on a world landscape. In G. G. Hamilton (ed.), *Cosmopolitan capitalists* (pp. 100–117). Seattle: University of Washington Press.

Skeldon, R. (ed.) (1994). *Reluctant exiles? Migration from Hong Kong and the new overseas Chinese.* New York: M. E. Sharpe, and Hong Kong: Hong Kong University Press.

Skeldon, R. (ed.) (1995). *Emigration from Hong Kong: Tendencies and impacts.* Hong Kong: The Chinese University Press.

Soh, B. E. (2003). The impact of acculturation on the level of depression among Chinese-American women. *Dissertation Abstract International: Section B:* The Sciences and Engineering, 63(8-B), 3939.

South China Morning Post. (April 22, 1990). Important to lure home the emigrants.

Steiner, H., and Haas, K. (1995). *Cross-cultural design: Communicating in the global marketplace.* London: Thames and Hudson.

Storti, C. (2001). *The art of coming home.* Yarmouth, ME: Intercultural Press.

Suda, N. (1999). Issues of adjustment abroad and readjustment to their home country of Japanese spouses. *Journal of Intercultural Communication, 3,* 75–86.

Sung, B. L. (1985). Bicultural conflicts in Chinese immigrant children. *Journal of Comparative Family Studies, 16,* 255–269.

Sussman, N. M. (1985). Corporate re-entry: A comparative look at returning home. Paper presented at the Japan Psychological Association, Tokyo, Japan, July.

Sussman, N. M. (2000). The dynamic nature of cultural identity throughout cultural transitions: Why home is not so sweet. *Personality and Social Psychology Review, 4,* 355–373.

Sussman, N. M. (2001). Repatriation transitions: Psychological preparedness, cultural identity, and attributions among American managers. *International Journal of Intercultural Relation, 25,* 109–123.

Sussman, N. M. (2002). Testing the cultural identity model of the cultural transition cycle: Sojourners return home. *International Journal of Intercultural Relations, 26,* 391–408.

Sussman, N. M. (2007). Identity shifts as a consequence of crossing cultures: Hong Kong Chinese migrants return home. In K. B. Chan, J. W. Walls, and D. Hayward (eds.), *East-West identities: Globalization, localization, and hybridization* (pp. 121–147). Leiden: Brill.

Sussman, N. M., and Sanzari, J. (2007). The effects of self-construal on re-entry adjustment of American study abroad students. Unpublished manuscript.

Sussman, N. M., Truong, N., and Lim, J. (2007). Who experiences "America the beautiful"? Ethnicity moderating the effect of acculturation on body image and risks for eating disorders among immigrant women. *International Journal of Intercultural Relations, 31,* 29–49.

Tajfel, H. (1978). Social categorization, social identity, and social comparison. In H. Tajfel (ed.), *Differentiation between social groups: Studies in the social psychology of intergroup relations* (pp. 254–267). London: Academic Press.

Tan, J., Hartel, C., Panipucci, D., and Strybosch, V. (2005). The effect of emotions in cross-cultural expatriate experiences. *Cross-Cultural Management, 13,* 4–15.

Tannenbaum, M. (2007). Back and forth: Immigrants' stories of migration and return. *International Migration, 45*(5), 147–175.

Triandis, H. C. (1995). *Individualism and collectivism.* Boulder, CO: Westview Press.

Tsay, C.-L. (2003). Taiwan: Significance, characteristics and policies on return skilled migration. In R. Iredale, F. Guo, and S. Rozario (eds.), *Return migration in the Asia Pacific* (pp. 112–135). Cheltenham, UK: Edward Elgar Publishing.

Tsuda, T. (2003). *Strangers in the ethnic homeland: Japanese-Brazilians return migration in transnational perspective.* New York: Columbia University Press.

Turner, J. C., Hogg, M. A., Oakes, P. J., Reicher, S. D., and Wetherell, M. (1987). *Rediscovering the social group: A self-categorization theory.* Oxford, UK: Blackwell.

UN Population Division, Department of Economic and Social Affairs. (2004). *World Population Prospects: The 2004 Revision.* http://esa.un.org/unpp.

Van Oudenhoven, J. P. (2006). Immigrants. In D. L. Sam and J. W. Berry (eds.), *The Cambridge handbook of acculturation psychology* (pp. 163–180). Cambridge: Cambridge University Press.

Virtanen, K. (1979). *Settlement or return: Finnish emigrants (1860–1930) in the international overseas return migration movement.* Turku, Finland: Migration Institute.

Waldorf, B. (1995). Determinants of international return migration intentions. *Professional Geographer, 47*, 125–136.

Wallis, K. (July 13, 2004). Hong Kong returnees on the increase. *South China Morning Post.*

Wang, G.W. (1991). *China and the Chinese overseas.* Singapore: Times Academic Press.

Wang, G.W. (1998). Upgrading the migrant: Neither *huaqiao* nor *huaren.* In E. Sinn (ed.), *The last half century of Chinese overseas* (pp. 15–34). Hong Kong: Hong Kong University Press.

Wang, L. L. (1991). Roots and changing identity of the Chinese in the United States. *Daedalus, 120*, 181–207.

Ward, C., and Kennedy, A. (1999). The measurement of sociocultural adaptation. *International Journal of Intercultural Relations, 23*, 659–677.

Ward, C., and Rana-Deuba, A. (1999). Acculturation and adaptation revisited. *Journal of Cross-Cultural Psychology, 30*, 422–442.

Ward, C., Bochner, S., and Furnham, A. (2001). *The psychology of culture shock (2nd edition).* East Sussex, UK: Routledge.

White, M. (1992). *The Japanese overseas: Can they go home again?* Princeton, NJ: Princeton University Press.

Wilford, J. N. (2008). Pacific islanders' ancestry emerges in genetic study. *The New York Times*, A6.

Wilhelm, K., and Biers, D. (15 June 2000). No place like home. *Far East Economic Review*, 72–75.

Wong, S. L. (1988). *Emigrant entrepreneurs: Shanghai industrialists in Hong Kong.* Hong Kong: Oxford University Press.

Wong, S. L. (1999). Deciding to stay, deciding to move, deciding not to decide. In G. G. Hamilton (ed.), *Cosmopolitan capitalists* (pp. 135–151). Seattle: University of Washington Press.

Wong, T. W. P. (1991). Inequality, stratification and mobility. In S. K. Lau, et al. (eds.), *Indicators of social development: Hong Kong, 1988* (pp. 145–171). Hong Kong: Hong Kong Institute of Asia-Pacific Studies, the Chinese University of Hong Kong.

Wu, A. (July 12, 2000). Why this boomerang happily came back. *The Standard* (Hong Kong).

Wu, C. T., Ip, D. F., Inglis, C., Kawakami, I., and Duivenvoorden, K. (1998). Settlement experiences of recent Chinese immigrants in Australia. In E. Sinn (ed.), *The last half century of Chinese overseas* (pp. 391–422). Hong Kong: Hong Kong University Press.

Wu, H. (2002). Contesting global/local: Chinese experimental art in the 1990s. *Orientations, 33*(9), 62–67.

Wyman, M. (1993). *Round-trip to America: The immigrants return to Europe, 1880–1930.* Ithaca, NY: Cornell University Press.

Yang, K. S. (1986). Chinese personality and its change. In M. H. Bond (ed.), *The psychology of the Chinese people* (pp. 106–170). Hong Kong: Oxford University Press.

Yik, M. S. M., Bond, M. H., and Paulhus, D. L. (1998). Do Chinese self-enhance or self-efface? It's a matter of domain. *Personality and Social Psychology Bulletin, 24,* 399–406.

York, G. (August 5, 2004). Canadian opts for Hong Kong vote. *Globe and Mail* (Toronto).

Zhang, A. (1998). Timothy Mo. In M. Moseley (ed.), *Dictionary of literary biography. Vol. 194: British novelists since 1960* (pp. 216–219). Asheville, NC: Gale Research.

Zheng, X., and Berry, J. W. (1991). Psychological adaptation of Chinese sojourners in Canada. *International Journal of Psychology, 26,* 451–470.

South China Morning Post (April 22, 1990.) Important to lure home the emigrants.

Zweig, D. (1997). Return or not to return? Politics vs. economics in China's brain drain. *Studies in Comparative International Development, 32,* 92–125.

Index

acceptance
  after remigration, 127–128
  by host country natives, 103–104
accommodation, cultural, 73
acculturation
  of affirmative identity remigrants,
    188
  of Australian immigrants, 25
  of Canadian immigrants, 24–25
  domains of, 57
  of Hong Kong Remigration Project
    respondents, 265–267
  of immigrant students, 55–56
  and religious choices, 87
  of United States immigrants, 28–29
  see also cultural adaptation
acculturation theory, 53
adaptability
  as Confucian value, 242
  of East-Asian peoples, 262
  as hallmark of maturity/good
    character, 237
  in home vs. host countries, 101
adaptation
  by acting Chinese, 110–111
  by additive identity emigrants, 132
  by adopting local social behaviors,
    106–110
  defined, 73
  by global identity remigrants, 181–
    184

sociocultural, 73–74 (*see also* cultural
    adaptation)
  to Western work style, 228–230
additive identity, 74–76, 79–81
  bicultural, 148–150, 152
  combined with affirmative identity,
    194–196
  combined with global identity, 182,
    184
  combined with subtractive identity,
    163–168
  and distress of returnees, 152–153
  in European remigrants, 154–155
  in Hong Kong remigrants, 131–154,
    261
  and housing choices, 139–143
  hybrid, 150–152
  in Indian remigrants, 156–158
  and interpersonal relations, 143–147
  in Israeli remigrants, 155–156
  in Japanese remigrants, 158–160
  in other Hong Kong studies, 154
  postadjustment, 113–114
  quantitative data on, 148, 149
  and school choices, 136–139
  and self-concept/self-naming, 133–
    136
  subprofiles of, 148–153
adjustment
  in country of settlement, 111–113
  cultural, 73

52218232R00202

Made in the USA
Lexington, KY
21 May 2016